Going Downtown

OSPREY
PUBLISHING

THOMAS
McKELVEY CLEAVER

Going
Downtown

THE US AIR FORCE OVER VIETNAM,
LAOS AND CAMBODIA, 1961–75

OSPREY PUBLISHING
Bloomsbury Publishing Plc
Kemp House, Chawley Park, Cumnor Hill, Oxford OX2 9PH, UK
29 Earlsfort Terrace, Dublin 2, Ireland
1385 Broadway, 5th Floor, New York, NY 10018, USA
E-mail: info@ospreypublishing.com
www.ospreypublishing.com

OSPREY is a trademark of Osprey Publishing Ltd

First published in Great Britain in 2022

This paperback edition was first published in Great Britain in 2023 by Osprey Publishing.
For legal purposes the Acknowledgments on p. 345 constitute an extension of this copyright page.

ISBN: HB 9781472848765; PB 9781472848758; eBook 9781472848789;
ePDF 9781472848772; XML 9781472848741

23 24 25 26 27   10 9 8 7 6 5 4 3 2 1

Maps by www.bounford.com
Index by Zoe Ross

Typeset by Deanta Global Publishing Services, Chennai, India
Printed and bound in Great Britain by CPI (Group) UK Ltd, Croydon CR0 4YY

Osprey Publishing supports the Woodland Trust, the UK's leading woodland conservation charity.

To find out more about our authors and books visit www.ospreypublishing.com. Here you will find
extracts, author interviews, details of forthcoming events and the option to sign up for our newsletter.

CONTENTS

LIST OF MAPS AND ILLUSTRATIONS

FOREWORD

Heavy combat is brutal, and combat over Hanoi was brutally heavy. You were busy the whole time, dodging flak, SAMs, and the occasional MiG. If you survived, you pieced together what happened during the debrief, after all the flight members had their say. It wasn't always perfect. With *Going Downtown: The US Air Force over Vietnam, Laos and Cambodia, 1961–75*, Tom Cleaver does his best to separate fact from fiction, and he does it well. Anything less, and you fail to have the lessons learned. For example, lost in the euphoria over the outcome of Operation *Bolo* is the fact that it really did not accomplish the intended mission, which was to wipe out the North Vietnamese air force. The lesson: if you need reasonable weather to get the job done, but do not have it, you scrub the mission. Another lesson learned the hard way is that once you let the enemy know your trick, you do not soon try the exact same thing again. The newspapers recounted the ruse pulled off by Olds, yet, before the month was out another *Bolo* was scheduled. Colonel Olds was vehemently against this second effort, but Seventh Air Force was adamant. Colonel Vermont Garrison led the mission this time. He pressed on in with bad weather once again, and the aircraft were met by a flock of SAMs that knocked one of the Phantoms out of the sky. That ended a sorry episode in higher-headquarter stupidity. No MiGs took off.

I think of the words bravery and courage in different ways. With bravery, one is presented with a danger and has to make an immediate choice: run or fight. With courage, there is time. In the case of Robin Olds, courage was the operative word. He was never scheduled for the Hanoi area without his approval. Though his predecessor never once went "Downtown," Olds went 54 times, way more times than this lieutenant. And before any one of those runs for the roses, he had plenty of time to find a reason to excuse himself from the mission. Let there be no doubt to anyone who might claim he hogged these missions, every "downtown" go was a hair-raiser filled with appalling violence and frequent death. Olds was the bravest, most courageous fighter pilot I ever encountered.

Tom Cleaver's effort adds to the body of work that defines the war and its heroes over North Vietnam. Reading it gave me chills. Its lessons will serve any aviator well, now and in the future.

Ralph F. Wetterhahn
Colonel, USAF (Ret.)
"Olds Two"

"ZORRO-16 – NAIL-43: YOU ARE ON FIRE. WHAT ARE YOUR INTENTIONS?"

"Roger, Nail-43. Understood – on fire." Air Force Captain Charles Brown didn't need the forward air controller (FAC) to know he was on fire. He could see the glow of the fire out the exhausts of his AT-28D! Whatever his intentions, the decision had to be fast. "I was in a burning aircraft, at night, over the Ho Chi Minh Trail in Laos – these were not the ingredients for a good night." It was January 27, 1968.

Flying out of Nakhon Phanom (NKP) air base in Thailand in the 606th Special Operations Squadron, the mission of the AT-28D pilots was to find and stop the North Vietnamese supply convoys moving down the Ho Chi Minh Trail at night. Brown's patrol area was the section where the trail exited North Vietnam at Mu Gia Pass and turned southeast through Laos before crossing into the mountains of northwestern South Vietnam. Arriving on station around 2015 hours that night, Brown had watched two jets miss with their bombs before the FAC, call sign "Nail-43" flying a twin-engine Cessna O-2A, cleared him in hot. "I saw strings of 37mm fire in the area where I thought the FAC was holding. I was about to call him when my aircraft shook, jumped, and burst into flame."

Brown's tour with the 606th was not his first experience with the T-28 in Southeast Asia. As a first lieutenant he had arrived in South Vietnam with the 4400th Combat Crew Training Squadron in May 1962 as part of what was called "Farm Gate," a detachment of the 4400th Combat Crew Training Squadron assigned to train South Vietnamese pilots. "The T-28s we first took to South Vietnam were ex-Navy T-28Cs with the tail hook," he recalled. Farm Gate had been the first group of US

Air Force (USAF) pilots to fly combat in Vietnam, though they did so under a unique set of rules: "We were supposed to always have a South Vietnamese person in the airplane with us. At first that meant having a pilot, but pretty soon it was anyone. I had a South Vietnamese cook who really liked to fly and he'd go with me every chance he had." Brown's first tour in South Vietnam lasted six months.

With the development in the late 1950s of a strategy of "counterinsurgency" to deal with "wars of national liberation" in the formerly colonized nations of what was called at the time the Third World, the Air Force had been directed in 1960 to decide what aircraft in the inventory could be used for such operations and had chosen the vast fleet of T-28A trainers then in storage at Davis-Monthan Air Force Base (AFB). Taking Wright R-1820 radial engines with nearly twice the horsepower of the Wright R-1300-7 that powered the T-28A from recently retired HU-16 Albatross amphibians, 321 T-28As were converted by Pacific Airmotive to the T-28D in three versions depending on the engine used, armed with two .50-caliber machine guns and underwing hardpoints capable of carrying 2,000 pounds of ordnance, and deemed suitable for use by smaller air forces, though both the airframes and engines were weary from the start. By 1964, the Air Force was officially out of the T-28 business in Southeast Asia, with the airplane replaced in the Republic of Vietnam Air Force (VNAF) by the Skyraider. The T-28s were then transferred to the "neutral" Royal Laotian and Thai air forces.

In 1966, the Air Force realized that the fast jets were not ideal for the mission of going after North Vietnamese trucks on the Ho Chi Minh Trail, which operated at night. "We were needed because the fast-movers had trouble seeing trucks at night," Brown later explained. "The objective was to jam them up by hitting the first and last trucks in the convoy, then let the fast-movers or the A-26s work on them." The airplane chosen for the job was the AT-28D, a modification of the T-28D produced by Fairchild, powered by the R-1820-80 producing 1,535hp, and fitted with six underwing hardpoints to carry 3,000 pounds of ordnance. To this day, officially, the USAF never operated the AT-28D, and the 606th Special Operations Squadron, whose pilots dyed their flight suits black and wore the red "Z" made famous in the Disney TV series *Zorro* on their chest as "heroes who fought bad guys in the dark," never flew combat missions in Southeast Asia. According to the Air Force, the pilots in Thailand were there to train pilots of the Royal

Thai Air Force. This was because their missions were illegal violations of the terms of the 1964 international agreement that ended the "Laotian Crisis" by making Laos a "neutral" country in Southeast Asia. In the years following that agreement, none of the United States, the Democratic Republic of Vietnam, or the Laotian Pathet Lao guerillas ever followed any of those terms as the war in Southeast Asia expanded. As Brown explained, "Our families had no idea what we were doing."

While Brown contemplated his near future, Nail-43 suggested that he try to head to the "Rooster Tail," an area of rough terrain in southwestern Laos away from the Trail, since there was no reported military activity at the time:

> My aircraft's control response seemed okay. The engine and prop were still turning. I was indicating 140 knots and losing altitude. The windscreen was covered with oil, but I could see out the sides. I told Nail-43 I was going to stay with it as long as I could and he told me it was fifty miles to the Rooster Tail. I contacted NKP, gave them my position, told them my aircraft was on fire, and reported I was going to ride as far away from the target in the direction of the Rooster Tail as possible. They confirmed my position and reported my condition to my unit and Air Rescue.

Brown then reviewed his checklist and prepared for a night bailout on the wrong side of the bomb line in Laos. It would be his second such experience, having been shot down north of Tchepone in Laos on January 27, 1962 while flying with Farm Gate, and picked up the next morning. "Times were easy back then, compared to this situation. By 1968, Tchepone in Laos was the most heavily defended part of the trail."

Five minutes later, Brown's T-28 was a dozen miles west of the main part of the trail, with still a long way to go to the "Rooster Tail." At that moment, the fire ate its way through the firewall into the cockpit. "Nail-43, Zorro-16 — I am leaving this sonofabitch!"

Checking trim, Brown rolled in a little more nose-up, opened the canopy and threw himself out, aiming to pass over the wing trailing edge as he fell into the stygian darkness of the night sky over southeastern Laos. "WHAM! I hit something. It seemed like the fuselage under the horizontal stabilizer. All I knew for sure was I was rolling at a fairly fast rate. I extended my arms to stop the roll and tried to pull my D-ring to no avail." Rolling again, but not as fast, Brown stabilized, grabbed the

D-ring with both hands, and jerked hard. He looked up to see that the parachute was now partially deployed. Looking down, he could see a river and a road. "I remember thinking 'my wife will kill me if I screw this up.'"

In the next instant, he hit a tree and fell through the triple canopy into the jungle. "I don't know how far I fell, but it felt like a long way, banging into a few things on the way down. I hit the ground so hard I flipped completely over."

Brown was disoriented and dizzy. He staggered to his feet and tried to gather his senses. Suddenly, the surrounding jungle was lit by a bright glow from his airplane as it penetrated the jungle canopy and hit the ground nearby with a large explosion. His legs tingled, his lower back burned, and his head throbbed from hitting the tail. He tried to climb the tree and pull the parachute out of it to no avail. Now fearful that pursuers would find the parachute and know he had survived the crash, he moved into the jungle's darkness. Stepping only a few yards away, he froze at the sound of voices. "They were from my right and were moving towards the glow in the sky."

In the dark sky above, Nail-43 circled, anxious, hoping to hear from the downed pilot. Brown pulled out his AN/PRC-90 emergency radio and came up on the emergency radio channel. "The FAC said it had been quite a few minutes from the time I left the aircraft until I called. They were worried they might draw attention, if they stayed directly overhead. It was not yet 2100 hours and the night had already really gone to hell." Brown remembered looking up through the trees to see a small patch of the night sky with a portion of the Milky Way visible. "It looked beautiful and I sure wished I could be up there to see it better."

Since the squadron had begun operations in the fall of 1966, eight pilots of the 606th had been shot down over the Trail. Only one, Major John Pattee, had been rescued:

If you went down, it was a pretty good bet you'd be caught by the Pathet Lao guerillas. A trail-watcher had told me about seeing an A-26 crash, and the guerillas pulled the two guys out of the plane and beheaded them on the spot. Nobody knew what would happen if the North Vietnamese caught you, but it couldn't be good. We were told we likely had a 50–50 chance of surviving to become POWs [prisoners of war] if that happened.

Brown was glad he was wearing his black flight suit, which allowed him to melt into the dark shadows of the surrounding jungle.

Afraid the searchers would hear his radio, Brown put the speaker inside his mouth and turned it up just enough to allow him to hear it through his ear bones. Nail-43 reported that rescue forces could not get into the area for a night pickup. Brown was now truly on his own as he began a night of evasion while the guerillas searched the jungle for him. Stumbling on, he came to a bamboo grove and crawled inside. After an hour spent hiding in the bamboo while he tried to move further from the crash site:

> The voices were moving again. As they came closer I could see they had lights. One person with a light was coming almost directly toward my location. I tried to get as small as I could and thanked god I had listened to what the road watch team said about not wearing deodorant, after shave, or cologne, because they could use them to smell you out and find you even if they couldn't see you. Just when I thought the next swing of his flashlight would hit me, the next guy down the line yelled out and he turned away.

Remembering to breathe, Brown tried to become invisible, as he listened to the two searchers converse. Then the first resumed his search. "He came so close I thought he'd hit me, but he moved on." Gradually, the noise faded and Brown found a larger bamboo grove to hide in next to a fallen tree trunk. He pulled the bamboo over him and curled up to spend the rest of the night. "I could feel large insects or small animals brush against me and climb over me. I made no attempt to find out which or what they were."

Dawn's light through the bamboo awakened him. As he squirmed out of his hiding place, he discovered he had spent the night in a bamboo grove right at the foot of a watchtower! Fortunately, he was able to quickly ascertain it was unoccupied. This was a piece of good luck, since the watchtower was visible from the air, which would give his rescuers an aim point to find him. Pulling out the rescue radio, he re-established contact with Nail-55, the FAC who had replaced Nail-43 and was orbiting over the jungle a distance from his location.

The good news was that the rescue force was on its way. Looking up in the trees, Brown was amazed to discover that with all the evasion he had engaged in during the night, he was only some 400 yards from where his parachute still hung in the tree.

Minutes later, he heard the sound of aircraft engines approaching. "I looked up and saw two A-1Hs making spiraling vapor trails in the damp morning air. I informed them where I was relative to the watchtower, then Sandy Lead called 'Smoke NOW!'" Brown popped his orange smoke grenade to make his exact position.

"A moment later four F-4s attacked what turned out to be an NVA [North Vietnamese Army] camp less than a kilometer [approximately half a mile] from my position. Then the Sandys dropped white phosphorus to either side of the watchtower." The Skyraiders then strafed the jungle as the big Sikorsky HH-3E Jolly Green Giant rescue helicopter came in and hovered over Brown's position. "I never saw anything that looked as good as that penetrator as it came through the canopy. All I had to do was pull down the seat, zip open the bags holding the body straps, climb into the straps, and onto the seat. I heard a few rounds of small arms fire, but the penetrator ride up was fairly quick."

Once aboard the helicopter, Brown's first request was to get by the open door to relieve himself. "I had held it all night because I was afraid they'd smell me, and I had to go real, real bad."

The welcome Brown received on his return to Nakhon Phanom was tumultuous. Over the rest of the war, only one other pilot who went down over the Ho Chi Minh Trail would be rescued. The fall through the trees and the night in the Laotian jungle stayed with Brown for the rest of his air force career and his life after. "I have had physical problems ever since – hip replacement, knee replacements, shoulder repair. A Navy surgeon said I had bruises on all five areas of my chute harness."

The "Zorros" would end their war against the North Vietnamese transport system by that summer of 1968. "By then, they had every kind of gun you could imagine along the trail. Our T-28s were too slow and what armor we had wasn't sufficient for protection." The 606th would trade in its trainers for A-1E and A-1H Skyraiders. "But while we were there, we were so successful that Seventh Air Force stopped separating their reports into prop and jet categories, because 80 percent of the successes were going to the props – to us." A squadron that never numbered more than 12 aircraft was more successful in its mission than the rest of the Seventh Air Force.

2

GOOD INTENTIONS AND IGNORANCE

One cannot begin to either comprehend or understand anything that happened during America's involvement in the Southeast Asian wars of the 1960s without understanding that those events did not arise *de novo* with the election of John F. Kennedy as president in 1960. America's wars in Southeast Asia were a long time coming. The United States had been effectively at war in Southeast Asia since 1950, and in many ways for much longer than that. Perhaps the best description of what Americans would bring to the region is the famous line in Graham Greene's novel of the First Indochina War, *The Quiet American*, in which the novel's protagonist, cynical British journalist Thomas Fowler – a stand-in for Greene, who wrote from experience – describes the title character, Alden Pyle: "I never knew a man who had better motives for all the trouble he caused... impregnably armored by his good intentions and his ignorance."

John F. Kennedy, who could well be seen as the embodiment of Pyle and was perhaps more responsible than any other American for involving his country in Southeast Asia's wars, had visited South Vietnam as a young congressman on a fact-finding investigation in 1952. After two weeks of meetings with officials and dinner conversations with French *colons* in Saigon, and taking a quick tour of the countryside, he returned home and wrote presciently in his diary: "We are more and more becoming colonialists in the minds of the people. Because everyone believes that we control the U.N. [United Nations] and because our wealth is supposedly inexhaustible, we will be damned if we don't do what the new nations want." Ten years later, one could argue he had forgotten every moment of his visit, every sight seen, every conversation engaged in. American Marines first arrived in Vietnam on May 10, 1845 – 120 years before they landed on Da Nang's White Beach in April 1965 – when Captain John "Mad Jack" Percival, commanding USS *Constitution*, then on a "show the flag tour" of Asia, dropped anchor in Da Nang Harbor and landed a detachment of the ship's Marines in the closest port to Hue, the Vietnamese capitol. He was responding to news that the Vietnamese were about to execute French bishop Dominic Lefèbvre, the Catholic religious leader in Vietnam. This was part of an ongoing persecution of native Catholics on orders from Emperor Trinh, son of Emperor Gia Long who had considered Christianity subversive to the nation he was building before his death in 1832. In 1827, Gia Long began the greatest Christian persecution since Rome, with 130,000 Vietnamese Catholics murdered by 1856.

The American Marines quickly took captive several local Vietnamese officials – who had never heard of the United States of America – holding them hostages for four days until Emperor Trinh assured Captain Percival that the bishop was safe. Percival then sailed away and matters remained quiet until the government in Washington finally heard of the event and sent the American consul at Singapore, in 1849, to apologize for the captain's audacious behavior. In a similar situation to the events of 120 years later, Captain Percival and his Marines had never heard of Vietnam until two weeks before they landed, when they learned of the Christian persecution while in Singapore and the captain decided to unilaterally intervene.

France first became involved with Vietnam when it established a trading post in 1680, which was abandoned in 1682. However, French Jesuit missionaries had first landed at Da Nang in 1615. Their initial success in evangelizing the Buddhist Vietnamese led the pope to appoint Monsignor Alexandre de Rhodes leader of a permanent mission in 1627. By the time he was banished in 1649, more than 20,000 Vietnamese had converted. Rhodes also transliterated the Vietnamese language from Chinese characters to the Latin alphabet, with the use of diacritical marks to note the multi-tonal character of the language.

The 18th century saw the physical conquest of south Vietnam by the Nguyen Dynasty. However, the Tay-Son revolt broke out against them in 1771, with the goal of restoring the Le Dynasty in the north; by

1776 only one Nguyen prince, 18-year-old Nguyen Anh, was left alive. His son, Prince Canh, accompanied Monsignor Pigneau de Béhaine to Paris in 1784 to seek support from the French monarchy. The French Revolution prevented this, but the monsignor and the prince returned to Vietnam in 1789 in a privately purchased warship with 300 French adventurers. While the Tay-Son rulers were engaged by another Chinese invasion that prevented them from delivering their promised reforms, this force overthrew them. In 1802, Prince Nguyen Anh declared himself emperor. Taking the name Gia Long, he established control of the entire country by the Nguyen Dynasty. He founded Saigon, designed for him by French military engineers Theodore Lebrun and Olivier de Puymanel in 1792. His resolute adoption of Confucianism led inevitably to conflict with the Catholic minority and the 1827–56 persecutions.

In response to the Catholic persecution, a French military force landed at Da Nang in 1856. By 1866, the French had secured the coast to Saigon and controlled the Mekong Delta. By 1870 they had broken Vietnam into three provinces as a Protectorate in Indochina, a colony that included the kingdoms of Laos and Cambodia. By the early 20th century, French-built irrigation systems had eliminated the floods and droughts that the country had previously experienced, turning the Mekong Delta into a major agricultural-exporting region. French marginalization of the Vietnamese intellectual and entrepreneurial classes led to the formation across the country of secret political societies advocating resistance to foreign rule.

Nguyen That Thanh ("Nguyen the accomplished"), son of a former imperial magistrate and Confucian scholar, was accepted in 1908 for study at the Collège Quoc Hoc (High School for the Gifted) in Hue. His classmates included two fellow believers in independence, Pham Van Dong and Vo Nguyen Giap, and a young Catholic, Ngo Dinh Diem.

In the summer of 1919, US Secretary of State Robert Lansing, then in France for the Versailles peace conference to settle World War I, received a letter addressed to President Wilson from a young Vietnamese exile living in Paris, Nguyen That Thanh, now known as Nguyen Ai Quoc ("Nguyen the patriot") to disguise himself from French authorities after joining le Groupe des Patriotes Annamites (the Group of Annamite Patriots). The letter included a petition, *Revendications du Peuple Annamite* (Claims of the Annamite People), calling for reform of the French colonies and the independence of Vietnam in accordance with the Fourteen Points that President Wilson had proposed as the reasons for American involvement in the war and that later became the terms of the peace agreement. The term "Annamite" was used because the term "Vietnamien" (Vietnamese) was forbidden by France for its nationalist connotation. Annam was the French name of the central Vietnamese province in French Indochina.

The petition specifically cited Point Five of the Fourteen Points, which called for "A free, open-minded, and absolutely impartial adjustment of all colonial claims, based upon a strict observance of the principle that in determining all such questions of sovereignty the interests of the populations concerned must have equal weight with the equitable government whose title is to be determined." Nguyen Ai Quoc sought to enlist the president's support for Vietnamese independence as part of the Treaty of Versailles then being negotiated.

Woodrow Wilson had been born and raised in Civil War-era Virginia, and was well known in Democratic Party politics as a "narrow-minded Southern bigot"; during his presidency he had nationalized Jim Crow racial segregation with the full force of the federal government. He was no believer in granting political independence to the non-white colonies of European empires. His Fourteen Points applied to the white European nations being formed from the German and Austrian empires. Secretary Lansing replied that the letter would be shared with the president, but there was never any formal response.

Turned down by the leader of the country founded by an anti-colonial revolt that he had believed meant what it said about all men being equal, Nguyen Ai Quoc returned to Paris. Here he and the other members of le Groupe des Patriotes Annamites joined other French revolutionary socialists to found the French Communist Party because of Vladimir Lenin's declaration of support for all colonial people struggling for independence. When he visited Moscow, he was recruited as an agent of the Communist International (Comintern) to work for independence in the colonized nations of Asia, which he did for the next 20 years in China and throughout Asia. In the late 1930s, he took the revolutionary name Ho Chi Minh ("He Who Has Been Enlightened").

Meanwhile, the United States promptly forgot about Vietnam again for the next 20 years. Following the French defeat in June 1940, the collaborationist Vichy regime signed an armistice on June 22, 1940. Three days before, on June 19, Japan took advantage of the impending armistice to present a demand to Georges Catroux, governor-general of Indochina, that the French close the Haiphong–Yunnan railway and refuse to allow the Republic of China to import war materials through the port of Haiphong, and admit a 40-man Japanese inspection team under General Issaku Nishihara to insure this was done. American intelligence became aware that the "request" was actually an ultimatum through intercepts when the Japanese informed their German allies of the details through the Japanese diplomatic "Purple Code" that the Americans had broken earlier that year; upon which they informed Catroux of the actual situation. Catroux, initially reluctant to acquiesce, learned from his intelligence service that Japanese military units were moving into threatening positions; moreover he knew the Vichy government was unprepared to engage in defense of the colony.

On June 20, Catroux submitted. The last munitions train crossed the border two days later. On June 23, Catroux was replaced by Admiral Jean Decoux and defected to London to join General De Gaulle. On June 22, while Catroux was still governor-general, a demand was presented for naval basing rights and complete closure of the Chinese border by July 7. General Nishihara arrived in Hanoi on June 29 and issued a demand on July 3 for use of air bases and the right to transport combat troops through Indochina. Admiral Decoux, who arrived several days later, urged Vichy to reject the demands, supported by General Jules-Antoine Bührer, Chief of the Colonial General Staff. The neutral United States was prepared to provide aircraft, and there were 4,000 *Tirailleurs Sénégalais* in Djibouti at the Horn of Africa who could reinforce the 32,000 ill-equipped French army regulars and 17,000 reservists in Indochina.

Japanese Foreign Minister Yōsuke Matsuoka approved a proposal submitted by Vichy Foreign Minister Paul Baudouin on August 30, allowing Japanese occupying forces and to transit through Indochina for the duration of the Sino-Japanese War. Negotiations between General Maurice Martin, supreme French commander in Indochina, and General Nishihara began at Hanoi on September 3. Acting on their own, Decoux and Martin looked for help from the American and British consuls in Hanoi, even going so far as to consult the Chinese government in Chungking on a joint defense against a Japanese attack.

On September 6, an infantry battalion of the Japanese 22nd Army based in Nanning in southeastern China violated the Indochinese border near the French fort at Dong Dang in an attempt to force their superiors to take more aggressive action. Decoux ended negotiations, but on September 18 Nishihara warned him Japanese troops would enter Indochina, regardless of any French agreement, at 2200 hours on September 22. Decoux demanded a reduction in the number of Japanese troops to be stationed in Indochina. A few hours before expiration of the ultimatum, Martin and Nishihara signed an agreement authorizing 6,000 troops in Tonkin Province north of the Red River and use of four airfields in Tonkin; also the right to transit 25,000 troops through Tonkin to Yunnan and to send one division of the 22nd Army through Tonkin via Haiphong for other use in China.

When the ultimatum expired, Lieutenant General Akihito Nakamura sent the 5th Infantry Division across the border near Dong Dang. There was an exchange of fire that spread to other border posts overnight. Aircraft from *Kaga* and *Akagi* in the Gulf of Tonkin attacked French positions along the coast on September 24. Long Son was surrounded and surrendered on September 25. Among the units surrendering at Long Son was the 2nd Battalion of the 5th Foreign Infantry Regiment, the first Foreign Legion unit to surrender without a fight. The unit's 179 German and Austrian volunteers, all anti-Nazi exiles, refused efforts to induce them to join the Japanese.

On September 26, the Japanese landed at Dong Tac, south of Haiphong, and moved on the port while aircraft bombed the city. By early afternoon 4,500 troops and 12 tanks were outside Haiphong. By that evening, the Japanese had taken possession of Gia Lam Airbase outside Hanoi, the marshaling yard at Lao Cai, and Phu Lang Thuong on the railway from Hanoi to Long Son, stationing 900 troops in Haiphong and another 600 in Hanoi. This led President Roosevelt to impose an embargo of aviation gasoline and other supplies, which resulted in the outbreak of the Pacific War 15 months later.

Indochina was the most important staging area for Japanese military operations in Southeast Asia at the outset of the Pacific War, with naval and army air forces based there for operations against Malaya and the Dutch East Indies. The Vichy administration cooperated throughout the war with the Japanese until it was ousted and its armed forces disarmed in March 1945, due to the Japanese fear that the French forces might turn against them as their defeat approached. Following this, Bao Dai, the last French-appointed emperor of Vietnam, was allowed to proclaim the independence of his country as the Republic of Vietnam. A Vietnamese "national government" was installed in the old imperial capital of Hue, but the Japanese retained all real power.

A resistance movement operated against the Japanese throughout the war. The Republic of China supported formation of a Vietnamese nationalist resistance movement, the Dong Minh Hoi, at Nanking in 1935–36. The organization included communists, but was not controlled by them; its most important act was to free Ho Chi Minh, who had been jailed in 1938 for working with the Chinese communists. He returned to Vietnam in the summer of 1941, following the German invasion of the Soviet Union and the Soviet call for all communist parties to join in fighting the Axis powers, creating a resistance centered on the communist Viet Minh; this was the only "indigenous" anti-colonial force in Southeast Asia that did not collaborate with the Japanese and their "Greater East Asia Co-Prosperity Sphere" against the former European colonial powers, which was due to the Viet Minh's adherence to the Soviet wartime alliance with the Western powers.

The Viet Minh drew their initial inspiration from the writings of the great Vietnamese military leader Tran Hung Dao, author of *The Essential Summary of the Military Arts*, leader of the resistance to the Mongol invasion of 1284 CE. His principles expressed in the *Summary* were: "The enemy must fight his battles far from his home base for a long time. We must further weaken him by drawing him into protracted campaigns. Once his initial dash is broken, it will be easier to destroy him." The strategy had worked with the fearsome Mongols, who destroyed civilization from Beijing to Baghdad, withdrawing from Vietnam in 1287, their only defeat in Asia.

In January 1945, Admiral William F. Halsey, Jr., led the US Third Fleet on a series of strikes against Japanese positions in Formosa, southern China, and Indochina, designed to cut off Japan from the oil and other raw materials of its Southern Empire, for which it had originally gone to war in 1941. Task Force 38 struck Indochina from Hanoi to Saigon on January 12, leaving the Japanese reeling. Following this, Indochina retreated from American military planning over the rest of the war.

Following the overthrow of the Vichy French in March 1945, an Office of Strategic Services (OSS) "Deer Team" (a code word) arrived in Indochina on May 16, 1945, to train Viet Minh guerillas. The OSS operatives worked closely with Ho Chi Minh and Vo Nguyen

Giap, whom they knew only as "Mr. Hoo" and "Mr. Van." In July, the OSS team participated in capturing the Japanese garrison at Tan Trao. The Americans accompanied the Viet Minh into Hanoi following the Japanese surrender.

On September 2, 1945, Ho Chi Minh proclaimed the independent Democratic Republic of Vietnam in Hanoi's Ba Dinh square. His speech began with a verbatim recitation of the second paragraph of the American Declaration of Independence: "We hold these truths to be self-evident, that all men are created equal, that they are endowed by their Creator with certain unalienable Rights, that among these are Life, Liberty and the pursuit of Happiness."

What to do with French Indochina in the aftermath of the war had not been a high priority in Allied planning until the Potsdam conference held in Berlin in July 1945, following the defeat of Germany. It was necessary to divide the liberated territories that had been conquered by the Germans and Japanese in order to take the surrender of Axis forces. Outside of the OSS operatives on the ground in Indochina, few Americans knew anything about Vietnam and none knew any part of the history of resistance to French colonial rule; it was a situation much like that regarding postwar Korea. Like Korea, the dividing line between forces was made on the basis of geography. The 17th parallel divided Vietnam approximately in half, as the 38th parallel divided Korea. In the case of Vietnam, troops of the Republic of China were to move into Vietnam north of the parallel to take the Japanese surrender, while British forces would move into the region south of the parallel.

In the aftermath of Ho Chi Minh's declaration of independence, Republic of China forces in northern Vietnam, reverting to the traditional Chinese position regarding Vietnamese independence coupled with anti-communism from their own civil war which had blossomed anew following the end of the Sino-Japanese struggle, did their best to frustrate the Viet Minh in their region. The British, unwilling to promote the fortunes of an Asian independence movement as they struggled to justify their position in India and their return to Burma and Malaya to re-establish Imperial rule, also acted against the Viet Minh. French forces returned to Indochina by the end of the year. Almost a year to the day following the Vietnamese declaration of independence, a full-fledged military struggle broke out between the French and the Viet Minh.

The French forces were led by General Philippe Leclerc, liberator of Paris. He declared Ho Chi Minh an "enemy of France." Within a matter of months, seeing the universal hatred of France and Frenchmen held by both communist and non-communist Vietnamese, Leclerc became convinced that Indochina could not be held. Unfortunately, while flying back to France where he intended to report his views, he was killed when his airplane crashed in Algeria. High Commissioner Georges Thierry d'Argenlieu, a thoroughgoing believer in the French Empire, convinced De Gaulle that Ho's movement could be crushed. That November, following a breakdown in negotiations, the French unleashed a naval and air bombardment of Viet Minh strongholds in Haiphong that devastated the city, killing several thousand Vietnamese, while leaving the city's European quarter intact. The First Indochina War had begun.

Initially, over the next four years, the United States did nothing to support the French return to Indochina. The United States would not allow use in Indochina of World War II Lend-Lease aircraft supplied to the French air forces, which meant they could only use war-weary aircraft that had been supplied outside Lend-Lease. By 1949, all these aircraft were old and tired. Serviceability was poor, and spares were getting hard to find.

US policy changed toward the French in early 1950 before the outbreak of the Korean War following the Chinese communist victory in the Chinese Civil War in October 1949, though nothing was publicly stated in Washington. On January 11, 1950, USS *Boxer* (CV-21) departed San Diego for the first deployment of a US aircraft carrier west of Hawaii since 1948, a "show the flag" deployment to Japan, Korea, and the Philippines. On March 5, 1950, *Boxer* and the Seventh Fleet Striking Force became the first US Navy warships to enter the Tonkin Gulf since January 1945. All five squadrons were launched to fly a "parade formation" from Haiphong in the north to the mouth of the Mekong and the city of Saigon in the south. Lieutenant (jg) Ed Phillips, a Skyraider pilot in VA-195, recalled, "We were told the flight was a statement by the United States regarding the situation that existed in Indochina."

This otherwise-unknown flight was the first indication of the change in US policy. The war was now seen as a part of the confrontation with the "international communist conspiracy" led by the Soviet Union and People's Republic of China. President Truman's Economic Survey Mission wrote a report finding that Indochina was strategically important as an invasion route to greater Southeast Asia via the Mekong River, which could lead to the fall of Thailand, Malaya, Burma, and Indonesia. Thus was born the "domino theory" that would guide US policy in Southeast Asia for the next 20 years.

Not all senior Americans were in favor of picking up France's falling banner. Around the same time that Ed Phillips and his fellow aviators were holding their aerial parade, Undersecretary of State Raymond Fosdick in a long memorandum urged against the United States "becoming allied with reaction," stating that despite any residual delusions of French grandeur, it was obvious that all of Indochina would soon become independent. He went on to explain that it did not matter that the French had sufficient strength not to lose to the Viet Minh, but rather that they offered nothing any intelligent Vietnamese might want. "Why, therefore, do we tie ourselves to the tail of their battered kite?" he ended. A week after he wrote this, the junior Senator from Wisconsin, Joseph McCarthy, who was due to stand for re-election in 1952 and was desperate to find an issue on which to ride to victory, settled on telling an audience at a Republican fund-raiser in West Virginia that he possessed a list of "known communists" working at high levels in the US State Department and other places in Washington. Over the next two years, the "Old Asia Hands" in the State Department, men like Fosdick and Edmund Clubb, who understood the political upheaval happening in the post-colonial world, would depart government service, taking their clear-eyed views and leaving Foggy Bottom populated by "Asian specialists" like Dean Rusk, Undersecretary for Far Eastern Affairs, who had never set foot in Asia, in charge of developing American policy.

Following the outbreak of the Korean War in June 1950, the Military Defense Program was modified by President Truman that December, when the United States signed a Mutual Defense Assistance Agreement with France, the Republic of Vietnam, and the kingdoms of Cambodia and Laos to oppose the Viet Minh. With this, the United States provided France with $100 million in military aid previously earmarked for use in China. Direct American military involvement began with the creation of the American Military Advisory Group Indochina; this would coordinate the provision of US military equipment, which the United States had previously promised to provide France for service in the war.

Under the terms of the agreement, the Eisenhower Administration was footing the bill for 80 percent of the cost of the war in Indochina,

$1 billion for 1953 alone. In August 1953, British Foreign Secretary Selwyn Lloyd wrote, "There is now in the United States an emotional feeling about communist China, and to a lesser extent Russia, which borders on hysteria."

In November 1953, Dien Bien Phu, a mountain-ringed basin near the Laos frontier, was chosen to become the major French army base in the north, in an attempt to block the transport of material from China. It was also hoped that the bulk of the Viet Minh forces would be contained within this area and neutralized, or even annihilated. On learning of this, General Giap decided to give the French the battle they sought with the Viet Minh. The Chinese supplied the Vietnamese with American artillery and antiaircraft guns that they had inherited from the departed Kuomintang troops; they just had to be brought to the scene. Viet Minh Captain Tran Do recalled the effort:

> Each night when freezing fog descended into the valleys, groups of men mustered. The track was so narrow that the slightest deviation of the wheels would have caused a gun to plunge into a ravine. By sheer sweat and tears we hauled them into position one by one, with men playing the part of trucks... It became the work of a whole torchlit night to move a gun five hundred or a thousand meters.

The effort to move the artillery 500 miles through the mountainous jungle terrain took 100 days. Once in position, they waited while ammunition was transported the same distance in conditions as difficult; 40-pound howitzer shells were brought down narrow paths by bicycles, each gun had 1,000 rounds.

The French were aware of Giap's effort but did little to stop the Viet Minh. Had they acted on the intelligence and evacuated their obviously indefensible position, no one would have known of it. Unfortunately, the French army and government were led by men who had borne the humiliations of World War II, who could not bear the thought of retreat and a loss of reputation, who were driven to restore national honor. They created a military fiasco that echoed for the next 20 years.

On March 13, 1954, the Viet Minh began their attack. They shelled the airfield, destroying aircraft and exploding the bomb storage area, wrecking command positions located during the waiting period. The nearest air support was 186 miles away. That night, French positions were attacked from hidden positions that had been dug within yards of their targets. Only 100 Foreign Legionnaires escaped the assault on Hill Beatrice. In the morning, air support was mobilized but it was too late. With the airfield destroyed by the end of March, the defenders were completely dependent on air-dropped supplies. The beginning of the rainy season brought torrential rains, reducing flights. The heavy-lift C-87s were manned by American "civilian" crews provided by Civil Air Transport (CAT), a CIA company created to provide "deniable" American air support to anti-communist operations throughout Southeast Asia that would be better known in later years as Air America.

Among the pilots was former Flying Tiger Erik Shilling, who later remembered:

> Why they chose Dien Bien Phu is a mystery to me. They put their main base in a valley and never took control of the hills that surrounded them. We came in high, then throttled back and dove straight into the flak. You'd begin your pullout at about 2,500 feet so you were at 1,000 feet and minimum speed when you dropped, or the parachutes would drift into enemy territory. Then you poured on the coals and climbed out of that basin, all the while under fire. Sometimes it seemed like the flak was coming *down* at us.

They were forced to make night drops; most of the supplies fell into enemy hands.

In spite of reinforcements from the United States, after 56 days of battle 11,000 French troops surrendered on May 8, 1954. Giap had committed three-quarters of his army to the battle. The surrender marked the end of the French fight in Indochina.

President Eisenhower considered mounting American air strikes to support the French. Despite eager support from Chief of Naval Operations Admiral Arthur Radford, who wanted to send B-29s of the 19th Bomb Group at Clark AFB to bomb the Viet Minh at Dien Bien Phu and proposed the use of up to three "properly employed" tactical nuclear weapons, there was no commitment to united action from Britain and Australia. British concern grew when Americans casually spoke of "nuking" China for supporting the Vietnamese. Secretary of State John Foster Dulles attempted to muster domestic support for opposing the "communist advance." *U.S. News & World Report* editorialized, "Blunt notice is given to the communists that the U.S. does not intend to let Indochina be gobbled up."

On April 3, Dulles attempted to get a congressional commitment for intervention, but had to admit to Senator Richard Russell that the British did not support this; Admiral Radford admitted to Democratic Senate Leader Lyndon Johnson that he was the only member of the Joint Chiefs of Staff (JCS) in favor. Johnson stated, "We want no more Koreas with the U.S. providing 90 percent of the manpower." On April 7, President Eisenhower for the first time articulated the domino theory: if the United States did not stand against the communists, all Southeast Asia would fall. New Massachusetts Senator John F. Kennedy urged that it was time to tell the American people the truth: "To pour money, materials and men into the jungles of Indochina against an enemy that has the sympathy and covert support of the people will achieve nothing."

Faced with the lack of allied support, Eisenhower grew wary of "another Korea," finally convinced against intervention by Army Chief of Staff General Matthew Ridgway, the primary commander in Korea. Even Dulles had to concede when French Foreign Minister Georges Bidault refused to consider a unilateral grant of Indochinese independence, a precondition for US intervention. Winston Churchill's opposition finally stopped Dulles when the old warrior convinced his friend the president to hold off.

At a conference of foreign ministers in Berlin in January, Soviet Foreign Minister V.I. Molotov had proposed an international conference to address issues in Asia. Negotiations regarding Southeast Asia began in Geneva, Switzerland on April 26, before the Dien Bien Phu surrender, and ran until July 20, 1954. Columnist Walter Lippmann wrote on April 29 that "The American position at Geneva is an impossible one, so long as leading Republican senators have no terms for peace except unconditional surrender of the enemy and no terms for entering the war except as a collective action in which nobody is now willing to engage."

French Foreign Minister Bidault opened the conference on May 8, the day after the Dien Bien Phu surrender, proposing a cessation of hostilities, a cease-fire in place, release of prisoners, and disarming of irregulars. On May 10, Pham Van Dong, leader of the Democratic Republic of Vietnam (DRV) delegation, proposed a cease-fire, the separation of forces, a ban on new forces in Indochina, an exchange of prisoners, and independence for Vietnam, Cambodia, and Laos, with elections in each country, withdrawal of all foreign forces and inclusion of the Pathet Lao and Khmer Issarak representatives at the conference. On May 25, he proposed a temporary partition of Vietnam, though the anti-communist Republic of Vietnam had rejected partition on May 12, with the United States following the next day.

Behind the scenes, the Americans and French discussed terms for US intervention; on May 29, they agreed that if the conference failed to deliver an acceptable peace deal, Eisenhower would seek approval for intervention. Australia and New Zealand declined to support American intervention. By mid-June, the United States concluded that it might be preferable for the French to leave while the United States supported the new states, removing the taint of French colonialism. The United States then withdrew from the conference.

On June 15, Molotov proposed a cease-fire monitored by an International Control Commission, headed by India. On June 16, Chinese premier Zhou Enlai stated that Vietnam, Cambodia, and Laos were not the same and should be treated separately, proposing that Laos and Cambodia be neutral nations with no foreign bases. On June 18, Pham Van Dong stated the Viet Minh would withdraw forces from Laos and Cambodia if no foreign bases were established. The softening of the communist position arose from a meeting among the DRV, Chinese, and Soviet delegations on June 15 in which Zhou warned the Viet Minh that its presence in Laos and Cambodia threatened to undermine negotiations regarding Vietnam. Zhou was following traditional Chinese policy, seeking to ensure that Laos and Cambodia were not under the influence of its ancient enemy Vietnam, but rather under that of China.

On June 18, the Laniel government fell in Paris, replaced by a coalition led by Radical Party leader Pierre Mendès France as prime minister, a long-time opponent of the war, who pledged that he would resign if he failed to achieve a cease-fire within 30 days. France had recognized Vietnam as "a fully independent and sovereign state" on June 4. The new government abandoned earlier assurances to the Republic of Vietnam that France would not accept partition, and negotiated secretly with the Viet Minh delegation in order to meet the deadline. On June 23, Mendès France secretly met with Zhou Enlai, who outlined the Chinese position: the Chinese demanded an immediate cease-fire; that the three nations be treated separately; and recognition that two governments existed in Vietnam.

The following day, Mendès France returned to Paris. General Paul Ély outlined the deteriorating military position in Vietnam, and Jean Chauvel suggested partition at the 16th or 17th parallel. They agreed that the Bao Dai government of the Republic of Vietnam would need to consolidate its position and that US assistance would be vital. On June 16, Bao Dai appointed Ngo Dinh Diem – former high school classmate of Ho Chi Minh – prime minister. He was a staunch nationalist, anti-French, and anti-communist, with strong political connections in the United States. He and Foreign Minister Tran Van Do opposed partition.

On June 28, Britain and the United States issued a joint communiqué, stating that if the conference failed, "the international situation will be seriously aggravated." They agreed to a secret list of minimum outcomes that they would "respect": preservation of a non-communist South Vietnam; future reunification of divided Vietnam; the integrity of Cambodia and Laos with removal of all Viet Minh forces. On July 10, Mendès France arrived to lead the French delegation. The Republic of Vietnam continued to protest the now-inevitable partition, in which the only issue was where to draw the line. Former Central Intelligence Agency (CIA) Director Walter Bedell Smith arrived in Geneva on July 16, but the Americans were instructed to avoid direct association with the negotiations so as not to be "tainted" by association with the French.

The negotiators were unable to agree on a date for the reunification elections, with the North Vietnamese arguing that the elections should be held six months after the cease-fire, while the Western allies favored no deadline. Molotov proposed June 1955, later agreeing to July 1956. The Diem government supported reunification elections with effective international supervision, arguing that genuinely free elections were impossible in the communist North. Privately, everyone agreed the Viet Minh had the prestige to win overwhelmingly in open elections. By July 20, the remaining outstanding issues were resolved.

The "Final Declaration of the Geneva Convention on the Problem of Restoring Peace in Indochina" focused on settling military rather than political issues. The states of Vietnam, Cambodia, and Laos were created, with Vietnam temporarily separated into two zones at the 17th parallel, with a general election to be held by July 1956 to create a unified Vietnam. The International Control Commission was created to oversee the agreement.

Significantly, the agreement was not signed or accepted by the Republic of Vietnam or the United States. The Eisenhower Administration had restored Republican rule in Washington the year before for the first time since 1932, and wanted to ensure that it could not be accused of allowing another "Yalta" or of having "lost Vietnam" to the communists as they had accused the Truman Administration of "losing China" after the communist victory in 1949. Walter Bedell Smith announced that the United States would abide by the agreement, but would view "any renewal of aggression in violation of these agreements with grave concern and as seriously threatening international peace and security."

On August 12, 1954, President Eisenhower convened the National Security Council (NSC) to review Far Eastern policy. It was agreed that the United States had experienced significant loss of prestige backing France; recouping that prestige would be vital for success in the region. The domino theory was specifically mentioned as motivation for US involvement in Southeast Asia; loss of the region would imperil even US retention of its position in Japan and developing the offshore island chain of bases to contain China. On August 20, Eisenhower approved NSC 5429/2, which set US policy in the Far East, stating, "the U.S. must protect its position and restore its prestige in the Far East by a new initiative in Southeast Asia, where the situation must be stabilized as soon as possible to prevent further losses to communism through (1) creeping expansion and subversion, or (2) overt aggression." A CIA National Intelligence Estimate (NIE), issued the same month, concluded that the communists would continue to pursue their objectives in the Republic of Vietnam, that Ho Chi Minh would most certainly win an election in 1956, and that the future of Southeast Asia depended on what happened in Vietnam.

In September, Secretary Dulles convened a meeting of the United States, the United Kingdom, France, Australia, New Zealand, Thailand, Pakistan, and the Philippines, to sign the Southeast Asia Collective Defense Treaty, establishing the South East Asia Treaty Organization (SEATO) to resist communist expansion. Vietnam, Cambodia, and Laos were considered "associated states" for mutual defense. Though modeled on NATO, SEATO did not have an Article V that pledged joint action in the face of aggression. Instead, Article IV Paragraph 1 stated that aggression by armed attack would endanger each signatory's peace and safety, and that the signatories would "act to meet the common danger in accordance with its constitutional processes." This was due to opposition by the US Joint Chiefs to any formal commitment to any unilateral action that would restrict US freedom of action. Secretary Dulles presented a formal US declaration of readiness to act, but there was no similar commitment by the others, and the declaration did not constitute a formal US commitment.

The United States signed bilateral agreements with the Republic of Vietnam, formally replacing France as the country's guarantor. The Military Assistance Advisory Group (MAAG) was established to train an army and air force. President Eisenhower sent a letter to Ngo Dinh Diem expressing an explicit quid pro quo that American assistance would be provided so long as there existed a "legitimate and meritorious government." In 1955, the US Operations Mission was established as an adjunct to the American Embassy, to coordinate financial aid with an initial commitment of $322 million.

Over the next two years, with American support, the Diem government claimed that it had solved the problems facing the country, including resettlement of refugees from the North, while it neutralized internal opposition. Diem's government blatantly favored the Catholic minority, seen by the Buddhist majority as "pro-French" and not to be trusted. Senator John F. Kennedy joined other congressional leaders to call on the administration never to approve the nationwide elections that the Geneva Accords called for, citing Diem's progress in creating an anti-communist independent Vietnam. Despite everything, Ho Chi Minh remained the most respected political leader in Indochina, and would undoubtedly win the election; there was no rebuke over Diem's announcement that the elections were canceled since a "free and fair" election could not be held in North Vietnam.

The officer corps of the newly formed Army of the Republic of Vietnam (ARVN) was stacked with Catholics, while Catholic-owned or Catholic-run businesses were favored to receive government assistance for expansion, and Catholics were appointed as village chiefs. Opposing political parties were banished and the press was strictly censored, while opposition newspapers and periodicals were closed. Joseph Buttinger, a State Department employee involved in establishing a modern civil service, reported in 1957 that the Diem government was opposed by intellectuals and the educated non-Catholic middle class, rejected by the majority of the business class who did not have access to government support owing to not being Catholic, and hated by non-communist nationalist politicians who were excluded from political participation. In a country 80 percent Buddhist, Diem was dangerously isolated, though neither he nor his American supporters took any notice. Buttinger's report was soon forgotten.

Resistance grew in the countryside; peasants turned to independence leaders who had remained in the south. Acts of resistance against Catholic landlords spread as non-communist nationalists took up the cause. Repression by the armed forces and police increased.

The North Vietnamese government took note of the resistance in the south that had begun in 1958; in January 1959 the Politburo decided to commit the Viet Minh political and military apparatus remaining in the south to overt support of the new resistance and the North Vietnamese government called for forceful liberation of all of Vietnam from foreign domination. Southern political and military cadres who had come to the North were sent back to build an independence movement able to overthrow Diem. Infiltration increased and on September 10, 1960, the National Liberation Front for the Liberation of South Vietnam was born. The Second Indochina War had begun, though few took notice.

These developments were well reported in Washington, but American support for Diem was unwavering. On October 26, 1960, President Eisenhower formally assured Diem that the United States would continue supporting him. This promise meant that, regardless of the presidential election outcome then two weeks away, this commitment would continue. For the United States, the immediate objective of preventing a communist takeover had been achieved by improving the stability of the anti-communist governments in Vietnam, Laos, and Cambodia. The Republic of Vietnam had a constitution and a constituent assembly (with members selected by Diem rather than by democratic vote) and promoted social and economic reform; that such reforms only benefited the pro-Western Catholic minority was ignored in Washington.

The day before his inauguration, President-elect Kennedy met with President Eisenhower. Kennedy advisor Clark Clifford later recalled that Eisenhower spent no time talking about Vietnam, rather concentrating on preservation of Laotian neutrality as the linchpin of the Southeast Asia domino theory; he stated that the Russians and Chinese were determined to destroy Laotian independence, leading to the fall of the region, and that the United States should obtain support from SEATO allies, but should intervene unilaterally to block communist expansion if necessary.

The next day, President Kennedy declared in his inaugural address:

Let the word go forth from this time and place, to friend and foe alike, that the torch has been passed to a new generation of Americans – born in this century, tempered by war, disciplined by a hard and bitter peace, proud of our ancient heritage – and unwilling to witness or permit the slow undoing of those human rights to which this nation has always been committed, and to which we are committed today at home and around the world... Let every nation know, whether it wishes us well or ill, that we shall pay any price, bear any burden, meet any hardship, support any friend, oppose any foe to assure the survival and the success of liberty.

Americans of the World War II generation were now in charge, and their ability to successfully face any issue would not be questioned.

The "New Frontiersmen," as the Kennedy Administration came to be known, prided themselves on being "men of action." Those at the highest levels believed they were able to assess, understand, and solve all problems. They really believed they were what journalist David Halberstam – who by experience knew more than any of them what they would soon face in Vietnam – would call them: "the Best and the Brightest."

In 1968, State Department East Asia specialist James C. Thomson, who worked in the White House from 1961 to 1966 under Presidents Johnson and Kennedy, wrote *How Could Vietnam Happen? An Autopsy*, published in *The Atlantic* magazine. In it, he asked, "How did men of superior ability, sound training, and high ideals – American policy-makers of the 1960s – create such costly and divisive policy?" His answer was found in the legacy of the 1950s, "the so-called 'loss of China,' the Korean War, and the Far East policy of Secretary of State Dulles." Most prominently:

in 1961 the US government's East Asian establishment was undoubtedly the most rigid and doctrinaire of Washington's regional divisions in foreign affairs. This was especially true at the Department of State, where the incoming Administration found the Bureau of Far Eastern Affairs the hardest nut to crack. It was a bureau that had been purged of its best China expertise, and of farsighted, dispassionate men, as a result of McCarthyism. Its members were generally committed to one policy line: the close containment and isolation of mainland China, the harassment of "neutralist" nations which sought to avoid alignment with either Washington or Peking, and the maintenance of a network of alliances with anti-Communist client states on China's periphery.

The 1950s legacy was broad and deep. All of the incoming administration had been seared by McCarthyism. None were willing to risk being called "soft on communism," the charge that had destroyed careers and affected policy since the night in March 1950 when Senator McCarthy had first charged that the government had been subverted by secret "communists." Thus, there were no New Frontiersmen – despite their public commitment to bringing "new ways" to Washington – who questioned the Cold War policies and worldview now locked into American government and politics. The new administration was immediately involved in the Laotian Crisis, and there were no changes in the Far East Bureau, other than renaming it the Bureau of East Asian and Pacific Affairs, until late 1961 when Averell Harriman made minor personnel changes at the top. The new administration both inherited and shared a view of an aggressive China, "a sense of China's vastness, its numbers, its belligerence; a revived sense, perhaps, of the Golden Horde." The one lesson for anyone from the Korean War was the danger of another Chinese intervention like the one that had happened in 1950.

Thus, it would in retrospect have been impossible for Kennedy to act other than he did in Southeast Asia. Thomson pointed out that the underlying cause of ultimate failure was "the replacement of the experts, who were generally and increasingly pessimistic, by men described as 'can-do guys,' loyal and energetic fixers unsoured by expertise." What became even more central to the failure was what Thomson described as:

persistent confusion as to what type of war we were fighting and, as a direct consequence, confusion as to how to end that war... Was it, for instance, a civil war, in which case counterinsurgency might suffice? Or was it a war of international aggression? Who was the aggressor – and the "real enemy?" The Viet Cong? Hanoi? Peking? Moscow?

International Communism? Or maybe "Asian Communism?" Differing enemies dictated differing strategies and tactics.

The week after his inauguration, General Edwin Lansdale, who had "saved the Philippines from communism" in the 1950s, presented Kennedy with an evaluation of South Vietnam in which he described the state of low-level crisis under Diem and the potential for communist victory. The report clearly reflected the possibility of South Vietnam falling under communist control in the coming year, but recommended continued support of Diem since the alternative was a clear communist victory.

When Lansdale finished, Kennedy turned to Walt Rostow, saying, "This is the worst we've got, isn't it? You know, Eisenhower never mentioned this. He talked about Laos but never mentioned Vietnam." The administration had campaigned on remaking American policy, foreign and domestic, in a new and different way. During the first year, events happened and decisions were made that affected American policy worldwide for the rest of the 20th century. Three events in particular affected American policy on Vietnam, though only one specifically involved Southeast Asia.

In a matter of weeks, events threatened to spiral out of control in Laos, which appeared to hold the potential for direct military confrontation between the United States and the USSR, since both supported the factions they were allied with. Laos was the last place to fight a modern war, covered by heavy jungle and lined with difficult mountain ranges. There was no modern internal transportation or infrastructure; the country was landlocked. The Soviets could only supply their forces by air from North Vietnam, while the United States could only provide supplies through Bangkok and then undertake difficult aerial resupply. The northern border was with China; those who had lived through the Chinese Korean intervention in 1950 had no appetite for a replay of the most catastrophic American near-defeat since the Civil War.

Despite Eisenhower having urged a unilateral military intervention, President Kennedy moved cautiously. The Joint Chiefs advised that any military action taken with sufficient force to insure success could involve a large-scale land war, suggesting a minimum of 60,000 troops. When Secretary of State Rusk asked JCS Chairman General Lyman L. Lemnitzer if "we can get the 101st Airborne in there," he responded,

"We can get it in all right. It's getting out that I'm worried about."
Kennedy saw his task as convincing the communists he would fight
if necessary while working toward a political settlement. At a White
House press conference on March 23, 1961, he called for an end to
hostilities and a move towards negotiations, saying that all Southeast
Asia would be endangered were Laos lost and that he sought "real
neutrality, observed by all." The statement marked his unambiguous
commitment to defending Southeast Asia as a whole.

The next day, a Marine landing team on Okinawa was ordered to
prepare for deployment to Laos. Nikita Khrushchev now believed
he would have to accept a cease-fire and neutrality. Even as world
attention was on Laos, the administration had determined to make its
Southeast Asian stand in South Vietnam, which was accessible with
its ports on the South China Sea, and seen as more unified than Laos.
Importantly, North Vietnam was between the potential battlefield and
China; there were no plans for an invasion that might result in Chinese
military intervention. On April 23, an interagency task force, headed
by Deputy Secretary of Defense Roswell Gilpatric, was ordered to
study the communist effort to dominate South Vietnam and present
military, political, economic, and overt/covert options to prevent the
communists from taking power.

The report was submitted on May 6, 1961. The central conclusion
was that the United States must take whatever action was necessary
to defend South Vietnam. National Security Memorandum 52 was
approved on May 11; 400 Special Forces troops were sent to advise and
train the ARVN. The memorandum ordered planning and execution
of covert operations in North Vietnam. Financial aid to increase the
ARVN from 170,000 to 200,000 was approved. On May 13, a joint
US–South Vietnamese communiqué announced the United States'
commitment to defend the independence and territorial integrity of
South Vietnam against communist aggression, pledging increased
American aid to accomplish this.

These decisions played out against the failure to topple the Castro
government in Cuba in the invasion at the Bay of Pigs on April 17,
1961. President Kennedy was deeply depressed and angered by the
failure. Several years after his assassination, it was reported that he had
expressed a desire "to splinter the CIA into a thousand pieces and scatter
it to the winds." In the event he did not. The Bay of Pigs invasion set a

course of increasing escalation that would bring the world to its nearest brush with nuclear holocaust.

As Cuba and Laos played out, a crisis over the status of West Berlin became "hot." Nikita Khrushchev had issued an ultimatum in November 1958 that the Western Allies leave in six months, when he would give control of all lines of communication with the city to the German Democratic Republic. When he had conferred with President Eisenhower at Camp David, Khrushchev had come away believing that a deal could be made at the Paris Summit in May 1960; however, that had been canceled after Francis Gary Powers was shot down in a U-2 over Sverdlovsk on May 1, 1960.

Kennedy and Khrushchev were scheduled to attend a summit meeting in Vienna on June 4, 1961. Kennedy flew there aboard the new Air Force One, a Boeing 707 jetliner. No leader had ever flown through so many time zones so fast before and no one realized that "jet lag" existed. Kennedy did not realize how mentally disoriented he was. His attempt to debate Marxism with Khrushchev was a disaster; the Soviet leader said to his interpreter, "This man is very inexperienced, even immature. Compared to him, Eisenhower is a man of intelligence and vision." Khrushchev then berated Kennedy about US failures and he bragged that the "war of national liberation" in South Vietnam was the "blueprint" for future Soviet action and that American power would be of no value in such a war. He ended by renewing his Berlin ultimatum, stating that he would sign a separate peace treaty with the German Democratic Republic by December 31, 1961.

The Berlin threat was made good at midnight on August 9, 1961, when East German border guards sealed off all contact with West Berlin and began constructing the Berlin Wall. This marked the coldest part of the Cold War.

Kennedy left Vienna believing that Khrushchev had bested him and convinced that supporting South Vietnam was the conflict that would define the Cold War; in a few months, he would order direct involvement of US troops in combat there. Khrushchev came away believing that Kennedy could not stand up to him, and began the actions that led to the Cuban Missile Crisis. The Vienna Summit is perhaps the most consequential diplomatic failure of modern history.

In 1962, the Geneva conference on Laos produced the "Declaration on the Neutrality of Laos," establishing a coalition government composed of pro-American, pro-communist and neutral factions. The United States believed that the arrangement would fail in the long term, but was the best of current options. Soon after, civil war resumed; neither side made any attempt to support the agreement, though officially they all accepted it.

On November 11, 1961, President Kennedy authorized providing the ARVN with more military advisors than allowed under the 1954 agreement. On December 22, 1961, Army Security Agency technician Spec/4 James T. Davis was killed in a Viet Cong ambush near the village of Cau Xang.

The situation was worse than the "men of action" knew. French scholar Bernard Fall, the Westerner most knowledgeable about Southeast Asian politics, visited South Vietnam in January 1962. In 1953, he had traveled throughout North Vietnam independent of French officialdom; in interviews with local leaders, he demonstrated that the Viet Minh controlled far more of the country than was officially admitted. Fall's book, *Street Without Joy*, was considered the most accurate account of the First Indochina War, but was ignored in both Paris and Washington. This time, he made a similar study. His attempt to inform officials in Washington that the Viet Cong (Vietnamese communists) already controlled most of the South Vietnamese countryside was pushed aside by the CIA, who declared him either an active communist or a "French dupe." Army Chief of Staff General Earle Wheeler returned from a January 1963 tour to report confidently that things in South Vietnam were "on the right track."

The Kennedy Administration soon confronted the failure of the South Vietnamese government to contain the Viet Cong. By July 1963, the American advisor force had grown from 1,100 sent in December 1961 to 16,500; American army advisors entered combat with the ARVN units they were assigned to, while American pilots flew combat missions with their Vietnamese "pilot counterparts" mere passengers in the back seat. The official optimism didn't stop American advisor Major John Paul Vann from expressing his disillusionment with the state of things to reporters like the *New York Times'* David Halberstam. Those advisors who truly cared about the outcome knew the ARVN had been defeated in the countryside by the spring of 1963. The Diem government increased repression of all dissent.

The war changed forever in May 1963, when the Buddhist revolt against Diem's government began. The first self-immolation of a monk occurred in June. The more the government cracked down, the stronger the movement became. American attempts to initiate talks leading to inclusion of more Buddhists in the government were rebuffed by Diem and his brother No Dinh Nhu, head of the security forces. By mid-September the ARVN leadership was moving towards removal of Diem. Ambassador Henry Cabot Lodge cabled Secretary Rusk that "we are now launched on a course for which there is no respectable turning back: the overthrow of the Diem Government." Rusk, blaming Diem for the reversal of favorable conditions in the first six months of the year, gave Lodge a free hand so long as there was "no appearance of collusion with the Generals."

Secretary McNamara and General Taylor were dispatched in early October to insure there was no loss of commitment to fighting the communist enemy. President Kennedy instructed the ambassador to suspend some American aid to dissuade Diem from further repression. On return, Taylor warned Kennedy that ousting Diem would impede the war effort. Attorney General Robert F. Kennedy supported Taylor's position while his brother appeared ambivalent.

The coup began shortly after noon local time on November 1. Diem appealed for support to Ambassador Lodge, who put him off. By early evening, Diem and his brother Nhu were in army custody. Hours later, they were dead.

On November 22, 1963, John F. Kennedy was assassinated in Dallas, Texas. Vice President Lyndon Baines Johnson became the new president. A man with limited experience in foreign affairs, he was willing to support the Kennedy foreign policy team about continued involvement in Vietnam.

Seen in hindsight, the American war in Southeast Asia was as inevitable and inexorable as World War I. After 1954, the only real question was what event would set it off and when. As with the earlier conflict, those who were believed at the outset to know what they were doing were proven the least knowledgeable of all. And like the events of 1914–18, the result was a disaster with long-lasting effects.

3

PLANNING THE WRONG WAR

From the moment the future leaders of the United States Air Force could claim they had "won" the Pacific War through the atomic bombing of Hiroshima and Nagasaki, after their successful strategic bombing campaigns against Germany and Japan, Douhet's true believers reckoned they had been proven correct in their belief that air power was now the primary force projection through the strategy of "strategic bombing" in any future war. This belief was solidified in the overall policy adopted by the United States in National Security Council memorandum NSC68 in 1952, which directed that the United States would aim to achieve "strategic dominance" in its ability to fight a nuclear war. Despite the Air Force experience in Korea, where the service was unable to develop a war-winning strategy, continued belief in this policy meant that when the next war came, the Air Force was not equipped, from strategic planning through combat crew training to aircraft available for use, to effectively fight another limited war against a non-industrial opponent. Almost all Air Force technical development between the end of World War II and the commitment of American military forces to combat in Vietnam was expended on the development of aircraft that were not usable in such a conflict. Following the revelation that the USSR had exploded its own nuclear device in September 1949, years ahead of the date that US intelligence had believed such a development would be possible, the idea of a nuclear war seemed to become a much more distinct possibility. Throughout the 1950s, following the achievement of nuclear capability by the Soviet Union, the Air Force consistently overestimated the threat of nuclear war. The production of over 2,000 jet-powered nuclear bombers during this period was justified by claims that the Soviets were producing vast numbers of intercontinental bombers, creating what was called the "Bomber Gap."

The "big stick" that became the embodiment of "strategic bombing" was the B-52 Stratofortress. It began with a request for proposals issued on November 23, 1945, by the USAAF's Air Materiel Command (AMC) for a new strategic bomber "capable of carrying out the strategic mission without dependence upon advanced and intermediate bases controlled by other countries." Boeing, Consolidated Aircraft, and the Glenn L. Martin Company submitted proposals.

Boeing's Model 462, a large straight-wing aircraft powered by six Wright T35 turboprops, weighing 360,000 pounds, with a combat radius of 3,110 miles, was selected for further development on June 5, 1946. A letter of contract for $1.7 million was issued for what was designated the XB-52. The fact that the Boeing proposal failed to meet the original design requirements elicited concern from the Air Force. Boeing responded with several alternatives, none of which really answered the problem. The performance requirements were updated and in September 1947 Boeing presented the Model 464-29, with 20-degree swept wings and four Pratt & Whitney PT-4 turboprops. New Air Force requirements issued in November for a top speed of 500 miles per hour and a range of 8,000 miles were far beyond the 464-29.

Boeing managed to avoid outright cancellation in December with a personal plea from Boeing president William M. Allen to Secretary of the Air Force Stuart Symington. Boeing was instructed to explore recent technological innovations. In May 1948, turboprop power was discarded, when the Air Force opted for turbojet power. The resulting Model 464-40 substituted Westinghouse J40 turbojets; while this received a favorable response from the Air Force project officer, Deputy Chief of Staff for Material General Howard A. Craig believed jet engines were not yet ready; Boeing was directed to use the turboprop-powered Model 464-35 for the XB-52.

On Thursday October 21, 1948, Boeing engineers George S. Schairer, Art Carlsen, and Vaughn Blumenthal presented a refined 464-35 to Colonel Pete Warden, chief of bomber development; disappointed by what he saw, he asked if they could come up with a proposal for a jet-powered bomber. Joined by Vice-President of Engineering Ed Wells, they worked overnight to turn 464-35 into a jet bomber. Warden looked at what they had and asked for something better by Monday.

Faced with the knowledge that failure would mean cancellation of the project, that night the team roughed out what was essentially a new airplane which featured 35-degree swept wings, with eight engines in four underwing pods. On Saturday morning, Schairer visited a hobby shop for supplies and created a model. A secretary worked on Sunday to type a clean proposal. Monday morning, Warden was presented with a neatly bound 33-page proposal and a 14-inch scale model of an aircraft that exceeded all design specifications. The B-52 had been saved.

On April 15, 1952, well-known test pilot "Tex" Johnston took off in the YB-52 for a two-hour, 21-minute proving flight from Boeing Field in Seattle to Larson AFB near Moses Lake. The smooth flight led the Air Force to increase its order to 282 B-52s, the first of which entered service in 1956. Eventually, 742 B-52s were manufactured by the time production ended in 1962. However, the bomber designed to fight thermonuclear war would only ever deliver conventional bombs in Southeast Asia.

The West had underestimated Soviet military capability before World War II. However, when three B-29s – which Western observers at first believed were the three known to have landed in Siberia during the war – appeared over Tushino airfield in Moscow for the Soviet Aviation Day Celebration on August 3, 1947 and were followed minutes later by a fourth bomber, panic set in at the Pentagon. This, followed in 1949 by the appearance of the MiG-15, a jet fighter fully equal to Western equivalents, with the achievement months later of nuclear capability years before Western intelligence had believed it possible, led to massive overestimation. Combined with the closed nature of the Soviet system and a very effective Soviet disinformation strategy throughout the Cold War, such intelligence overestimation prevailed right up to the Soviet collapse in 1989.

The four bombers seen over Tushino were the result of an incredible feat: the reverse-engineering of the most complex aircraft in the world at the time. The three combat-damaged B-29s that landed in Siberia in late 1944 and early 1945 were interned, since the USSR was at the time neutral in the Pacific War. After repairs, they were flown to Moscow and delivered to the Tupolev OKB, where Stalin personally ordered designer Andrei Tupolev to create an exact copy as rapidly as possible. All design work was completed by the summer of 1945. By the end of 1946, 20 aircraft, designated Tu-4, were ready for state acceptance trials. The first flew on May 19, 1947; serial production began that summer, and the Tu-4 entered service in 1949.

What wasn't known in the West was that only 847 Tu-4s were built, of which no more than 500 ever served in the Aviatsiya Dal'nego Deysviya (ADD), the Soviet strategic bombing force. Not only that, it was the only mass-produced Soviet long-range manned bomber to see service. However, a series of prototypes appeared over the next few years to convince the West that a massive, highly capable bomber force was being created.

On May 1, 1954, 12 Tu-16 bombers, powered by two enormous Mikulin AM-3 turbojets, appeared over Tushino. To the USAF, this was the Soviet B-47, which had only entered service a year before. In 1955, ten M-4 bombers, powered by four AM-3s, flew over the Tushino crowd; several minutes later, a second ten-plane formation, followed by an eight-plane formation, appeared. The USAF believed that the Soviets had just flown their B-52 equivalent in public a matter of months after the XB-52 had flown. In 1956, the Tu-95, powered by four Kuznetsov NK-12 turboprop engines and the size of the B-52 that had not yet entered USAF service, flew in a similar set of formations to that of the M-4 the year before.

What the Air Force didn't know was that the multiple formations were actually one each. Once flown past the reviewing stand, they circled for the second, then two dropped off before the third. It was a masterpiece of Soviet disinformation that convinced the US Air Force their enemy would have 800 bombers by 1960. The Pentagon proclaimed a "bomber gap."

President Eisenhower was skeptical. In 1956, the U-2, a long-range high-altitude reconnaissance aircraft developed for the CIA by Lockheed became operational; it could confirm or deny the estimates. As it operated at 70,000 feet, interception was believed impossible. The missions to find out what really existed in the riddle wrapped in a mystery inside an enigma that was the Soviet Union were among the most important intelligence-gathering flights ever flown.

The first U-2 overflight of the Soviet Union occurred on July 4, 1956, a mission to Minsk flown by CIA pilot Hervey Stockman. The intruder was spotted by Soviet radar, but the MiG-17s sent to intercept it stalled out 20,000 feet below Stockman's airplane. On July 9, Martin Knutson left England on Mission 2020. He photographed 30 M-4 bombers at an airfield southwest of Leningrad. The mission resulted in

National Intelligence Estimate NIE 11-4-57, issued in November 1957. Extrapolating from the number of bombers photographed on Mission 2020, multiplying by the number of known bases capable of operating such aircraft, the analysts stated that the ADD would have 150–250 operational M-4s by 1958, and more than 600 by 1965. The Air Force claim of a "bomber gap" was true.

Follow-up in 1957–58 found no other M-4s. The missions revealed that the Red Air Force was actually operating at a very low activity level. Further intelligence from the CIA showed that M-4 production had slowed. In April 1958, CIA analyst Sherman Kent stated that production of the M-4 appeared to have slowed in anticipation of ending, and force estimates should be cut by 80 percent.

The Air Force refused to listen and issued a counter-report in May 1958, suggesting that M-4 production was taking place at Kyubyshev in Kazakhstan and Irkutsk in Siberia, with the aircraft delivered to Engels-2, Bila Tserkva, and Balbasovo air bases – none of which had been overflown. In December 1959, Engels-2 and Kyubyshev were overflown by a U-2 flown by an RAF pilot; there was no sign of bombers or factories. Dino Brugioni, then a CIA photo interpreter, remembered, "Within several months, we could positively produce facts that the bomber gap didn't exist. We solved the main problem facing President Eisenhower."

Eisenhower's frustration with the Air Force and the aircraft industry that supported the fight for more bombers and interceptors to meet a threat he knew never existed resulted in his farewell address in January 1961, in which he warned of the "military-industrial complex" as a threat to the republic.

What was ignored throughout this time was that every Aviation Day celebration from the first appearance of the MiG-15 on featured flights by fighters of ever-increasing sophistication, designed to meet the very real threat posed by Strategic Air Command (SAC) and its leader, a general was often quoted as hoping that some incident would finally allow him to fight World War III "while we can."

The appearance of the Tu-4, based on an aircraft known to be able to carry and drop an atomic bomb, panicked the US Air Force since it had the range, flown trans-polar, to fly a one-way mission as far as Chicago or Los Angeles. The result was an industrial mobilization second only to the Manhattan Project to create the technological and industrial base to support the design and production of what came to be known as "the Century Series," revolutionary supersonic fighters that changed the face of aviation. The revolution began in 1953.

A clear spring dawn over the California High Desert is always spectacular. The sun rises out of the Sonoran Desert to the east and the deep clear blue of the sky becomes progressively more visible. So it was the morning of May 25, 1953, when two pilots approached the aircraft they were to fly, parked on the ramp at the Air Force Flight Test Center, otherwise known as Edwards AFB. The smaller was the well-known North American F-86D Sabre. The hulking monster sitting next to it made the Sabre look small. North American chief test pilot George Welch turned to his "chase" pilot, Air Force Flight Test Centre (AFFTC) commander Lieutenant Colonel Frank K. "Pete" Everest, known as "the fastest man alive" for his record-breaking flights in rocket-powered experimental aircraft, and bet him two beers they'd "do it," on the new airplane's first flight.

Welch, who had shot down four Japanese aircraft over Pearl Harbor on December 7, 1941, climbed up the ladder and swung into the cockpit. The two taxied onto the dry lake, the longest, widest runway in North America, and accelerated. A moment later, Everest became the first human to see the gout of flame with the diamond shock waves within spout from the exhaust of Welch's airplane when he lit the afterburner and climbed into the desert sky like the proverbial homesick angel, leaving Everest far behind.

Twenty minutes later, Everest finally caught up. The two were high over Edwards at 35,000 feet; Everest used full afterburner just to keep station with the big jet. "Hang on, here we go," Welch's voice echoed in Everest's headset. The gout of flame with the diamond-shaped shockwaves erupted again as the J57 went from 9,870 pounds of thrust to 14,000 pounds in 20 seconds with a "whoomp!" so loud Everest could hear it through his canopy and helmet. In less than a minute, Welch was out of sight.

Below, the North American engineers and everyone else heard the echoing sonic boom seven miles overhead. George Welch had just gone supersonic in level flight in a jet-powered airplane, the North American YF-100. That afternoon, just to prove it wasn't a fluke, he did it again. Less than 50 years after the first flight of the Wright Brothers, operational supersonic jet-powered flight had arrived and aviation would never be the same.

North American first began thinking about a supersonic fighter in 1948. At the time, there were two ways to go: a very big airframe powered by a very big engine, or Something Else, only seen dimly at the time. Edgar Schmued and Raymond Rice, the premier fighter designers in the United States as the creators of the P-51 Mustang and F-86 Sabre, were offended aesthetically by a big airplane that wouldn't be able to do what their two war-winning designs could do in air combat.

By June 1948, they had determined that the optimum wing sweepback was 45 degrees; the project became known within North American as the "Sabre-45." Had they proceeded, the airplane likely would have been powered by the General Electric J53, which later provided 23,000 pounds of thrust with afterburner. Schmued and Rice thought the best alternative light engine would be the afterburning J40, a Navy design which ultimately proved to be one of the major disappointments of early jet engine development.

In early 1949, Pratt & Whitney told them about the JT3, which would prove to be the most significant gas turbine engine since Whittle's W1. The JT3 was a jet development of an engine that began life as the PT4 turboprop, the second powerplant choice for the B-52. In developed form as the J57, it would power the F-100, the F8U Crusader, and the F4D Skyray, as well as the Boeing 707 and Douglas DC-8 jetliners, with more than 21,000 engines produced. It was light and yet as strong as anything Pratt & Whitney ever made, providing reliability second to none. Looking at its specifications, North American engineers saw the drag rise was well beyond Mach 1.

North American's formal proposal for a supersonic fighter was presented in January 1949. The Air Force made the program official on February 3, 1949, though it was still a company-funded project. The name "Sabre" was kept for emotive value, though it was obvious that the new design would have little to do with the airplane that came before.

The F-100 was the first beneficiary of an industry–government alliance which provided more money for more basic aerodynamic research and advanced machine tool development than had been spent in all the years since the Wright Brothers, to create operational supersonic flight. Only a country that produced 52 percent of the planetary Gross Economic Product in 1950 could have done so while at the same time taking the German autobahn to its penultimate development in the Interstate

Highway System and simultaneously creating the modern American middle class through the GI Bill.

Using public funds, North American built the first supersonic wind tunnel in April 1949.

Based on the German Kochel system, it had a sphere of dry air exhausting into a vacuum chamber; the peak attainable Mach number was 5.25. The wind tunnel tests led to a radical redesign, with the fortunate result that the horizontal stabilizer was pulled off the vertical fin and put where it belongs on a supersonic airplane: low on the fuselage, where it cannot be blanked by the shockwaves coming off the wing. At the same time, Pratt & Whitney developed the variable nozzle for use on an afterburner, resulting in a reliable engine that never failed to ignite. With these developments, Raymond Rice knew he could go supersonic.

The supersonic fighters that were developed could not have been created without the development of the physical industrial plant to build such aircraft. This involved advances in structures, materials and techniques, propulsion systems, and aerodynamics eclipsing all aviation development since the Wright Brothers. The aerodynamic research bill alone was $375 million in 1950s dollars, which included the X-1 series, the X-2, X-3, and the Skyrocket. Engine research and development costs came to $280 million. The Air Force spent $397 million to create a heavy press capable of squeezing large light-alloy forgings that otherwise would have been constructed in separate parts or "hogged" (sculptured) from a solid slab. The press allowed lightweight single-piece aircraft skins to be produced in a matter of minutes. Radical new machine tools that could remove vast amounts of metal at high speed with extreme precision and for automatic precision machines capable of drilling, countersinking, dimpling, riveting, reaming, bolting, and sealing, doing these operations in sequence – and all before computers – were developed at a cost of $180 million. A brand-new industry was created to produce 500–600 tons of wrought titanium a month; supersonic fighters used prodigious amounts of this metal. Developing electrical and hydraulic systems that could operate reliably after being soaked for extended periods at up to 300 degrees Celsius, in addition to reliable miniaturized electronic devices still using vacuum tubes in the days before the transistor revolution, cost several hundred million dollars.

In the five years between 1950 and 1955, $2 billion in 1950s dollars was spent merely to create an industry that could produce supersonic fighters. It was the second most-expensive government sponsored scientific research program after the Manhattan Project.

Air Force enthusiasm about the F-100 was such that Air Force pilots led by Everest performed Phase II tests while North American was in Phase I testing. Approval for 110 F-100As was given 90 days after the first flight. On October 29, 1953, Everest flew the second YF-100 at the Salton Sea and hit 753 miles per hour at sea level to officially demonstrate the Super Sabre's supersonic capability.

At this point, North American made a nearly fatal decision to chop the vertical fin at a point just above the rudder to lessen the wetted surface. Ultimately, the result would affect the way every supersonic airplane built after was designed.

The 479th Day Fighter Wing at nearby George AFB, southeast of Edwards in the California Desert, received the first F-100As in the spring of 1954. The first unexplained loss happened weeks later, and within 60 days four F-100s crashed out of control. At the conclusion of Phase II testing, Everest's team identified an area of the flight envelope where dynamic coupling could occur; it was dismissed as something a service pilot would never experience. Everest counseled delay in putting the airplane into service until this anomaly had been thoroughly investigated. Contravening every previous policy for introducing new technological breakthroughs, the Air Force allowed senior service pilots to wring out the airplane; they all said it was wonderful and Everest was wrong. Everest nearly lost his career for sticking to his guns no matter the top brass's anger. At the 479th, then-First Lieutenant Ed Rasimus later recalled that squadron pilots were actually afraid of their airplanes.

At 1030 hours on October 12, 1954, George Welch took off from Edwards in F-100A FW-764, to fly the maximum structural test, a Phase I test that should have been completed prior to any Phase II testing, long before the airplane entered squadron service. A "maximum structural test" is the traditional maximum velocity dive from maximum altitude with a maximum performance pullout. Welch had flown the test earlier and hadn't hit the limit load factor of 7.5G in his pullout. At 1100 hours, he radioed North American's Flight Test center at Edwards that he was over the Mojave Desert town of Rosamond and starting the dive. At 1102 hours, radio contact was lost. Palmdale Airport Tower informed the team that two parachutes had been spotted. The engineers took off in two Navions, and soon discovered the F-100's braking parachute trapped around the remains of the tail, with a dying Welch under the second.

Welch's crash resulted in an accident investigation rivaled only by that following the Comet 1 crashes. Fortunately, the airplane was instrumented. When the pieces were recovered it was determined that everything had been working perfectly until the airplane exploded, which had been witnessed by the crew of a B-47 transiting the area. The answer was found in a camera mounted in the fin that kept running on inertia after it lost power. The film showed the sharp shadow of the fin and rudder racing across the right horizontal stabilizer. Griffith Park Observatory provided the sun's exact bearing and azimuth, making it possible to calculate that the airplane had yawed violently to the right, resulting in a supersonic sideslip that exceeded the airframe design limit. Finding the oscillograph provided confirmation.

The investigation ultimately revealed that, as Welch pulled harder on the stick to pull out, the F-100 yawed to the right, giving a vertical acceleration of 8Gs and suddenly increasing from 8 to 15 degrees right yaw, which stabilized, then went off the scale. The airplane had been designed to survive an 8-degree yaw and 7Gs of side force. Essentially, what happened was the airplane lost directional control. Chuck Yeager once explained that the "supersonic tumble" that happened to him in the X-1A in December 1953 resulted from the supersonic shock waves off the nose blanking the small tail, with the result that the airplane acted as if it had "lost its tail." During Welch's attempted pullout, the F-100's short vertical fin had been blanked by the supersonic shock waves in the same way, resulting in a catastrophic loss of directional stability.

The original tall vertical fin was immediately reinstated on the production line, and the existing aircraft were quickly retrofitted, solving the problem. Ever since, all supersonic airplanes have had large tail surfaces, because something has to stick out beyond the supersonic shock wave to keep everything going in the same direction under control.

The F-100 was the only supersonic airplane that did not conform to Richard Whitcomb's "Area Rule" for supersonic aircraft, which stated that the drag on an airplane flying at high speed is a function of the aircraft's entire cross-sectional area. The similarly powered F8U Crusader, the design of which fortuitously did conform to the yet-to-be-discovered area rule, was some 300 miles per hour faster than the F-100 as a result, with the same engine.

Within a year of Welch's crash, the fully capable F-100C arrived, followed shortly by the even-better F-100D, which became the most widely produced sub-type. Originally designed for air superiority, the Super Sabre served most of its career as a fighter-bomber, seeing more direct combat than any other Century Series fighter, including the F-105, as the main jet fighter-bomber in South Vietnam between 1964 and 1971, and served with the Air National Guard (ANG) until 1979. The 3,850 F-100s flew more combat hours than the 16,000 P-51s that North American produced. In Vietnam, they maintained an 80 percent serviceability rate over seven years and flew 1.2 sorties per aircraft per day, a record no other Air Force Fighter came close to.

The F-100 found its shortcomings in the early *Rolling Thunder* missions when the "Huns" were deployed as fighter escorts. The J57 engine suffered violent compressor stalls when the afterburner was engaged in high angle-of-attack maneuvers used in aerial combat. Lieutenant Colonel David Williams, who flew some of the early F-100D MiG Combat Air Patrol (MiGCAP) missions, recalled experiencing a compressor stall so violent that fire exited the nose intake and tailpipe simultaneously while shaking the rudder pedals so hard he lost foot contact with them.

The F-100D's empty weight of 22,300 pounds was more than twice the MiG-17F's 8,373 pounds, meaning that the "Hun" lacked the acceleration or maneuverability to oppose the nimble MiG. Colonel Williams, who later scored a MiG kill in an F-4D Phantom, stated:

I feel confident that the F-100 would not have fared well in the MiGCAP role because I do not believe that it could either out-turn or out-climb the MiG-17 or MiG-21, or out-dive or out-run the latter fighter. The F-100 suffered from a low thrust-to-weight ratio, and in a hard turn the aircraft would shudder, approaching a stall even with the leading-edge slats extended. The airspeed would then bleed off quickly, leaving the pilot in a terribly vulnerable position.

Whereas the F-100 got everything right the first time, the fighter that followed it got nearly everything from initial design concept onward wrong. In November 1951, famed Lockheed designer Kelly Johnson visited Korea, spending time asking pilots flying combat in the F-86 what they wanted in a future fighter. The F-86A was inferior to the MiG-15 in high-altitude performance and gunpower; its avionics were difficult to maintain. Many of the pilots felt that the MiG was superior to the larger and more complex Sabre and asked for a small, simple aircraft with good speed and high-altitude capability. Johnson returned to Lockheed committed to a lightweight fighter that would fly faster and higher than any other in the world. Unfortunately, almost all air combat since 1953 has happened below 20,000 feet at subsonic speed. Johnson's F-104 Starfighter is still one of the most dramatic designs to see the light of day; sitting in a museum, it still looks as if it's going a million miles an hour.

Johnson chose a small, simple design, weighing 12,000 pounds, powered by the new General Electric J79, an engine with dramatically improved performance. He presented the Model 83 to the Air Force on November 5, 1952. The Air Force was sufficiently interested to create a general operational requirement for such a fighter. Republic Aviation responded with the AP-55, an improvement on the XF-91 Thunderceptor, while North American's NA-212 ultimately became the F-107, and Northrop submitted the J79-powered N-102 Fang. Lockheed's insurmountable head start resulted in a contract on March 12, 1953, for two prototypes designated XF-104. Unlike the F-100, the F-104's horizontal stabilizer was atop the vertical fin in a "T" position, where it could be blanked at high angles of attack, limiting flight maneuvers.

The mock-up was inspected in late April. Following approval, work began on two prototypes. With the J79 unready, both used the J65, a license-built Armstrong Siddeley Sapphire. The first prototype flew on March 4, 1954 with Tony LeVier in the cockpit for a 21-minute flight at Edwards, less than a year after work began. The second was lost several weeks later during gun-firing trials when the hatch to the ejection seat blew out, depressurizing the cockpit; the pilot ejected, mistakenly believing that an accident with the cannon had crippled the airplane.

Powered by the J79, production F-104As were "placarded" at Mach 2 to prevent overheating the J79 and deforming the aluminum skin due to air friction. The downward ejection seat meant that the pilot couldn't eject until he was at 1,500 feet. This was considered responsible for the loss of Korean War ace and test pilot Iven C. Kincheloe during testing of the production version, the first of 20 other Air Force pilots who would die trying to use this system.

Once operational in 1958, lack of an onboard radar other than the ranging radar and limited fuel capacity adversely limited the F-104A as an interceptor, while its small wing limited maneuverability. The M61 Vulcan cannon suffered problems, with its linked ammunition being prone to misfeed and presenting a foreign object damage hazard as discarded links were occasionally sucked into the engine. A linkless ammunition feed system was developed for the upgraded M61A1 in the F-104C, which had ammunition for a maximum seven seconds. After 90 days of operations, the 83rd Fighter-Interceptor Squadron's F-104As were grounded due to engine-related accidents. In the August 1958 Formosa Straits Crisis, F-104As were airlifted to Taiwan, where they made high-speed flights between Taiwan and the Chinese mainland to awe the People's Liberation Army Air Force.

The F-104As were removed from the Air Force inventory and turned over to the Air National Guard beginning in 1960 except for two squadrons in Florida whose purpose was to counter Cuban MiG-21s. Two ANG squadrons stood quick-reaction alert in West Germany during the 1961 Berlin Crisis. Rather than the thousands of F-104s that Lockheed had believed they would produce, the Air Force ordered only 153 F-104As. Lockheed upgraded the F-104C, which had an improved AN/ASG-14T-2 fire control radar and a centerline pylon capable of carrying the Mark 28 or Mark 43 tactical nuclear bomb. Range was increased through air refueling capability. The Air Force ordered a disappointing 77. Altogether, including the two-seat F-104B and D trainer versions of the F-104A and C respectively, total production was only 296.

In September 1958, the 479th Tactical Fighter Wing received F-104C nuclear strike fighters. They saw major success in the 1962 William Tell competition. The 479th's Captain Charles E. Tofferi was considered an interloper, given the 479th's primary mission of tactical nuclear strike, but competing against ten other pilots in F-100s, and three in F-105s, he scored 19,018 points out of a possible 24,000 – 2,000 points ahead of his nearest competitor. Three close-support missions were perfect 1,000s and he scored the maximum 3,000 points in aerial gunnery by shooting down the towed target in 63 seconds. That fall, the wing transferred to Florida with the potential assignment of flying strikes into Cuba had the Cuban Missile Crisis turned into an invasion.

While popular history claims that the F-104 was unsuccessful in Southeast Asia, 100-mission F-104 veteran Tom Delahunt disagreed, recalling:

After the disastrous battle at the Dragon's Jaw on April 4, the Air Force determined that there was a need for an airborne early warning capability to provide coverage in North Vietnam. An EC-121D College Eye unit was dispatched, and TAC [Tactical Air Command] was asked to deploy F-104s to escort the EC-121s over the Gulf of Tonkin and to provide a MiG screen for strike aircraft. The 479th TFW [Tactical Fighter Wing], then based at George AFB in California, received the deployment order on April 7, 1965 as part of Operation *Two-Buck Charlie*, which assigned fighter units to Southeast Asia on TDY [temporary duty]. The first 24 F-104Cs of the 476th TFS [Tactical Fighter Squadron] were delivered to Kung Kuan Air Base on Taiwan, on April 11 after being disassembled and loaded aboard C-124s for the trans-Pacific flight. Kung Kuan was to serve as the main operating base for the F-104s, with regular rotation of 14 aircraft to the forward operating base at DaNang every ten days. After a work-up period of seven days, 14 F-104s arrived at DaNang on April 19, and flew their first escort mission the next day.

The typical EC-121 escort mission involved three flights of four F-104s, supported by two KC-135 tankers. Sorties typically lasted two to five hours, with the operating area 250–300 miles north-northwest of Da Nang, off the North Vietnamese coast over the Gulf of Tonkin. MiGCAP missions involved two or three four-plane flights deployed at various altitudes between the strike area and Hanoi–Haiphong, and on-station times varied from 40 to 90 minutes with aerial refueling required for longer-duration missions.

Delahunt recalled:

The effect of F-104 deployment on North Vietnamese and Chinese communist MiG operations was immediate and dramatic. The North Vietnamese avoided contact with strikes covered by F-104s, and Chinese MiGs gave the EC-121s a wide berth despite the proximity to Hainan Island, from where their harassment flights had previously originated. Much to the frustration of the pilots of the F-104s, during the entire deployment of the 476th only two fleeting encounters between F-104s and enemy fighters occurred.

With a decrease in the MiG threat, the F-104s were used on weather recce and ground attack missions. Weather recce involved two F-104s flying near enough to a target area to report the pre-strike weather without revealing the target's identity. Antiaircraft artillery (AAA)-suppression sorties were flown against targets in North Vietnam; however, the majority of ground attack sorties were in-country close air support missions controlled by airborne forward air controllers (FACs). The F-104s quickly gained a reputation for accuracy and FACs specifically requested them due to their fast reaction time. Such missions took their toll. One F-104 went down 100 miles south of Da Nang on June 29; the pilot was rescued with minor injuries. The 476th Tactical Fighter Squadron completed its 96th day of TDY on July 11. In all, the Starfighters flew 1,182 sorties, with 52 percent being EC-121 escort; 24 percent MiGCAP; 5 percent weather recce; and 18 percent ground attack missions. The in-commission rate was 94.7 percent, testimony to both the quality of maintenance personnel and the maintainability of the systems.

Of the fighters that the Air Force developed during the decade before Vietnam, the F-105 Thunderchief – originally developed as a nuclear strike fighter – flew the majority of Air Force bombing missions during Operation *Rolling Thunder*. It was the only American aircraft ever removed from combat due to high losses; of 833 produced, 382 were lost including 62 non-combat losses.

What became the F-105 began as a Republic Aviation internal project in 1952 for a dedicated photo-reconnaissance aircraft replacing the RF-84F. It later morphed into a fighter-bomber because the Air Force was uninterested in a dedicated photo-reconnaissance airplane. Designer Alexander Kartvelit settled on the AP-63-31 design for the AP-63FBX (Advanced Project 63 Fighter Bomber, Experimental). It was designed for low-altitude supersonic penetration, delivering a nuclear weapon carried in an internal bomb bay, with design emphasis on low-altitude speed and flight characteristics, range, and payload. Its heavy weight and relatively small wing provided a high wing loading for a stable ride at low altitude; with only secondary consideration given to traditional attributes like maneuverability, it was more bomber than fighter.

With urgency from the Korean War, Air Material Command awarded Republic a contract for 199 F-105s "off the drawing board" in September 1952. Six months later, with the end in sight in Korea, the order was reduced to 37 fighter-bombers and nine tactical reconnaissance versions in March 1953. With design refinement, it grew so large by the time the mock-up was ready for inspection, the

J71 engine was abandoned for the more powerful Pratt & Whitney J75. A month later, due to continued uncertainty about the final design, the contract was officially canceled. Kartveli's design team persisted and finalized a design that resurrected the project in June 1954, with two YF-105As, four YF-105Bs, six F-105Bs, and three RF-105Bs ordered under the Weapon System designation WS-306A.

The first YF-105A flew on October 22, 1955, followed by the second on January 28, 1956. Due to extended development of the J75, which provided 24,500 pounds of thrust with afterburner, these aircraft used the less-powerful J57-P-25 which gave first flight. Further testing revealed problems associated with transonic drag, as had been experienced with the F-102. With the area rule now known, the fuselage was modified with a "wasp waist," resulting in the F-105B; the first to use the J75, it hit Mach 2.15 on its first flight. The first production F-105B was accepted on May 27, 1957 and in August the Air Force named it "Thunderchief," continuing the Republic tradition of "Thunder"-named aircraft.

To meet the need for all-weather strike capability, in 1957 Republic proposed the F-105D, with the AN/ASG-19 Thunderstick bombing/navigation system designed around an Autonetics R-14A radar that operated in air-to-air and air-to-ground modes, and the AN/APN-131 Doppler navigation radar. The cockpit featured vertical-tape instrument displays for adverse weather operation. The capacity to carry the TX-43 nuclear weapon was added. The F-105D first flew June 9, 1959. Plans to procure 1,500 F-105Ds were cut short in November 1961 when Secretary of Defense McNamara directed the Air Force to adopt the Navy's F-4 Phantom, with long-range strike capability met by the new TFX program that became the F-111. Thus the Thunderchief equipped only seven wings. Of 833 produced, the final 143 were the two-seat F-105F conversion trainer, which proved faster than the single-seater due to increased fuselage fineness ratio.

Designed for operation in a short-term nuclear campaign in which it would fly no more than one strike mission, the F-105 would reveal shortcomings in extended operations in Southeast Asia where each airframe was expected to fly more than 100 missions, including a poor hydraulics layout that resulted in complete control loss if any part of the system was hit by enemy fire; lack of self-sealing fuel tanks, allowing the airplane to catch fire easily when hit; and limited overall operational readiness in the tropical environment thanks to its vacuum-tube avionics. Thus, while a single F-105 could deliver a heavier bomb load than the B-17 or B-24 Liberator, it was not suited to an extended conventional bombing campaign. But because of the lack of an alternative, it became the primary Air Force attack aircraft during Operation *Rolling Thunder*; over 20,000 sorties were flown between 1965 and 1968. Despite the aircraft's lack of air combat maneuverability, F-105s were credited with 27.5 MiG victories, the most of any Air Force fighter type. The two-seat variant became the backbone of Air Force suppression of enemy air defense (SEAD) capability in the battle against surface-to-air missiles (SAMs), flying the Wild Weasel mission.

The fighter pilot community had a lukewarm reaction to the F-105 when first introduced. Between its enormous size and the troubled early service experienced, it gained the nicknames "Thud" (the sound made when it hit the ground), "Squat Bomber," "Lead Sled," and "Hyper Hog" or "Ultra Hog." Due to operational problems the F-105D fleet was grounded in December 1961, then again the following June. Its capability was sarcastically referred to as a "Triple Threat": "it could bomb you, strafe you, or fall on you." Over time, the positive aspects, such as responsive controls, good performance at high speed and low altitude, and its electronics won over some pilots, particularly after the completion of the Project Look Alike upgrades after 1964. Famed F-105 pilot Colonel Jack Broughton said: "The Thud has justified herself, and the name that was originally spoken with a sneer has become one of utmost respect through the air fraternity."

Following McNamara's decision to stop production in 1961, the mission was gradually changed from nuclear interdiction to conventional bombing. Bomb capacity was increased through the Look Alike upgrades from four to 16 750-pound bombs on underwing and fuselage centerline hard points, with an upgrade to use the AGM-12 Bullpup air-to-ground missile.

That the F-105 was even designated a "fighter," showed how little importance the bomber generals leading the Air Force accorded to air superiority. The Thunderchief was a bomber, with a very secondary air combat capability. It was the largest, most complex, single-seat attack bomber of its generation; in Vietnam it was used as a strategic bomber. It had an M61 "Vulcan" 20mm gun (which the Phantom did not) and sometimes carried a missile or two, but the fact that its pilots

considered themselves "fighter pilots" did not make it one. Captain
Murray Denton recalled the F-105:

> My first impression of the F-105 was how large it was and how
> roomy the cockpit seemed. Coming from the F-106 Delta Dart, I
> couldn't believe the long takeoff roll. I remember the night flights
> with three bags of fuel and water injection for more thrust. We would
> use all 9,000 feet of runway and milk the flaps up. It was a very stable
> platform, and the faster it flew the better it got. It operated well from
> sea level to 15,000ft, and in military power the jet would run faster
> than any other aircraft at low level – it just didn't turn much. It also
> had a great gun and was a very stable bomber that could take hits and
> come home.

While the F-105, like its predecessors the P-47 and F-84, was a tough
airplane that could take hits and bring the pilot home, the airplane's
Achilles' heel was its complex hydraulics system. There were two
primary systems, one for each side of the airframe, that operated the
flying controls. These were backed up by a ram air turbine that provided
limited control of an emergency system with which to power the primary
systems, if it could be deployed in time. The landing gear and brakes,
flaps, speed brakes, gun, variable inlet control plugs, refueling probe, and
water injection pump were operated by the utility system. All the lines
were in close proximity to each other in the lower fuselage, making them
highly susceptible to AAA damage. If the primary system was hit and the
ram air turbine was not quickly activated, the all-flying tail would lock
in the nose-down position, putting the airplane out of control. If a pilot
did not eject immediately, it would be impossible as the Thunderchief
went into an ever-steeper dive. Lack of a backup located some distance
from the primary system meant that if the F-105 took a good hit over
the target there was little chance of it being flown any distance to give
the pilot an opportunity to eject where he might evade capture.

After several losses due to loss of hydraulic fluid, an automatic lock
which kept the stabilator in the neutral position when hydraulic control
was lost was added, allowing the aircraft to fly straight and level and get
some distance before the pilot was forced to eject. A more comprehensive
fix was a third, back-up hydraulic system to allow basic flight control,
housed in a slim ridge fairing on the fuselage spine. The fuel tanks were
made self-sealing and were lined with fire-retardant polyurethane foam.

When the K-17 reflector sight was set for bombing, it had no accuracy for air-to-air combat. The system was poorly designed, requiring the pilot to move several switches in disparate locations to switch from bombing to air-to-air mode. Doing this took valuable time, allowing the enemy MiG to get away before the pilot was able to engage. The air-to-air mode was included only with the understanding that the pilot might be forced to briefly engage enemy interceptors en route to the target, rather than as an air combat system. Ten F-105 pilots made gun kills by centering the target in the windscreen, then tapping the rudder pedals to "spray" gunfire into the airspace occupied by the enemy fighter.

The provision to carry and use the AIM-9B Sidewinder was premised on its being more a deterrent to an enemy interceptor than a weapon for air combat. By the end of the 1966, one F-105 in a flight of four carried two Sidewinders, while the other three carried jamming pods for SAM protection. The AIM-9B Sidewinder had to be fired within a cone behind the target 5 degrees to either side of the exhaust at a range of 3,000–3,500 feet. If either the F-105 or the target maneuvered at more than 2G, the missile would break lock and go ballistic. The infrared sighting system worked best with the target against a clear sky background; lock-on could fail if the target went between the launch aircraft and the sun, or through ground heat if the target was in a dive or against a cloud backdrop. A MiG-17 pilot who spotted a Sidewinder launch could time a sharp, high-speed 70-degree turn or start a shallow dive. With attitude relative to the missile changing as a result, either maneuver would break the AIM-9B's lock. An F-105 pilot's best chance of scoring was to fire from behind and below, climbing into the MiG's blind spot with the enemy fighter against a clear sky background while maneuvering within the launch parameters. This was almost impossible in the usual high-G maneuvering of a fighter-vs-fighter battle. The situation as regards the Sidewinder was also true for the F-4 Phantom. Thus, F-105 pilots only managed to get three of their 27 MiG-17 kills with missiles.

Because of the Sidewinder's unreliability, the M61A1 cannon became the preferred weapon for air combat. The cannon and its ammunition only added 800 pounds to the F-105D. The six-barrel Gatling gun fired 20mm ammunition at 6,000 rounds per minute in 2.5-second bursts, at a muzzle velocity of 3,380 feet per second, with cooling time between bursts. While the total firing time was only ten seconds, a well-aimed burst fired at 100 rounds per second could saw the wing off the target.

The M61 was reliable, with a 10 percent failure rate due to jamming, which would happen if a round slipped out of position in the drum or on the conveyor belts.

The key to the F-105's air-to-air success was its engine. The J75 was the largest turbojet ever installed in a single-seat fighter and was thoroughly reliable by 1965. At low altitude, the F-105 was extremely difficult for a MiG-17 or MiG-21 to catch, with a top speed in excess of 700 miles per hour. MiG-17s were forced to attack from ahead once the F-105s dropped their ordnance, requiring close guidance from their ground control. The MiG-21 could catch the F-105 from the rear, but only if it had been favorably positioned by ground control to dive on the formation. While the J75 was tremendously powerful, its acceleration from low speed in a combat situation was the slowest of any jet's, unless the pilot went into a dive. The heavy weight and high wing loading meant it would rapidly bleed off speed in a high-G turn or steep climb. In the United States, the crew chief started the ground power unit, which spun the turbine blades to the start speed, at which point the "start" button was pushed and the igniter plugs started the flame from fuel spraying into the igniter chamber. In Thailand, F-105s used a starter cartridge the size of a three-pound coffee can, which burned and created expanding gases that spun the turbine. It was more dangerous than ground power, with the potential for a hang-fire, and even an explosion, but it cut down starting time for a formation since they could all start simultaneously without waiting for the starter cart. Ed Rasimus remembered, "One always knew when there were planes starting up out on the line by the explosions and the clouds of black smoke issuing from the airplanes and blowing across the field."

In air combat, the weak point of the Thunderchief was its wing, which was swept at 45 degrees and had a total area of 385 square feet, which was small for the overall aircraft size. It was thin for high speed, provided stable, high speed flight at low altitudes, and was good for the tactical nuclear mission that the aircraft was originally designed to perform, but not for missions where turning performance was important. The wing thus limited the ability of the F-105 to engage the much more maneuverable MiG-17. One Thunderchief pilot noted ruefully after successfully evading enemy aircraft sent to intercept his flight that "air-to-air combat is still a turning game. The airplane that turns the best has the advantage." Also, crucially, the F-105 cockpit had very poor rear visibility, giving the initial advantage of surprise to the attacker.

The second strike against the Dragon's Jaw on April 4, 1965, marked the end of the F-100 in air-to-air combat. The replacement was the new McDonnell F-4C Phantom II.

The Navy-developed F-4 had such superior performance to the Air Force's Century Series, that when the service proposed development of a new fighter, the top leaders of the Defense Department, led by a Secretary of Defense constantly looking to simplify acquisition and promote "commonality," directed the generals to accept the admirals' airplane while promoting the need for a new fighter into a program known as the "TFX" – ultimately the F-111 – the fighter of the future for both services. The Air Force took the Phantom in 1962 under protest, designating it F-110 to become a member of the Century Series, and naming it "Spectre" to avoid notice that this was the first fighter originally developed by the Navy to be used by the Air Force since the Boeing F4B series of biplane fighters were adopted by the Air Corps as the P-12 in 1929. The adoption of the tri-service designation system in late 1962 meant that the Air Force operated an F-4 Phantom, albeit an F-4C differing from the Navy F-4B in details such as larger main wheels that resulted in a noticeable "bulge" in the upper wing to house the gear.

Unlike the Navy, which put rated pilots in the front cockpit and non-pilot-rated naval aviation observers (NAOs) in back to operate the complex radar as radar intercept operators (RIOs), the F-4C had flight controls in both cockpits and both were rated pilots. This could lead to difficulties in delegating authority and responsibility between the two since often the pilot more comfortable and experienced with the airplane and its capabilities was the junior officer in back. This only began to change in late 1965 after the Phantom entered combat. The Air Force had a surplus of navigators, and it was realized that they could be trained to operate the weapon system, leading to the creation of weapon systems operators (WSOs) who replaced second pilots in the latter part of 1966. Captain Ralph Wetterhahn, who was assigned to the 8th Tactical Fighter Wing, explained, "Navs began coming to Ubon about half way through my tour '66–'67. I never flew with one. My backseater, First Lieutenant Jerry Sharp, was a pilot, so sharing stick time was always at issue."

The F-4 Phantom, like every other US "fighter" designed after Korea, with the exception of the F-8 Crusader, had not been designed with air combat maneuverability in mind. The original concept was a "fleet defense fighter" which would engage nuclear-armed bombers at long range from the fleet and shoot them down with beyond-visual-range (BVR) missiles. For both the interceptor and missiles, the target was always assumed to be large, flying straight and level, and unable to perform evasive maneuvers. Thus, when a Phantom did engage in air combat maneuvering (ACM), it was subject to uncontrollable roll coupling if forced into high angle-of-attack maneuvers. Its primary weapon, the AIM-7 Sparrow, was designed for use against a non-maneuvering target, rather than a smaller highly maneuverable opponent. The J79 engines emitted so much smoke that Phantoms were identifiable at more than 20 miles on a clear day.

The Phantom set over a dozen world records between December 1959 and April 1962, including absolute altitude of 98,557 feet; flight at sustained altitude of 66,443.8 feet; and climb to 50,000 feet under two minutes. The important record, which revealed the F-4's design focus, was 1,606.3 miles per hour top speed. The F-4 confirmed its versatility by setting more records than any previous aircraft. However, none evaluated it in air-to-air combat. Its particular vulnerability was its hydraulic control system; with no manual backup, a minor hit led to loss of control, forcing immediate crew ejection before control was completely lost.

The F-4's most dangerous problem was "adverse yaw," also known as "departure," a situation that develops during maneuvers involving high angles of attack or hard turns in which the airflow over the airframe is disturbed, leading to complete loss of control. While control can be regained by reducing angle of attack, doing so in air combat could give the advantage to the opponent. The result was that pilots became reluctant to "fly to the limits," which is almost always the difference between winning and losing a fight.

The radar-guided AIM-7 Sparrow took seven seconds to lock on to a target; once fired, the aircraft had to hold position to put its radar on the target so the missile could guide to it. Designed as a BVR weapon, used against targets flying straight and level, it had never been tested against a maneuvering target. Due to price and budget restraints, very few were fired before the war; this meant it was unknown before the war that the Sparrow was fragile, with its internal systems subject to failure in the air combat environment. Since the rules of engagement (ROE) required that a target be identified visually, this reduced the Sparrow's usefulness. If the target could be picked up at long range, before the enemy pilot knew the Phantom was anywhere near, he would be flying at the optimum straight-and-level for successful firing; this situation happened very infrequently.

It is surprising that the Air Force stuck with the AIM-9B Sidewinder throughout the war, despite the Navy having deployed the more capable AIM-9D in 1966, and the even better AIM-9G in 1972.

Once crews engaged the far more agile MiG-17s, complaints regarding the F-4's deficiencies became common. The most frequent complaint was the poor rear visibility, since an attack from the rear was common. Others highlighted the danger from adverse yaw and departure in air combat maneuvering. Crews complained how the lack of air combat training (ACT) meant that they were ignorant of how to best use the F-4. Despite the fact that the Air Force knew the value of ACT as a result of the Project Feather Duster tests in 1965, the service resisted introducing ACT into the curriculum throughout the war.

To the Air Force leadership, the war in Korea had been a distraction from deterring the inevitable Soviet nuclear attack by the threat of massive retaliation. None of the Korean War's lessons were taken to heart, with the result that when the next war that wasn't World War III broke out in Southeast Asia a decade later, the strategy and tactics used were those that had failed in 1950–53, while most of the Air Force aircraft in use were ill-suited for the conflict.

The result of fixation on the war that the United States never fought was that the most effective aircraft used in Southeast Asia were not Air Force designs. In addition to the F-4, lack of an effective battlefield close air support (CAS) aircraft resulted in adoption of the piston-engined Douglas A-1 Skyraider as the Navy removed the venerable tactical bomber from its inventory after 1961. When the Navy commenced development of the A-7 Corsair II light attack bomber, the Air Force ordered its own specialized variant, the A-7D, which replaced the Skyraider in the final years of the conflict.

4

EARLY DAYS – 1962–65

As the two super powers engaged throughout the 1950s in a Europe-centered cold war in which each threatened the other with nuclear annihilation – though in reality during the period only the United States was capable of fighting such a war – the weaker Soviet side looked for other ways in which to engage their enemy. Leninism had always held a position of anti-imperialism, and during the period between World Wars I and II the Comintern had acted wherever possible to provide support to independence movements. In the postwar period, de-colonization became a popular movement in the European colonies. The greatest communist anti-colonial success was the victory of Mao Zedong in China in 1949.

When de-colonization accelerated in the 1950s, it appeared that the Soviets were increasing their influence in these newly independent countries. For Western military leaders, the use of the nuclear threat, which was seen as viable in preventing further Soviet encroachment in Europe, was not a viable deterrent to communist-led anti-colonial movements. In the late 1950s, military strategists in the United States developed the theory of "counterinsurgency." Communist-led insurgencies would be countered by the United States providing training to local militaries as well as technical and material support, to defeat the insurgency.

The theory did not see full flower until the Kennedy Administration came into office in 1961, perhaps the tensest year of the Cold War to date. Soviet pressure over the status of West Berlin was building. On January 6, 1961, Nikita Khrushchev gave a speech to the Soviet

Presidium that would have a far-ranging effect on East–West relations for the next 20 years. In the speech, Khrushchev announced his belief that the likely-catastrophic results of a general war did not suit communist ends, while limited wars such as the Korean War could too easily escalate to general wars and should therefore be avoided. Instead, the Soviet Union would support "wars of national liberation" and would "help the peoples striving for their independence" to overthrow colonial governments.

The speech was an open challenge to the West, and was taken exactly that way. President-elect Kennedy, only two weeks away from taking office, took particular notice. It became increasingly important within weeks of his inauguration as he faced multiple crises in Laos, South Vietnam, and South America, owing to Fidel Castro's threat to export the Cuban Revolution throughout Latin America.

In January 1961, the war in Vietnam was still a Vietnamese conflict, with no direct US involvement other than the 685-man Military Assistance Advisory Group (MAAG) responsible for training the Republic of Vietnam Armed Forces since 1955. By 1961 the ARVN had 170,000 troops, organized along US lines and using US equipment. Although it outnumbered the Viet Cong by a factor of ten, the war was not going well for the Diem government.

Kennedy quickly called for a review of Southeast Asia, where the Eisenhower Administration had focused on Laos. The resulting report by Air Force Brigadier General Edward G. Lansdale warned that the South Vietnamese government was close to being overwhelmed by an estimated 15,000 communist guerillas. In response, Kennedy signed National Security Action Memorandum (NSAM) No. 2, directing the US military to develop counterinsurgency forces capable of resisting Soviet-backed guerillas.

The three services reacted differently. The US Army had already created the "Special Forces," known as the Green Berets for their distinctive head gear, as a continuation of the World War II OSS "Jedburgh Teams" – specialist paramilitary groups to organize and train local resistance groups. Expanding their role to include training local military units in nations experiencing a communist insurgency was not hard.

The Navy's initial contribution was to emphasize the commando role that their Underwater Demolition Teams – the famous "frogmen" of World War II — had taken on during the Korean War. The result was the SEALs — an acronym for SEa Air Land. Formally organized in the Atlantic and Pacific fleets in 1962, the teams would conduct unconventional warfare, counter-guerilla warfare and clandestine operations.

The Air Force response directed Tactical Air Command (TAC) to form a counterinsurgency force which could train allied and friendly air forces to fight limited wars against guerilla forces.

On April 14, 1961, TAC activated the 4400th Combat Crew Training Squadron at Hurlburt Field, part of Eglin AFB, with a strength of 124 officers and 228 enlisted men. The squadron took the code name "Jungle Jim," which became their nickname. The declared mission was training indigenous air forces in counterinsurgency and air operations. Air Force Chief of Staff Curtis LeMay personally chose Colonel Benjamin H. King, a World War II combat veteran and recognized combat leader, as unit commander.

The call for volunteers required that pilots have at least 5,000 hours' flight time, while mechanics, armament specialists, and combat controllers must rank in the top two percentile in their specialties. There were 3,500 volunteers.

Not all were volunteers. One of the earliest members was Lieutenant Colonel Robert L. Gleason, who recalled that he was attending the Air War College at Maxwell AFB, Alabama in March 1961, when he was told to report to the base commander's office, where he was asked a series of questions and cautioned not to repeat them to anyone. Two in particular grabbed his attention: Would you be willing to fly and fight in support of a friendly foreign nation in situations where you could not wear the US uniform? Would you be willing to fly and fight on behalf of the US government and to agree to do so knowing that your government might choose to deny that you are a member of the US military, or even associated with this nation, and thus might not be able to provide you with the protection normally given to a US citizen? Gleason answered yes to both. A month later, he was assigned to the 4400th Combat Crew Training Squadron at Hurlburt.

Then-recently promoted Captain John "Pete" Piotrowski, who retired 28 years later as Air Force Vice Chief of Staff, recalled the interviews as "the most unique in my 38-year Air Force career." When his turn came, "I was ushered into a small office, dark except for a light that shone on

[handwritten margin note: I HAd This interview Also]

the interviewee. The officer conducting the interview was barely visible, a shadowy figure in the darkness." He was asked three questions: Are you willing to fly old obsolete aircraft? Are you willing to fly combat? If shot down and captured, are you willing to be disowned by your government? Piotrowski had some hesitation with the third question, but answered yes to all three.

Then-Captain Richard V. Secord recounted that a few weeks after his initial interview, a special Air Force team met with him. He concluded after this interview that only "crazy guys" were wanted. He thought that was a good thing, and was happy to see that, for reasons unclear at the time, he fit the profile.

Following the second interviews, those who made that cut received orders to Hurlburt Field where Colonel King told them, "All I can promise you are long hours and hard work in preparation for what lies ahead." Over the next month, the special Air Force team conducted psychological evaluations designed to identify unstable personalities who might not successfully handle the rigors of the assignment. There were increasingly bizarre tests; one involved standing for long periods on ice while naked. The final test was a three-week mountain survival course and an excruciatingly realistic mock prisoner-of-war camp. Then-First Lieutenant Bill Brown remembered spending three hours stuffed inside a refrigerator-size cubicle. "It was torture treatment in a way, but I stuck it out."

In the end, of 3,500 who answered the first call, 350 were accepted. Once chosen, they learned that they were in a special operations unit and would be called "air commandos," following the tradition of a similar unit organized by the legendary Colonel Phil Cochran that had operated behind enemy lines in Burma during World War II. Colonel King also told them that they would not be able to talk to anyone about what they did while in the unit for the next 25 years.

The unit would work with friendly air forces facing domestic insurgencies. Since the United States had provided these air forces with obsolete aircraft, the 4400th Combat Crew Training Squadron would operate a composite force of World War II aircraft that initially included 16 C-47s, eight B-26 Invaders, and eight T-28s modified as fighter-bombers. These were among the most common – and most expendable – aircraft in the inventory, and considered optimal for air combat in a primitive environment.

The North American T-28 was chosen in 1960 to equip small air forces with a fighter-bomber that was simple to fly and maintain. It had begun life in 1946 as the XSN2J-1, to replace the SNJ trainer. The design failed to interest the Navy, but the Air Force issued a specification for a new trainer in 1947 to replace the T-6. It would use the 800hp Wright R-1300 radial engine, which was essentially an R-2600 cut in half, and would use tricycle landing gear to provide familiarity with jet aircraft. North American modified their failed Navy design, and in May 1948 the Air Force selected it as the BT-28. After two prototypes flew successfully in 1949, the Air Force ordered 266 T-28A "Trojans" with the first of an eventual 1,948 entering service in April 1950. The last T-28A was produced in 1957 and it began leaving service in 1958. Norm Crocker, who would fly T-28s in three Southeast Asia tours, remembered "When I was graduating flight school in 1959, I saw the T-28As being taken to the boneyard."

The T-28As were "weary" from their years in training command and would need a bigger engine. Wright R-1820s removed from recently retired SA-16 Albatross aircraft were installed in the T-28s, which became T-28Ds – the Navy's trainers being designated T-28B and C – with the wings strengthened to allow up to 4,000 pounds in underwing stores. Fifty-caliber gun pods developed for gunnery training were used, with two underwing pylons on each wing in addition to the self-contained gun pods. Top speed was 345 miles per hour, with a rate of climb of 3,780 feet per minute. North American received 13 production contracts to convert 371 T-28As to T-28Ds between 1961 and 1969.

The twin-engine A-26 Invader – designated B-26 after 1948 – first entered combat in 1944. After World War II, it saw combat in the Korean War and several Cold War conflicts with American and other air forces. The B-26B's nose carried six and later eight .50-caliber machine guns; late production aircraft had three machine guns installed in each outer wing, giving 14 .50-caliber machine guns firing forward. After the Korean War, the wing guns were generally removed. The airplane had high performance, useful in the mountainous areas of Southeast Asia and operated from primitive airfields. By 1961, they were well-used, weary airplanes; a program to modernize the airplane with rebuilt wings by On-Mark Aviation at Van Nuys Airport, California resulted in the B-26K.

Flight training featured air-to-ground gunnery as the primary focus. Colonel King specifically directed that crews hone their flying skills for night operations. Missions were flown to Fort Bragg, North Carolina, for training with Army Special Forces where procedures and tactics were developed and implemented to work out airlift and fire support, and a strong bond grew between the two groups. Speculation about where they might go when the training was completed erroneously focused on Cuba.

Military conditions in South Vietnam continued their deterioration as the ARVN proved themselves unable to successfully meet the enemy due to poor leadership by officers whose positions were obtained through political influence and outright purchase, along with massive corruption in army administration, leading to demoralization of the conscript soldiers. Secretary of Defense McNamara – oblivious to the underlying problems – considered dispatching the new counterinsurgency forces to test the utility of such strategy and techniques in Southeast Asia. General LeMay was quick to point out that the 4400th was ready to serve as the Air Force contingent in that proposed force.

The French organized the first Vietnamese air units in 1951, as part of the army. The Khong Quan Viet Nam, the Vietnamese Air Force (VNAF), was created on July 1, 1955, initially equipped with 58 ex-French transport and liaison aircraft, organized into five squadrons. In June 1956, the 1st Fighter Squadron was created with 23 ex-Armée de l'Air F8F-1 Bearcats. President Diem also requested creation of a B-26 squadron; however, French and US advisors thought the VNAF lacked the ability to operate a bomber unit, and refused the request. By the time the Second Indochina War began in 1958, the Bearcats were worn out. Since the Geneva Accords prohibited introduction of jet aircraft, replacements would also be piston-engined aircraft. After again considering the B-26, the United States decided to provide AD-6 Skyraiders that the US Navy was in the process of replacing. The first arrived in late 1960 with a group of naval aviators to train the VNAF pilots. By mid-1961, the VNAF had only mustered 25 Skyraiders in the 1st Fighter Squadron. The 2nd Fighter Squadron was scheduled to be formed with T-28s later that year, but there was little likelihood of further VNAF expansion. This was the background to the initial deployment of American-manned combat aircraft to South Vietnam.

On October 11, 1961, President Kennedy signed NSAM 104, which directed the Secretary of Defense to "introduce the Air Force 'Jungle Jim' Squadron into Vietnam for the initial purpose of training Vietnamese forces." The 4400th were to maintain a low profile in-country and avoid the press. Their aircraft carried VNAF insignia, while pilots wore plain flight suits minus anything identifying them as American. They did not carry military ID or Geneva Convention cards. This was because introducing foreign military forces into South Vietnam violated the 1954 Geneva Accords. The administration needed plausible deniability that it had military forces operating in the region.

At this time, a Concept of Operations was developed for the 4400th:

> To develop and improve tactics and techniques for COIN [counterinsurgency] operations and to train the VNAF in such operations. Fulfillment of this task will greatly enhance the Republic of Vietnam (RVN) in-country capability to eliminate the communist threat. Operational tasks in RVN include combat and combat support flights as an extension of the training mission. All FARM GATE operations are limited to within the borders of South Vietnam. Combat missions will only be flown when the VNAF lack the capability to conduct the mission and then only with a combined USAF/VNAF crew aboard the aircraft. Such missions will be for the purpose of providing training for RVN personnel so that the VNAF can perform the missions required at the earliest possible time.

The 4400th Combat Crew Training Squadron Detachment 2A consisted of 41 officers and 115 enlisted men, each given a top secret clearance and authorized to bear arms. Eight T-28C Trojans, obtained from the Navy while North American modified T-28As to T-28Ds, joined four modified SC-47 Skytrains. Following their arrival, the unit received four B-26s after their rebuild at a repair facility in Taiwan. Their supply code name was "Farm Gate." The unit departed Hurlburt on November 5, 1961, headed for California. From there, the SC-47s staged across the Pacific via Hawaii, Midway, and Guam to Clark AFB in the Philippines. The T-28s were loaded into C-124s and flown to the same destination. After reassembly, the T-28s flew with the SC-47s to Tan Son Nhut Airport at Saigon, then on to the VNAF base at Bien Hoa airfield. They took up residency in a separate "tent city" over Thanksgiving weekend. The B-26s arrived the week before Christmas, 1961.

Yes & we felt stupid

The men arrived on 179-day temporary duty (TDY) assignments and were less than impressed by Bien Hoa. They were instructed to avoid reporters; if that was impossible, they were to say they were civilians. They could not inform their families where they were or what they were doing. Bien Hoa was originally built for the French air force in the 1930s, and was one of the main air bases in the First Indochina War. Six years later, it was in bad shape. The 5,800-foot runway was covered with pierced-steel planking (PSP), with many gaps badly in need of repair. The airfield was home to the VNAF's 1st Fighter Squadron which was quartered across the field from the Americans, still learning the intricacies of the Skyraider.

While Farm Gate was assigned operationally to the Air Force section of the MAAG Vietnam, administratively it reported directly to the office of the Air Force Chief of Staff in Washington through the "Jungle Jim" command at Eglin AFB. This led to an incident that defined "air commandos" ever after. At first, their only headgear was baseball caps, which proved of little use when the monsoon rains came. They began wearing the "bush hats" that VNAF crews at Bien Hoa wore, similar to Australian Army bush hats. When Admiral Harry D. Felt, the top US commander in the Pacific, visited Bien Hoa, he was unfavorably impressed by the sight of Americans wearing Vietnamese "cowboy hats." Assuming they were under his command, on his return to Pearl Harbor he issued an order forbidding the hats. A back-channel message was sent from Bien Hoa to "Jungle Jim" headquarters. Within a day, an official message signed by LeMay stating that the bush hats were official headgear for Farm Gate arrived on Admiral Felt's desk. Since then, all air commandos have worn the bush hats as a distinctive part of their uniform, similar to the Green Berets. *with a " Sorry About That Patch*

The command structure initially confused Colonel King, who later recalled:

> There was the matter of who we reported to. A lot of people had a lot of questions about that, including me. We were serviced and supplied theoretically through Ninth Air Force. I never met anyone in Ninth Air Force. I took my orders from two lieutenant colonels in the bottom of the Pentagon building. It seemed odd to me at the time, given that I was a full colonel.

72

Richard Secord later wrote, "The only people who knew the truth about our assignment besides the 4400th commanders and the deployed troops themselves were the Joint Chiefs and President Kennedy, and they weren't talking either."

By December 1961, the T-28s and their pilots were ready for orientation flights. The first Farm Gate combat mission was flown with the VNAF on January 13, 1962. Farm Gate aircraft began operating from airfields further north at Pleiku in the Central Highlands and at Da Nang where the SC-47s flew airdrop and "psyop" leaflet and loudspeaker broadcast missions to camps and "strategic hamlets" where Green Berets worked with the growing South Vietnamese Civilian Irregular Defense Groups. On February 12, 1962, a Farm Gate SC-47 on a leaflet drop mission in the highlands near Bao Loc was shot down, killing six airmen, two soldiers, and one Vietnamese crewman on board. This was the first USAF combat loss in the Vietnam War.

By the end of January, 229 sorties had been flown, with the missions reported as "training" for reconnaissance, surveillance, interdiction, and close air support; Farm Gate pilots dropped ordnance and made strafing runs to demonstrate to their "trainees" how it was done. When the reports arrived at MAAG headquarters in Saigon, the unit was quickly ordered not to conduct independent air operations, since officially it was there only to train South Vietnamese pilots. The truth was, at least in the beginning, that the French-trained VNAF pilots didn't need much additional training.

On December 26, 1961, orders from Washington directed that all Farm Gate missions would include a South Vietnamese national aboard the aircraft. Colonel King recalled 30 years later that his first mission involved dropping propaganda leaflets from one of the SC-47s. The VNAF officer assigned was a colonel named Nguyen Cao Ky. "Neither of us could speak the other's language, so that day's mission, like many others, was conducted with little clear communication. When we were done, I headed back to land at Bien Hoa. I had to abort the landing on my first attempt since I was too long and too hot." King added power and went around, but the second try was no better. "I was still too hot, so I went around again. As I prepared for my third try, I looked over at the colonel. He was just sitting there, shaking his head. I took my hands off the wheel and asked in English, 'Can you do any better?'" Ky nodded and King handed off control. "He went around and landed that airplane so short, he had to give it power to get it to the end of the strip. And I was supposed to be teaching him to fly." Looking back on his time with Farm Gate, King stated, "I can say this: We never trained a Vietnamese pilot."

The "backseat rider" requirement was political. In the event that an aircraft was shot down in hostile territory, the presence of a Vietnamese crewman would be enough to dodge accusations of the United States violating the Geneva Accords. However, as the VNAF grew and demand for pilots expanded, the experienced French-trained pilots returned to their own units. Many replacements were cadets awaiting orders to flight school. Captain Bill Brown recalled that his Vietnamese riders "never were allowed anywhere near the controls of the aircraft." Then-Lieutenant Charles Brown remembered, "We were supposed to always have a South Vietnamese person in the airplane with us. At first that meant having a pilot, but pretty soon it was anyone. I had a South Vietnamese cook who really liked to fly and he'd go with me every chance he had." B-26 pilot Roy Dalton recalled that the Americans eventually flew with any Vietnamese in the other seat, regardless of their experience or ability. Richard Secord and his Vietnamese copilot barely escaped a crash when the terrified backseater repeatedly grabbed their T-28's controls.

In March 1962, the 4400th Combat Crew Training Squadron became the 4400th Combat Crew Training Group. The following month it was reformed as the 1st Air Commando Group, and Farm Gate became Detachment 2A of the 1st ACG.

Although President Kennedy had issued a flat denial at a press conference held in January 1962 that US troops were engaged in combat in Vietnam, in March 1962 *New York Times* reporter David Halberstam wrote that US pilots were "engaged in combat missions with South Vietnamese pilots in training them to fight communist guerrillas." With that, Farm Gate became increasingly subject to public scrutiny. Farm Gate medic Sergeant Hap Lutz remembered, "Reporters were snooping around, and they would watch the airplanes take off. They soon discerned that the Vietnamese on board weren't pilots." Ironically, the VNAF insignia so closely resembled that of the US Air Force, with only a variation in color to distinguish the difference, that reporters described the aircraft at Bien Hoa as having US markings, inadvertently revealing the truth about which nation actually owned them.

On August 28, 1962, a Farm Gate T-28 became the first US fixed-wing attack aircraft lost during the Vietnam War when Captain Robert L. Simpson and VNAF Lieutenant Hoa were lost when they were shot down flying close air support.

Farm Gate pilots operated under the requirement that all strikes be made at the direction of an airborne VNAF FAC who could "authenticate the target," according to Dalton. "Once we showed up on the scene, if the FAC wasn't there, we didn't strike. We were totally at the mercy and the direction of the FAC. We had no intelligence of our own, no hard intelligence, on who we were hitting."

The Americans also had to deal with the fact that the only VNAF unit that could perform air strikes was the 1st Fighter Squadron, which wasn't equipped for night flying. The T-28-equipped 2nd Fighter Squadron had no night-qualified pilots. The enemy took advantage to make nearly all attacks at night. Captain John L. Piotrowski obtained magnesium flares and one of the SC-47s was rigged to drop them. A few days later a South Vietnamese outpost came under night attack. The SC-47 and two T-28s broke the attack when they strafed and dropped bombs under the SC-47's flares. As the tactic was refined, three or four flares would be dropped by parachute from the SC-47 at an altitude of about 1,500 feet. The accompanying T-28s or B-26s immediately strafed or bombed the target. By 1963, C-47 flareships were on constant night alert, and ARVN units in IV and southern III Corps, the tactical zones nearest Bien Hoa, received night illumination and close air support within 20 to 60 minutes. An Air Force report stated, "It was merely sufficient for a flareship to appear over a besieged position and expend flares to cause the VC to break off an attack."

The ground units devised a "fire arrow" consisting of flare pots or electric lights on a large platform which could be rotated to show the enemy's direction, providing guidance for supporting pilots, with those on the ground radioing instructions to drop ordnance by distance from the lighted arrow. In a 1973 Air Force interview, former Captain Frank Gorski recalled one night mission in support of a besieged ARVN fort shrouded in fog:

We could circle above and pick up the fire arrow, but as soon as you tried to get some sort of angle on it, you lost it. Of course, the flareship was dropping flares and they would go down in the fog and that would really play havoc with your sight. But we would try everything we could because we had a limited resource, and we did things that maybe now we would say were a little bit harebrained or foolish.

Once the C-47 had dropped flares, the B-26 dropped napalm on the first attack run. This provided sufficient light to give a better ground reference so that rockets, bombs, and guns could then be used on subsequent runs as required. Working at night, under flares in poorly lit cockpits with bad weather or light reflecting off water filled rice paddies, was guaranteed to give a pilot a severe case of vertigo; only extensive training made the missions possible. They were seen as the most rewarding because they challenged a crew's skill with the results immediately obvious. Flying with a navigator in the right seat was a decided advantage, since he could give the pilot a tap on the shoulder when approaching minimum altitudes.

Flying conditions in 1962 were primitive, with virtually no navigation aids. Gorski remembered, "We flew in all kinds of weather. If you wanted to get someplace, you just picked up a canal and went. That was your navigation system. Flew time and distance. Kept one eye on the fuel and one eye out the window and pressed on."

The American involvement grew rapidly in 1962. Following the formation of United States Military Assistance Command – Vietnam (MACV) from the MAAG, Farm Gate's status in the larger Air Force regarding command and control became confused. Air Force units were reorganized under the control of 2nd Advanced Echelon (2nd ADVON) of Thirteenth Air Force in November 1961 with the assignment "to conduct sustained offensive, defensive, and reconnaissance air operations aimed at the destruction or neutralization of Viet Cong forces, resources, and communications within the borders of South Vietnam." Farm Gate's official role did not include these missions and Colonel Gleason, who had relieved King, resisted attempts by the 2nd ADVON detachment commander at Bien Hoa to take operational control. When 2nd ADVON was replaced by 2nd Air Division of Thirteenth Air Force that summer, enemy attacks were increasing, with increased calls for air support to ARVN units with American advisors. Forward operations began at Qui Nhon and Soc Trang airfields. With the VNAF unable to meet demands for air cover, 2nd Air Division commander Brigadier General Rollen H. Anthis increasingly turned to the Farm Gate crews, putting stress on the small unit.

Theoretically the B-26 could carry 7,500 pounds of ordnance but seldom carried more than 6,000 pounds and often less. Due to mountainous terrain, it was important to have extra performance from a lighter load. A typical load was two 500-pound napalm bombs and two LAU 3A 2.75-inch rocket launchers underwing, plus six 100-pound general-purpose (GP) bombs and six 120-pound fragmentation clusters in the bomb bay. The eight nose guns had 350 rounds of .50 ammunition each, giving a total load of 4,000 pounds. Alternatively, six napalm bombs underwing with 12 fragmentation clusters in the bomb bay, or two rocket pods and four 500-pound GP bombs underwing, and six more bombs in the bomb bay were carried. The minimum release altitude was 1,600 feet, with pull-out at 1,000 feet to avoid blast damage. Dive bombing was the typical delivery method, with level runs rarely if ever flown. Rockets and guns were fired at considerably lower altitudes, while napalm was dropped from as low as 200 feet.

The B-26s improved during 1963, as they were rotated to Air Asia on Taiwan or Clark AFB for Inspect or Repair As Necessary (IRAN) major maintenance. However, a report claimed, "To term the present B-26 an unsophisticated aircraft is to pay it an unwarranted compliment."

B-26 pilot Captain Roy Dalton kept a personal diary, which provides a window into what the air war in South Vietnam was like during the early days:

Monday 8 October 1962: Out on strike this morning. Terrain very difficult. A valley about one and a half miles long by a half mile wide with one end closed by mountain and other open. Stream in the middle with rice paddies and hooches. The steep sides of the mountains are covered with jungle. The FAC marked at each end and stated that all in between was target area plus one village on the rim. This was a reported VC [Viet Cong] Battalion training area. We destroyed the village and set lots of fires up and down the valley. Very difficult to get in close and pull up. We saw zip but FAC reported ground fire. The valley was very pretty. I sometimes wonder if we aren't making more enemies for the local government than we are doing good. Sure hope their intelligence was right. On the way back we lost number one engine. Feathered and returned home.

Friday 16 November 1962: Flew strike in Delta. Was giving close air support to ground operation when five hidden boats were found. Got three. Couldn't hit my butt. Everyone else busy so even though I have duty officer, Charlie and I pull alert. Got scrambled at 2300 hours. Fort under attack at Can Tho. Covered it for two hours. Appeared to be good mission. Fort called flareship and told them to thank us. Had been up since 0600 Friday morning. Finally got to bed at 0330 Sat morning.

Saturday 17 to Monday 19 November 1962: Slept most of Saturday. Duty officer Sunday. Poker Sunday night. Lost $12. Flew mission number 100 Monday. Made a total of 25 passes on a large target area. Hit boats, hooches and personnel. Word came in on Friday night's fort defense mission. 18 VC confirmed KIA.

Tuesday 20 November 1962: Zip today. Yesterday's mission – six structures, 14 boats and 25 VC confirmed KIA. They certainly were everywhere. Dave told me about one of their missions. The FAC directed them at VCs under trees. Just before they dropped Dave saw women under a tree. They didn't drop and pulled off. We agreed that it sometimes gets to be a gut call. The FAC, who is Vietnamese, is in a position to see and he directs the fire, still it's pretty bad sometimes. Some time I'm going to add up the total KIAs and destruction and then again it would probably be better if I didn't.

While B-26s were considered superior to T-28s for close air support, many were old and considered "maintenance nightmares" by the ground crews. This was largely due to the airplanes' age and the limited overhauls they had received prior to arriving in Vietnam. They had 1,800–4,000 flying hours each, and all went through varied modifications. A report in April 1963 stated:

> None of the B 26s at Farm Gate are configured alike. Each IRAN depot and each work package change within each depot resulted in some variation in electrical wiring, communications equipment, location of cockpit controls, etc. As one result, valid wiring diagrams do not exist for many of the aircraft. Armament switches for the various stores and stations are placed in five separate locations in each of the four different armament switch configurations within the fleet.

Servicing was difficult. During the second half of 1962, serviceability was approximately 54.5 percent at any given time, the lowest figure for any USAF aircraft in Vietnam. By comparison, serviceability for the T-28s was an average 80.3 percent.

Ray Dalton explained:

Keep in mind that these were aircraft that had probably been used in WW II and certainly in Korea. They were old and had little modification. However, every man associated with the operation was dedicated to make it work. Therefore we had few qualms about flying aircraft that might not be 100 percent. Had we not done so, operating under the conditions with which we were faced, we would not have been effective.

Dalton's diary recorded 13 malfunctions over a three-month period in 1962:

16 August: Six bombs stuck in bomb bay.

20 August: Bombs in bomb bay failed to release.

22 August: Could get only 50 inches manifold pressure on number 1 engine, number 2 engine backfired if throttle was moved rapidly, gear handle came up only when manual detent button used (Aircraft flown anyway).

2 September: Rockets failed to fire.

5 September: Airborne radio failure.

20 September: Bombs fell out of bomb bay when battery switched on.

26 September: Hydraulic line on brakes blew on landing.

28 September: Number 2 engine failed on pull out from bomb drop.

30 September: Brake failure on landing.

2 October: Left magneto failed on run up.

7 October: Hydraulic leak in left wheel well on start up, right generator out, right cowl flap inoperable, only two of eight guns would fire (Aircraft flown anyway).

8 October: Number 1 engine failed on return from strike; feathered.

12 November: Unsafe gear indicator (bad switch).

Invader crews in Korea had experienced the same problems. They had also operated aircraft that had been in storage several years and had been given only a minimum of rehabilitation before being sent to combat units. The lessons were forgotten by the time the B-26s were taken out of storage a second time. Despite these difficulties, Farm Gate B-26s had flown 1,135 combat sorties by December 1962; some crews completed 100 missions in less than four months. On New Year's Day 1963, Farm Gate operated 24 aircraft, nearly 40 percent of USAF aircraft in South Vietnam.

Most B-26 missions in 1962 involved a single aircraft, while the T-28s usually flew in pairs. With the near-doubling of B-26s in 1963, it became common to fly in pairs, with one suppressing ground fire while the other carried out the strike.

The last four B-26s arrived at Bien Hoa in June 1963. All were survivors of the CIA effort to overthrow President Sukarno in Indonesia in 1958 and were in storage with Air Asia in Taiwan as CIA assets. All these aircraft had been struck off charge as "obsolete" in 1957, and officially no longer existed.

In October 1962, McNamara ordered US commanders in Vietnam to develop a campaign plan to defeat the communist forces. This was completed in March 1963; it called for significant VNAF expansion with two additional fighter squadrons flying A-1 Skyraiders, one reconnaissance squadron, several squadrons of FACs, and five more cargo squadrons operating C-47s. This was at odds with reality since it was clear that the South Vietnamese were far from ready to fight independently. During 1962, neither the Viet Cong nor the South Vietnamese forces had achieved any decisive victories; however popular resentment of the Diem regime grew due to the creation of the "strategic hamlet program" that forced large numbers of the rural population from their ancestral lands to newly constructed villages under strict control by government agents who were nearly universally corrupt.

On January 2, 1963, the ARVN were defeated at the Battle of Ap Bac in the Mekong Delta; five of 15 US helicopters ferrying ARVN troops into the battle zone were shot down and destroyed, along with several US-supplied M-113 armored personnel carriers. The defeat resulted from poor American intelligence regarding enemy strength. Despite the ARVN force outnumbering the enemy by five to one, ARVN commanders were reluctant to close with the enemy when they stood against the initial ARVN advance. Ap Bac signaled a new willingness by the enemy to stand and fight rather than melt away into the jungle; that they could be successful shook the Diem government in Saigon.

In July 1963, 2nd Air Division commander General Anthis requested an additional ten B-26s, five T-28s, and two SC-47s. McNamara's goal was to build up the VNAF to operate without American assistance; thus he was initially cool to expanding Farm Gate for combat use. However, he approved the request for aircraft in August, adding two U-10 Helio Couriers. Eleven B-26s arrived in December 1962; all had undergone a thorough IRAN at Hill AFB in Utah, and were in good condition. The force continued growing; by April 1963, there were 12 B-26Bs and 13 T-28Bs and personnel had doubled to 350, though there was still only one air crew per aircraft. These 25 airplanes, with 50 Skyraiders operated by the VNAF 1st and 2nd Fighter Squadrons, were the total air strike capability in South Vietnam.

By June 1963, the Air Force presence had increased to 5,000 personnel. As the buildup continued, a new outfit – the 1st Air Commando Squadron – was activated at Bien Hoa.

On July 20, 1963, a Farm Gate SC-47 crew flew an emergency night mission to Loc Ninh. Disregarding enemy fire, strong winds, and a blacked-out dirt runway, they landed and rescued six badly wounded ARVN troops. The crew received the Mackay Trophy for performing the most meritorious air mission of 1963. On July 28, the 1st Air Commando Squadron was activated and Farm Gate disappeared into the new organization. However, the term "Farm Gate" remained in use for supply purposes, eventually replaced by other code names as the war continued to expand. One crew chief explained, "Things just got bigger. It wasn't Farm Gate anymore. It was war." Between October 1961 and July 1963, 16 Farm Gate aircrew were killed, while one SC-47, four T-28s, one U-10, and four B-26s were lost.

Despite the fact that, by 1963, US units were actively engaged in combat in South Vietnam, there were times when even the pilots didn't know what they were being used for. Captain Joe Kittinger recalled a mission flown on November 1, 1963: "I had just taken off from Bien Hoa in a B-26, when I happened to look over to the side and saw the most amazing thing: Airplanes were bombing the palace in downtown Saigon! I said, 'My Lord, what is happening?'" Kittinger radioed the Air Force command center and was instructed to report what he saw, which was the beginning of the coup that overthrew President Ngo

Dinh Diem. "I could see tanks and bombing, and a battle was going on. They kept running me from place to place to see what was going on. I was an airborne command post." He remained over Saigon nearly four hours before running low on fuel.

By the spring of 1963, the T-28Bs, which had come from the Navy and were approaching their maximum airframe fatigue life, began to show stress from carrying underwing ordnance and the stresses of combat flying. Kittinger recalled, "The T-28s had made a lot of takeoffs and landings in Training Command. They were tired, and we were using them as fighter-bombers. The wings started coming off." He explained that, "If a wing comes off, there is a violent roll. The G-force would preclude you from doing anything. You can't get out. You don't have a chance." Farm Gate crews began to speak of the "folding wing versions" of the T-28s and B-26s.

Time finally caught up with the B-26s by 1964. The heavy underwing loads imposed high negative G-forces on the wings when they were taxied on the bumpy airfields. Their use as dive bombers did not help, especially as they had no G meter to tell the crew how much load they put on the wings. After a B-26 lost a wing on August 16, 1963, strict limitations were imposed on maneuvers allowed during missions.

On February 11, 1964, following several B-26 losses in Vietnam, the left wing failed on B-26 44-35665 during a demonstration at Hurlburt Field, killing Captains Herman S. Moore and Lawrence L. Lively. When the news reached Vietnam, one B-26 was on a strike mission. The crew were ordered to return to Bien Hoa immediately, being certain not to put any undue stress on the bomber during their return. The Farm Gate B-26s were grounded. In April, they were flown to Clark Field for disposal. Soon after the Hurlburt incident, *U.S. News & World Report* published several of Jerry Shank's letters home, in which he detailed complaints about conditions in Vietnam. The letters were supplied by Shank's wife shortly after he was killed when one wing of his T-28 sheared off during a bomb run.

Even after the creation of the 1st Air Commando Squadron, the official legal status of the US operation in South Vietnam remained ambiguous. According to Admiral Ulysses Grant Sharp, leader of the Pacific Command, as late as July 1964, US units in South Vietnam were still acting as "an advisory mission, and our personnel were not participating in military action at that point." That fiction disappeared

a month later with the passage of the Gulf of Tonkin Resolution. By
that time, the 1st Air Commando Squadron had gotten rid of the B-26s
and SC-47s and many T-28Bs were grounded. In May 1964, 25 A-1J
and A-1E Skyraiders were received as replacements. The 602nd Air
Commando Squadron deployed to South Vietnam that fall, equipped
with A-1Es.

The arrival of the regular Air Force soon overshadowed the air
commandos. In the fall of 1964, B-57s, F-100s, C-130s, and F-102s,
as well as surface-to-air Hawk missiles and a formal Air Force medical
unit, arrived at Bien Hoa while US leaders in Washington debated a
formal US combat role. Farm Gate crews had flown a few missions
against the supply and transport system that the North Vietnamese had
begun constructing in 1962 which would become known in 1962–63
as the Ho Chi Minh Trail. Captain Jack Drummond, a C-130 pilot at
the time, arrived that fall. "We started working 'Blind Bat' missions,
dropping flares for B-57s attacking the Ho Chi Minh Trail in Laos and
South Vietnam. When we first went up, no one was flying at night, and
the North Vietnamese were driving with their lights on."

After Farm Gate was unclassified in 1963 and officially came under
regular Air Force control, the 4400th Combat Crew Training Squadron
was awarded the Air Force Outstanding Unit Award for the period
May 1961 to May 1962, though no operations were cited in the award.
Farm Gate can now be seen for what it really was: the first step in a very
long war, with the unit's arrival in South Vietnam in November 1961
providing an exact date for the war's start. During the course of its
existence, the unit proved the special operations mission, resulting in
the creation of 11 special operations squadrons during the Vietnam War
as well as the Special Air Warfare Center, which inherited the original
"Jungle Jim" mission and is still operational today.

5

GOING UP NORTH

Looking at the decisions leading the United States into full-scale war in Southeast Asia, and the way it would be fought, two things become obvious: the lack of understanding of the nature of the enemy by US leadership, and the extreme ambivalence over initial engagement by the same people.

Throughout the Cold War, US political leaders failed to understand the true nature of their opponents; this was the result of failure by the military and intelligence specialists on whom they depended for information to develop a nuanced understanding of the communist world, which changed after 1945 from the simplistic Soviet-domination of the Comintern, which was disestablished in 1943, to nation-states led by communist parties. That communist states would follow Prince Metternich's admonition that "nations have no permanent friends or permanent enemies, only permanent interests" was not considered as an organizing principle to understand the world situation during the entire Cold War. Thus, the intentions, capability, and commitment of the opposing forces were consistently underestimated. This lack of knowledge and understanding, what Graham Greene described as "good intentions and ignorance," was the foundation for the consistent failures in Southeast Asia up to 1975.

Throughout the Cold War, US policy proceeded from the belief that the country's communist opponents were part of a monolithic world system dominated by the Soviet Union. In fact, the only time the Soviet Union dominated the communist movement in the rest of the world was before World War II, when it was the only communist

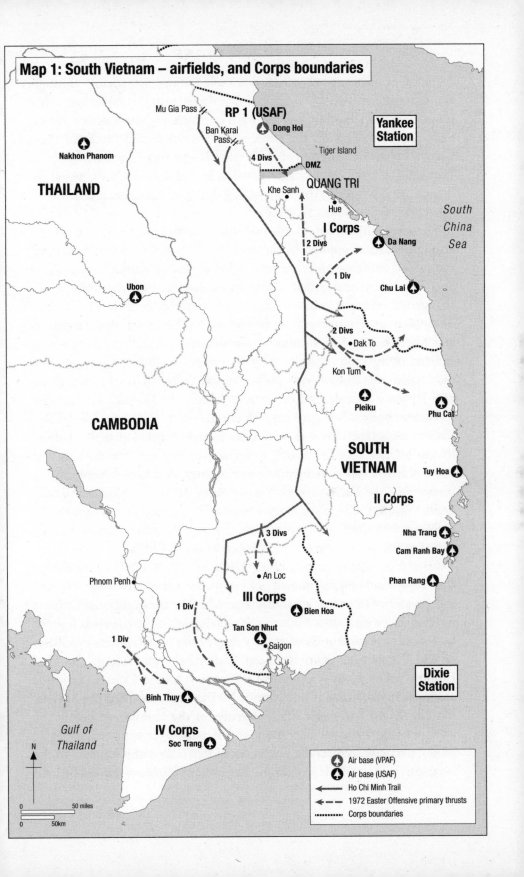

Map 1: South Vietnam – airfields, and Corps boundaries

Nakhon Phanom

THAILAND

Mu Gia Pass

Ban Karai Pass

RP 1 (USAF)

Dong Hoi

Tiger Island

4 Divs

DMZ

QUANG TRI

Khe Sanh

Hue

I Corps

2 Divs

Da Nang

South China Sea

1 Div

Chu Lai

Ubon

2 Divs

Dak To

Kon Tum

Pleiku

Phu Cat

CAMBODIA

SOUTH VIETNAM

Tuy Hoa

II Corps

Nha Trang

Cam Ranh Bay

Phan Rang

Phnom Penh

3 Divs

An Loc

III Corps

Bien Hoa

1 Div

Tan Son Nhut

Saigon

1 Div

Binh Thuy

Gulf of Thailand

IV Corps

Soc Trang

Yankee Station

Dixie Station

N

0 ___ 50 miles
0 ___ 50km

Air base (VPAF)
Air base (USAF)
Ho Chi Minh Trail
1972 Easter Offensive primary thrusts
Corps boundaries

country, controlling all other national communist parties through the Comintern. After World War II, Soviet-installed communist-led governments in Eastern Europe were creatures of Soviet policy whose existence depended on the presence of Soviet armed forces in their national territory. Attempts to change this – in East Germany in 1953, Hungary in 1956, and Czechoslovakia in 1968 – were suppressed by Soviet armed forces. Thus, regarding Europe, the strategic belief of Soviet domination was accurate.

However, this belief in "monolithic communism" was completely wrong-headed as applied to the communist nations of Asia and most radical-left movements in the post-colonial "Third World." Both China and Vietnam became independent nation-states led by communist parties that genuinely represented the desires of the majority of the population. The Asian communist regime closest to the Eastern European model was North Korea; Kim Il-Sung's government was installed during Soviet military occupation of the country. However, Kim himself led a genuine nationalist movement with public support due to his history as an anti-Japanese guerilla. His decision to launch the Korean War was due to Korean nationalism, not communist ideology; the Soviet Union and China supported him due to Stalin's mistaken belief that the United States did not consider South Korea a vital interest after Secretary of State Acheson failed to mention the country in a speech defining US interests in the Pacific shortly before Kim's arrival in Moscow to seek Stalin's support. China's military involvement was due not to communist ideology but rather to a centuries-old Chinese commitment to a friendly Korea to prevent its use as a path for invasion of China.

Like Mao Zedong in China, Ho Chi Minh came to power as the legitimate representative of popular nationalist support for independence from foreign domination. Unlike the traditional Chinese relationship with Korea, China's relationship with Vietnam was fraught by several thousand years of enmity, beginning with Chinese expulsion of the Vietnamese from southern China by expansion of the Han Empire, followed by Vietnamese opposition to the Chinese Empire's attempts to dominate if not control Vietnam. As regarded the Soviets, Ho Chi Minh had made many enemies in the Comintern before the war, pressing national liberation of Vietnam over supporting Soviet policy, particularly after the Soviet decision to ally with Germany in the Nazi–Soviet Pact. The Democratic Republic of Vietnam was led by men adamantly committed to independence of all of Vietnam, who were not prepared to back down to opposition by stronger powers, regardless of any other nation's policies.

For the Johnson Administration, the main risk of "going North" was possible war with China. Misunderstanding the complex political dynamic among North Vietnam, China, and the USSR, they typecast the North Vietnamese as Chinese and/or Soviet pawns. Even after China descended into the chaos of the Cultural Revolution after 1966, they continued to fear Chinese intervention. Their lack of understanding led them to believe that the Soviet Union could help broker peace among Hanoi, Saigon, and Washington. General Westmoreland later recounted his astonishment over Ambassador Averell Harriman's statement during the Manila war conference in October 1966, when Soviet SAMs, radars, advisors, and technicians were in direct combat against the United States, that "The Russians are doing everything they can to bring peace in Vietnam."

The North Vietnamese leaders were not people American politicians were used to dealing with; they did not respond to American actions as expected. Once the air campaign was approved, which by decision of the top leaders would be administered "humanely" without intending regime change, American leaders – civilian and military – consistently underestimated the North Vietnamese commitment despite consistent evidence of their rapidly evolving technical, operational, and tactical war-fighting capability. Two months after the campaign began, Soviet SAMs and associated crews arrived to fight while training the North Vietnamese to operate them. Pleas by US commanders in Vietnam to strike the sites while under construction were turned down due to fear that any deaths or injuries to Soviet personnel could lead to direct Soviet involvement. Two months later, after a Soviet-fired SAM shot down the first US aircraft, American military leaders were astounded when the number and quality of AAA had already grown by hundreds and then thousands. By the time the first bombing halt was ordered in December 1965 to get North Vietnamese commitment to negotiations, the People's Army of Vietnam (PAVN) had grown to 400,000 troops, while 50,000 regular troops sent down the Ho Chi Minh Trail had already engaged US ground forces in direct combat.

Coupled with failing to understand their opponents, US leaders had long been ambivalent about engaging in a Southeast Asian war.

The US military opposed any land war in Asia, and this reluctance was reinforced by the Korean War, and by the discovery that China was more fearsome than expected. Leaders in the Democratic Party recalled that the failure to win in Korea had ended 20 years of domestic political domination. Simultaneously all the leaders in the 1960s had survived McCarthyism in the 1950s and were loath to provide Republicans with an opportunity to attack them with the charge of being "soft on communism." The result was a campaign resembling the joke about a camel being a horse designed by a committee: it was unsuccessful both as a political campaign designed to have a military result and as a military campaign designed for a political result.

The only American leader who looked at what would really be necessary to block the North's intention to unify the country was CIA Director John McCone. An air power advocate, he saw that the sporadic, unstructured incrementalism of what was now called *Rolling Thunder* would never convince the enemy to abandon their goals, and feared what a large American commitment of ground forces to combat in the South would mean for domestic politics. At the end of April 1965, concluding that he could no longer in good conscience support the administration's policy, he took the extraordinary step of resigning. In a final letter to McNamara, Rusk, Bundy, and Taylor, he wrote:

> We must change the ground rule of the strikes against North Vietnam. Instead of avoiding the MiGs, we must go in and take them out. A bridge here and there will not do the job. We must strike their air fields, their petroleum resources, power stations and the military compounds promptly and with minimum restraint. We must hit them harder, more frequently, and inflict greater damage.

Almost the entire American military leadership agreed with him, yet none ever followed his example.

While the Vietnam War is generally thought of as a singular event, in reality, it was a series of interlinked conflicts involving expanding US commitment in response to growing insurgencies in Laos and South Vietnam in the late 1950s and early 1960s, which became a full-blown war throughout Southeast Asia. Many more countries than the United States and the three countries in Indochina – North and South Vietnam and Laos – were involved. Supporters of South Vietnam included the United States, Australia, Canada, Britain, the (non-communist)

Republic of China, the Republic of Korea, Japan, Malaysia, New Zealand, the Philippines, Spain, Thailand, and West Germany, with active military engagement by Australia, New Zealand, and Korea in addition to the United States. North Vietnam was supported by the Democratic Republic of Korea, the (communist) People's Republic of China, the Soviet Union, Czechoslovakia, Cuba, East Germany, Hungary, Poland, and Romania. The Soviet Union, China, and Cuba sent military advisors in addition to material assistance, while the Vietnam People's Air Force (VPAF) received direct assistance from the North Korean People's Air Force, which sent a combat unit.

Operation *Rolling Thunder*, the three-and-a-half-year aerial bombardment of North Vietnam, which was carried out between March 3, 1965 and November 1, 1968 was the longest, most controversial campaign ever waged by the US Air Force. It revealed serious strategic, tactical, doctrinal, training, and technological deficiencies and outright failures in the organization. The close control of the campaign by political leaders resulted in an incoherent operational strategy. The ultimate failure of the stated goal to deter North Vietnam from supporting the war in South Vietnam should not be surprising. There was little that those advocating a traditional military campaign could have done differently that would have brought a different result. Perhaps the only tactic that might have done so would have been to use B-52s over North Vietnam in 1965 as they were at the end of the war. Writing after the war, General Vo Nguyen Giap stated, "We always knew we would have to cease the struggle the day the B-52s arrived over Hanoi." US leaders were unwilling to do so out of fear that it would result in direct Chinese intervention as had happened in the Korean War. This was the result of failure to understand the different histories of China and Korea as allies and China and Vietnam as traditional enemies. The troubled history of *Rolling Thunder* shaped the theory and practice of how the US Air Force conducts an air war – radically changing the doctrine, training, planning, and operational execution in comparison with what existed before.

What became *Rolling Thunder* began in March 1964 when Admiral Harry D. Felt, Commander in Chief Pacific Command (CinCPac) ordered his staff to develop a plan for a sustained air campaign which would escalate in three eight-week-long stages. It included what came to be known later as the "94 target list" of sites that US intelligence believed were crucial, the destruction of which would end the war. Whether or not to bomb North Vietnam split the Joint Chiefs; Air Force Chief of Staff General Curtis LeMay and Marine Commandant General Wallace Greene favored a comprehensive campaign, while Army Chief of Staff General Harold Johnson, Chief of Naval Operations Admiral David McDonald, and Joint Chiefs Chairman General Maxwell Taylor demurred.

In mid-April 1964, the JCS offered Secretary McNamara three options: first, intensified air and ground action in South Vietnam with "hot pursuit" into Laos and Cambodia; second, reprisal actions against North Vietnam in answer to actions in South Vietnam, including air strikes, airborne and amphibious raids, and port and harbor mining; and third, Admiral Felt's graduated air campaign, which was finally published following the Tonkin Gulf Incident, the event that led to direct US military involvement, as CINCPAC OPLAN 37-64. Secretary of State Rusk stated that he believed the plan "emphasized the bombing of the North more than I was entirely comfortable with." There was widespread concern that this could bring involvement by the USSR or the People's Republic of China in a wider conflict. General Westmoreland referred to "an almost paranoid fear of nuclear confrontation with the Soviet Union" and a "phobia" that the Chinese would invade, the only lesson learned from the Korean War.

The Tonkin Gulf Incident in August 1964 resulted in Congress authorizing more direct US involvement in the war. The next six months saw increased action against Americans in South Vietnam. A mortar attack at Bien Hoa on November 1 killed four Americans and wounded 72, destroying or damaging 20 of 33 B-57s, and 12 other aircraft. Ambassador Maxwell Taylor, MACV commander Westmoreland, and the JCS favored retaliation. Taylor advocated an attack on the VPAF's MiG base at Phuc Yen and barracks associated with infiltration "preferably within 24 hours, at latest within 48 hours." On November 2, the JCS recommended strikes against the targets they had identified following the Tonkin Gulf Incident. General Wheeler met with Secretary McNamara and warned him that if President Johnson continued delaying action in Vietnam, "most of the chiefs believed the United States should withdraw from South Vietnam." With the election two days away and the president ahead of his opponent Barry Goldwater as the man who would keep the country out of war, Johnson held off taking any action. Secretary Rusk later said, "It's entirely possible that Hanoi said to themselves 'Lyndon Johnson says "we don't want a larger war," therefore, we, Hanoi, can have a larger war without an increase of risk.'"

Following the election, which Johnson won in the largest political landslide in American history to that time, he finally committed to undefined air action in response to continuing communist action, rationalizing that the strikes would signal American resolve, boost South Vietnamese morale, and "impose increased costs and strains" on the North Vietnamese. In October, before the election, Undersecretary of State George Ball had published an article that revealed that the Johnson Administration was "considering air action against [North Vietnam] as the means to a limited objective – the improvement of our bargaining position with the North Vietnamese." The article openly signaled that the intent, limits, and end-goal were to improve the American negotiating position, not to achieve a decisive military result. On December 3, Ball told Maxwell Taylor that South Vietnam and the United States should "execute prompt reprisals for any unusual hostile action," including a "series of air attacks on the DRV progressively mounting in scope and intensity for the purpose of convincing the leaders of [the] DRV that it is to their interest to cease to aid the Viet Cong and to respect the independence and security of South Vietnam."

The United States finally began combat air operations with what would become an eight-year-long interdiction program in Laos, starting in the northern part of that supposedly "neutral" nation against segments of what was becoming the Ho Chi Minh Trail that crossed the Laotian "panhandle" – the piece of geography that made the country resemble a cooking pan – out of North Vietnam before turning back into northern South Vietnam; these were given the code name *Barrel Roll*.

Laotian "neutralist" leader Prince Souvanna Phouma authorized the United States to fly unpublicized "armed road reconnaissance" missions on December 10, 1964. The first Air Force mission was flown on December 14, followed on December 17 by the first Navy mission. *Barrel Roll* was followed in April 1965 by *Steel Tiger* strikes in southern Laos. Initial restrictions were severe. All missions required approval by the JCS, with a two-week wait for pre-planned targets and a three-day wait for damage assessment flights. Overflying North Vietnam was prohibited, and there was a two-mile-wide buffer zone along the

Laos/North Vietnam border. Use of napalm was prohibited "regardless of target." Strikes on "armed road recce" missions were allowed only within 200 yards of such roads. Attacks on secondary targets were prohibited. Finally, no Thailand-based aircraft could be used.

On December 24, the Brinks Hotel in Saigon, which provided quarters for US officers, was bombed. Two Americans were killed and 107 injured. On Christmas Day, F-105s of the newly arrived 44th Tactical Fighter Squadron flew their first mission in retribution for this attack. The Thunderchiefs struck a barracks at Tchepone, located on one of the main Laotian supply corridors of the Ho Chi Minh Trail. Squadron commander Lieutenant Colonel William Craig led four F-105Ds in an inaccurate dive-bombing attack that inflicted no damage.

On December 28, a pitched battle broke out near Binh Gia, 40 miles east of Saigon. Two regiments of the 9th Division of the National Liberation Front (NLF, the official name for the Viet Cong) ambushed and nearly destroyed two Vietnamese Marine Corps battalions, then fought ARVN armor and US air attacks until January 1, 1965, inflicting heavy casualties on units attempting to relieve the two units originally ambushed. Westmoreland reported that Binh Gia marked "...the beginning of an intensive military challenge which the Vietnamese government could not meet with its own resources." Secretary Rusk recalled, "As 1965 opened, the military situation in South Vietnam was dire indeed."

Following the Binh Gia defeat, McGeorge Bundy and Secretary McNamara finally agreed with other advisors that they must change course; Bundy warned the president on January 27 to either expand the war or disengage. Johnson was reluctant to commit to direct US involvement, stating that "a weak government in Saigon would have difficulty surviving the pressures that might be exerted against the south if we bombed the north." He ordered Rusk to explore exit strategies, while Bundy went to Vietnam to "take a hard look at the situation on the ground."

On February 7, a sapper attack on Pleiku airfield killed eight Americans and wounded 108, destroying 25 USAF aircraft. The attack surprised Soviet premier Alexei Kosygin, who was visiting Hanoi. Soviet Ambassador to Washington Anatoly Dobrynin accused the North Vietnamese of "doing their utmost to foster enmity between Washington and Moscow," adding that "the Soviet leaders were well aware of the game the Vietnamese were playing and cursed them behind their backs."

On February 8, President Johnson met with McNamara, General Wheeler, Cyrus Vance, George Ball, William Bundy, and Senate Majority Leader Mike Mansfield, telling them "the enemy was killing his personnel and he could not expect them to continue their work if he did not authorize them to take steps to defend themselves." He then authorized Operation *Flaming Dart I*: air strikes by *Hancock* (CVA-19), *Ranger* (CVA-61), and the VNAF 1st Fighter Squadron against barracks complexes around Dong Hoi which largely achieved nothing. On February 9, an enlisted billet in Qui Nhon was bombed, killing 23 and injuring 100, and triggering *Flaming Dart II* on February 11. These strikes in the North Vietnamese panhandle were more an exercise in presidential pique than an actual military operation, and had no effect on the North Vietnamese.

Bundy reported to the president on February 12 regarding his Vietnam trip:

The situation in Vietnam is deteriorating, and without new US action defeat appears inevitable. To be an American in Saigon today is to have a gnawing feeling that time is against us. The best available way of increasing our chance of success in Vietnam is the development and execution of a policy of sustained reprisal against North Vietnam... It implies significant US air losses even if no full air war is joined, and it seems likely that it would eventually require an extensive and costly effort against the whole air defense system of North Vietnam. US casualties would be higher – and more visible to American feelings – than those sustained in the struggle in South Vietnam. Yet measured against the costs of defeat in Vietnam, this program seems cheap. And even if it fails to turn the tide – as it may – the value of the effort seems to us to exceed its cost.

He concluded: "The object would not be to 'win' an air war against Hanoi, but rather to influence the course of the struggle in the South." The proposal was a policy to avoid committing ground forces to the war in the South by committing air power to a campaign in the North with no commitment to a victorious outcome.

Overcast skies hindered the *Flaming Dart* strikes and flak destroyed five aircraft though the North Vietnamese claimed 14 shot down. On

January 12, the JCS submitted a plan for air strikes against barracks, bridges, depots, ferries, and bases below the 19th parallel, and armed reconnaissance flights along Route 7 near the Laotian border. Aircraft would strike two to four targets per week over an eight-week period. Should the VPAF intervene, 30 B-52s from Andersen AFB on Guam would bomb the VPAF airfield at Phuc Yen on the night of such an event, followed by an attack by 48 F-105 fighter-bombers at dawn.

On February 13, President Johnson authorized commencement of the air campaign against the North in a presidential directive calling for "a program of measured and limited air action" against "selected military targets" in North Vietnam, noting that "attacks might come about once or twice a week and involve two or three targets on each day of operation." It would begin with an eight-week air campaign in the panhandle below the 19th parallel. Targeting would be consistent with the restrictions imposed by the president. If North Vietnam continued the insurgency in South Vietnam, the campaign could be expanded north of the 19th parallel, but south of Hanoi and Haiphong for an additional eight weeks. Should the North persist, the campaign would be extended to Haiphong, and eventually Hanoi.

This was OPLAN 37-64. There were four political/military objectives: to boost morale in South Vietnam; to persuade the North to cease support for the insurgency without sending ground forces into North Vietnam; to destroy the transportation system, industrial base, and air defenses; and to halt the flow of men and material into South Vietnam. On February 18, the JCS sent an "execute" order to Pacific Command (PACOM) for *Rolling Thunder I* on February 20 against Quang Khe naval base and the Vu Con barracks.

Following the Tonkin Gulf Incident, the Air Force deployed 54 F-100Ds of the 416th and 428th Tactical Fighter Squadrons and 28 B-57B light jet bombers of the 8th and 13th Bomb Squadrons to Bien Hoa and Da Nang to join 48 A-1Es of the 601st and 602nd Special Operations Squadrons. The main force was the F-105Ds of the 18th Tactical Fighter Wing's 12th, 36th, 44th, and 67th squadrons at Korat Royal Thai Air Force Base (RTAFB) and the 355th Tactical Fighter Wing's 354th, 562nd, and 563rd squadrons at Takhli RTAFB.

The foundational *Rolling Thunder* strategy was selective pressure, controlled by Washington and combined with diplomatic overtures to compel North Vietnam to end aggression against the South. Known as "gradualism," it was based on belief that threatening destruction would be a better signal of American determination than the destruction itself. Thus, important targets would be "held hostage" by bombing trivial ones. The targeting choices made bore little connection to military logic, since the sequence of attacks was not coordinated to provide any reinforcement and targets were approved randomly – even illogically. The airfields used by the VPAF, which would have been hit first in any rational campaign, were off-limits under the "hostage" strategy. Second Air Division commander Major General Joseph H. Moore, Jr. – in charge during the first 18 months – later stated:

> I was never allowed in the early days to send a single airplane north without being told how many bombs I would have on it, how many airplanes were in the flight, and what time it would be over the target. And if we couldn't get there at that time for some reason (weather or what not) we couldn't put the strike on later. We had to cancel it and start over again.

When the campaign was expanded country-wide in September 1965, strikes were strictly forbidden within 30 nautical miles of Hanoi and within ten nautical miles of Haiphong, while a 30-mile buffer zone extended the length of the Chinese frontier. The result was that strikes from Thailand were forced to follow almost exactly the same route for every attack, following what was known as "Thud Ridge" on the way to Hanoi. This "chute" was known to crews as "Slaughter Alley," the most heavily defended region of North Vietnam, with 150 SAM sites and 1,000 AAA sites along its length by December 1966. The "no bomb" zones around Hanoi and Haiphong allowed positioning of SAM sites that could target aircraft outside the zones, which couldn't strike back.

Rolling Thunder was more a series of individual operations conducted in fits and starts than a coherent campaign like the bombing of Nazi Germany. Civilian political aims dominated planning, oversight, and execution. In World War II and Korea, the military leadership was responsible for developing and directing a military campaign to achieve the political goals of the civilian leadership; this was turned on its head by the Johnson Administration. Civilians from the president on, inexperienced and uneducated in military strategy and operational tactics, took direct control of target selection and approval, frequently overruling input from the commands directly involved, resulting in little rhyme or reason in specific actions taken. From the outset, military leaders at all levels expressed reservations regarding *Rolling Thunder*, dissent that became stronger the closer one got to the levels tasked with carrying out the orders. A pilot who flew the early missions wrote home, "It seemed as if we were trying to see how much ordnance we could drop, without disturbing the country's way of life."

Rolling Thunder I was initially scheduled for February 20, 1965. However, this and the next four strikes were aborted due to a new military coup led by General Lam Van Phat and Colonel Pham Ngoc Thao (who was actually a communist agent) against General Nguyen Khanh, who had unseated General Duong Van "Big" Minh, who in turn had overthrown Diem. Unrest among the South Vietnamese leaders had broken out in December 1964. By January, Ambassador Taylor implicitly supported a coup against Khanh, believing that the general was too reliant on the pro-negotiations Buddhists, which prevented implementation of the air campaign that Taylor supported. Initially, the plotters believed that VNAF chief Air Marshal Nguyen Cao Ky would remain neutral, not knowing that Ky was planning a coup of his own. When the coup began on February 19, Ky ended it by threatening air attacks on Saigon; General Khanh departed for exile in Paris; Ky was now "first among rivals" and head of state in a government more unstable than that which was overthrown.

The air campaign finally began on March 2, with *Rolling Thunder V*. The North Vietnamese were not surprised, because the Americans and South Vietnamese had issued a joint communiqué on February 28 announcing "a continuous limited air campaign against the North to bring about a negotiated settlement on favorable terms." The strike involved 160 US Air Force and VNAF aircraft, supported by six KC-135 tankers – 25 F-100Ds, 20 F-105Ds, and 19 VNAF A-1Hs struck the Quang Khe naval base while 41 F-105Ds, 20 B-57Bs, and 12 F-100Ds bombed an ammunition depot at Xom Bang. Success was "moderate." North Vietnamese gunners shot down three F-105Ds, two F-100Ds, and one VNAF A-1H. The three F-105Ds from the 12th and 67th squadrons were assigned to flak suppression. All the downed pilots were rescued, including Captain Robert Baird, who ejected seconds before his F-105D struck the ground. The other two F-105s demonstrated the Thunderchief's toughness when pilots Captain Karl Spagnola and Major

George Panas flew their badly damaged airplanes out of North Vietnam to Thailand before ejecting. The two F-100Ds were lost making second passes at AAA positions. First Lieutenant J.A. Cullen from the 428th Tactical Fighter Squadron managed to get over the Tonkin Gulf before ejecting and was picked up, but First Lieutenant Hayden Lockhart of the 613th Tactical Fighter Squadron became the first USAF prisoner of war when he was finally captured after evading for seven days.

McNamara, alarmed by the surprisingly high losses, ordered a review by Deputy Secretary Cyrus Vance. The review was completed in mid-March, reporting that loss rates so far were less than those experienced during World War II, though double the overall loss rate in Korea. The losses were ominous, given that they resulted from limited numbers of light and medium AAA manned by inexperienced crews. Throughout the early phase, both Air Force and Navy pilots employed low-level attack formations devised for the proposed invasion of Cuba during the Cuban Missile Crisis.

While the reason for commencing an air campaign in the North was to avoid involvement in a ground war in the South, on March 8, 1965 the 9th Marine Expeditionary Brigade became the first US ground combat force in Vietnam when the unit landed at Da Nang's White Beach to defend the air base. As McNamara later wrote in his memoirs, "President Johnson's authorization of Operation *Rolling Thunder* not only started the air war but unexpectedly triggered the introduction of US troops into ground combat as well." Although MACV stated that "The US Marine Force will not, repeat will not, engage in day-to-day actions against the Viet Cong," the first firefight between a Marine patrol and an NLF force happened at the end of March. On May 7, the 173rd Airborne Brigade arrived to defend Bien Hoa air base.

Rolling Thunder soon came under criticism. Ambassador Taylor wrote on March 8, a week after the first strikes and the day the Marines landed in <u>Da Nang</u>: Actually CHO My DONG Beach

It appears to me evident that to date DRV leaders believe air strikes at present levels on their territory are meaningless and that we are more susceptible to international pressure for negotiations than are they. We must convince Hanoi authorities they face prospect of progressively severe punishment. I fear that to date *Rolling Thunder* in their eyes has been merely a few isolated thunderclaps.

On March 13, he reiterated that Hanoi had "the impression that our air strikes are a limited attempt to improve our bargaining position and hence are no great cause for immediate concern." This was a retort to Undersecretary Ball's December memo, urging that the administration "begin at once a progression of US strikes north of 19th parallel in a slow but steadily ascending movement."

Rolling Thunder VI, a two-day series of Air Force–Navy–VNAF strikes, began on March 14. Protected by F-100Ds flying top cover and F-105Ds to attack AAA sites, 24 VNAF Skyraiders, personally led by Nguyen Cao Ky in the only case known in history of a sitting head of state personally leading an air strike, struck barracks on Tiger Island. The Skyraiders dropped 250-pound, 500-pound, and 750-pound bombs and inflicted what was determined as 70–80 percent damage. On March 15, 64 A-1s and A-4s from *Hancock* and *Ranger* and 20 F-105Ds from Thailand, supported by 51 other USAF and USN aircraft, bombed the ammo depot located southwest of Phu Quy with bombs, rockets, strafing, and the first use of napalm over North Vietnam. They damaged or destroyed 20 of 23 buildings while losing one A-1 and its pilot. Bomb damage assessment (BDA) photos showed 30 percent destruction.

By mid-March, *Rolling Thunder* was one mission a week in southern North Vietnam. Nothing had been hit that seriously harmed the war effort, and a joke made the rounds of American units that the North Vietnamese were unaware there was a war going on. That soon changed.

Rolling Thunder VII, flown from March 19 to 25, involved Air Force, Navy, and VNAF strikes against North Vietnamese targets "decoupled" from direct relation to provocations in the South, with similar results. On March 22, the first "all-American mission" saw eight 67th Tactical Fighter Squadron F-105s led by squadron commander and Korean War ten-victory MiG ace Lieutenant Colonel Robinson Risner hit the "Moon Cone" radar site at Vinh Son. The hard-charging Risner had flown a mission every day over Laos or North Vietnam since arriving at Korat, frequently taking hits. This time, Risner's F-105D was badly damaged by AAA. He managed to hold things together until the burning plane was over the Tonkin Gulf, where he ejected and was picked up by an HU-16B that almost didn't make it back into the air after picking him up, due to a faulty engine.

Less than a month after *Rolling Thunder* began, the VPAF appeared in combat. The air force had arrived in North Vietnam on August 6,

1964, when the first group of pilots trained in the Soviet Union and China brought 16 MiG-17s to Hanoi's Gia Lam airfield. On April 3, 1965, the MiGs intercepted A-4 Skyhawks escorted by F-8 Crusaders from the carrier *Hancock* attacking the Dong Phuong Thong Bridge. In the confused action, the VPAF claimed two F-8s shot down; these were two different attacks by the inexperienced pilots against the same airplane.

McNamara remained determined to limit *Rolling Thunder*. He defended this in contentious congressional hearings in mid-summer 1967 and after resigning as Secretary of Defense and leaving office in 1968. To McNamara, *Rolling Thunder* was only a campaign to coerce the North Vietnamese to end support of the insurgency. After the war, Seventh Air Force commander William Momyer recalled, "Neither the President, the Secretary of State, nor the Secretary of Defense yet conceived of *Rolling Thunder* as a strategic air offensive. The Secretary of Defense continued to maintain that the primary role for air power should be to support ground forces in South Vietnam as it was here that the enemy must be denied a military victory."

Between March 2, 1965 and November 1, 1968, less than 30 percent of all US attack sorties in all of Southeast Asia were "up North." The specific numbers were 594,702 sorties over South Vietnam, 306,618 sorties over North Vietnam, and 183,812 sorties over Laos.

According to The Pentagon Papers, the secret history of the war commissioned by Secretary McNamara later leaked to the public in 1971, "After a month of bombing with no response from the North Vietnamese, optimism began to wane." In a phone conversation recorded by the White House taping system on March 6, 1965 – four days after the first strikes – between the president and Georgia Senator Richard Russell, Chairman of the Senate Armed Services Committee, Johnson exclaimed, "Airplanes ain't worth a damn, Dick! A man can fight if he can see daylight down the road somewhere. But there ain't no daylight in Vietnam. There's not a bit." The senator, who never publicly waivered in his support for the war, replied, "There's no end to the road. There's just nothing. We're going to wind up with the people mad as hell with us." Truer words were never spoken.

6

FEATHER DUSTER

A month after *Rolling Thunder* began, *Rolling Thunder 9* was flown on April 3, 1965. It was the first of many strikes against the Thanh Hoa railroad and highway bridge which spanned the Song Ma River three miles northeast of the provincial capital of Thanh Hoa in Annam Province. The Vietnamese knew the bridge as "Ham Rong," or "Dragon's Jaw" which came from the shape formed by a jagged ridge that rose from the surrounding flat terrain west of the bridge known as Rong Mountain and a small hill east of the bridge named Ngoc (Jade) Hill; together they resembled the jawbones of a dragon's mouth.

The bridge, designed by Nguyen Dinh Doan and built by the French, was destroyed in 1945 by Viet Minh guerillas running two TNT-laden locomotives together at the midpoint. It was reconstructed between 1957 and 1964, and now spanned 540 feet and was 56 feet wide and 50 feet tall. It was overbuilt with two steel truss spans resting on a gigantic reinforced concrete pier 16 feet thick between massive reinforced concrete abutments at each end. A railway track ran down the center, with 22-foot-wide reinforced concrete highways to either side. To call it massive was an understatement.

The largest strike to date saw 45 F-105Ds take part, escorted by 24 F-100Ds of the 416th Tactical Fighter Wing and supported by KC-135 tankers. Lieutenant Colonel Risner's squadron led, carrying AGM-45 Bullpup-B missiles. Despite scoring hits on key structural points, they only caused superficial damage since the early Bullpup's 250-pound warhead was far too small to crack concrete 40 feet thick in places. It was not a "fire and forget" weapon, being visually guided by the pilot with a joystick using radio signals, who had to stay on course behind the Bullpup as he steered it to its target, exposed to enemy fire.

Third flight leader Captain Bill Meyerholt fired his Bullpup and watched it streak toward the bridge. When it exploded and the smoke cleared, he was shocked to see no visible damage. "Those things were as effective as shooting BBs at a battleship," he recalled. Due to an unexpected strong crosswind, the others were frustrated as the Bullpups drifted and exploded against the hillside. They fired 32 Bullpups and dropped 120 M117 750-pound bombs; all of the structure was charred, yet the damage was insufficient to drop it. The unsuccessful attack cost the life of Major George Smith of the 615th Tactical Fighter Squadron, shot down while attacking an AAA site.

A second strike was scheduled for the next day with 46 F-105Ds escorted by 21 F-100Ds. This time, the VPAF were ready for them.

Lieutenant Colonel Risner was leader again. All 48 attackers carried 750-pound bombs. Delays with the tankers over Laos and poor target visibility resulted in several F-105 flights having to orbit ten miles south to await their bombing times. The 354th Tactical Fighter Squadron Zinc Flight had just received the call to attack the bridge when four VPAF MiG-17s of the 921st Fighter Regiment, led by 32-year-old Senior Lieutenant Tran Hanh with Lieutenants Pham Giay, Le Minh Huan, and Tran Nguyen Nam, appeared out of the haze. Tran Hanh, considered one of the best MiG-17 pilots at the time, recalled:

> The weather was very cloudy, with considerable fog patches. My flight received orders from ground control to descend to low altitude and head east, then, again on orders, changed our heading to south-east. As my flight approached the area of the anticipated interception, we quickly climbed to gain advantage. I reported at 1030 hours that we had visual contact with the Americans. I had spotted a group of four F-105Ds which had just started dropping their bombs, and I ordered my wingman, Pham Giay, to cover me in the attack. I closed on the enemy and at a distance of 400 meters, I opened up with all three cannons.

Zinc 03 element leader Major Vernon M. Kulla, an experienced former F-100 pilot, and his wingman, squadron gunnery instructor Captain Richard P. Pearson in Zinc 04, saw the enemy fighters emerge from the haze and called warnings to flight leader Major Frank Bennett in

Zinc 01. Neither he nor wingman Captain James Magnusson heard the calls since the radio circuit was jammed with transmissions from others, and they continued to orbit. Kulla jettisoned his bombs, which Tran Hanh saw, and switched his gunsight to air-to-air mode to use his M61 Vulcan gun, but Pearson failed to complete the complex sequence in time and lost sight of the MiGs.

Tran Hanh closed on Bennett and opened fire. The shells set the Thunderchief on fire. Bennett turned and headed out to sea where he ejected from his burning bomber near Hon Me Island. He became tangled in the parachute when he hit the water and drowned before the HU-16 rescue amphibian could reach him.

Tran Hanh recalled, "The Americans turned to attack us, and we split into two groups. My wingman and I stayed on the southern side of the Ham Rong Bridge, while Le Minh Huan and Tran Nguyen Nam flew across to the northern side." Huan and Nam fired on and damaged Zinc 03. Kulla evaded with a snap roll that slowed him and forced the MiGs to overshoot, a tactic he'd learned from his Fighter Weapons School instructor, the legendary John R. Boyd, developer of the Energy-Maneuverability Theory of air combat. At the time, Kulla had dismissed Boyd's idea, but it put one MiG in his gunsight, surprising him so he missed a sure kill. Coming out of the roll, Kulla accelerated to maximum speed and descended to 500 feet, taking himself out of the fight.

Le Minh Huan then turned on Magnusson's tail, firing a burst that set the Thunderchief on fire. Magnusson was unable to eject before he struck a nearby hillside. Huan and Nam turned toward their base at Noi Bai. At that moment, MiGCAP Purple flight leader Lieutenant Colonel Emmett Hays, commanding officer (CO) of the 416th Tactical Fighter Squadron, and wingman Captain Keith Connolly, who had spotted the MiGs when they attacked Zinc Flight, closed to Sidewinder range of Huan and Nam. Connolly's AIM-9B narrowly missed Huan's right wing; he fired a second Sidewinder that also missed, then closed and fired his guns but Huan and Nam evaded. However, they never made it back to Noi Bai. Neither did Hanh's wingman, Pham Giay.

Sole survivor Tran Hanh reported:

In the ensuing combat, the numerical superiority of the Americans resulted in the loss of my wingman, as well as Le Minh Huan and Tran Nguyen Nam. I was only able to escape through hard maneuvering, but I lost contact with ground control in the process. Short on fuel, I successfully put my MiG down in Ke Tam Valley, but was immediately arrested by the locals, who mistook me for an enemy when they heard my southern accent. I was only able to regain my freedom after showing them my VPAF badge. I was taken to the provincial capital, where the commander turned out to be my friend with whom I had fought against the French in the 320th Army Division.

Tran Hanh flew throughout the war, rising to command the 921st Fighter Regiment in 1966 and becoming deputy commander of the VPAF in 1972, then commander two years later. He retired in 2000 as a lieutenant general after four years as Deputy Defense Minister and member of the Party Central Committee.

Captain Don Kilgus from the 416th Squadron's Green Flight claimed a MiG-17 shot down, though he lost it in haze before it crashed, which was denied. It is believed that the three pilots were lost to "friendly fire" near the bridge, becoming the first VPAF combat losses. Heavy flak was also responsible for the loss of Captain "Smitty" Harris in Steel Flight from the 67th Tactical Fighter Squadron, who became the second USAF prisoner of war when he ejected near the target and was captured.

President Johnson saw Kilgus' claimed MiG as politically inflammatory, stating that he "...did not want any more MiGs shot down." He was still obsessed with avoiding Russian or Chinese intervention. Air Force Chief of Staff General John P. McConnell was "hopping mad" on learning that two F-105s had been shot down by "Korean War-era MiGs."

The Thanh Hoa Bridge became the most-bombed target in North Vietnam, site of more US losses than any other location during the remainder of *Rolling Thunder*. It would finally be destroyed by a strike using laser-guided 2,000-pound bombs during Operation *Linebacker* in 1972.

The first engagement with enemy fighters revealed many shortcomings in the proficiency of US pilots in air-to-air combat. Amazingly, it was known before *Rolling Thunder* that there was trouble. In 1964, Colonel Abner M. Aust, Jr., a staff officer at Pacific Air Forces (PACAF) headquarters, complained:

One item that concerns me as much as anything is air combat tactics. I don't think we have any F-105 or F-100 pilots in Southeast Asia who could fight their way out of a paper bag if they were really contested by MiGs today. There has been no real training on air-to-air tactics for a good five years. Because of the emphasis on nuclear attack by tactical fighters, our tactics and techniques lessons learned during Korea and World War II have been pretty much discarded.

The decision after the Korean War to completely de-emphasize air-to-air combat training, and the absolute ban on any unofficial "hassling" – the informal aerial competitions between pilots – meant that Air Force fighter pilots lacked the necessary skills and knowledge to be successful fighter pilots in the traditional sense. There had been attempts to maintain those capabilities. In 1957, several articles on air-to-air combat for the F-100 Super Sabre – then TAC's primary fighter – were published by the Air Force Fighter Weapons School (FWS) in *Fighter Weapons Newsletter*. The primary recommendation was seven one-hour sorties for its fighter weapons instructor course. However, the 1959 FWS syllabus contained three-and-a-half flight hours on correct employment of the new Sidewinder missile, three hours of intercepts, and three more for air-to-air gunnery against a slow towed target, but no air combat maneuvering training. This was the state of affairs as a second war involving none of the elements that the service had organized itself to face in combat began.

Then-First Lieutenant Ralph Wetterhahn graduated from the Air Force Academy in 1963 and recalled that his initial assignment after flight school was to F-4 Phantom training:

After a few months filling squares, I was awarded a Combat Crew Badge. At that point in time, not only did I not know how to do even such a simple maneuver as a hi-speed yo-yo, I had never even heard the term, no less any other fighter tactics. Our front seaters were a mix of guys recalled during the Cuban Missile Crisis, and navigators who had flown as radar operators in the F-101, and were offered pilot training. The thinking was the latter would become excellent F-4 pilots given their time spent looking at a radar tube. Almost all of those guys were weak, to say the least. In 1965, things began heating up in Vietnam. The first MiG shot down since the Korean War was claimed on April 9, 1965. All of a sudden dogfighting was a topic. One of our good front-seaters produced a tattered copy of Boots Blesse's *No Guts, No Glory*. I opened the book and was shocked. This Designated Combat Crewman had never *heard* of any of these maneuvers! In March, 1966, I was called into the squadron commander's office along with two other backseaters and offered the front seat if we would accept a combat tour. We jumped at it. It was probably safer than flying with most of the guys we sat behind.

After arriving at Ubon RTAB to join the 8th Tactical Fighter Wing, known as "the Wolfpack" and led by the legendary Colonel Robin Olds, Wetterhahn and the other pilots in the wing got some limited experience in air combat maneuvering with 76 Squadron of the Royal Australian Air Force (RAAF), which maintained a detachment of the Australian version of the F-86, the CA-32 Sabre, the most powerful and capable sub-type of that legendary fighter, against a possible VPAF attack. Wetterhahn explained:

> When we were returning from a mission up North, if we had enough fuel we'd put in a radio call to base and the Aussies would be launched to intercept us and we'd hassle for a few minutes before arrival back home. The only thing I learned from that, and it was important, was not to try and turn with those guys. The first time I engaged in full-on "dissimilar air combat maneuvering" was as Robin Olds' wingman, and the dissimilar aircraft were MiG-21s!

Thus, in the years before Vietnam, TAC's "fighter pilots" trained to deliver tactical nuclear bombs in a World War III that never happened, while Air Defense Command's (ADC's) "fighters" were interceptors whose expected targets were enemy bombers similar to the B-52, flying straight and level with the interceptors guided from the ground to the point where they fired a single-shot volley of rockets. In truth, in 1965, there were neither "air superiority fighters" in the Air Force inventory, nor pilots with skills to fly them.

Although the Air Force was rightly condemned in later studies of the air war over North Vietnam, with the service excoriated for opposing development of a real air-to-air combat capability, an effort was made in the aftermath of the Dragon's Jaw battle in 1965 to analyze Air Force combat tactics in a more realistic training environment, to develop a more effective means of engaging the enemy air force.

By the summer of 1965, TAC was aware of every point that Lieutenant Wetterhahn had discovered during his introduction to the

F-4 Phantom. Not only that, direct experiments clearly demonstrated the need of pilots for formal training in air combat maneuvering and that pilots who received such training were more likely to succeed in air combat. This was the result of a project code named "Feather Duster," which tested the air combat capabilities of the F-100, F-104, F-105, and F-4C against the F-86H, acting as a substitute for the MiG-17. The information was in a report from the Fighter Weapons School, published in May, 1965, titled *TAC Mission FF-857: Air Combat Tactics Evaluation – F-100, F-104, F-105 and F-4C versus MiG-15/17 type aircraft (F-86H).*

Colonel Tom "Sharkbait" Delahunt, a 300-mission F-104 and F-4 pilot in Vietnam, who participated in Feather Duster, later recalled:

> Project Feather Duster was instigated by TAC to help develop proper tactics against likely opponents that TAC aircraft might face in Southeast Asia. The TAC aircraft of concern were the F-100C/D/F, F-4C, F-105D and F-104C. Opponents included the F-102A and F-106A to simulate the MiG-21, F-86H to simulate the MiG-17, and F-8C/D to simulate the MiG-19. The TAC aircraft were also flown against each other to practice dissimilar air combat training (DACT) and to further evaluate their individual strengths and weaknesses.
>
> It should come as no surprise that the F-8s did pretty well against the F-100s. It probably won't surprise too many to learn that the F-4s generally beat up on the F-105s. The big shock to most, however, was the fact that the F-104C ended up at the top of the heap. It not only bested all the other aircraft, but it did so regularly and by a surprising margin. Only when dictated to fly high altitude, subsonic turning engagements did the F-104 fall short of its opponents.

Feather Duster 1 Part 1, Mission FF-857, was carried out between April 26 and May 7, 1965, mere weeks after the embarrassment at the Dragon's Jaw where experienced Air Force pilots were bested by less experienced North Vietnamese pilots flying an inferior fighter. The F-100D, F-104C, F-105D, and F-4C were alternated in "attacker" and "defender" positions, with the Air National Guard F-86H opponents similarly alternated in "attacker" and "defender" positions. Most engagements were one-on-one, with a limited number of two-on-two engagements to analyze a defending unit's defensive-split capability. The individual flight profiles were either "defender" at 35,000 feet at typical combat patrol speed, adjusted to 0.9 Mach so the F-86H could make an attack, or "defender" at 20,000 feet with typical ordnance-loaded airspeed for the type of fighter involved, for example 360 knots for the F-105D. A total 128 sorties were flown, each lasting approximately 45 minutes, during which the aircraft were involved in two to four engagements per sortie, for a total 180 engagements.

That was followed by Feather Duster 1 Part 2, conducted June 28–July 2, involving two new F-5A "Freedom Fighters" from the 4441st Combat Crew Training Squadron versus ANG F-86Hs, to demonstrate the new fighter's ability to its intended foreign users, who were primarily interested in its air-to-air capability. A total of 62 sorties were flown, with the F-5s fighting 35 engagements as the "defender" and 47 as the "attacker." The report concluded, "F-5 agility was impressive."

Feather Duster 2 Part 1, conducted August 16–September 22, involved tests to demonstrate proper usage of the AIM-7B Sparrow and AIM-9B Sidewinder in the low-altitude combat environment. The same four TAC fighters flew versus the F-86H. Typical setups had the "defenders" at 5,000 feet, 1,000 feet, and 500 feet above ground level (AGL), flying airspeeds ranging from 360 to 420 calibrated airspeeds in knots (KCAS). This revealed that in 80 percent of the engagements, TAC crews did not properly deploy and use their missiles, due to lack of familiarity with proper usage.

The three Feather Duster tests involved 298 sorties, with over 200 engagements. Interestingly, during all three tests, the new tactics based on "energy management" proposed by then-Lieutenant Colonel John Boyd, which are today the "bible" for air combat maneuvering by every fighter pilot in the world, were tested and found to be accurate, leading to improvement in fighting capability by each pilot who trained in their use and then employed them in the tests. Faced with these reports, TAC made no changes to either basic pilot training or the advanced training provided at the Fighter Weapons School throughout the Vietnam War until 1971; "energy management" was only adopted following introduction of the F-15 and F-16 into the inventory in the mid/late 1970s.

The results of Feather Duster cast doubt on the combat effectiveness of the "fluid four" combat formation, in which two pairs of fighters gave mutual support to each other. In this formation, each pair had a leader and a wingman, with the latter flying behind and to one side in "fighting wing" formation, with the assignment to stay with and protect his leader, the "shooter." The Feather Duster fights clearly demonstrated that the formation was ineffective against MiGs. However, the "fluid four," or "welded wing" as some dubbed the inflexible arrangement, had dominated Air Force tactics since its adoption in 1942. The formation was retained throughout the war and the Air Force resisted adoption of the Navy's more effective "loose deuce" pairing, in which either fighter could be the "shooter," depending on who first spotted the enemy. The first fighter pilots to adopt this tactic were Don Gentile and Johnny Godfrey of the famed 4th Fighter Group during World War II, explained by Godfrey in his autobiography *The Look of Eagles* thus: "Whoever sees them first, takes them." Using the tactic, the two became the most successful pilots in the group during the battles over Berlin in the spring of 1944, though they were criticized by others in the unit for failing to follow the rules of the "finger four," as the "fluid four" was known then.

Pilots of all four fighters that went up against the ANG F-86Hs learned the folly of getting "low and slow" in a turning fight. The tests also proved that the four types fought better at lower altitudes, though their missiles were less effective in the denser air, and defined the areas of their performance envelopes in which they would have the best chance against the MiG-17 and MiG-21. It was found that keeping speed up allowed pilots to use "energy maneuverability," rather than suffer the disadvantage of reduced lift in a high-G turn which left a steep dive the only way of recovering energy. The report recommended that US pilots make fast, slashing attacks on the enemy to overcome the MiGs' advantage below 0.9 Mach. Unfortunately, Feather Duster did not receive the wide distribution it deserved in the fighter wings of TAC that could have made best use of the information.

Legendary F-105 pilot Ed Rasimus, veteran of 100 missions over North Vietnam in the Thunderchief and later a noted historian of the war he fought, knew several of the F-105 pilots involved in Feather Duster and later wrote about the tests. In explaining why TAC was reluctant to accept the results of Feather Duster, particularly regarding the "fluid four," he noted that in the 1960s the Fighter Weapons School was fragmented in operation; pilots of different type fighters didn't interact, either on the ground or in the air, thus eliminating any possibility of informal "hassling" between different types stirring thoughts in the minds of pilots that dissimilar air combat training might be valuable:

> The overall pilot's worldview there was purely a reflection of the ingrained training. The senior instructors were World War II and Korean War vets, and the "Fluid Four" was what was done. Criteria for attendance at the school started with a requirement that the candidate have 1,000 flight hours in type. When you went to FWS, you were going to be a leader, not a fighting wing hanger-on. You were going to be the shooter. The mere idea that a junior lieutenant could be capable of maneuvering on his own and then being authorized to pull the trigger was anathema. The concept was well established even through the Korean War that senior pilots, as flight and element leads did the shooting, while junior pilots were supposed to fly fighting wing and "clear lead's six." Really, the wingmen merely became the alternative target for the attacker and thus protected the lead. One obvious result of the "Fluid Four" formation was that the majority of MiG kills were scored by flight or element leaders, who could concentrate on their shots while their wingmen protected them.

Regarding the validation of John Boyd's theories of air combat in the tests, Rasimus said:

> The thinking that most fighter types take for granted today was revolutionary at the time. Understanding that energy was both potential and kinetic, that the two were interchangeable, that the vertical offered some advantages, and that there were chartable corners of the performance envelope that revealed strengths and weaknesses were all new ideas. The Air Force at that time was led by senior generals who were predominantly from SAC. The senior fighter leadership was secondary overall in organizational influence, and most dated back to World War II when the fight was considerably different. Worst of all was the reluctance to accept an element of risk in training. Air-to-air requires maximum performance maneuvering, close to another aircraft that is trying to be unpredictable. That smacks of mid-air potential.

The pilots Rasimus spoke with all thought the most important Feather Duster lesson was the value of DACT:

> Probably the most critical aspect of Feather Duster, but largely ignored until the '70s was the identification of the value of dissimilar

training. Rather than fighting your own type, which inevitably leads
to an "I can fly slower than you" contest, the dissimilar battle requires
understanding of both aircraft's potential and maximizing your own
performance while minimizing your opponent's.

Despite Rasimus' dismissal of World War II fighter pilots, some of them
saw the problem. Former Air Force Vice Chief of Staff and noted World
War II China–Burma–India Theater ten-victory fighter ace General
Bruce K. Holloway wrote: *I Served on his STAFF for*
Swift strike 2

Between 1954 and 1962, the USAF training curriculum for fighter
pilots included little, if any, air-to-air combat. This omission was partly
a result of doctrine, which then regarded tactical fighters primarily as
a means for delivering nuclear ordnance. It was partly a reflection of
concern for flying safety. In any event, as late as October 1963, it was
reported that only four of 30 pilots in one fighter squadron had ever
shot aerial gunnery.

There were others in the Air Force advocating for new, more effective
tactics. Tom Delahunt recalled that the F-104 pilots he served with at
Homestead AFB were very interested in finding a way to stretch their
numbers as they considered their possible opponents across the Florida
Straits:

The F-104 bunch that did so well was predominantly from the
435th TFS "Black Eagles" of the 479th Tactical Fighter Wing
at Homestead. They were one of few day fighter units in the Air
Force at the time and were leaders in the development of "fluid
attack" tactics in which, rather than fighting wing, the element
flew as a mutually supporting team, not chasing the leader's tail but
maneuvering counter-plane and positioning to deny counters and
swap roles to maintain pressure on the defender. They were leaders
in vertical maneuver application.

Zipper pilots at Homestead all read the same books, mainly
Boyd, Riccione and Rutowsky. I was squadron weapons officer in
1964–1966 and got "double attack" adapted. The way I sold it was
describing it as "fluid four with no wingmen." We normally flew in
pairs anyway. Since we had 28 F-104Cs looking at 125 MiG-21s down
in Cuba, pairs maximized flexibility. We also had a comprehensive

combat crew training program to get new pilots up to flight lead as soon as possible. This of course made "double attack/loose deuce" eminently practical.

In 1968, two late-production F-104A-19-LO Starfighters were used in air combat maneuvering tests in Nevada with the former-Iraqi MiG-17F and MiG-21F-13 secretly given to the Air Force by the Israelis. Delahunt recounted how he was told by the pilots that "Even with the old F-104As, there was no contest. The Dash-19 couldn't be attacked in high cruise by the MiG-17 and the MiG-21 couldn't sustain energy in maneuvering."

While TAC was reluctant to adopt DACT, ADC was very interested in doing so with its F-106A squadrons. The command developed its own program for DACT in 1966 to be ready for a new supplementary mission providing air defense overseas, when the Air Force began to consider that ADC squadrons could be deployed to hot spots outside of the continental United States, as had been done with deployment of PACAF F-102As to Vietnam in 1964. The requirement became real during the *Pueblo* Crisis, when the intelligence ship USS *Pueblo* was captured by the North Koreans in 1969, when F-106As from the 48th Fighter-Interceptor Squadron were assigned to Operation *Fresh Storm* and sent to South Korea.

ADC/ADOTT Project 66-1, code named "College Prom," took place at Minot AFB, North Dakota, from August 22 to September 17, 1966. F-106As from the 5th Fighter-Interceptor Squadron engaged with F-102As and F-104As operating as adversaries. Specific tests included formation flying, basic fighter maneuvers, visual identification of enemy MiGs, discovering which tactics were most appropriate and which least effective for the F-106 against fighters, the effects of air combat maneuvering on the airplane itself, and developing modifications to the fire control system in order to engage MiGs. College Prom involved 127 F-106A sorties, 40 F-104A sorties, and 40 F-102A sorties.

The rule "Safety will be paramount during this test" was reflective of the long-time Air Force concern over mid-air collisions that had been such an effective barrier to pilots' learning how to fight other aircraft. Safety requirements included a minimum speed of 150 knots indicated air speed (IAS), a minimum altitude of 10,000 feet AGL, visibility of five miles and 2,000 feet vertically from clouds, a common radio channel, and that the wingman maintain sight of his leader at all times during maneuvers.

At its conclusion, College Prom was declared a success. As a result, the Air Force revised Air Force Manual (AFM) 3-16 *Intercept Tactics for Air-to-Air Operations* by adding the chapter "Air Superiority-Air Combat Tactics," providing procedures for air defense interceptors in the air superiority role. Importantly, ADC made DACT training a priority for F-106 pilots, requiring 12 sorties for qualification. In May 1967, the 71st Fighter-Interceptor Squadron became the first F-106 unit to undergo the new training. When the 318th Fighter-Interceptor Squadron commenced DACT training in July 1967, the squadron historian noted:

This is a completely new type of training for the aircrews who have been in ADC all their careers. This program requires 12 missions be flown utilizing the F-106 as an Air-to-Air Day Fighter. For most of us in the squadron, Tactical Formation and Element Engagements were both challenging and very exciting. This program has been very beneficial to the aircrews both in morale and operation of the F-106 in its optimum capability.

As a follow-on to College Prom, the Interceptor Weapons School began "College Dart" at Tyndall AFB, Florida, in 1968. This involved use of the Homestead-based F-104As as adversary aircraft. When the pilots of the 319th Fighter-Interceptor Squadron fought against F-106s in March 1969, the squadron historian wrote, "The results of this engagement were eye-catching as the Starfighter proved superior in the 'eyeball-to-eyeball' contest by scoring four 'mission accomplished' against the enemy force." The F-106 pilots learned as a result of fighting F-104s that the similarly sized MiG-21 would be hard to see, and that the F-106 radar did not detect them at great distances. Pilots from the 94th Fighter-Interceptor Squadron found that a formation of four F-106s "line-abreast" gave the best visual lookout, but that the "finger-four" did not provide the protection for the lead element it was supposed to, and did not place the formation "in a position to offensively command." Fighting invariably ended up in two-plane elements.

With ADC leadership enthusiastically supporting such training, the Air Force made DACT a priority for interceptor pilots; the 12-sortie requirement was standardized for qualification, with post-qualification continuation training to consist of two DACT sorties per month, of "approximately 30–45 minutes devoted to DACT maneuvering of which only five to ten minutes maximum would be at other than normal flight loads." While the program prepared F-106s to go up against MiGs, during the 71st Squadron's deployment to South Korea, its most-noted missions were two intercepts of Tu-95 Bear bombers in a winter snowstorm over the Sea of Japan. Following the founding of the Navy's Top Gun program in 1969, F-106 squadrons joined in with their Navy and Marine cousins for extensive DACT training. Pilots in VF-96, who scored the best one-day combat total of the Vietnam War on May 10, 1972, credited their success to flying against the DACT-experienced F-106 pilots.

Fortunately, while engagement of the F-105 in air-to-air combat was not considered likely, at the outset of US air operations over North Vietnam, many of the pilots in the F-105 squadrons initially deployed to Southeast Asia had previous air combat experience. Colonel Jack Broughton, vice commander of the 388th Tactical Fighter Wing, who eventually flew 105 missions over North Vietnam, had fighter experience going back to his initial Air Force assignment to fly the P-47 Thunderbolt in 1946, as well as a tour flying the F-80 Shooting Star in the Korean War, in addition to experience in the F-86 Sabre after the war. As he explained:

> Most of us "old heads" in the "Thud" business had a good grasp on aerial combat. I don't think air-to-air was ever considered irrelevant in training, at least not at our level. We didn't have many trainees join us during my time in Southeast Asia. We needed experienced guys to go North, and if we got a new guy we taught him all we could on-scene.

For the newer pilots, what air-to-air practice they had experienced had involved other F-105s and was frequently done on an informal basis since senior commanders were still opposed to such training. Their knowledge of the MiG-17 was primarily from reading translations of its flight manual. Surprisingly, the F-105 – an airplane never designed for air-to-air combat – had the best overall victory ratio of any US fighter used in the war, with 27 enemy fighters credited as shot down – with an additional half-claim shared with an F-4 – by F-105 pilots, for a loss of only three F-105s to fighters of the VPAF in air combat conditions during *Rolling Thunder*.

The bureaucratic seniority involved in the "welded wing" didn't apply just to air-to-air combat. Ralph Wetterhahn recalled a bombing mission flown in 1966:

We had two targets, both bridges, located within a half mile of each other, 25 miles from Hanoi in the southwest corner of Route Package VI-A. Captain Clarence "Bull" Fulkerson was flight lead assigned to hit the bridge to the south with his number two Bill DeLuca, while I was element lead, assigned the bridge to the north. Given there were towns nearby, SAM rings, AAA gun pits, and MiG air bases well within range, we expected it to be well defended.

We arrived over the target and suddenly, Bull radioed, "One's up!" He lit his afterburners and began a climbing turn away from me to the northwest. I looked left and spotted a bridge, but something didn't look right. For one thing, I saw only one bridge. DeLuca followed, "Two's up."

As I began my climb, my backseater, First Lieutenant Jerry Sharp, called, "Ain't our target." Our target bridges were oriented mostly east–west, while this bridge was oriented northwest–southeast. By that time, Bull was into his dive-bomb run. I called, "Lead, that's not our target." Bull did not respond, but his bombs did, as his M-117 750s left the racks and arced toward the bridge, hitting short. DeLuca was coming over the top. "What do you want me to do, Three?"

He didn't ask Bull the question, putting me in a quandary for a second or two. Just before the mission, Robin Olds had given us a tongue-lashing about hitting the wrong targets up here. "Go through dry," I finally managed. DeLuca pulled out without dropping. I radioed Bull, "Lead, my inertial shows we're six miles from the target." He responded, "Do whatever you want, Three," irritation evident in his tone. I picked up a heading of 220 degrees, as Two and Four moved to rejoin. I saw Bull off to the side, trailing us. A minute later, I began my pull up, having spotted the correct bridges. "I'm in on the pontoon," I radioed.

The target was hot and tracers began searching us out from numerous gun batteries. I hit the pickle button at 4,500 feet and began the pullout, then left, jinking all the way out. I never looked back. Two and Four called "in" and "off," and we all headed home, with Bull assuming the lead once again.

After landing, Bull was waiting in the debrief room, and he was not happy. The intel NCO was already there, so Bull bided his time. The sergeant asked Bull for his BDA on the target. "I hit short," he said. Sharp leaned over to me and whispered a bit too loud, "Yeah, by six miles!" Bull heard it and looked like he was about to leap over the debriefing table.

The sergeant then asked for my BDA. "I rolled on the northern target, the pontoon, but didn't look back because of the triple-A." DeLuca piped up, "You blew the shit out of it. We both went after the other one, and I think we hit it, too." Four backed DeLuca up. The intel NCO rolled up his papers and headed out. Bull then unloaded. "When I drop on a target, you drop on *that* target. Got it lieutenant?" "Yes, sir," I replied. "And you don't ever take over my flight like that!" He then announced there would be more to this once he had a talk with the Squadron Commander.

The first two units to achieve initial operational capability (IOC) in the F-4C Phantom were the 12th and 15th Tactical Fighter Wings, both based at McDill AFB in Florida, in October 1964. The 12th Wing's 555th "Triple Nickel" Tactical Fighter Squadron was the first to go to the Pacific when they arrived at Kadena AFB, Okinawa, that December. The new fighter first deployed for combat in Southeast Asia the day of the embarrassing air battle over the Dragon's Jaw, when the 15th Tactical Fighter Wing's 45th Tactical Fighter Squadron arrived for TDY at Ubon RTAB.

By July 10, the pilots were veterans, but they were frustrated by the enemy's lack of interest in picking a fight. That day, in a cleverly devised "sting" operation, the squadron sent a flight north masquerading as late-arriving F-105s. The VPAF frequently went after the last elements of a strike, knowing any escorts would be low on fuel, and took the bait, sending MiG-17s to intercept the "unescorted bombers." The result was a fight in which the F-4's first two air-to-air victory claims were confirmed.

Four F-4Cs of Mink Flight took off 20 minutes later than the rest of the squadron's escorts and flew to the target at Yen Bai at 20,000 feet and 0.85 Mach, the speed and altitude usually flown by loaded F-105s.

Once over Yen Bai, Mink Flight orbited several times before Mink flight leader Major Richard Hall and "Guy In Back" (GIB) First Lieutenant George Larson in Mink 01, and element leader Captains Kenneth Holcombe and Arthur Clarke in Mink 03 made radar contact with "bogeys" at a range of 33 miles as Larson searched "high" and Clarke "low." Wingmen Captains Harold Anderson and Wilbur Anderson in Mink 02 and Captains Tom Roberts and Ronald Anderson in Mink 04 flew a weaving pattern to the rear as they concentrated on a visual search. Mink 01 and Mink 02 were low on fuel when they pulled ahead of Holcombe and Roberts and finally made a visual ID of the bogeys as two MiG-17s. These were flown by the 921st Regiment's Lieutenants Phan Thanh Nha and Cuong Cuong. Hall and Anderson turned aside, allowing Holcombe and Roberts to drop back and fire their AIM-7D missiles at minimum range. However, the maneuver did not provide separation sufficient for the second element to fire without hitting the lead element, and the two MiGs passed the Phantoms head-on.

Now drawn into a turning fight, instead of the intended "textbook" interception, flight leader Hall and Anderson orbited outside the fight to cover for the arrival of other enemy aircraft while Holcombe and Roberts were soon taken under fire when the MiGs easily out-turned them and attacked from their six o'clock. The two Phantoms used afterburner to gain separation from the enemy, then dived apart, forcing the enemy jets to break their formation as one took after each Phantom, Phan Thanh Nha chasing Holcombe while Cuong Cuong followed Roberts.

Holcombe lost Nha by climbing vertically while his opponent attempted to follow. As the enemy fighter lost energy, Holcombe reversed into it and fired an AIM-9B Sidewinder that failed. He quickly fired his remaining three, the last two without the correct launch "tone." Surprisingly, both these Sidewinders tracked and detonated close enough to the MiG that it exploded in a fireball, killing Lieutenant Nha. Holcombe and Clarke had scored the first USAF Phantom victory.

As this was happening, Roberts accelerated away from Cuong and pulled into a climb, leaving the enemy fighter several thousand feet below. Timing his maneuver closely, Roberts turned back into the MiG as it fell away in a descending turn. At a range of one mile, Roberts fired an AIM-9B that exploded close to the enemy's left wing tip, setting fire to the rear fuselage. Roberts followed up quickly with three more Sidewinders and the fire intensified as Cuong ejected. The MiG traced a smoky trail toward the ground below. Unfortunately, Lieutenant Cuong's parachute failed to deploy and he was also killed in the engagement.

Mink Flight turned back for Udorn RTAB, where Holcombe landed with only 275 pounds of fuel aboard. Unknowingly, the four Phantom crews had just successfully demonstrated every lesson that had been learned in Project Feather Duster two months earlier. The MiGs had out-turned them horizontally, but the Phantoms had been able to use their power to outmaneuver their opponents in the vertical plane and gain victory.

In 1943, British bomber crews flying at night over Germany reported seeing what appeared to be other bombers catch fire and leave a fiery trail across the night sky before impacting the ground. Bomber Command told the crews these were "scarecrow" antiaircraft artillery rounds, fired to scare them into thinking they were under heavy German attack. In truth, these were other RAF bombers, shot down by German night fighters that homed on the radiation signature of their H2S radar, which most crews used throughout their mission for ground-mapping to successfully find their target. The practice was officially discouraged because it "over-used" the delicate radar sets, but Bomber Command was content since it improved accuracy. Using radar this way was the equivalent of waving a flashlight in a dark room, giving away a bomber's position and leading to a loss rate approaching 50 percent, yet the lie about "scarecrow shells" was told until the end of the war. In the Vietnam War, TAC failed to make use of the information widely used by ADC, that could have improved the combat performance of TAC aircrews as well as increasing their chances of survival in the most dangerous air combat environment in the history of air warfare, on the grounds that knowing how to fight would distract them from their bombing mission. This failure is as indefensible as the lies told to the crews flying over Germany two decades earlier.

7

BRIDGES, SAMs, AND MiGs – THE WIDENING WAR

Ed Rasimus graduated from undergraduate pilot training in August 1965 in the top ten of 350 flight school graduates and was one of nine newly commissioned pilots to receive orders for training on the F-105. Looking back afterwards, he knew just when it was he decided that the Thunderchief was for him:

> I was driving my '63 Impala out Route 66 from Illinois to Williams AFB in Arizona to start undergraduate flight training. Just west of Holbrook, Arizona, with a blink of a shadow over the car and a nearly mind-numbing roar, two Thunderchiefs blasted not more than a hundred feet above me, straddling the highway as they disappeared in the distance with the dust blowing behind them. I thought "That's for me. I've gotta fly '105s."

After eight months' training at Nellis AFB, Rasimus graduated as a qualified "Thud Driver" in a class that included his friend Karl Richter, who would become one of the "names" forever associated with the air war over North Vietnam. Both men arrived in Korat in April 1966, assigned to the 421st Tactical Fighter Squadron of the newly created 388th Tactical Fighter Wing. Five minutes after he met his roommate and fellow squadron pilot – and veteran of 30 missions north – Captain Glen Nix nearly burst into tears as he told Rasimus what he could expect in a squadron that had lost eight pilots (of 20) including the squadron commander in the previous ten days. "The SAMs aren't so bad. The MiGs hardly ever bother us. It's the flak. It doesn't care. It's the flak. The goddamn guns. There's so many goddamn guns. They just shoot everywhere, and you get hit by the golden BB. You can't jink, you can't avoid it. You never know. There's so many goddamn guns..."

By the time Rasimus arrived at Takhli, Karl Richter had already flown several missions, due to the losses that accelerated the pace of a new pilot's introduction to combat. On his third mission north in April 1966, Richter demonstrated what he was made of, and what the airplane could do when damaged. The target was the Bac Giang railway bridge, a critical interdiction point on the line from Hanoi to China, a few miles from the enemy air base at Kep. The bridge was well defended by SAMs and AAA; several F-105s had been lost on previous missions the week before. Targets here were chosen by the National Command Authority, and were hit until destroyed. Richter had been assigned as a spare, too new to be considered ready for such a show. In the attack, Richter lost his leader when he pulled out of his run and mistakenly joined up on an F-105 on its bomb run. The pilot dropped his two M118s directly on target and Richter – flying too close – flew directly above the blast. His plane was knocked tail up then righted itself. Rejoining his flight, he quickly learned what was wrong. Shrapnel holes peppered the underside of the rear fuselage around the afterburner; the airplane kept wanting to fall off to the left because the left horizontal stabilator was blown off. He later told Rasimus that returning to Korat "just took a bit of trim." He landed safely and flew another mission the next day. His coolness in the emergency marked him as a "comer." The damaged F-105 spent six weeks in a major IRAN and also returned to combat.

On the ground, F-105 pilots were recognizable by their head gear – the Vietnamese "cowboy hat" first adopted by the air commandos. Rasimus recalled a superstition about the hats:

The hats were the "official" source for authenticating your mission count. When you successfully flew a mission, you inked a hash mark on the band. When you had a hundred hash marks, you went home. If you didn't get a hundred hash marks, someone sent your hat home without you. By common agreement, if there was ever any question about your mission count, your hat was the primary source document. You had to have a hat.

The North Vietnamese Air Force was very different from the USAF. The North Vietnamese air defense forces were unified in June 1963, when the VPAF and the Air Defense Forces were combined as the Air Defense Forces–Vietnamese People's Air Force (Phong Khong – Khong Quan Nhan Dan Viet Nam) on October 22, 1963, joining the artillery, radar, and ground control units under a single command. When war came in 1965, VPAF pilots were less trained and greatly outnumbered by their American opponents. Soviet advisors and crews manned the SAM sites and the heavy antiaircraft artillery while the Vietnamese were trained. For the VPAF's pilots, the danger of "friendly fire" was acute. In 1965, at least three MiG-17s and their pilots were lost when fired on by their comrades on the ground during the battle over the Dragon's Jaw on April 4; several others were shot down in the summer of 1965, and two MiG-21s in 1966. By late 1966, over 200 radars were installed throughout the country and were coordinated at regional centers that fed information on enemy formations to the centralized Air Force ground control in Hanoi.

Creating the infrastructure to support an air defense force was difficult in a country as primitive and underdeveloped as North Vietnam. The size and shape of the country made defense difficult. In the North, where the major cities and population were located, the country was only some 200 miles wide, while it was only about 35–40 miles wide in the southern panhandle. This meant that attack forces coming from either east (the US Navy from the carriers in the Tonkin Gulf) or the west (Air Force units from Thailand attacking from Laos) would be over their targets within a matter of minutes after crossing the borders. Additionally, outside the Red River Valley in the North, the rest of the country was mountainous and some 60 percent of its area was jungle-covered, which made it difficult to construct and supply radar sites for sufficient early warning.

Following the end of the First Indochina War, the only airfield able to operate modern aircraft was Gia Lam, the civilian airfield outside Hanoi. The others were primitive dirt strips that the French had used to cover their armies. In 1954, none could operate jet aircraft; even Gia Lam had only one paved all-weather runway. In 1955, runways at Gia Lam and Cat Bi were extended and paved. The next year, airfields at Vinh, Dong Hoi, Lang Son, Lao Cai, and Tien Yen were rebuilt though none to fully modern status. In May 1960, construction of the first fully modern airfield, Noi Bai (Phuc Yen) began; this was the only MiG base in 1965. This work required experienced engineers from China to deal with earth-moving and concrete laying; a workforce of over 10,000 was involved. The airfield was completed in June 1964 and the first MiG-17s flew in from China to operate there the week following the Tonkin Gulf Incident.

In May 1965, the airfields at Hoa Lac, Yen Bai, Tho Xuan, and Kep were modernized, while Gia Lam and Kien An were rebuilt to allow modern larger aircraft to use them. The airfield at Kep was planned as the base for the newly organized 923rd Fighter Regiment and took top priority. Eventually, 4,000 workers at the Bac Giang fertilizer factory were drafted for the work. The nearby mountain was leveled using dynamite on July 8, 1965 to speed construction. The airfield was completed on September 7, three months early. The base was ready on September 7, and Major Nguyen Phuc Trach's 923rd Fighter Regiment arrived a week later. Work on the others was finished by December.

Air defense became easier when the air war began because there were a limited number of routes that low-flying attackers could follow, combined with the restrictions of the American rules of engagement that precluded attacks on Hanoi and Haiphong, and the "no fly zone" along the Chinese border. The most common path for US Air Force strike missions into the Red River Valley from bases in Thailand involved flying down what aircrews called "suicide alley" along the long escarpment known as "Thud Ridge" to hit targets near Hanoi. Eventually, this became the most heavily defended piece of real estate on earth, with several thousand guns ranging in size from 20mm to 85mm, and many active SAM sites. More US planes and crews would be lost there than anywhere else in Southeast Asia.

The 30 early-type MiG-17 "Fresco-A" fighters that arrived as original equipment in August 1964 were reinforced with the delivery of 23 more in the fall of 1964. These 53 fighters bore the brunt of the initial air combats in 1965 until they were reinforced that summer by 30 more, these being the definitive "Fresco-C" type with an improved afterburner, as well as pilots to fly them from the second class of trainees who returned from the Soviet Union with the airplanes.

Tactically, the VPAF soon determined that their main goal was not to shoot down enemy aircraft; initially, VPAF pilots frequently made the mistake of engaging the escorts, rather than flying through them to attack the bombers. This was due to the Vietnamese pilots' lack of experience; at first it was difficult to identify the different American aircraft. Since gaining air superiority was out of the question, the VPAF leadership decided to implement a policy of air deniability. Much as their army fought as guerillas, and refused to meet an enemy force in battle without a good likelihood of victory due to the relative strength of forces, the VPAF interceptors focused on denying the Americans the opportunity to make their attacks by forcing them to abort the mission, dropping their ordnance to get away from the MiGs. Overall during *Rolling Thunder*, the VPAF were able to force enemy formations to abort by their presence on approximately 50 percent of the missions flown. For the Vietnamese, a bomber that didn't hit its target was out of action as effectively as if it had been shot down. This also suited the VPAF pilots, since their training and experience level was far below that of their opponents.

Despite the discovery that the VPAF pilot might be better than anticipated, following the first air battle over the Dragon's Jaw Bridge on April 4, 1965, the US air war expanded when railroads and bridges elsewhere in Vietnam below the 20th parallel were added to the target list.

During the early stages of *Rolling Thunder*, Air Force units were sent to Southeast Asia on four-month TDY tours from units permanently based in Japan and Okinawa. Squadrons assigned to bases in Thailand were controlled by two provisional wings. The 6234th Tactical Fighter Wing (Provisional) was established at Korat on April 5, 1965, with the 6441st Tactical Fighter Wing (Provisional) established at Takhli that May, following the arrival of the F-105-equipped 36th Tactical Fighter Squadron; they were part of the Yokota, Japan-based 6441st AD on a second TDY tour, arriving on March 6 in Operation *Two Buck Charlie*. The squadron joined the 354th Tactical Fighter Squadron at Korat for operations over the North. Several flights from the 23rd Tactical Fighter Wing's 561st and 563rd Tactical Fighter Squadron on TDY from Shaw AFB, South Carolina, arrived at Takhli to reinforce the 36th Tactical Fighter Squadron. Operational experience soon demonstrated that sending units on TDY was unnecessarily expensive. Even worse, four months was about the time it took pilots to become sufficiently experienced in combat operations to be really effective.

Following success in the initial bombing missions in March, the campaign was expanded in a second phase starting in April 1965 which targeted the North's many road and railway bridges. After failing to knock down the Thanh Hoa Bridge on April 3 and 4, the 354th Tactical Fighter Squadron went back to attacking rail and road lines. On April 5, 16 F-105s hit rail lines and Route 9, knocking out two locomotives and a truck convoy. Captain Thomas Gay was shot down, though he was rescued by an HH-43 Husky helicopter.

Bridges and railways were struck repeatedly during April and May, before the first bombing halt on May 15. F-105s knocked out highway bridges at Khe Kienm, Qui Vinh, and Phuong Can during *Rolling Thunder 10*, flown April 9–15. The F-105s flew the biggest one-day assault of the war to date on April 16, when the Dien Chau and Thai Hai bridges were partially dropped with 296 M117 750-pound bombs. The units were finally allowed to plan the bombing runs as "successive waves," rather than being forced to fly in a single, closely spaced attack. The rules of engagement were modified to reduce restrictions on armed reconnaissance missions, allowing more targets of opportunity to be found and attacked. Although five F-105s took damage from AAA on these missions, there were no further losses that month.

Rolling Thunder 13 and *14*, flown in May, included another strike at the Thanh Hoa Bridge on May 7. Major Charles Watry of the 354th Tactical Fighter Squadron led 28 F-105s in a 64-aircraft package that dropped 356 M117s on the structure and fired 304 2.75-inch rockets at the increased AAA sites. Watry's F-105 took a hit that started serious fuel leakage, but he stayed to direct the strike and was awarded a Silver Star for his action. Major R.E. Lambert's F-105D was lost, but he was able to eject over the gulf and came home in an SA-16 Albatross. As a result of the strike's failure, tactics were revised. Since the 750-pound M117s were unable to penetrate the reinforced concrete, further attacks were delayed until the new AGM-12C Bullpup with its 1,000-pound warhead was available. Post-strike debriefings showed that putting a large formation of F-105s over the target made it difficult for pilots to concentrate on their aiming points. Attacking with a smaller formation of two flights at a time in a series of attack waves the next day, 28 F-105s were able to demolish the Xom Trung Hoa barracks.

Attacking in a large formation meant that radio discipline in the heat of battle was a persistent problem; radios were overloaded with warnings from pilots in the strike force and from airborne and land-based sites transmitting warnings with increased power that often interrupted what pilots needed to hear. An additional communication problem was that if a pilot ejected, his rescue beeper blotted out the frequency with a shrill wail. Signals from radar-homing and warning (RHAW) equipment in the aircraft could also fill a pilot's headset. Colonel Jack Broughton recalled:

> We did brief that pilots were to speak on the radio only when necessary. Often, in tense times, flight leaders would have to tell individuals to shut up, but excited chatter was often a fact of combat life. When you packed lots of fast-moving machinery into a small ballpark, with good buddies getting blown up or punching out, it was difficult not to become a bit emotional. The worthless SAM and MiG calls from our four-engined radar observers flying out over the water were a pain. They usually came at the wrong time, and they blocked all other transmissions.

Improved weather allowed the first attack on a target above the 20th parallel on May 22, following the bombing halt. Forty F-105s struck and seriously damaged the barracks at Quang Soui, 60 miles from Hanoi, and the Phu Quy ammunition depot. The "thunder" steadily rolled north in response to Hanoi's refusal to act in accordance with what planners expected. As had been the case with Operation *Strangle* in North Korea ten years earlier, the enemy displayed real efficiency at repairing tracks and bridges. The bitter truth was that bridges and highways were repaired within a week to a month of an attack. Furthermore, Ed Rasimus remembered that many times when they were assigned to bomb a bridge, they arrived over the target to find that the bridge had not been rebuilt, but there were dirt trails leading to the water's edge, and reappearing on the other side of the river, where the trucks that drove through the shallow area of the river emerged to keep heading south. "We dropped our bombs as ordered, but with the certainty the enemy would not be deterred that night."

This was not a coincidence. Several North Korean and Chinese veterans of the road battles in the earlier war were sent to North Vietnam, along with teams from both countries to take responsibility for repair and teach their Vietnamese allies how to make do. Bridges that were hit were replaced with simple wood structures or pontoon bridges which were more difficult to attack successfully, and also easier to repair. In 1965, China sent the first of an eventual 310,000 Chinese to work in North Vietnam, preserving the rail system that allowed Chinese supplies to make it to Hanoi. Railway specialist Colonel Guilin Long, a veteran of maintaining railroads in North Korea during the Korean War, arrived with five regiments of the People's Liberation Army Railway Corps, to maintain the section of road from Hanoi to Lao Cai through Huu Nghi Quan, "Friendship Pass." The Chinese hated life in North Vietnam — the weather, the insects — as much as Americans did in South Vietnam. Over the course of *Rolling Thunder*, 771 Chinese railway workers were killed in US airstrikes, while 1,675 were sent home wounded.

By the summer of 1965, F-105s were responsible for 55 percent of bombing missions flown "up North." They were coming under increasing threat from the VPAF, which had been reinforced with more MiG-17s and pilots. When the Joint Chiefs pushed for permission to strike the VPAF airfields, McNamara refused their requests.

Following the battle at the Dragon's Jaw, F-105 pilots did not see MiGs again until June 24, when a flight of F-105Ds was pursued by two MiG-17s after bombing a bridge near Son La. The Americans had the advantage of a MiG warning from an EC-121 Big Eye radar picket orbiting offshore over the Gulf of Tonkin. With the warning, the flight split into high and low elements. The pilots of the second "high" element spotted two MiG-17s approaching their "six o'clock" position and all four dropped their tanks. The lead MiG followed the fourth F-105, firing repeatedly but very inaccurately as the two aircraft turned, forcing the US wingman to escape by lighting his afterburner and diving away at Mach 1.1 to low altitude. The lead F-105 element, flying 5,000 feet below the second, climbed to meet the enemy jets as the second MiG closed on the F-105 element leader. The F-105 flight leader closed on the second MiG, but his gunsight did not acquire a radar lock-on and he was only able to fire a few rounds before the MiG disappeared into low clouds.

The *Rolling Thunder* campaign continued through the summer with a weekly cycle of two attacks against the North, one Air Force and one by Task Force 77. The Yen Bai and Yen Son ordnance depots were hit by big F-105 strikes. The Thunderchief added new weapons over the summer. On July 11, F-105s from the 12th Tactical Fighter Squadron dropped delayed-action MLU-10 mines along the main rail route to Hanoi for the first time. On July 28, the squadron flew their first mission carrying the 3,000-pound M118 Low Drag General Purpose Bomb on yet another strike against the Dragon's Jaw. The new bombs caused serious damage but no spans were dropped. On August 10, the squadron destroyed the Vinh Tuy Bridge near Dien Bien Phu.

The Vinh Tuy mission also saw the first use of the AGM-12C Bullpup-B by F-105s. Carrying a 1,000-pound warhead instead of the 570-pound warhead of the AGM-12B, the new missile could be fired from up to ten miles from the target. However, while the AGM-12B was fired straight off the pylon, the AGM-12C had to be dropped first, then fired via a frangible cable. This process was hazardous, as was shown on July 27, 1966, when Ed Rasimus' flight leader, Captain John R. Mitchell of the 388th Tactical Fighter Wing's 421st Tactical Fighter Squadron, dropped a Bullpup that failed to release from its front shackle. With the missile canted tail-down far enough to break the cable, it fired and shot through the leading edge of the wing, causing severe damage and draining hydraulic fluid. Mitchell was forced to eject when the F-105 went out of control after losing all hydraulic fluid five miles from Nakhon Phanom RTAB. As Rasimus recalled, "Our gung-ho flight leader joined that exclusive fraternity of fighter pilots who shot themselves down. The squadron declared it his last combat mission, with the helicopter ride after he was picked up being his hundredth, and he left for home. We didn't miss him."

After only a few missions with the new Bullpup, North Vietnamese gunners learned to fire into the missile's smoke trail, knowing that close behind was the F-105 guiding it. Jack Broughton recalled the Bullpup thus: "The only memory I have of the missile is firing it, then watching it rock and roll through the sky heading nowhere close to what I had aimed at, with a pretty good assurance that it would hit the surface... someplace." The Bullpup quickly became the most-disliked weapon that F-105s carried.

While North Vietnam's air defense system was still comparatively primitive in 1965 compared to what would exist a year later, the ever-increasing AAA strength began to exact a serious toll on the F-105s, over both North Vietnam and Laos. During May and June, 1965, ten were shot down. Radar-directed AAA was now a serious threat, though most guns were still aimed visually. The first RB-66C and EB-66E Destroyers – a twin-jet light bomber developed for the Air Force from the Navy's A-3 Skywarrior – flown by the 9th Tactical Reconnaissance Squadron arrived at Korat on April 2 to provide airborne radar jamming to support *Rolling Thunder* missions. Four RB-66Bs and six RB-66Cs arrived at Tan Son Nhut on April 6. Initially, the RB-66Bs were used as pathfinders for F-105 formations, allowing them to attack in the poor weather conditions associated with the spring and summer monsoon period over the North. This allowed bombing strikes against AAA positions since the gunners firing visually had difficulty finding their targets. Known as "Brown Cradle" missions, an RB-66B led several flights of F-105s, using its K-5 bombing/navigation equipment to find the target. The navigator in the RB-66 would give the fighters "heads up" on the radio prior to the bomb run, finishing with a ten-second tone. When the tone stopped, the F-105s dropped in unison.

On April 5, 1965, a month after the opening strikes, US reconnaissance aircraft discovered that the North Vietnamese were constructing positions for SAM batteries. These were the SA-2, NATO code name "Guideline," designated S-75 Dvina by the Soviets, a medium- to high-altitude surface-to-air missile system that first surprised the West by shooting down Francis Gary Powers' U-2 spyplane over Sverdlovsk in May 1960. The SA-2 missile was highly effective against non-maneuvering targets such as aircraft on bombing runs, and those whose crews did not keep a sharp lookout for a missile launch. The Air Force and Navy asked Washington for permission to strike the sites before they went operational, but they were refused since most of the sites were near the restricted urban areas. Ed Rasimus later recalled that according to the rules of engagement regarding SAM sites in 1966: "They were off-limits while under construction but could be attacked once they were completely built. To confirm that they were actually no longer under construction, the SAM site had to be observed firing a missile at you. Sure, that makes a lot of sense."

The United States made a very temporary bombing halt on May 13, 1965, in hopes that the North Vietnamese would respond by either announcing cessation of support for the war in the South or showing willingness to engage in negotiations; instead, the North Vietnamese used the five days to speed work on the first SAM sites, which became operational the next month. Once the Americans announced the restrictions on bombing of Hanoi and Haiphong, SAMs were sited there and near population centers in order to take advantage of US restrictions against bombing urban population areas.

In July 1965, five active SA-2 sites went operational. On July 24, four F-4Cs from the 15th Tactical Fighter Wing participated in a strike against the Dien Bien Phu munitions storage depot and the Lang Chi munitions factory west of Hanoi. One was shot down and three were damaged when SA-2s were fired unexpectedly. Although McNamara and the rest of the government leadership had known of the existence of SAMs since the first photos of sites under construction were taken in April, they were surprised that a missile had been fired, believing the SAMs were merely intended as a threat. On July 26, President Johnson ordered an attack on all known SAM sites outside the 30-mile Hanoi bombing exclusion zone. Operation *Spring High* was set for July 27.

The strike was flown by 48 F-105s armed with CBU-2s, napalm, and rockets. The force approached at 500 feet, below the SA-2's "operational envelope." Unfortunately, that put them in range of several hundred light and medium AAA. Eleven F-105s hit SAM Site 6 while 12 hit Site 7. The SA-2 operators' barracks were hit by 23 others. Eight F-105s were assigned to flak suppression, since the sites were surrounded by 37mm, 57mm, and 85mm AAA batteries. The attacks were made in four-plane line-abreast flights, flying at 50–100 feet. What they didn't know was that the mission was not a surprise to the North Vietnamese, because there was a communist agent at 2nd Air Division headquarters in Saigon. The sites were empty "flak traps." One American pilot described the action that followed as "looking like the end of the world" as flak bursts and tracers filled the sky.

The first flight came under immediate fire from the expectant gunners. Captain Walt Kosko of the 563rd Tactical Fighter Squadron was hit and drowned in the Black River near Site 7 after he ejected. In a follow-up attack on the same target an hour later, the 563rd's Captain Kile Berg was hit as he dropped napalm. He ejected and was quickly captured. The 357th's Captain William Barthelmas was hit as he pulled off his run at Site 6. He stuck with the F-105, which was slowly leaking hydraulic fluid. A few miles from Ubon RTAB, he lost control as the last of the hydraulics drained out, and collided with Major Jack Farr, who was escorting him. Both died in the collision, but were officially

Legendary Thud ace 1st Lieutenant Karl Richter flew more missions over North Vietnam before his death than any other Air Force pilot. (USAF Official)

WSO Captain Jeffrey Feinstein was the third Air Force ace of the Vietnam War. (USAF Official)

The McDonnell RF-101C Voodoo was the primary photo-recon aircraft used for Bomb Damage Assessment during *Rolling Thunder*. (USAF Official)

Four VPAF MiG-21 pilots in their Soviet high-altitude pressure suits. The Soviet suit was a copy of the USAF T-2 suit used in the 1950s. (VPAF Official)

A B-26B flown by "Farm Gate" in 1961–64. The B-26s operated by Farm Gate in the early days of US involvement in Vietnam were the best ground-support aircraft used at the time. (USAF Official)

Ex-USN T-28B armed trainers were flown by USAF crews in Project Farm Gate, the first direct US combat involvement in the Vietnam War, 1961–64. (USAF Official)

F-104Cs of the 470th TFW provided escort for RC-121D Constellations over the Tonkin Gulf off North Vietnam in 1965. (USAF Official)

The venerable A-1E Skyraider became the USAF's primary battlefield close support aircraft in Vietnam after the US Navy removed them from service. This A-1E is dropping two napalm cannisters. (USAF Official)

An A-1E of the 1st Special Operations Squadron at DaNang air base in 1966. The aircraft is carrying Zuni rocket pods. (USAF Official)

This heavily armed A-1J "Sandy" prepares for takeoff on a search-and-rescue (SAR) mission. (USAF Official)

The HH-53C "Super Jolly Green Giant" was a development from the HH-3C, with higher-power engines, additional armament and defensive weapons, and larger fuel supply. "Super Jolly Greens" penetrated North Vietnam close to Hanoi itself to pick up downed fliers. (USAF Official)

The AT-28D armed trainers flown by the "Zorros" of the 606th Special Operations Squadron for night interdiction of the Ho Chi Minh Trail were so successful that Seventh Air Force stopped separating successful missions by "prop" or "jet" since the obsolete trainers out-scored the jets. (USAF Official)

An HH-53C "Super Jolly Green Giant" maneuvers to hook up with a C-130 aerial tanker. C-130s orbited over Laos just outside North Vietnamese territory to provide refueling for HH-3Cs and A-1 Sandys operating over the North on SAR missions. (USAF Official)

A B-26K of the 609th Special Operations Squadron starts up at Nakhan Phanom RTAB prior to a mission over the Ho Chi Minh Trail. The B-26K used cut-down DC-7 propellers. (USAF Official)

The B-52G Stratofortresses flown during Operation *Linebacker II* were from the SAC nuclear strike force. The crews were not experienced in operations over North Vietnam and incorrect tactics used by SAC planners led to severe losses over Hanoi to the North Vietnamese air defense system. It is estimated that over 20 B-52s were lost in the two-week campaign, though Air Force records have been deliberately modified to cover this fact. (USAF Official)

Captain Charles "Chuck" DeBellvue, the top-scoring US ace of the Vietnam War. DeBellvue was WSO with Steve Ritchie for all five victories and scored his sixth flying with a different pilot. (USAF Official)

Colonel Daniel "Chappie" James, Jr., deputy wing commander of the 8th TFW under Robin Olds. James and Olds were popularly known as "Blackman and Robin." James began his Air Force career as a Tuskegee Airman and flew F-51Ds in the early, difficult days of the Korean War. (USAF Official)

The Air Force's first supersonic fighter, the F-100D provided escort for bombing missions over North Vietnam during the first months of *Rolling Thunder*. (USAF Official)

The first Wild Weasel anti-SAM aircraft were 2-seat F-100Fs. Their electronic search equipment was so primitive that the SAM site could only be detected by flying directly over it. Third from left in rear row is WSO 1st Lieutenant Sam Peacock, who would remain in the "Weasel business" throughout a 30-year Air Force career. (USAF Official)

A formation of F-105s releases their bombs over the target. The F-105s flew in tight formation so their jammers would mask them from the North Vietnamese SAM radars. (USAF Official)

A flight of F-105Ds is led in "blind" bombing by an EB-66 electronic warfare bomber.
(USAF Official)

This then-top secret MiG-21F-13 was given to the US by the Israeli Air Force in 1967 after its Syrian pilot defected with the aircraft in 1966. US pilots flew the aircraft to learn how to fight against it with the F-4 Phantom. (USAF Official)

Colonel Robin Olds, a World War II ace, reinvigorated the 8th TFW during his time in command of the wing in 1966–67 by "leading from in front." He was the top-scoring USAF pilot with 4 victories over MiGs during his tour. Pilots who flew with him called him "inspirational." (USAF Official)

MiG-17 pilot Nguyen Van Bay (the elder) was the most successful VPAF ace of the *Rolling Thunder* period, scoring seven victories. (VPAF Official)

Steve Ritchie, the only USAF pilot ace of Vietnam. All five of Ritchie's kills are confirmed in official VPAF records. (USAF Official)

F-4C Phantoms of the 8th TFW in their revetments at Udorn RTAFB in 1967. (USAF Official)

Phantom crews begged from the beginning of the war for an internal gun on the F-4 Phantom. McDonnell fitted a 20mm M61 Vulcan cannon under a slimmed-down nose in the F-4E, which arrived in Vietnam just too late to see combat in *Rolling Thunder*. (USAF Official)

The F-105G was the ultimate F-105 Wild Weasel, developed from the F-105F with superior electronic detection gear. F-105Gs were used in the Christmas Bombing in December 1972. This F-105G carries a "Standard ARM" anti-radiation missile and an ARM-45 "Shrike" on the outer station. (USAF Official)

WSO Roger Locher and pilot Roger Lodge were the leading MiG killers in the 555th TFS at the time of their loss on May 10, 1972. Lodge stayed with the burning F-4 and died in the crash to keep safe the information he possessed regarding Combat Tree. Locher survived on his own for 29 days in North Vietnam before being rescued in the largest SAR battle of the Vietnam War. (USAF Official)

Captain Roger Locher the day of his rescue on June 9, 1972, after 29 days alone in North Vietnam. Locher's rescue was one for the records: the longest time on the ground by a shot-down pilot, the deepest penetration of North Vietnam by SAR aircraft, and the biggest rescue battle of the war. (USAF Official)

Captain Tran Hanh was one of the first VPAF fighter pilots. On April 4, 1965, he became the first VPAF pilot to shoot down an F-105 Thunderchief in the first air battle of the war over "The Dragon's Jaw," the Than Hoa Bridge, flying a MiG-17C. (VPAF Official)

ABOVE Four pilots of the 923rd Fighter Regiment in front of their MiG-17Cs. (VNAF Official)

RIGHT A VPAF instructor demonstrates attack techniques to other VPAF pilots. (VPAF Official)

1st Lieutenants Ralph Wetterhahn and Jerry Sharp in "Olds-2" as they prepare for takeoff in Operation *Bolo*, where they would shoot down the first MiG-21 destroyed in battle. Note that this F-4C was repainted "in the field" over the original grey-white scheme, which is wearing through the camouflage paint. (Wetterhahn Collection)

Wetterhanh pre-strike and post-strike photos of the bridges struck by Wetterhahn and Sharp after their flight leader bombed the wrong target. (Wetterhahn Collection)

A VPAF MiG-21PFM lands after a mission in which it did not intercept American bombers, with its AA-2 Atoll missiles still on the wing racks. (VPAF Official)

listed as lost in an "operational accident" to avoid any public linkage of Thailand to *Rolling Thunder*.

Dogwood Flight from the 12th Tactical Fighter Squadron, assigned to destroy anything not hit by the main force, were fired on with a volley of SAMs from a different site as they began their run and came under fire from AAA. Captain Robert Purcell was hit as he bombed the operators' barracks and captured when he ejected. Captain Frank Tullo was also hit but managed to stick with his F-105 long enough to get away from the targets before ejecting. He was the only pilot rescued, when a newly deployed HH-3 Jolly Green Giant helicopter staging out of Laos from the secret Lima Site 36 flew farther into North Vietnam than had any previous search and rescue (SAR) helicopter and pulled him to safety.

Losing six F-105s on a single mission was shocking; better tactics were badly needed. The SA-2, according to 2nd Air Division CO General Joseph Moore, "had precluded medium-altitude air operations." The launchers were highly mobile and could be moved in a few hours, making it nearly impossible to discover which sites were real, rather than carefully contrived flaktraps. While prewar planners were right that individual gunners on the ground could not track low-level attackers flying at high speed, they neglected what 50–100 guns or more could do, firing into an area of sky the attackers had to fly through to bomb their target. Once an attack force committed, the gunners knew immediately where to shoot. Ed Rasimus remembered that he never got over the fear that came from looking at a sky filled with the black clouds of explosions through which he had to fly to release his bombs. "That kind of combat was strictly a matter of the rules of chance. My skill and ability had nothing to do with my survival once I committed to that dive."

Of 2,300 US aircraft shot down during the war, flak claimed 1,600. The traps were deadly, with batteries of 37mm and 57mm guns aimed at the "perch" of a "pop-up" where the attackers rolled into their dive to start their bomb runs, or at the point where the attacker pulled up from its run. The guns were capable of putting 1,000-plus rounds into such a box of airspace in less than five seconds. At lower altitudes "barrage fire" with hundreds of small arms or 23mm AAA could put up a curtain of bullets through which the attacker had to pass.

On August 9, the 12th Squadron's Major James Hosmer led three flights of CBU-carrying F-105s to hit the newly discovered SAM

Site 8 near Hanoi. Hosmer was awarded the Silver Star for leading a well-executed attack, but it was empty. On August 12, Air Force and Navy units received authorization to attack SAM sites whenever found. The Air Force adopted the "Iron Hand" anti-SAM strategy that the Navy used for flak suppression missions. This involved a flight of four F-105s, with one element the "hunters" and one the "killers." Flying at low altitude where they could spot a site, the "hunters" attacked the radar control van with napalm, which knocked out the missile guidance and acted as a target marker for the "killers," who attacked the launcher with M117 750-pound bombs. The squadrons began operating a dedicated quick-reaction Iron Hand flight on August 16 when they attacked a SAM site at Binh Linh. Unfortunately, few sites were located over the rest of the summer.

"Robbie" Risner, who led the April 4, 1965 attack on the Thanh Hoa Bridge, became a rising star in the Air Force and was soon on the cover of the April 23, 1965 *Time* magazine issue; he was one of ten Americans then fighting in Vietnam profiled in an article titled "The Fighting American." Three days later, he received the Air Force Cross just before his squadron returned to the 18th Tactical Fighter Wing at Kadena. On August 16, the squadron returned to Korat. Between August 18 and September 16, Risner flew a mission a day, later recalling: "During one week, I was hit four missions out of five."

On August 23, McNamara finally approved a strike against North Vietnam's hydroelectric network. The 12th Tactical Fighter Squadron dropped eight M118s on the Ban Thach generating plant while the 67th went after the AAA defending the plant. Risner received the Silver Star for leadership.

In September, Risner took on flak suppression for his squadron. On September 9, as he bombed the Yen Khaoi army base he took a hit head-on that blew off his canopy; a piece of red-hot shrapnel burned his shoulder before stabbing into his headrest. Risner stayed with his "open cockpit" jet and tanked successfully on the way home.

SAM site attacks intensified. On September 16, the 67th again went after the Thanh Hoa Bridge. When a pilot scheduled for the Iron Hand flight was medically grounded, Risner assigned himself the mission, leading a four-plane "hunter-killer" flight for his 55th mission. Risner's F-105D carried napalm for use against the radar unit, while wingman First Lieutenant Mike Stevens carried M117s to destroy the launcher.

The flight approached what turned out to be a flak trap so low that Risner had to climb to avoid a 100-foot hill. Momentarily silhouetted against the sky, he took multiple hits. Stevens warned him of a raging fire in his main fuel tank. Risner lit afterburner, dropped ordnance, and sped for the Gulf of Tonkin, hoping to repeat his March rescue. When the hydraulic system drained empty three miles short, the controls froze and the F-105 went into an uncontrollable dive. Risner ejected and was quickly captured. His captors, aware of his fame from the *Time* cover, repeatedly tortured him to obtain a compromising statement during seven years as a prisoner of war. He was awarded a second Air Force Cross for his courage and leadership as a POW, following his release from prison in 1973. Soviet Senior Lieutenant Valery Miroshnichenko, who trained Vietnamese SAM operators in 1965–66, remembered, "You told them to learn something and they did so, even if they did not understand what they had learned... they were driven by discipline, thoroughness, striving for victory." More senior Soviet advisors in the country complained that, once trained, the crews fired their expensive weapons "like firecrackers." Those in the Soviet embassy believed that the North Vietnamese regarded them only as important for providing war supplies.

Anti-SAM measures were frantically developed by the United States. On September 23, F-105 pilots first used the hair-raising "SAM break" tactic, which involved spotting the site, then watching for the missile. A pilot turned towards the SAM, then split-essed at the last moment to defeat the radar lock. Warning was crucial to survive, and this came from electronic countermeasures (ECM) added to the aircraft. The Navy had some success, using AN/ALQ-51 jammers to break the Fan Song radar lock, successfully defeating six SAMs on September 16. Despite these changes, the 4th Tactical Fighter Wing's 334th Tactical Fighter Squadron commander, Lieutenant Colonel Melvin Killian, became the first F-105 pilot shot down by a SAM on September 30. His F-105 caught fire and exploded before he could eject.

The Navy's AGM-45 "Shrike" was first used in August 1965. In 25 attacks on Fan Song radars that month, it only scored two "probables." It had to be tuned to a known frequency before takeoff, and fired more than five miles from the target. The SA-2 crews soon learned to switch off the fire control radar units when a Shrike was launched, which broke its lock.

The jammer's value was demonstrated on October 31, when eight Iron Hand 562nd Tactical Fighter Squadron F-105s were led by Navy Commander Richard Powers as "pathfinder" with his jammer-equipped A-4E to go after SAMs while 65 Navy aircraft bombed a bridge near Kep. Powers detected Fan Song emissions from one site and he spotted two SA-2s when they were launched from a second. He made a run on the first, taking hits and ejecting while the F-105s hit a third site. The jammers allowed the F-105s to avoid the 28 SA-2s fired at them. F-105s were finally wired to use the AN/ALQ-51 in 1966.

Following the first F-4 victories on July 10, the VPAF fighters were withdrawn to China for additional training in new tactics of making feint attacks and dry firing passes under GCI vectoring, breaking off before US fighters could engage. This period of training allowed the inexperienced pilots and ground controllers to develop an effective intercept capability, which was demonstrated when they returned on October 14, when Captain Robert H. Schuler of the 36th Tactical Fighter Squadron became the third and last F-105 pilot shot down by a MiG-17 in air-to-air combat.

The final VPAF victory of 1965 confirmed by both sides happened on November 6 when four MiG-17s led by Senior Lieutenant Tran Hanh and Lieutenants Ngo Doan Hung, Pham Ngoc Lan, and Tran Van Phuong were scrambled to intercept a search for and rescue operation to pick up Lieutenant Colonel George C. McCleary, who had been hit by an SA-2 while in clouds.

After takeoff, Tran's flight was directed toward My Duc. They were unable to spot the target in the poor weather in two attempted interceptions. On the third attempt, Ngo Doan Hung spotted a helicopter low over the jungle and was cleared to attack by ground control. Coming in low, he hit the CH-53, which was searching for McCleary. The big helicopter crashed six miles southwest of Cho Ben, the first US helicopter shot down over North Vietnam.

Following the shoot-down of the last F-105 lost to MiG-17s in October, F-105 pilots only infrequently sighted MiGs for the rest of 1965, except on December 20, when a flight of F-105s spotted two MiG-17s. The F-105 flight leader turned in behind the MiGs, but they flew on at high speed and the F-105s were unable to engage.

During 1965, the VPAF scrambled fighters 156 times, and was credited with shooting down 15 American aircraft. The USAF had the nasty surprise of discovering that the "obsolete, Korean-era" MiG-17, a simple, subsonic fighter, was able to successfully take on the technologically superior F-105 and F-4s. The smaller, lighter MiG was more maneuverable at altitudes below 15,000 feet, and was easily able to out-turn them. They were vulnerable to the MiG's all-gun armament, which allowed it to fight close-in, where the all-missile armament of the F-4 was unusable. The MiG's guns were reliable, while the missiles were unreliable and often used incorrectly by crews who had not been adequately trained in proper deployment. Though the F-105 had a gun, the difficulty in changing the sighting system from bombing to air-to-air modes meant that the MiG could attack and be gone before the American was set up to fight with the gun.

On December 10, the United States divided North Vietnam into six "route packages." Initially, the USAF and Navy planned to exchange "packs" every week, but operational experience led to the Navy taking the coastal area of Route Packages I, III, and VIB, including the Haiphong docks. Air Force units were assigned Route Packages II, IV, V, and VIA, which included Hanoi, Thai Nguyen, and the MiG airfields at Kep and Noi Bai. With the arrival of PCS squadrons, the aircrew tour of duty became one year, or 100 missions, whichever came first. After flying a full 100-mission tour, a pilot would not be required to fly a second tour until all Air Force pilots had flown a tour. When losses mounted in 1966, pilots wondered if such a tour was feasible. A joke among Thunderchief pilots at the time was, "The most optimistic man in the world is an F-105 jockey who gives up smoking because he's afraid of cancer."

By December 1965, when the first 30-day bombing halt was announced in an effort to stimulate negotiations, the US Joint Chiefs acknowledged that after the nine and a half months of the campaign, not only had the war-making ability of North Vietnam been scarcely impaired by the US effort, but the enemy was now more capable of resistance than at the outset.

The VPAF was reinforced by the arrival of the MiG-21F-13 "Fishbed-C" which carried two Sidewinder-based R-3S missiles (known as the K-13 "Atoll" in the West) at the end of 1965. These were reinforced by MiG-21PF "Fishbed-D" all-weather fighters which arrived in April, 1966. When encounters occurred, the MiG-21 pilots used their superior speed and maneuverability to make passes on bomb-carrying F-105s and forced them to jettison their ordnance and take evasive action.

When the northeast monsoon season came to an end in April 1966, US air activity increased. Seven F-4s and one F-105 shot down eight MiGs between late April and June.

Over the course of May and June, the original pilots of the 421st Squadron, whom Ed Rasimus later described as "the somewhat reluctant warriors we had never quite become accustomed to," flew their final missions and left Korat. The new replacements had flown F-105s in the nuclear strike mission at Bitburg and Spangdahlem in Germany. Rasimus remembered, "They were eager and aggressive, well-trained and willing to get the job done. The squadron quickly became a new machine assembled from well-oiled parts, smoothed and trued by careful use." Major Fred Tracy became the 421st's new commander despite his low rank, due to the heavy losses in the F-105 force. Rasimus recalled that the pilots with whom he had arrived in the squadron were happy with Tracy's policy of equity in flight assignments. "The favoritism and avoidance of high-threat missions by a few we had experienced with the leaders from McConnell would end."

The "bomb shortage" came to the Thailand-based units in the spring of 1966. While Secretary McNamara was denying such a shortage existed, Rasimus recalled how F-105s were sent to bomb targets in North Vietnam carrying as few as two 250-pound bombs due to the severe shortage of Korean War-vintage M117 and M118 750 and 3,000-pound bombs respectively, as well as the 250-pound Mk. 81 "Lady Finger"and the 500-pound Mk. 82. "We occasionally were sent north carrying mines, rocket packs, and other strange ordnance underwing as we maintained the battle of the sortie rates with our naval enemies on the aircraft carriers in the Gulf of Tonkin." Once, Rasimus' flight went on a road-recce mission in the Mu Gia Pass armed with nothing but their M61 guns.

The first air-to-air victory scored by an F-105 pilot happened on June 29, 1966, when six-victory Korean War Sabre ace Major James H. Kasler led 46 F-105s from the 354th Tactical Fighter Squadron on the first strike of the newly approved campaign against petroleum, oil, and lubricant (POL) sites. Iron Hand SAM suppression was provided by Crab Flight from 421st Squadron, led by Crab 01, an F-105F Wild Weasel flown by Major Richard D. Westcott and

Captain Herbert L. Friesen. Friesen spotted the Fan Song radar on his gear and Westcott killed it with an AGM-45 Shrike while the F-105Ds made rocket attacks. As they pulled up from their attack, four MiG-17s began to close from behind. Belatedly, Crab 04 spotted them and called a warning that the first element did not hear. Major Kenneth D. Frank, Crab 03, led Crab 04 in a dive as the lead MiG opened fire. The MiGs turned on the lead element just as Westcott spotted them and called for the flight to go to afterburner and clean off ordnance as he and Tracy broke left. Tracy was hit by nine cannon shells, with one 23mm shell forcing his hand away from the throttle and canceling his afterburner. The instruments, oxygen equipment, gunsight, and entire left side of the cockpit were knocked before the shell lodged in the AC power pack without exploding.

As Tracy slowed, the attacker overshot. Tracy aimed by superimposing his pitot boom over the MiG and squeezing the trigger, firing 200 rounds. He reported "I squeezed the trigger and saw the 20mm rounds sparkling along the left fuselage and wing root of the MiG. His left wing folded over the tail and in an abrupt left turn he went into a cloud at about 2,500 feet." A later flight discovered MiG-17 wreckage, and Tracy's victory claim was confirmed, making him the first F-105 MiG killer.

MiG activity increased between July and September 1966, with six shot down by F-4s and F-105s. North Vietnamese tactics continued to improve. US pilots determined that they were most vulnerable during the three minutes before they dropped their ordnance and the first two minutes afterwards, and trained to fly a rejoin maneuver allowing them to get back in a mutually supporting formation quickly. The VPAF concentrated their attacks on the Iron Hand and Wild Weasel flights, which were separate from the rest of the force.

Starting in July, one or two flights of F-4s flew directly with an F-105 strike. Because they were faster than the loaded F-105s, they were forced to S-turn to stay with their charges, using more gas. This meant that one flight had to refuel from tankers just before ingress; they also had to depart before the mission was completed due to low fuel if they became involved with MiGs. North Vietnamese MiG-21s flying in two-plane sections were guided by ground controlled interception (GCI) to make a pass on the escorts to draw them off and waste their fuel before the F-105s were attacked.

The Da Nang-based 480th Tactical Fighter Squadron scored their second and third MiG kills on July 14, when two F-4Cs flown by lead Captain William J. Swendner and First Lieutenant Duane A. Buttell, Jr., and wingman First Lieutenants Ronald G. Martin and Richard N. Krieps got involved in a fight with two MiG-21s flown by Lieutenants Hoang Bieu and Ta Vanh Thanh when they attacked the Iron Hand flight. The two F-4 crews sighted Hoang Bieu just as he fired his missile at the third F-105 when it fired a Shrike, and spotted Ta Vanh Thanh. Swendner jettisoned his wing tanks and headed straight for Ta Vanh Thanh as he closed on the F-105s. Swendner fired two AIM-9Bs; one failed and one smoked past the MiG's canopy without exploding, alerting Ta to the Phantom's presence; he went into afterburner and climbed away. Swendner fired a third Sidewinder with a perfect "hot" target of the afterburner flame against a plain sky background. It blew the MiG-21's rear fuselage apart. Ta ejected but his parachute failed to open when his seat failed to separate from the canopy.

In the meantime, Martin and Krieps got behind Hoang Bieu's MiG-21 as he attacked the fourth F-4C of the MiGCAP flight. He fired his second Atoll and missed again when the F-4 made a hard turn and the missile passed in front. Martin fired a Sidewinder which impacted the MiG's tail. The explosion knocked Bieu unconscious for a moment. When he came to, he ejected at once, parachuting safely.

On July 19, Major Jim Kasler engaged in a 20-minute life-or-death battle that was the longest fight yet in the war. Leading a 16-plane strike against a fuel storage target just north of Hanoi, his flight was intercepted by three MiG-17s just short of the target. The F-105s jettisoned their ordnance and Kasler's element leader, the only pilot in the flight with Sidewinders, fired his one at the departing MiGs, but it failed to guide. A second missed when fired outside its G-limits. He then fired a burst but the MiG dived away; Kasler and the others lost sight of it.

Kasler and wingman First Lieutenant Steve Diamond were then set on by Nguyen Bien and Vo Van Man of the 923rd Regiment. Kasler was forced to use every maneuver he had learned over the Yalu River, turning as tightly as he could as he and Diamond dropped from 7,000 feet to well below 500 feet while the two MiGs remained glued to their tails.

Their calls for help went unheard because the radio frequency was used by their strike, a Navy strike, and ECM aircraft calling warnings.

Vo Van Man scored a mortal hit on Diamond's fighter. As he closed for a second attack, Kasler got on his tail and opened fire, damaging Man's rudder, but he hit Diamond a second time, forcing him to eject. As Man headed for Phuc Yen, Kasler punched in afterburner and pursued him, but heavy AAA and the rule that MiGs could not be attacked at their airfields forced him to turn away. As he did, Nguyen Bien turned in behind and opened fire, damaging Kasler's fighter. At that moment, the second F-105 flight leader and his wingman spotted Kasler and closed for a gun attack to shoot Bien off his tail. Despite being hit in his wing, Bien managed to break away in a 6-G left turn that the F-105 couldn't follow.

Diamond was never found and is still listed as missing in action (MIA). Kasler demonstrated that even though the F-105 was no dogfighter, an experienced pilot could exploit its air-to-air capability to the maximum when given the opportunity. He was awarded the Air Force Cross for his performance.

Eighteen days later, Kasler led another low-level strike; his wingman, First Lieutenant Fred R. Flom, was hit and ejected. Kasler located him and flew Rescue Combat Air Patrol (RESCAP) at low altitude until he was forced to break away to meet a tanker and refuel. Returning, he went to treetop level trying to relocate Flom and was badly hit by ground fire. He ejected and was captured. Having been singled out as "the war's hottest pilot" in press reports of the July 19 fight, Kasler was repeatedly tortured to get him to cooperate with their propaganda efforts, which he never did. He was awarded a second Air Force Cross for the attempted rescue and an unprecedented third Air Force Cross for his leadership in prison.

The F-105 scored a second air-to-air victory on August 18, when Honda 01, the Wild Weasel F-105F flown by Majors "Robbie" Robinson and Pete Tsouprake, and Honda 02, their F-105D wingman Major Kenneth T. Blank, were fired on by a SAM site they were hunting, the missile exploding between them and blowing out Blank's afterburner. Honda 01 fired two Shrikes at the site, then were warned by Schlitz 01, the lead attack flight, that two MiG-17s were closing on their rear. Robinson, who had flown 50 Wild Weasel missions without meeting enemy fighters, called Blank, "Get him off my ass!" as he passed below with the MiG still shooting. Blank instructed Robinson to break left, as he quickly got on the MiG's tail. Though he had 53 missions and 600 F-105 flying hours, Blank found the complicated armament switching sequence impossible to complete in time. Closing until the MiG filled his windscreen, Blank "hosed" the MiG till it caught fire, flipped inverted, and dived into the ground without the pilot ejecting. VPAF records name Captain Pham Thanh Chung as the only pilot lost that day.

Robinson, who came from ADC, where he had had ACM training in College Prom, reported:

> The F-105 needs a quick, sure method to select guns-air. It is a good aircraft for this type of war, but any new aircraft should be able to maneuver in high-g conditions. The F-105 can fight with the MiG-21 at low altitudes according to Maj John Boyd's Energy Maneuverability Charts. It can hassle with MiGs in clean configuration with less than 5000 pounds of fuel. It needs tracer ammunition in the guns. The gunsight camera also needs to be improved as it currently produces hazy images. Combat is a tough place to learn what a pilot must know to survive in engagements with enemy fighters.

Beginning on September 4, MiGs were spotted nearly every day for the rest of 1966. F-105s were involved in several fights, but lack of maneuverability and lack of pilot training in air combat maneuvering left most who tangled with the MiGs frustrated. On September 21, First Lieutenant Karl Richter became the youngest air force pilot to shoot down a MiG when F-105s shot down two MiGs in a battle over the Dap Cau Bridge. Richter's demonstrated ability had resulted in an unprecedented promotion to element leader despite the fact that he was only a first lieutenant less than a year out of pilot training on his first tour. Ford 01, the F-105F Wild Weasel, had just fired a Shrike at a SAM site when Richter's wingman – Ford 04, Captain Ralph Beardsley – spotted a pair of MiG-17s closing on the lead element.

Richter quickly set up "guns air" while all four F-105s cleared their ordnance. He and Beardsley went to afterburner, cutting off the MiGs as they turned away. Closing, Richter fired two bursts and saw pieces of the lead MiG's right wing fly off as pilot Do Huy Hoang rolled level and lit his afterburner. Hit badly, the MiG-17 rolled right uncontrollably while Beardsley fired at his wingman without seeing hits. Richter closed on Hoang and fired the rest of his ammunition, chopping off more of the wing, smashing the instrument panel and wounding Hoang. Richter reported, "I saw my 20 mm rounds start to sparkle on his right wing the second time I fired. His right wing fell off. As I flew past I saw the MiG's canopy pop off." Richter was happy to see Hoang successfully eject. "He's a 'jock' like I am, flying a plane, doing a job he has to do." Hoang's MiG exploded when it hit the ground, while the second MiG enemy fighter reappeared and moved towards them. Out of ammo and short of fuel, Richter followed the others as they exited the area.

At the end of September, the F-105 units were equipped with the QRC-160 ECM pod. With these, flying formations that provided full coverage, the Thunderchiefs could finally deter the SAM radar. The downside was that use of the pod required a tight formation. Only one QRC-160 equipped F-105 was hit by a SAM by December. The tighter "pod formations" also reduced the time over the target and exposure to AAA.

The 480th Tactical Fighter Squadron scored a fifth MiG kill on November 5. "Opal flight" escorted an EB-66 northwest of Hanoi. Following their new strategy, North Vietnamese controllers waited until the EB-66 and its escorts were low on fuel. A formation of MiG-21s was detected 18 miles distant. When warned, the EB-66 executed a left turn to depart. Opal 01, Major James E. "Friar" Tuck, spotted the MiGs and called them out. The first launched an Atoll at the EB-66 as it broke into a diving spiral and the missile missed. A second MiG got on Tuck's tail and Opal 02, First Lieutenants Wilbur J. Latham, Jr., and Klaus J. Klause, maneuvered to fire on it.

Klause later described the fight:

Towards the end of the mission there was one F-105 flight – call sign "Lincoln" – that hadn't checked in yet, and we later found out that they had never shown up. We had an outrigger formation of Opal 03 and 04 above us at 27,000 feet, and we were hanging about a mile from the EB-66's left wing, with Opal 01 on its right wing. We were at about 25,000 ft, cruising at 0.72 Mach.

I picked up a radar contact at 18 miles, and the EB-66 crew picked up a coded indication of a MiG-21 radar, so they decided to turn back towards the northwest and leave. There was also a MiG call from an EC-121, but that was after we engaged. The first MiG-21 came from our deep six in a 30-degree climb from low altitude, and this started the engagement. I called out, "There's a MiG down there!" and Tuck called "I'm on him too." The lead MiG was pursued by Tuck, and there was another MiG-21 chasing him.

I told Joe (my GIB) to lock on to this last MiG. We had the 'burners cooking, so we ate up the two miles distance. This MiG must have realized we were behind him, he entered a left-hand turn and pulled up. We were at a range of 3000 ft, so I said, "Hey – shoot!" As he pulled up against a clear blue sky, we fired an AIM-9B. The missile jinked and exploded. The MiG looked as if it had just blown up and been punched over. We broke back left and almost ran over the pilot in his 'chute.

Meanwhile, Tuck jumped the lead MiG and fired two Sparrows, but he was inside minimum range. He was going pretty fast, and was soon almost flying close formation alongside the MiG. However, its pilot still wouldn't break off from the EB-66's six o'clock, so Tuck practically shoulder-charged it to one side. Finally, the MiG broke and dived, so Tuck fired another AIM-7. It appeared to explode just ahead of the MiG, making its engine flame out, or maybe the pilot just lost control of it and bailed out.

Renewed MiG aggressiveness in December resulted in a final F-105 kill. Lacking the F-105's ECM pod, the F-4 escorts had suffered heavy losses to SAMs; thus MiGCAP escort flights no longer entered the heavy SAM belts around Hanoi, leaving the Thunderchiefs alone at the most dangerous part of the mission. Almost 90 percent of December MiG encounters involved attacks on F-105s. The "pod" formation minimized chances to maneuver and check the rear.

On December 4, Major Roy S. Dickey led a flight from the 469th Tactical Fighter Squadron, assigned to strike a railroad yard two miles north of Hanoi. As they rolled in, they spotted four MiG-17s over the target, several thousand feet lower. Pulling out of his run, Dickey spotted one MiG attacking his element leader. Pulling behind and slightly above the MiG, he opened fire, closing to within 700 feet. The MiG caught fire at the wing roots and the fuselage aft of the cockpit caught fire as the MiG rolled right and fell into a spin, killing Lieutenant Luu Duc Sy in the crash. Dickey was forced to take evasive action when another MiG opened fire from his rear and he dived away. When he leveled out at 50 feet, the second MiG was nowhere in sight.

The first two years of air war over North Vietnam reinforced the findings of Project Feather Duster. Of 69 Phantoms lost in 1965–66, only four were victims of MiGs, and only one was destroyed by an Atoll missile. In return, F-4s claimed nine MiG-17s and five MiG-21s, all but one with missiles. The North Vietnamese defenses had steadily improved, with SAMs and increasing light and medium AAA making accurate bombing more difficult.

As was discovered in Britain and Germany during World War II, the effect of bombing on the civilian population was to increase popular support for the government. Project Jason, a top secret 1966 Pentagon study of *Rolling Thunder*, concluded: "A direct, frontal attack on a society tends to strengthen the social fabric of the nation, to increase popular support of the existing government, to improve the determination of both the leadership and the populace to fight back." RAND Corporation analyst Oleg Hoeffding wrote:

Hanoi has reaped substantial benefits from its response to what was seen as an exaggerated threat assessment. As to the effects on public morale and the effectiveness of government control, the curious guess would be that they have redounded to the regime's net benefit. The bombing has produced enough incidental damage and civilian casualties to assist the government in maintaining anti-American militancy, and not enough to be seriously depressing or disaffecting.

8

BLACKMAN AND ROBIN

Despite the F-4 Phantom's success since scoring the initial victories in June 1965, the airplane suffered real difficulties in aerial combat. The missile armament and lack of an internal gun were its greatest weaknesses. During 18 months of air combat since the first scores, there had been numerous engagements where either technical failure of the weapons or their misuse by the crews had denied a victory.

The AIM-7D Sparrow, the Phantom's primary weapon around which it had been designed, had only scored one kill in the first 12 months of service in Southeast Asia. It had been replaced after April 1966 by the AIM-7E, which scored only one victory despite being fired in several engagements. The central problem was that the AIM-7 had been designed as a mid-range/long-range radar-guided weapon intended for use against large, relatively slow targets flying predictable flight paths at medium to high altitude. The Sparrow was never intended to be used against a maneuvering target at close range, which was exactly what it was called on to do over North Vietnam.

Designed for use by a fleet defense fighter, the Sparrow took five seconds – a lifetime in aerial combat – to obtain necessary data from the airplane's radar and fire control system. Thus, the conditions of air combat seldom allowed the crew to fire the missile "properly" using the radar lock-on mode, which required that the AN/APQ-100 radar be "locked on" to its target during the missile's entire flight time. Even when it was possible to operate this way, the fact that the launching airplane had to pursue the target in order to guide the missile to get a hit, in conditions where other enemy fighters could force the F-4 to take evasive action that broke the lock, greatly lowered the prospect of success. "Boresight," a "dogfight" mode using a narrow radar beam lock-on allowing a one-second launch procedure, could be used in close-in fighting, but it was unreliable, with only one hit scored in the first 65 launches. Radar lock could be lost in either mode at altitudes below 8,000 feet due to ground clutter confusing the radar return. Over the course of 1965–66, the Da Nang-based 366th Tactical Fighter Wing's Phantoms fired 21 AIM-7s below 8,000 feet and scored no hits. Former "GIB" Steve Wayne recalled, "Although the F-4C's radar was the best we had in Vietnam, it was lacking greatly, particularly in the ground mapping mode, where it was worthless. We really had to do the old 'time and distance' navigation to go from hill to hill at low level."

Technical problems in airplane and weapon made things even worse, since a great many of the complex components within both the radar and the missile itself were subject to damage from robust handling and were not resistant to either the rigors of combat or the humid, dusty environment in Southeast Asia. In addition to radar failure, the year-round humidity could render the AIM-7 useless. Additionally, it also suffered from fusing problems, motor ignition failure, premature detonation, or failure to "self-tune" before launch. For the GIB responsible for arming and firing the missile, the cockpit radar screen displayed the launch parameters in symbology that was only correct for a target flying straight and level. When trying to fire at a maneuvering target, which was the more typical combat situation, the launch parameters changed and varied greatly, but the screen symbols did not provide the operator the figures with sufficient accuracy.

All this contributed to a lack of faith in the weapon; Sparrows were often fired in "ripple," with two or even four fired at a single target in hopes that one would work. Each missile left a very visible white smoke trail that allowed an enemy pilot to maneuver to avoid it, presuming he was not already aware of the F-4's presence by the dark smokey exhaust from the J79s when not in afterburner, which could be seen from a distance of up to 20 miles on a clear day. Additionally, the rules of engagement took away the most important element of the Sparrow's capability, that it could be fired "beyond visual range." The rules of engagement required visual identification, which added to difficulties. Steve Wayne explained: "Due to the need to make visual identification, combined with the wing's minimum airspeed rule of maintaining

400 knots in combat against MiG-17s, we were always launching AIM-7s out of parameters – too close, with too much overtake."

Due to the Sparrow's difficulties, during 1965–66, F-4 pilots generally favored use of the "secondary" armament, the four AIM-9B Sidewinders. The infrared-guided Sidewinder was easier to use, though it had a shorter range. Unfortunately, its prewar development led to a design able to hit targets flying straight and level, rather than the opponents found over the North. A MiG maneuvering at 5G meant the missile's turning capability was incapable of hitting the target, while even a modest 3-G turn on the part of a MiG reduced the deployment envelope by 50 percent. The infrared seeker head on the AIM-9B was also too small, resulting in an inability to distinguish the target from its exhaust wake, the sun, bright clouds, or the terrain below; a MiG could escape into the ever-present clouds, reducing their infrared signature so that a pursuing Sidewinder would break lock. If the missile was launched in more than a 2-G turn it would probably fail to guide. A pilot also had to remember that the growling signal in his headset, indicating that the missile had picked up a heat source ahead, would only give a chance of a kill if the Sidewinder was launched within its proper firing envelope. Reviews of action reports confirmed that more than 25 percent of AIM-9s fired were launched outside of design parameters. The AIM-9B's flat-fronted seeker head also caused drag and reduced range.

Despite these shortcomings, Sidewinders performed much better than Sparrows, scoring 11 kills. However, this only amounted to a kill probability of 0.15, far below the 65 percent success rate in prewar tests held in ideal conditions at high altitude against targets flying straight and level. In 1965, the Navy developed the AIM-9D with a larger seeker head that largely solved these problems. However, the Air Force refused to take up the Navy missile and used the AIM-9B throughout the war, only attempting to replace it with the even less-capable AIM-4 Falcon.

On top of technical problems, there was generally poor leadership at the wing and squadron level. A "Wing King" was not expected to fly missions as part of his command assignment, with the result that top leadership was not personally aware what the crews faced on their missions. Many crews viewed upper leadership with contempt, as they studiously avoided difficult missions, and were so rusty when they did fly a mission that their lack of experience made flying with them even on easy missions more difficult for experienced junior crews. The units that first came from the United States had crews which had been together for an extended period; newcomers frequently found that they received the more difficult missions, while the "old boys' club" took care of the originals. This even extended to the squadron level, where more than a few squadron leaders chose to avoid the more difficult and dangerous missions, leaving such responsibility to senior flight commanders. In the 8th Tactical Fighter Wing, the first wing commander never flew a "tough" mission to Hanoi, or any other Route Pack VI target.

There were exceptions, and none was more exceptional than the man who replaced the first "Wing King" in the 8th Tactical Fighter Wing in September 1966 and the deputy he brought with him. Robin Olds and Chappie James indelibly changed the game as it was played over North Vietnam. Olds was a leading World War II ace in the European Theater, a major by age 22, who fought the Air Force throughout his career for not creating fighter pilots who were indeed fighter pilots. Former Tuskegee Airman Chappie James had distinguished himself flying in the most difficult opening days of the Korean War. They were aided by the presence of Vermont Garrison as vice wing commander when they arrived. Garrison's combat career had begun in the Eagle Squadrons, the Americans flying in the RAF before US entry into World War II, and included service in the 4th Fighter Group, the most successful American fighter group ever, where he flew with their legendary leader, Don Blakeslee. He scored seven victories in Korea. The three formed the most air combat-savvy leadership of any Air Force wing in the Vietnam War.

Ralph Wetterhahn, who shot down a MiG as Olds' wingman in the epic Operation *Bolo* air battle recalled, "I was a 24-year-old first lieutenant when I met him. He was the most courageous leader I ever knew." If there was such a thing as "royalty" in the US Air Force, that described Robin Olds. Born in 1922, he was the oldest of four brothers born to Captain (later Major General) Robert Olds and Eloise Nott Olds, who died when he was four. His father was one of the leading advocates of strategic bombing in the Air Corps, and was appointed the first commander of a bomber group equipped with B-17s in 1938.

Growing up at Langley Field, Virginia, Robin Olds was in daily contact with the small group of officers who later commanded the USAAF in World War II. The family's next-door neighbor was Major Carl Spaatz. Eddie Rickenbacker was a frequent visitor; Hap Arnold once took him flying. In 1940, he tried to join the Royal Canadian Air

Force, but his father kept him home; he entered West Point that fall in the class of 1944. With the outbreak of war, the class graduated a year early in 1943.

As a cadet, he had ambivalent feelings about West Point, admiring the dedication to "Duty, Honor, Country," but disturbed by how the purpose of the Honor Code was distorted. In March, 1943, returning from leave in New York City he was braced by a tactical officer, and compelled on penalty of an honor violation to admit he had consumed alcohol. As a result he was reduced in rank from cadet captain to cadet private, and walked punishment tours until his graduation in June. When he later became Commandant of Cadets at the Air Force Academy, he changed the rules to promote the Honor Code as an instrument to promote integrity. He also became so contemptuous of the tradition of academy alumni networking, or "ring knocking," that he went out of his way to conceal having graduated from West Point.

After flight training, Olds received his pilot's wings personally from General Arnold on May 30, 1943, graduating 194 of 514, with orders to join the newly organized 479th Fighter Group.

The last fighter group to join the Eighth Air Force and the last to fly the P-38 Lightning, the 479th arrived in Britain in March 1944 and flew their first mission on May 26. First Lieutenant Olds' P-38J was named "Scat II," the name he would apply to all his airplanes. His crew chief, Technical Sergeant Glen A. Wold, remembered that – unlike nearly all the other pilots – Olds showed immediate interest in how his P-38 was maintained and learned emergency servicing, helping his ground crew carry out their tasks.

Promoted to captain and flight leader on July 24, Olds shot down two Fw-190s on August 14. During a bomber escort to Wismar on August 23, he ran across 40–50 Bf-109s. Undetected, Olds and his wingman dropped their wing tanks and attacked. Just as he opened fire, both engines quit from fuel starvation; he had neglected to switch to internal fuel. Continuing his attack in "dead-stick mode," he fatally damaged the Bf-109 then dived away and restarted his engines. He later reported:

> Still in a shallow dive, I observed a P-51 and an Me 109 going round. It seemed the '51 needed help so I started down. At about 4,000 feet the Jerry, still way out of range, turned under me. I rolled on my back and gave him an ineffective burst at long range. By this time I was

traveling in excess of 500 miles per hour. My left window blew out, scaring the hell out of me. I thought I had been hit by ground fire. I regained control and pulled out above a wheat field. I tried to contact the flight to get myself recognized, but observed an Me 109 making a pass at me from about seven o'clock high. I broke left as well as my plane could and the Jerry overshot. I straightened out and gave him a burst. He chandelled steeply to the left and I shot some more. He passed right over me and I slipped over in an Immelmann. As I straightened out at the top, I saw the pilot bail out.

At that point he turned for home, but a third '109 attacked him. Pulling hard on the yoke and turning hard left, he shuddered into a high-speed stall. As the enemy fighter passed under him, he pulled the nose down and fired a burst that set its engine afire. The score of three made him the 479th's first ace.

The next month the group re-equipped with the P-51D. Completing his tour soon after, Olds volunteered for a second after scoring two more victories in the Mustang. Returning to combat in 1945, he shot down six more Bf-109s and Fw-190s for a total of 13 air-to-air victories as well as 11.5 strafing victories. On March 25, 1945, at age 22 and less than two years out of West Point, he was promoted to major and became commander of the 434th Fighter Squadron. Robin Olds was the only pilot to become an ace in both P-38 and P-51 aircraft.

After the war, Olds became one of the first P-80 pilots, and developed the first jet flight demonstration team with fellow ace Major John C. "Pappy" Herbst. He married Hollywood actress Ella Raines in 1948. Despite his submitting many requests for orders to Korea, his wife used her connections with high places to keep him stateside.

Promoted to colonel and assigned as Deputy Chief, Air Defense Division at the Pentagon in 1958, Olds contributed to his reputation as an iconoclast, advocating for reinstatement of tactical air training in conventional warfare and upgraded production of conventional bombs, in the face of Air Force commitment to preparing for a nuclear war. His superiors informed him that air combat and conventional air warfare were a thing of the past. Assigned to the National War College in 1962, following graduation in 1963 he was promoted to command the 81st Tactical Fighter Wing, flying the F-101C Voodoo in the nuclear strike role from RAF Bentwaters, England. He brought

Colonel Daniel "Chappie" James, Jr., whom he had met while at the Pentagon, as deputy operations commander. Olds formed an F-101 demonstration team without official approval. Upon learning he was up for promotion to brigadier general, he and the team performed at an open house at Bentwaters in the summer of 1966. Brought up on court-martial charges by the commander of Third Air Force for the illegal event, his friend, US Air Force in Europe commander General Gabriel P. Disosway, "threw me in the briar patch," removing him as 81st Tactical Fighter Wing Commander, taking him off the brigadier general promotion list, canceling a recommended award of the Legion of Merit, and transferring him to Ninth Air Force HQ at Shaw Air Force Base, South Carolina.

In September 1966, Olds wangled assignment as commander of the 8th Tactical Fighter Wing. Told he was expected to fill the position as a more "traditional" Wing King, the 44-year old assured everyone he would only man a desk if it had wings. En route to his new command, he stopped at the 4453rd Combat Crew Training Wing at Davis-Monthan AFB, Arizona, where Chappie James was now deputy operations commander. He completed the 14-day checkout syllabus for the F-4 in five days under instruction by Major William L. Kirk, the 4453rd's standardization and evaluation officer, who had been a pilot in the 81st Wing at Bentwaters. Kirk then accompanied him to Point Mugu missile range for practice firing of AIM-7 Sparrow and AIM-9 Sidewinder missiles before he flew on to Travis Air Force Base for transport to Southeast Asia. Kirk later joined his old CO in Thailand in March 1967.

Rather than take the special treatment reserved for senior officers, Olds flew to his new assignment the way the other aircrew did, on an uncomfortable charter flight. Arriving at Ubon RTAB unannounced and without fanfare, he was unceremoniously dumped from the C-130 Klong Flight in company with several enlisted men and their luggage. On taking command, he changed the process for greeting new troops, with personnel to welcome them and give assistance. When he arrived at the Officer's Club in his flight suit with patches from ADC, two lieutenants who mistook him for an outsider pounced on him. By the time authority arrived, the three were having a drink at the bar.

When he took command, Robin Olds had not seen combat in over 20 years, and had only a few hours flying the F-4 Phantom. The day following his arrival, he called a meeting of the pilots, where he set the tone for how he would command by putting himself on the flight schedule as a rookie pilot, to be trained by officers junior, challenging them to train him properly because he would soon be leading them, and warning that he would soon be better than any of them. Ralph Wetterhahn later recalled, "He was right on all counts. The air we breathed suddenly became different."

Olds was very fortunate that Vermont Garrison had arrived the previous month, since he was the only senior leader solidly respected by the junior crews doing the fighting. Garrison was always older than those with whom he served, becoming an ace at age 28, an "old man" where the average age was 21–22. He shot down seven MiG-15s over the Yalu at age 37. As commander of the 335th Fighter-Interceptor Squadron, he was in charge of Project Gun-Val, a combat evaluation of seven F-86Fs with their armament changed to four 20mm cannon.

Shortly after turning 50, Garrison returned to combat in August 1965, as deputy operations commander of the 405th Tactical Fighter Wing, a composite wing of F-100Ds, F-102As, and B-57B bombers serving temporary rotations in South Vietnam. He became wing commander on January 5, 1966, remaining until August 4, 1966, when he was relieved by Colonel Chuck Yeager. In the "Wolfpack," Garrison flew 97 missions over North Vietnam and Laos, although he was never formally "checked out" in the Phantom, which meant he always flew with an instructor pilot in the rear seat. Olds remembered that Garrison "flew his 52nd combat mission on his 52nd birthday." Olds was forced to restrict Garrison from flying missions like Operation *Bolo* where they were purposely engaging MiGs, recalling:

> Garry was so nearsighted he carried about four different pairs of glasses with him, but by God, if you wanted a target bombed, he would hit it. He would hit it when everybody else missed. He got furious with me because I wouldn't let him get up there among the MiGs. I told him, "Pappy, every fighter pilot in the Air Force knows and loves you, and I am not going to be the guy that sends you up there to get your butt scragged." He just could not see anymore.

For his age and reputation as a gunnery expert, Garrison's call sign was "Gray Eagle." He completed his tour on June 5, 1967, and was replaced by Chappie James.

Garrison was described by USAF historian and author Walter J. Boyne as a "first-rate combat unit leader." Olds said of him, "Of the many hundreds I've served with, Garry was one of the greatest – as pilot, as gentleman, as officer, and as friend."

Daniel "Chappie" James, the man Olds brought with him to Southeast Asia, had an equally distinguished career. A member of the famed Tuskeegee Airmen, James' flying ability was such that he was retained at the school as an instructor, later taking part in the "Freeman Field Mutiny," in which the African-American pilots and crews stood up to bad actions on the part of their white commanders.

Following President Truman's 1948 executive order ending outlawing racial segregation in the armed forces, he was assigned to the 18th Fighter-Bomber Wing at Clark AFB six months before the outbreak of the Korean War and was among the experienced F-51 Mustang pilots sent to Korea during the war's first desperate month, where he joined the "Dallas Squadron," a scratch unit that was the only USAF fighter-bomber unit operating on the Korean Peninsula during the UN retreat. On one mission in August during the First Battle of the Naktong River in defense of the Pusan Perimeter, James' flight spotted several North Korean artillery pieces on a sand bar in the river. The napalm canisters they dropped failed to ignite because of bad fuses. He recalled, "Every third round in our fifties was an incendiary, so we came around in a strafing run. The incendiaries set the cans off and the entire area went up in flames, completely destroying the cannons."

North Korean troops had infiltrated crowds of refugees clogging the roads, forcing UN troops to fire into refugee crowds when the infiltrators opened fire on them. "Dallas Squadron" Major John Moreland remembered a mission flown with James:

We were in contact with a Forward Air Controller (FAC) who had spotted a large body of enemy troops coming down a road. He led us to a large group of people heading south, but before we attacked I decided to take a closer look and we made a low pass over the crowd. We both saw mostly women and children, who did not run for cover. We both felt they really were refugees and decided not to attack.

By the time he left Korea in 1951, James had flown in some of the most difficult battles of the war, including the terrible retreat out of

North Korea, surviving 101 battlefield close air support missions in
P-51 Mustangs and F-80 Shooting Stars with the 67th, 12th, and 44th
Fighter Bomber Squadrons. In his second war, James flew 67 missions
into North Vietnam and led a flight in Operation *Bolo*, the most
successful air combat until Operation *Linebacker*. He later became
the first African-American four-star Air Force general and retired
as Commander of North American Aerospace Defense Command
(NORAD).

Five days after Olds arrived, the wing became the first Phantom unit
to lose an F-4C to an air-to-air missile fired by a MiG-21. This loss
followed two other F-4 losses to MiGs over the two weeks before Olds
took command, which equaled the losses of the previous year. Olds was
convinced his pilots could take on the MiG-21 and prevail if the enemy
could be drawn into the air on even terms. An exponent of air combat,
Olds soon discovered that most of his pilots were as ignorant of how
to fight another airplane as was Ralph Wetterhahn. His philosophy of
command, learned from Colonel "Hub" Zemke, the commander he
respected the most during World War II, was to lead from the front
and bring energy and enthusiasm to personal involvement in every
level of activity. He quickly arranged with the Royal Australian Air
Force squadron that provided air defense at Ubon with their Sabres, to
provide ACM opportunities for his pilots whenever they had sufficient
fuel when returning from missions. The Australians, who were "dying
of boredom" as then-Flight Lieutenant Ken Bricknell later recalled,
were only too happy to oblige.

Since bombing North Vietnamese airfields was still forbidden, the
MiGs would have to be enticed to come up where the F-4s could get
at them. "Wolfpack" tactics officer Captain John B. Stone originated
the plan of how to accomplish this enticement by imitating F-105s
to the North Vietnamese defense system, which became Operation
Bolo. Olds liked Stone's idea and assigned responsibility for planning
to Major James D. Covington, Captain Stone, and First Lieutenants
Joseph Hicks and Ralph F. Wetterhahn to flesh it out as a formal plan.
Wetterhahn recalled:

> Colonel Olds and John Stone conceived the idea of the mission. Hicks
> and I worked with Stone and our intelligence officer J.D. Covington
> to plot out the details of the whole mission. Covington got the data

on how often the MiGs flew, how many generally took off and how long they stayed airborne. We worked together, deciding how long a flight could orbit over each target airfield and in blocking positions near the Chinese border, the fuel requirement and the total length of the mission. We had flights orbiting over all the MiG bases, with relief every five minutes or so except at Gia Lam, since it was overlapped by the Phuc Yen flights. We wanted to deny landings to the MiGs, so we needed 45–50 minutes minimum coverage after they scrambled. Hicks and I put colored tape over the map for the routes in and out. The beauty of Olds' way of doing things was that he refused to tell us where we would fly on that mission. We all wanted to be flight leaders, but not knowing where we might fly made us plan each line very, very carefully. Stone said, "You might be riding that train."

The completed plan involved equipping the F-4s with the QRC-160 jamming pods used by F-105s, communicating with the call signs and communications code words of the F-105 wings, and flying at the speed and altitude of a bomb-carrying F-105 formation through northwest Vietnam to entice the enemy to launch their MiG-21s to intercept the "bomb-laden F-105s," discovering too late that they were up against F-4s. Olds liked the proposals and the plan was presented to PACAF commander General Hunter Harris, Jr., who didn't like it. Persistent, Olds presented it to Seventh Air Force commander General Momyer, who rejected it initially but told Olds to work it up further after his director of operations, General Donovan Smith, became an ardent supporter.

The four planners went back to work between December 13 and 22 and developed the plan in detail. Wetterhahn recalled, "While we were working on it, the MiGs pulled some more of their interceptions on a strike force, and everyone became concerned with what the other side was doing." Now Momyer approved it. The code name "Bolo" referred to a tool used in the Philippines for cutting sugar cane, which was also sharp enough to be a weapon, though such use wasn't obvious until it was wielded that way.

The target date was January 1. To maintain tight security, since it was known the base was infiltrated by pro-communist spies, the pilots assigned to fly the mission were not briefed until December 30. The coordinated mission would be flown by a "west force" of seven flights of F-4Cs from the 8th Tactical Fighter Wing and an "east force" of seven flights of F-4Cs from the 366th Tactical Fighter Wing based at Da Nang. The West Force would simulate the F-105 strike force, flying altitudes, routes, and speeds typical of bomb-carrying F-105s. This force was responsible for bringing the MiGs up and covering Phuc Yen and Gia Lam airfields. The East Force was assigned to cover Kep and Cat Bi airfields, and to provide a barrier against MiGs attempting to flee to China. The task force included six flights of Wild Weasel/Iron Hand F-105s from the 355th and 388th wings for SAM protection, with airborne radar warning by College Eye EC-121s over the Gulf of Tonkin. Radar jamming support was by EB-66s escorted by four flights of F-104Cs from the 435th Tactical Fighter Squadron at Da Nang.

If the MiGs reacted, their fuel endurance from takeoff to landing gave a maximum flight time of 55 minutes. Thus, arrival times of the F-4 flights at the targeted airfields were set five minutes apart, providing continuous coverage and maximum opportunities for engagement, while preventing surviving MiGs from landing to refuel. No other US aircraft would be present over North Vietnam, allowing the first flight to engage without having to first identify the target, thus maximizing the Sparrow's effectiveness.

Maintenance crews spent the last week of December inspecting, cleaning, and repairing all equipment on aircraft assigned to the mission. Once the F-4s were equipped with the QRC-160 pods, the date of the attack was set for January 1, 1967.

Bad weather on New Year's Day scrubbed the mission, which was rescheduled for January 2. The weather report the next day showed solid overcast for Phuc Yen, Gia Lam, Kep, and Cat Bi. After an hour's delay, the F-4s launched from Ubon that afternoon. The pods were mounted on the right wing pylon, so they carried a centerline and single wing tank that created an asymmetric imbalance making takeoff difficult since the aircraft would roll to the side carrying the wing tank. Flying the tight F-105 four-plane wing-abreast formation and following the F-105 flight paths and tanker rendezvous on the ingress route used by F-105s, the mission drew no defensive reaction, despite the seven flights being assigned MiGCAP call signs: Olds, Ford, Rambler, Lincoln, Tempest, Plymouth, and Vespa, rather than F-105 call signs. Olds arrived over Phuc Yen at 1500 hours, where a floor of thick clouds blanketed the area below.

Unknown to the Americans, the GCI controllers had delayed takeoffs by 15 minutes in the expectation that the enemy would abort due to weather. A flight of MiG-21s, led by Vu Ngoc Dinh, with wingman Nguyen Van Thuan, element leader Nguyen Dang Kinh and his wingman Bui Duc Nhu were first to take off.

Robin Olds checked his watch as his flight began their turn. When three minutes had passed without contact, and with Ford flight expected to arrive at any moment, the missile-free option was canceled. Ralph Wetterhahn, Olds' wingman in Olds 02, recalled what happened:

It was Colonel Olds' first mission to Hanoi, and up to this point he had controlled the flight with a coolness I had never experienced. The Hanoi delta was a dangerous place to spend even a few minutes, let alone the 55 planned for Operation *Bolo*. Heavy undercast covered the target area. The peaks along infamous "Thud Ridge" poked through the cloud layer to the east. It was obvious that we would be unable to see the airfields, and the SAMs could fire at us through the clouds. It was advisable to abort the mission. Olds, however, was not to be denied. He continued directly for Hanoi.

Our radars swept the area and were greeted with an ominous absence of targets. As we neared the city, my jammer pod shut down. Of all the fighters over North Vietnam, only my F-4 could easily be detected by enemy radar. I notified Olds about my problem. "Tuck in close, Two," he ordered. "My jammer should cover us both." I moved closer with a knot tightening in my stomach. I'd seen what a SAM could do.

As we reversed course over Hanoi, MiGs were scrambling from all their bases. Olds Flight headed to the northwest and Number Three, Lieutenant Joe Hicks, locked onto a very low, fast target at our twelve o'clock. He was given the lead and he dove to engage, but the MiG passed underneath, still hidden in the clouds.

Just as Chappie James' Ford Flight arrived in the target area, Vu Ngoc Dinh's flight emerged from the clouds near Phu Ninh and spotted the four F-4s of Ford Flight approaching from the direction of Phu Tho. Flight leader Dinh went to afterburner, but the F-4s immediately initiated a violent combat weave maneuver, making it impossible to obtain a firing position. He turned left to return and the other three lost contact in the clouds.

Olds resumed lead, swinging the flight back toward Hanoi. Completing the turn, he heard James' call: "Olds, you got a MiG-21, he's at your six o'clock."

Dinh was looking for a hole in the clouds through which to descend when he spotted the second formation of four F-4s approaching. Wetterhahn recalled:

Olds broke sharply left. He had his eye on one MiG at eight o'clock while I thought he was maneuvering against a second MiG in sight at my ten o'clock. James was watching a third MiG at our six. Each of us thought there was only one enemy plane. Total confusion. Olds continued his turn and sandwiched us between two MiGs. I tried to keep tabs on the one sliding behind us. "Olds-One, break left, he's at your seven and firing!" "Get him off!"

Olds' radar broke lock before his AIM-7 could hit the target. He then fired a Sidewinder, but it misguided on the nearby clouds. He ceased acknowledging my warnings, and ceased firing missiles. The second MiG came in for a missile shot while Olds remained focused on the first MiG.

I moved laterally to avoid shooting from behind him. My GIB Lieutenant Sharp locked the radar on the MiG, and yelled "Shoot!" I fired two missiles. The first one never appeared, but the second popped into sight just left of the radome. It guided. The missile streaked across the two miles spacing and hit the MiG just forward of the stabilizer. A red fireball mushroomed and the MiG-21 flew through it, continued for an instant, and then swapped ends, shedding large sections of the tail. The stricken plane went into a flat spin, like a falling leaf, and disappeared in flames into the clouds.

Dinh did not have time to take evasive action before his aircraft was hit. When the missile exploded, his MiG-21 shuddered and became uncontrollable. Dinh ejected.

"I got one, I got one!' Wetterhahn announced with a huge release of tension:

Then I checked six. Another MiG was making a gun firing pass. No-holds dogfights erupted everywhere. The radio chatter went wild.
"Lead, there's one closing at five – fast – break right!" "Razz, he overshot – get him – ah, beautiful, tremendous." "Rambler Lead, there they are – two o'clock – two of 'em – slightly low."

"Okay, attacking."

Missile smoke trails snaked across the entire dome of the sky, like skeletal fingers whose touch meant death. "Rambler, look out, one coming in from three o'clock – break, break." "Rambler Three here – I've got two MiGs, three miles at twelve. Engaging. Four, take the one on the right."

Olds had seen my MiG explode and finally broke left while our Number-Four, flown by Captain Walt Radeker III and Lieutenant Jim Murray engaged the MiG chasing us. Olds spotted another MiG and began a barrel-roll to line up for a shot. He pulled up into the sun, and I lost sight of him for about twenty seconds.

Radeker was unable get a consistently good tone but launched regardless. His Sidewinder guided perfectly striking the MiG just in front of its tail, sending it into a spin. This was the MiG-21 flown by Nguyen Van Thuan, flight leader Dinh's wingman. He was able to eject successfully and parachuted to safety.

Olds then spotted the MiG-21 flown by element leader Nguyen Dang Kinh. He described what happened:

I pulled the nose up high, about 45 degrees, inside his circle. Mind you, he was turning around to the left so I pulled the nose up high and rolled to the right. I got up on top of him and half upside down, hung there, and waited for him to complete more of his turn and timed it so that as I continued to roll down behind him I'd be about 20 degrees angle off.

The vertical maneuver, known as a "vector roll," positioned Olds' Phantom above the tighter-turning MiG-21. When it completed its turn, Olds dropped in behind and fired two Sidewinders. "When I got down low and behind, and he was outlined by the sun against a brilliant blue sky, I let him have two Sidewinders, one of which hit and blew his right wing off." The MiG spiraled into the clouds below, the second kill of the battle as Kinh ejected successfully. Olds Flight had destroyed three MiG-21s without loss. Olds recalled, "It was over very quickly." Wetterhahn continued:

Not quite. We heard a warning, "SAMs coming up at your six o'clock." "Whose six o'clock!!" roared Olds. An SA-2 burst through the clouds trailing a two hundred foot plume of fire. The site had apparently zeroed in on my jammer-less aircraft. I spotted Olds below me, shoved the throttles to full afterburner, and dove for the protection provided by his jammer. The two-stage SAM went out of control as the booster separated. "It's not guiding. I'm right behind you chief. Don't worry. I'm covering your tail," James radioed.

Olds flight went into afterburner and we left the area in a supersonic dash. In all, the dogfight lasted nine minutes.

Ford Flight, led by "Chappie" James, entered the target area at 1505 hours, just as the MiGs began to engage. Though he did not score a victory, James witnessed the victory by his wingman, Captain Everett T. Raspberry:

At 1504 hours my flight was attacked by three MiGs, two from the ten o'clock and one from the six o'clock. Initially I didn't see this last one because I had been concentrating on those approaching head-on. My GIB excitedly warned me about this rapidly approaching MiG, which was within firing range of my number three and number four. I hesitated a moment before interrupting my attack against the two MiGs in front, because I had seen the Olds flight passing below us a few seconds before. I thought that the plane seen by my GIB could be one of them.

Despite that, I suddenly turned left and then right, and caught sight of the third MiG. I ordered my numbers three and four to break right. As they did so, the MiG broke left for some mysterious reason and for a split second we were side by side. We were so close that, besides the red stars in his wings, I could clearly see the pilot's face. I began a horizontal barrel roll to get away from him and into an attack position. Once in position, I launched a Sidewinder. The missile missed because the evading MiG broke left at full throttle. But when he did, he put himself in the line of fire of my number two, Captain Everett T. Raspberry. I ordered him to follow, because the two aircraft that I initially saw had been placed in my forward sector. I was in an advantageous position, so I fired two AIM-9s against them in a quick sequence, and I turned to place myself as wingman for Captain Raspberry. I kept on descending beside Captain Raspberry and I remember that I thought that he was still out of the optimal launching envelope. But he performed a barrel roll that placed him in a perfect position again and he launched an AIM-9 which hit against the tail section of the MiG-21. It was shaken violently and later fell in a slow, almost plane spin.

This was the MiG-21 flown by Kinh's wingman, Bui Duc Nhu, who also ejected as the missile exploded against his fighter. After Raspberry scored his kill, Ford Flight left the scene without loss.

As Olds and Ford flights engaged the first flight of MiG-21s, a second flight led by Nguyen Ngoc Do with wingman Dang Ngoc Ngu, and element leader Dong Van De with his wingman, the future VPAF leading ace Nguyen Van Coc, took off. The leader and element lead were both armed with Atolls, while their wingmen were carrying rocket pods.

Shortly after Rambler Flight, led by Captain John B. Stone, arrived, Stone spotted Nguyen Ngoc Do and Dang Ngoc Ngu as they popped through a break in the clouds. Flight leader Do spotted Rambler Flight; as Dong Van De and Nguyen Van Coc emerged from the clouds, Do ordered the flight to drop external fuel tanks and turn left. Deciding to pursue the lead enemy element, he closed to 6,500 feet and fired one missile.

Major Philip P. Combies, Rambler 04, recalled:

We were at 13,440 feet and our speed was 540 knots. A little bit after completing a turn to the northwest, we identified a patrol of four MiG-21s in spread formation at a distance of five miles at two o'clock and below us. Two more MiGs appeared, two miles behind. When they crossed in front of Stone, he followed, breaking left and losing height. The flight spread wide to the right, and I found myself higher and somewhat to the right of the others.

Stone closed on flight leader Do and fired a Sparrow that failed to ignite. He fired a second Sparrow that tracked perfectly. Do's first warning that he was in trouble was the explosion of Stone's missile, and he felt his aircraft become unstable. It then went into a side-slip spin and began dropping. At that point, Do ejected, landing safely.

Combies described what happened next:

I kept the throttle to the minimum during the first phase of the combat. So, when the MiGs broke to the left, and the engagement began, I chose one of the MiGs and followed him with my radar.

I don't think that we ever exceeded 4Gs during the whole engagement. I decided to follow the Navy pilots' tactics, stay at close range foregoing the radar tracking, but looking through the reticle instead. When I realized that I was in the right position, I pushed the fire button, released it, pushed it again, and waited. I did not even see the first Sparrow. However, I followed the entire trajectory of the second one, from launch to impact. I fired the missiles at less than 2,000 yards from the MiG's tail, at a height of 9,800 feet, while turning to the left. The second one hit the tail section of the enemy aircraft. A second later, I saw a huge, orange ball of fire.

A moment later, another MiG-21 turned in front of First Lieutenant Lawrence Flynn, Rambler 02, who fired a Sparrow that hit the MiG behind the vertical fin and it exploded in a fireball. Rambler Flight's third MiG raised the final score to 7:0 in favor of the F-4s. Five SA-2 missile launches threatened Rambler Flight and they disengaged. The entire combat lasted 12 minutes.

According to VPAF records, Dong Van De, Nguyen Van Coc, and Dang Ngoc Ngu were hit and damaged in this fight with Rambler Flight, but were able to successfully land their damaged fighters back at their airfield.

The last four flights arrived to find the battle over and quickly departed due to the SAM threat. The Da Nang-based East Force never entered North Vietnamese airspace due to the bad weather. Ultimately, only 26 of the 56 assigned fighters entered the target area, and only 12 engaged. Of the 16 MiG-21s that the VPAF had in their inventory, 11–14 had engaged, with seven destroyed and two others probably shot down by Combies and Major Herman L. Knapp, Rambler 03. After the war, the VPAF admitted that Operation *Bolo* was one of the worst days they experienced during the war, with a loss of seven MiG-21s for no enemy loss.

In 2012, Vu Ngoc Dinh, who had been shot down by Ralph Wetterhahn, recalled Operation *Bolo* from the Vietnamese side:

I do not know why the weather on January 2 was so unfavorable for our side. The clouds were thick, with the bottom of the cloud layer at 200 meters [656 feet] and the top of the cloud layer at 600 meters [1,969 feet]. This made it easy for the US Air Force to conceal their forces so that they could ambush our MiGs above the clouds. Because we had not figured out the enemy's plan, after we took off and popped through the top of the cloud layer, all four of our aircraft were shot down, but all four of our pilots were able to eject and land safely.

This is because the Americans were able to keep their plan totally secret, and we were not able to learn much from our intelligence reports about the American tactical schemes. In any case, we learned lessons from our experiences in this battle, and all four of us emerged unhurt so that we were able to rejoin the fight within a few days. I feel bad about this battle because the Americans took us by surprise and we were shot down before we even had a chance to engage the American aircraft.

On May 4, Robin Olds shot down another MiG-21 over Phuc Yen. He recalled:

Closing on the F-105 flight from their 7:30 position, I broke the rear flight into the MiGs, called the 105s to break, and maneuvered to obtain a missile firing position on one of the MiG-21's. I obtained a boresight lock-on, interlocks in, went full system, kept the pipper on the MiG, and fired two AIM-7's in a ripple. One AIM-7 went ballistic. The other guided but passed behind the MiG and did not detonate.

Knowing that I was then too close for further AIM-7 firing, I maneuvered to obtain AIM-9 firing parameters. The MiG-21 was maneuvering violently and firing position was difficult to achieve. I snapped two AIM-9's at the MiG and did not observe either missile. The MiG then reversed and presented the best parameter yet. I achieved a loud growl, tracked, and fired one AIM-9. From the moment of launch, it was obvious that the missile was locked on. It guided straight for the MiG and exploded about 5–10 feet beneath his tailpipe. The MiG then went into a series of frantic turns, some of them so violent that the aircraft snap-rolled in the opposite direction. Fire was coming from the tailpipe, but I was not sure whether it was normal afterburner or damage-induced.

I fired the remaining AIM-9 at one point, but the shot was down toward the ground and the missile did not discriminate. I followed the MiG as he turned southeast and headed for Phuc Yen.

At this point, Olds ordered his wingman, MiG-killer Captain Dick Pascoe in Flamingo 02, to get the escaping enemy fighter:

> The MiG-21 ceased maneuvering and went in a straight slant for the airfield. I stayed 2,500 feet behind him and observed a brilliant white fire streaming from the left side of his fuselage. It looked like magnesium burning with particles flaking off. I had to break off to the right as I neared Phuc Yen runway at about 2,000 feet, due to a heavy, accurate, 85mm barrage. I lost sight of the MiG at that point. Our number three saw the MiG continue in a straight gentle dive and impact approximately 100 yards south of the runway.

The kill was Olds' since Pascoe had not been able to close and fire a missile before the enemy fighter hit the ground.

On May 20, Olds shot down two MiG-17s in what one of his pilots called a "vengeful chase" after they shot down his wingman during a large dogfight, making him a triple ace – 12 in World War II and four in Vietnam. He later stated that after he shot down his fourth MiG, he intentionally avoided shooting down a fifth, despite at least ten opportunities to do so, because he learned that Secretary of the Air Force Harold Brown would immediately bring him to the United States for publicity if he became a two-war ace. He let his wingmen take any kills he set up until his tour ended. Ralph Wetterhahn recalled, "I think Robin Olds could have been a double MiG ace if he hadn't done that."

When the F-4D arrived several months after Operation *Bolo*, it was equipped with the more "advanced" but far less reliable AIM-4 Falcon rather than the Sidewinder. After missing what should have been an easy kill due to a Falcon malfunction, Olds had all the F-4Ds rewired so they could use Sidewinders. This was eventually done to all F-4Ds.

After Operation *Bolo*, the press descended on Ubon; Olds and Chappie James became famous, known as "Blackman" and "Robin," a play of words on the *Batman* TV show then playing in the United States.

Olds was awarded a fourth Silver Star for leading a low-level bombing strike on March 30, 1967, and the Air Force Cross for an attack on the Paul Doumer Bridge in Hanoi on August 11, one of five awarded for that mission. He flew his final mission over North Vietnam on

September 23, 1967. His total of 259 combat missions included 107 in World War II and 152 in Southeast Asia, 105 over North Vietnam. His F-4C "Scat XXVII" is on display at the National Museum of the United States Air Force at Wright-Patterson AFB, Ohio.

Olds' call sign in Vietnam was "Wolf." Tradition in the 8th Fighter Wing is for each wing commander to assume the call sign "Wolf," with a number to distinguish between particular Wolves.

Olds once described his feelings about air combat:

> Our basic job over there is to bomb targets, not chase MiGs. If they happen to get in the way, so much the worse for them. However, we liked them because they kept our morale up. All fighter pilots have a love for aerial battle. It's a great feeling to launch a missile at a MiG, even if the missile misses. At least you feel useful. After the mission you can tell terrible war stories about the scrap you had.

Looking back on Operation *Bolo*, Ralph Wetterhahn observed:

> The *Bolo* mission was designed to eliminate the North Vietnamese Air Force as an effective fighting force by shooting them all down or preventing any that took off from landing. To do that required decent weather. We didn't have it. Later we were told that 19 MiGs took off that day. Once they began losing planes, the rest were ordered to remain in the clouds and recover. In spite of the morale-boosting victory we accomplished that day, in truth, the mission failed in its goal. That failure would haunt us, since the Vietnamese pilots stood down, revised their tactics, and came back months later with a vengeance. Oh, and one of those who were shot down that day, Lieutenant Vu Ngoc Dinh, eventually made ace.

9

THE MiGs FIGHT BACK

As 1967 began, US leaders were optimistic about prospects in Vietnam. In President Johnson's State of the Union address on January 10, he stated that while the end was not yet in sight, he believed General William Westmoreland's assessment that the enemy could no longer succeed on the battlefield. The next day, US Ambassador Henry Cabot Lodge, Jr., predicted "tremendous success" and that US casualties would decrease. He predicated this on continued bombing of North Vietnam, which was "tremendously useful" in stopping the flow of personnel and supplies to the South. Testifying before Congress later that month, Secretary McNamara stated that air operations over North Vietnam were producing "good results," citing Operation *Bolo* as evidence for optimism.

The military leadership did not share this optimism. The Joint Chiefs believed that the enemy had not been able to prevail on the battlefield during 1966 because of increased B-52 "Arclight" bombing of the jungle where the enemy were hidden, which prevented them undertaking offensive military action. However, there was no "substantial trend" toward achieving the objective of ending North Vietnamese efforts to prevail in the South. The Air Force leadership in particular argued for lessening restrictions on targeting important installations such as airfields and most particularly allowing supplies to continue coming through Haiphong. They argued strenuously against Westmoreland's request to increase American troop levels, stating that this would become an unending demand; the United States could never win the war of attrition that the general advocated. Increasing American personnel would likely provoke North Vietnam into a larger military response, raise American casualties, and convince the South Vietnamese that this was not "their war." This argument continued to a final decision in June by the civilian leadership to muddle along with a small increase in forces.

In late February, Joint Chiefs Chairman General Earle Wheeler directed the staff to prepare a range of military proposals to "assure a definite and visible improvement" in the war by Christmas, 1967. The Air Staff responded with a plan for an escalating campaign against key targets in the prohibited and restricted zones of Hanoi and Haiphong, recommending that these operations begin with the onset of favorable weather in April in order to achieve the desired results by the end of the year. The civilian leadership approved some target changes on February 22, authorizing an increase in *Rolling Thunder* strikes. These approvals were welcome, but were still considered inadequate to achieving the goal. Air Force Secretary Harold Brown advocated continuing the *Rolling Thunder* campaign on the grounds that it caused a diversion of enemy manpower to man the air defenses and maintain the infrastructure repair organizations that might otherwise be sent to South Vietnam. The JCS air staff went back to further refining their requests for expanded effort.

On March 23, Admiral Sharp requested authority to initiate spoiling attacks on Hoa Lac and Kep airfields before MiGs from those bases became a serious threat. Hoa Lac was close to completion while Kep had been recently improved. The JCS included these targets in the proposal for *Rolling Thunder 55*. However, there was no response from those in the administration who approved targets during March and most of April.

Aerial engagements increased in April; Admiral Sharp renewed his request for authority to attack the MiG bases. On April 13, he stated in a cable to General Wheeler that such strikes could force the MiGs to move to airfields in China.

Rolling Thunder 55 was approved two days later, which gave permission to bomb Kep and Hoa Lac, but attacks were to be limited to "small and random harassment strikes designed to attrit aircraft and disrupt support facilities." Air Force and Navy commanders took immediate advantage to promptly launch major strikes against each airfield and deal a heavy blow to the enemy. Their success was such that

McNamara expressed immediate concern that the field commanders had attempted to achieve more than the stipulated harassment and attrition. JCS Chairman Wheeler suggested to Admiral Sharp that he exert a restraining influence on his subordinates. Despite the momentary success of the two airfield attacks, MiG sightings and encounters grew.

As soon as *Rolling Thunder 55* was approved, the commanders sought additional authority to bomb the power generation grid, specifically the powerplants in Route Pack VI-A and VI-B providing power to Hanoi and Haiphong. However, when *Rolling Thunder 56* was approved in May, the Hanoi generating plant was specifically excluded on grounds that there was too much likelihood of civilian casualties.

The MiGs were still a force to be reckoned with. Following the success of Operation *Bolo*, the VPAF challenged the daily "weather recce" mission on January 3 and 4, causing the RF-4Cs to abort. On January 5 and 6, a pair of 555th Tactical Fighter Squadron F-4C Phantoms flew the RF-4C's high-speed profile in close formation to appear as a single target on North Vietnamese radar. Four MiGs intercepted them on January 6. Crab 01, Captain Richard M. Pascoe and First Lieutenant Norman E. Wells, and Crab 02, Major Thomas M. Hirsch and First Lieutenant Roger J. Strasswimmer, each shot down a MiG.

Pascoe later reported: "I maneuvered the flight by use of airborne radar to effect a visual identification of four MIG-21C aircraft and fired two AIM-7 radar missiles at the enemy flight leader. The second missile struck the MIG aircraft in the fuselage midsection and detonated. The MIG-21 was seen to burst into flame and fell in uncontrollable flight through the clouds."

At nearly the same time, Hirsch launched an AIM-7 at the same target but the Sparrow did not guide. Pascoe attacked the second MiG, which disappeared into the clouds. Spotting the other two at Hirsch's six o'clock, he barrel-rolled onto their six o'clock, but before he could fire they also disappeared in the clouds. Continuing to turn, assuming they would continue their turns in the clouds, he spotted them when they emerged from the clouds in wing formation. As he barrel-rolled to drop on their rear, they spotted him. Completing his roll, Pascoe put his gunsight pipper on the fourth MiG's tailpipe and fired a Sidewinder to "keep their attention," even though his angle was too high. The missile passed about 300–400 feet behind the MiG. He fired a second that passed close to the enemy's tail but did not detonate. The fight turned into a slow-speed scissors when the two MiGs reversed. Pascoe fired a third Sidewinder that missed. The third MiG pilot saw he was getting into a disadvantageous position and departed, but the fourth MiG continued the scissors maneuvers.

Hirsch later reported:

> In rolling to watch one of the enemy aircraft dive away I lost sight of the flight leader. Approximately one minute later I picked him up and saw two MiG-21's reappear from the undercast in a climb. The lead F-4 engaged the MiGs as I turned to close on them. I obtained a radar lock-on to a MiG-21 which was in a right climbing turn. As I slid in to his five o'clock, I fired an AIM-7. The MiG steepened his climb to near vertical and lost airspeed. When next observed, it was in an 80-degree nose-down attitude and rolling slowly. Just prior he entered the undercast, the MiG pilot ejected and separated from the seat.

Spotting Pascoe's flight on radar and thinking they were the weather flight, the 921st Fighter Regiment launched four MiG-21s from Noi Bai airfield, led by Tran Hanh, with his wingman Mai Van Cuong, element leader Dong Van De, and his wingman the redoubtable Nguyen Van Coc. Suddenly, Tran Hanh heard Nguyen Van Coc report spotting four F-4s behind them. Realizing they were in an unfavorable position, he immediately ordered a hard right turn. Turning, he spotted the four F-4s, chasing them in afterburner. At the same moment he saw six smoke trails headed toward his flight. Element leader Dong Van De was hit by a Sparrow fired by Captain Pascoe and ejected when he was hit, but was killed when his parachute harness came loose.

Tran Hanh decided to pursue the two F-4s in the lead and closed on the wingman. When the range was 1,000 meters (3,280 feet), he launched one missile, then immediately broke left. Nguyen Van Coc, who was also chasing the second F-4, spotted missiles fired at him and took evasive action. Hanh shouted to the others to dive back under the clouds, but Mai Van Cuong's MiG-21 was hit by a missile fired by Hirsch and Strasswimmer. Cuong ejected and landed safely in the village of Tu Lap, Me Linh District. Tran Hanh and Nguyen Van Coc returned to Noi Bai, landing at 0942 hours.

In a 2012 interview, Lieutenant General Nguyen Van Coc, the leading VPAF ace with nine victories, recalled the fight:

> Right after we broke through the top of the cloud layer I heard Cuong report he had spotted F-4s behind us. At that moment, Hanh also spotted the enemy aircraft and ordered the flight to turn hard to the right. Because De and I were in the process of trying to form up on one another we were not yet able to make a hard turn. I was able to see two missiles trailing white smoke flash right under the belly of my MiG and head straight for De's MiG, which was on the outside of the turn. I shouted, "Eject!" three times. He ejected, but his ejection was not successful. Hanh ordered the flight to immediately dive back through the cloud layer. When I broke out below the cloud layer, I saw a MiG diving toward the ground and shouted, "Eject!" but did not see anything happen. It turned out Cuong had already ejected while he was still inside the clouds. The death of Dong Van De was a tremendous loss because he was an outstanding pilot.

The North Vietnamese were forced to withdraw to China for two months of retraining and development of new tactics. Operation *Bolo* had achieved its goal to eliminate or diminish the threat of MiGs to the strike formations, at least for the moment. The VPAF only engaged in combat on January 21, when a special flight of veteran MiG-17 pilots led by Ho Van Quy, with Phan Thanh Tai, Nguyen Van Bay (the elder), and Vo Van Man secretly moved down to Kep airfield to attack the F-105s outside the ground-based air defense umbrella. They intercepted 20 F-105s escorted by four F-4s. Spotting the MiGs, the Thunderchiefs jettisoned their bombs and the F-4s turned toward the enemy. In the confusion, Nguyen Van Bay shot down the F-105D flown by Captain W.R. Wyatt of the 421st Tactical Fighter Squadron. Wyatt ejected successfully and was picked up by a Jolly Green Giant.

The lull in the air war was only temporary. During March, the MiGs ventured forth as *Rolling Thunder* intensified with strikes against the newly approved targets. Now flying only in two-plane flights, the MiGs only patrolled their bases. A few MiG-21s did try single aircraft attacks against strike forces and MiG-17s continued to attack just as F-105s entered or recovered from a bomb run.

In March, F-105 pilots downed three MiG-17s, all of which were claimed by pilots of the 355th Tactical Fighter Wing, two to Captain

Max C. Brestel on March 10, and the third on March 26 to the 355th's wing commander, Colonel Robert R. Scott.

Brestel's victories were the first Air Force double kill of the war. Flying element lead as Kangaroo 03 in an Iron Hand flight, Brestel recalled his two victories:

We proceeded to the target via the Red River to a point north of the target, where we turned south. Numerous SAM and MiG warnings had been transmitted. Also, the 388th Wing, which had preceded us on the target, had encountered MiGs.

As the flight pulled up to gain altitude for delivering our ordnance, I sighted two MiG-21's making a pass at "Kangaroo 01," Lt. Colonel Philip C. Gast, from his 4 o'clock position. I was in his 8:30 o'clock position. I broke toward the MiGs and passed across his tail. They broke off the attack and I continued on my dive delivery. Flak was normal for the area. We delivered our ordnance as planned. As the flight pulled out at an altitude of approximately 3–4,000 feet, Gast called MiGs at two o'clock low. "Let's go get them," he called. "I'm with you," I replied.

Brestel spotted a flight of four MiG-17s in staggered trail heading north at an altitude of approximately 1,500 feet, followed by another flight of four:

I observed all the MiGs light their afterburners. Colonel Gast began firing at one of the first two. I observed the second two begin to fire at Colonel Gast. I called a break and closed to within 300–500 feet of the number four MiG. I fired an approximate two-second burst at him as he was in a right turn. I observed hits in the wing and fuselage. The MiG reversed into a left turn. I fired another two-second burst into him, observing hits in the left wing, fuselage and canopy, and a fire in the left wing root. The aircraft rolled over and hit the ground under my left wing. I then closed to 300 feet behind the number three MiG, which was firing at Colonel Gast. He was in a right turn and again I fired a two-second burst, observing hits in wing and fuselage. He also reversed to the left and I fired another two-second burst, observing more hits and pieces flying off. The aircraft appeared to flip back up over my canopy and disappeared behind me. We broke off the engagement at this time after approximately one or two minutes of combat.

A SAM was fired at us and more flak came up as we exited the area. I know I destroyed the first MiG, as I saw him crash. I did not see the pilot bail out and doubt if he was alive, since hits were observed in the cockpit and the canopy broke up. My wingman, First Lieutenant Robert L. Weskamp, also observed the MiG hit the ground. I feel I also destroyed the second MiG, as the range was the same and hits were observed in the same areas, i.e., fuselage, wings, etc. Also, his last maneuver could not be considered normal. The aircraft appeared to be in a violent pitch-up or tumble and out of control. However, because he pitched up and over and behind, I did not see him strike the ground.

Brestel was given credit for destroying both MiGs.

The VPAF's records state that this battle involved MiG-17s flown by the super-secret North Korean Air Force "Group Z" that had been sent to reinforce the VPAF, which used the newly developed "wheel" tactic for the first time to draw the enemy into low-altitude combat. This was based on the well-known "Lufberry" defensive circle. Flying at low altitude where they were close to the US aircraft in performance and more maneuverable, three to four MiGs would form the circle, turning in a continuous orbit to provide mutual support covering the tail of the airplane ahead. Each time an enemy fighter attempted to engage a MiG in the circle, another across the circle could tighten its turn and pull across onto the enemy's tail. F-4s and F-105s were at a disadvantage in this situation because of the MiG's tighter turn radius and the fact that they had bled off speed in order to engage.

The third MiG-17 was credited to 355th Tactical Fighter Wing commander Colonel Scott, leading a mission not far from Hoa Lac on March 26. The fight involved four MiG-17s from the 923rd Regiment led by Ngo Duc Mai with Vu Huy Luong, Phan Thanh Tai, and Truong Van Cung, operating from Noi Bai airfield. Colonel Scott reported:

I had acquired the target and executed a dive bomb run. During the recovery from the run, while heading approximately 250 degrees, altitude approximately 4,000 feet, I observed a MiG taking off from Hoa Lac airfield. I began a left turn to follow the MiG for possible engagement. At this time I observed three more MiG-17s orbiting the airfield at approximately 3,000 feet, in single ship trail with 3–5,000 feet spacing. The MiGs were silver with red stars.

I concentrated my attention on the nearest MiG and pressed the attack. As I closed on the MiG, it began a turn to the right. I followed it, turning inside, and began firing. I observed hits on the left wing and pieces tearing off. At this time the MiG began a hard left descending turn. I began an overshoot and pulled off high and to the right. The last time I saw the MiG it was extremely low, approximately 500 feet, and rolling nose down.

Scott's opponent was Lieutenant Vu Huy Luong, who was killed when his MiG-17 struck the ground after he failed to eject. The VPAF credits Luong with earlier shooting down the 8th Tactical Fighter Wing's 433rd Tactical Fighter Squadron F-4C flown by Lieutenant Colonel Frederick Austin Crow and GIB First Lieutenant Henry Pope Fowler, who were captured. The Air Force lists Crow and Fowler as having been shot down by a SAM.

While these battles raged, Wild Weasel pilot Captain Merlyn H. Dethlefsen of the 355th Tactical Fighter Wing's 354th Tactical Fighter Squadron flew his 78th mission as Lincoln 03 on an Iron Hand suppression mission with electronic warfare officer (EWO) Captain John Gilroy ahead of the strike at the Thai Nguyen steel mill. As the flight made a run on a SAM site, Lincoln 01, flown by Major David Everson and EWO Captain Dave Luna, took a direct hit by 85mm flak in the nose. Both ejected and were taken prisoner. Lincoln 02 was badly damaged and forced to withdraw. Dethlefsen evaded a MiG-21 by flying back into the heavy flak, where his F-105F was severely damaged. Though he could have declared an emergency and aborted, Dethlefsen determined that the Thunderchief could still fly. Accompanied by wingman Major Kenneth Bell's F-105D, he made several strike runs against the SAM complex, despite both taking further flak hits. Evading a second MiG-21 that shot up Bell's right wing as he made a final dive-bombing attack, Dethlefsen took more damage and strafed the site. Having destroyed two SAM sites, the two finally turned back for Takhli.

Captain Gilroy and Major Bell nominated Dethlefsen for a Medal of Honor, and President Johnson awarded it on February 1, 1968, the third for an airman in the Vietnam War.

To counter the new "wheel" tactic, pilots learned to coordinate their attack to break individual MiGs out of the orbit by maintaining high speed and staying in the vertical plane. Air Force and Navy pilots were warned not to enter a turning duel, but make only hit-and-run attacks. "The wheel" allowed the VPAF to use a small cadre of experienced pilots and large numbers of inexperienced pilots to maximum effect.

MiG-21 pilots now employed a climbing turn as a defensive tactic, using their maneuverability and climbing advantage. In a low-speed engagement, they often dived in a high-G turn in which the MiG-21 could turn much more tightly. Both MiG-17 and MiG-21 pilots would dive to avoid missiles, since the Sparrow would lose them in ground return while the Sidewinder lost the heat source due to the surrounding clutter.

April 19 saw a spectacular series of air battles between MiG-17s and F-105s. In a series of hard fights that afternoon, the 355th Tactical Fighter Wing's Thunderchiefs scored an amazing four victories. Three separate flights were involved in the area of the Xuan Mai army barracks.

The first kill was claimed by Kingfish 01, Major Leo K. Thorsness and Captain Harold E. Johnson, in a battle that clearly demonstrated that the F-105F encumbered by a second cockpit and gear of a Wild Weasel could still fight. Eight to ten MiG-17s attacked Kingfish Flight as they prepared to launch Shrike anti-radiation missiles against a SAM site.

Four of the 923rd Regiment's MiG-17s led by Nguyen Ba Dich intercepted the Weasel flight. Kingfish 03 and 04 engaged the MiGs while Thorsness and Kingfish 02 attacked the radar. Johnson recalled: "We found and delivered our ordnance on an occupied SAM site. As we pulled off the site heading west, 'Kingfish 03' called that he had an overheat light. He also headed west, and the crew, Majors Thomas M. Madison, pilot, and Thomas J. Sterling, EWO, had to eject." They had been shot down by Nguyen Ba Dich. "We headed toward them by following the UHF-DF steer we received from their electronic beepers and saw them in the chutes. As we circled the descending crew, we were on a south easterly heading when I spotted a MIG-17 heading east, low at our 9 o'clock position. I called him to the attention of Major Thorsness." This MiG-17 was from Nguyen Ba Dich's flight.

Thorsness remembered:

The MIG was heading east and was approximately 2,500 feet. We were heading southeast at 8,000 feet. I S-turned to get behind the MIG, which had progressed from the foothills over the delta southwest of Hanoi. The MIG turned to a northerly heading, maintaining approximately the same altitude and airspeed. Captain Johnson continued to give me SAM bearings, SAM-PRF status and launch indications as I continued to maneuver to attain a six o'clock position on the MIG. The first burst was fired from 2,000–1,500 feet in a right hand shallow pursuit curve. No impacts were observed on the MIG.

Within a few seconds we were in the six o'clock position with approximately 75 to 100 knots overtake speed. I fired another burst and pulled up to avoid both the debris and the MIG. While pulling up I rolled slightly to the right, then left. The MIG was approximately 100 feet low and to our left, rolling to the right. The two red stars were clearly discernible, and several rips were noted on the battered left wing. After turning approximately 130 degrees I again sighted the MIG, still in a right descending spiral. Just prior to the MIG's impacting the ground, Captain Johnson sighted a MIG-17 at our 6:30 position approximately 2,000 feet back. I pulled into a tighter left turn, selected afterburner, and lowered the nose. I again looked at the crippled MIG, saw it impact the ground in what appeared to be a rice field. I made a hard reversal and descended very near the ground, heading generally westerly into the foothills.

VPAF records did not support Thorsness' claim.

While Thorsness fought, Nitro Flight was attacked by 11 MiG-17s. Flight leader Major Jack W. Hunt, carrying two AIM-9s, missed the first MiG when he fired one AIM-9, then engaged a second MiG which he fired at but missed, and then became involved with a third MiG successfully. He later reported, "I observed numerous hits and flashes coming from the top of the fuselage just behind the canopy. My pipper at this firing position was just forward and a little high on his canopy. I observed no large pieces of materiel coming from his aircraft." The MiG then broke hard right and dived, trailing smoke. Hunt's gun camera failed to operate properly, but his victory was confirmed from other evidence.

While Hunt was engaged, element lead Major Frederick G. Tolman also encountered a MiG-17. He later reported:

I closed to gun firing range, at which time the MiG broke hard left. I fired at him and observed hits around his canopy section. The

MiG passed by my six o'clock position. I engaged afterburner and performed a high-climbing turn for re-engagement. I sighted the MiG again and saw a trail of white smoke from his tailpipe. He was climbing, about 40 degrees nose up, two miles away. I saw him roll slowly to the left and start a gentle descent.

Tolman's victory was confirmed by his gun camera film.

Low on fuel, Thorsness rendezvoused with a tanker, then returned to provide RESCAP for Madison and Sterling since both Kingfish 02 and 04 were damaged and forced to depart. Arriving back over the crash site, Thorsness broke through the cloud cover and found himself in a "Wagon Wheel" with five MiG-17s. He turned on one, later reporting:

I was able to track the MiG using 30 degrees of bank. I placed the pipper ahead and above the MiG and opened fire at 2000 feet. I allowed my pipper to slowly slide through the upper wing of the MiG. After two and a half seconds of firing the MiG evidently saw us, for he tightened his turn to the left. I observed large pieces coming off the aircraft. Shortly afterwards I saw two fuel tanks spraying fuel as they descended.

Thorsness' gun camera film had run out and the MiG was officially credited as a "probable," even though Major Tolman witnessed the engagement and also saw smoke streaming from the MiG.

At this time, a second flight of MiG-17s took off to replace Nguyen Ba Dich's flight. The pilots were experienced and had numerous victories between them. Captain Luu Huy Chao led, with Lieutenants Le Hai, Nguyen Van Bay, and Hoang Van Ky. Ten minutes later, a third flight took off to back up the second flight, led by Le Quang Trung with Nguyen Van Tho, Nguyen Xuan Dung, and Duong Trung Tan.

Le Quan Trung spotted two A-1E "Sandy" Skyraiders as they attempted to join Thorsness and maneuvered to attack. Nguyen Van Tho shot down Sandy 01, Major John Smith Hamilton; his burning Skyraider crashed before he could bail out. Hamilton's wingman, Sandy 02, was attacked by Duong Trung Tan and hit. He dived for low altitude and called for help. Duong Trung Tan attacked a second time and claimed a victory, though the Skyraider had evaded him.

Thorsness attempted to intervene, despite being out of ammo and flak-damaged, making two unsuccessful passes to try to distract the enemy. Approaching "Bingo" fuel he remained in the area and tried again to distract the enemy.

Panda Flight had encountered two separate MiGs over Xuan Mai army barracks in an encounter in which Captain William Eskew (Panda 01) and Captain Paul A. Seymour (Panda 02) each scored hits. They were short of fuel and rendezvoused with a tanker. As they were taking on fuel, Eskew heard Sandy 02's call for help. At first Red Crown refused their offer to help, since they did not have sufficient endurance without tanks. However, they were the only force available and were quickly ordered to fly back to the site, 200 miles away.

Eskew later reported:

As we were approaching the area of the downed aircrews, "Sandy 02" made a desperate call for help. He stated he had four MiG-17's making firing passes at him and they had just downed his leader, Sandy 01. I immediately headed for the area of Sandy 02. Spotting the four MiG-17s, I took my flight directly through them in an attempt to draw them off Sandy 02. I turned back in an attempt to engage the MiGs.

The lead MiG apparently decided to run for home. I pulled in behind him and fired my AIM-9B at him, which passed directly under him, but failed to detonate. At this time I broke off and observed Panda 03, Captain Howard L. Bodenhamer, firing at a MiG-17 while both were in a descending left turn. I saw him score numerous hits on the MiG. Also, there was a second MiG behind him, firing while he was firing. Panda 04 was behind this MiG, firing. I had a fourth MiG, with Panda 02 behind him.

The fight broke down into a Lufbery circle at approximately 3,000 feet. The order of the circle was MiG, Panda 03, MiG, Panda 04, MiG, Panda 01, MiG, Panda 02. Panda 02's fire caused the MiG behind me to break off. I then fired two short bursts at the MiG in front of me, which broke right and started a gentle climb toward the Hanoi area. I pulled in behind and opened fire at 800–1,000 feet. I continued firing to a range of 50 feet. I saw an estimated 50–75 hits on the upper fuselage directly behind the canopy.

The MiG started a slow, gentle roll to the left that could not have been an evasive maneuver as his rate of roll was quite slow. As I pulled up to avoid a collision, he exploded directly beneath me. I saw the red fireball and was shaken by the shock. At this time I broke back to help Panda 03, who was engaging two MiGs. Glancing back at the downed MiG, I saw the wreckage burning on the ground. As I passed behind the MiG firing at Panda 03, he broke into me. Captain Bodenhamer then turned and fired his AIM-9B. I did not see the missile impact. We then broke off the fight and proceeded to an emergency post-strike refueling.

Panda Flight was now desperately short of fuel, with Panda 04 down to 1,000 pounds, enough for only a few minutes' flight. Despite his own low fuel state, Thorsness, who had just hooked up, broke connection just before Panda 04 would flame out, allowing him to hook up. Climbing to 35,000 feet, Thorsness determined he could glide two miles for every 1,000-foot loss of altitude. Setting his throttle to idle, he headed for Udorn, 70 miles distant. The J75 cut out from fuel starvation as he set down on the runway.

For shooting down one MiG and a probable second, and attacking the enemy despite being out of ammunition, while attempting to coordinate the rescue of his element leader in the face of strong enemy ground and air opposition, Major Leo Thorsness was nominated for the Medal of Honor.

Despite the F-105 pilots' reports of seeing four MiGs that were claimed shot down either explode or impact the ground, the VPAF claims that none were lost from any cause on April 19 and that all eight MiGs that took off from Noi Bai returned safe. The US pilots may have engaged the secret North Korean "Group Z" which fought separately from VPAF units, and for which there are no records due to the secret nature of the unit.

On April 23, four F4C's of the 389th Tactical Fighter Squadron, flying as Chicago Flight, encountered two MiG-21s that had taken off from Kep to attack an EB-66 electronic countermeasures aircraft. In the event, the EB-66 and its escorts had been spotted northwest of Nghia Lo, but they turned away and the primary attack flight did not take off.

Pilots Nguyen Dang Kinh and Tran Thien Luon spotted Chicago Flight north of Viet Tri; the flight was assigned for attack and MiG suppression with other F-4s to support F-105s from the 388th Tactical Fighter Wing sent to bomb targets including the Thai Nguyen steel mill. The F-4s spotted the MiGs and turned to engage, dropping their fuel tanks and bombs. Ordered by ground control to break off, Nguyen Dang Kinh ordered Tran Thien Luon to go to afterburner and they climbed to around 35,000 feet over Thai Nguyen.

Chicago 03, Major Robert D. Anderson and Captain Fred D. Kjer, reported:

> Chicago Flight saw the MiGs turning into the strike force and jettisoned bombs and left outboard external wing tanks to engage. They were in a staggered trail formation and entered a left climbing turn to a general heading of west. Chicago was unable to turn tight enough to decrease angle-off and reversed to the right to rejoin the strike force.
>
> The flight immediately sighted two more in staggered trail passing off the right wing. (This was in fact the same pair, who had been ordered by ground control to break off their attack.) Chicago 01 turned right to set up an attack on the lead MiG. Chicago 01 fired a Sparrow that was tracking when both went into a cirrus cloud.
>
> Chicago 03 continued accelerating to attack the other MiG. A boresight radar lock-on was obtained and then a full system lock-on. The range was marginally close for a successful Sparrow shot. A climbing turn was initiated. The radar was still locked on. One missile was fired that struck the MiG in the right aft fuselage. A large explosion was observed and fire and fuel began streaming. It continued the left turn and bank increased until inverted and the plane went straight into the ground.

Nguyen Dang Kinh had descended to 32,000 feet and was turning when he felt his aircraft shake. He saw two F-4s flash past and realized he had been hit by a missile and damaged. Heading back toward Kep, he discovered he was on fire and ejected south of Huu Lung, landing safely. Anderson reported:

> No chute was observed prior to aircraft impact, approximately 16 miles northeast of Thai Nguyen. The one thing I learned is that you can't afford to be complacent up there. You have to keep looking around. He thought he was out of the fight, home free. He made no evasive maneuvers. I don't think he ever saw me or knew what hit him.

There were several engagements through late April and early May. A 366th Tactical Fighter Wing F-4 claimed another MiG on April 26 and 355th Wing F-105s claimed two MiGs on April 28 and a third on April 30.

The monsoon finally ended on April 27 and the weather improved considerably. US air activity shifted north with strikes against key targets. In response, the VPAF used the new tactics they had developed.

The 355th Wing's Spitfire Flight bagged the first of two MiG-17s shot down on April 28 during a strike on the Han Phong causeway, 12 miles west of Hanoi. Spitfire 01, Major Harry E. Higgins, pulled off his bomb run when nine MiG-17s attacked. Higgins later reported:

I observed a MiG-17 at my two o'clock and immediately turned into him and engaged in a series of turning maneuvers, finally gaining the six o'clock position. I completed my cockpit switch setting and when I was approximately 3,000 feet behind, fired my AIM-9. The MiG immediately tightened his turn to the right and the missile missed by 1,000 feet behind and below.

By this time my wingman, First Lieutenant Gordon Jenkins, had regained position and we continued our turn to the west to egress. Rolling out westerly, we immediately spotted two MiG-17's at one o'clock. They made a head-on pass, firing cannon. We also fired bursts at them without visible damage. We turned to pursue but they continued southeast and were well out of range as we fell into their six o'clock position.

Again we turned to egress heading, and I spotted a single MiG-17, heading south. I immediately turned into the enemy and engaged afterburner. I completed the switch settings for guns and began to close. The MiG tightened his turn, but was slow. This allowed me to gain a 30-degree cut-off angle and when I was approximately 1,500 feet behind, I opened fire. I saw the MiG began to smoke, and flames erupted from his left wing root. He began a steep descending turn with the left wing down. We were then chased by other MiGs until we finally outdistanced them. My last glance at the MiG showed him burning and spiraling toward the ground at less than 500 feet.

Lieutenant Colonel Arthur F. Dennis' Atlanta Flight encountered MiGs when the strike force departed the target area. He spotted a

MiG-17 on the tail of a Weasel flight F-105F and went to his assistance. He later recalled:

> I closed on the MiG-17, and when I obtained a missile tone in my headset, I fired the AIM-9. The missile did not guide. I continued closing until I was about 3-4,000 feet behind and opened fire, but I was still too far out. The MiG was in a shallow right turn and apparently did not see me because he did not attempt evasive action. I closed to 1,500 feet and opened fire again, closing to about 700 feet, and the MiG burst into a large ball of flame. It continued to burn and trail smoke as it went into a steeper turn to the right and nosed over into a wide spiral toward the ground.
>
> I continued to watch it spiral near the ground, but I had to move out of the target area because I was receiving SAM launch indications. When I rolled back to the left toward my egress route, the MiG impact with the ground should have been in my seven to eight o'clock position but I was unable to see it.

On the morning of April 30, the 355th's Captain Thomas C. Lesan, Rattler 01, downed a MiG-17 while leading the last flight of F-105s bombing railyards northeast of Bac Giang. Lesan recounted:

> Rattler flight was attacked by three MiG-17's while ingressing, prior to pop-up and again at the top of the pop-up prior to the bomb run. I continued my dive bomb run and jinked right after delivery at approximately 3,000 feet, then turned back left and started a shallow climb. At this moment I sighted two MiG-17's at my eleven o'clock position, approximately 3,000 feet above me and 3,000 feet out. I jettisoned my drop tanks and with afterburner engaged, took up pursuit of the two MiGs. I estimate that my overtake was in excess of 100 knots.
>
> As I started to track the number two MiG, they both started a rolling descending turn to the right and I followed. I tracked him and opened fire at 1,000 feet, noting hits impacting the left side of the forward fuselage and the left wing.

Lesan was forced to use the pitot boom to calculate lead, since his 4-G turn had toppled the gunsight pipper. "With such a great rate of closure, I had to break left to avoid collision. After clearing him and climbing to maintain an altitude advantage, I rolled right and observed the MiG slowly leveling out with his left wing in flames as his leader continued the right turn."

Major James H. Middleton, Jr., a mile behind Lesan, observed the flaming MiG spin out of control.

Lesan's victory didn't make up for the loss that the 355th sustained. Minutes before Lesan scored his victory, Wild Weasel Carbine Flight – three F-105Fs and an F-105D – with Medal of Honor nominee Major Leo Thorsness and Captain Harold Johnson flying as Carbine 03 were on their 93rd mission to do check-out for Carbine 01, Major Al Lenski, as Weasel lead. They were intercepted by two MiG-21s led by Captain Le Truong Huyen with wingman Lieutenant Nguyen Ngoc Do. MiG warnings were lost in the clutter of radio chatter and Carbine Flight were unaware of their danger until Huyen climbed behind Thorsness' F-105 and fired an Atoll that exploded in the Thunderchief's tailpipe. After his release from prison at the end of the war, Thorsness recalled "It felt like we'd been smacked by a giant sledgehammer." The cockpit quickly filled with smoke while the controls froze. Thorsness and Johnson ejected at 690 miles per hour.

The rest of Carbine Flight immediately began RESCAP until the Sandys could escort a helicopter in for pickup, but it was not to be. Nguyen Ngoc Do gained position on Carbine 04, First Lieutenant Bob Abbott, and blew off the F-105D's rear with his Atoll. Abbott ejected in the vicinity of Thorsness' and Johnson's loss. Tomahawk Flight joined the RESCAP and was attacked by another pair of MiG-21s. Tomahawk 04, Captain Joe Abbott, was hit by an Atoll fired by Lieutenant Nguyen Van Coc to become the Ace of Aces' first victory. Coc's wingman attacked Carbine 01 Al Lenski; the Atoll badly damaged his F-105F, though he was able to make an emergency landing at Ubon. The 388th lost their leading aircrew and two other experienced pilots while all the MiG-21s returned safely.

When the F-105s departed, Thorsness was still in contact on his emergency radio. The next morning, Colonel Jack Broughton led a sweep to search for Abbott, with the eight F-105s each armed with two Sidewinders and a full ammo load. The weather was bad and they were unable to establish contact with Abbott, who had been captured overnight, along with Thorsness and Johnson. Broughton ran across eight MiG-17s. In the ensuing fight, the VPAF pilots used tight turns to keep the Thunderchiefs from more than quick snapshots, staying close enough to neutralize their Sidewinders. In response, the Thunderchief pilots kept their speed up to avoid low-speed turning fights where the MiGs were superior. The fight ended inconclusively, though the mission restored morale at Takhli.

By the end of April, 225 F-105s had been lost in two years of combat. The Thunderchief had gone out of production in 1964. There was thought of re-starting production until it was discovered that Republic Aviation had gotten rid of the assembly jigs, which would take a year to replace. As a result, the missing numbers were made up by increasing the number of F-4 Phantoms in bombing missions.

10

BLOODY MAY AND JUNE

Throughout the spring, the *Rolling Thunder* strike forces had increased their efforts. In March, 1,781 targets were destroyed or damaged; in April it was 2,722; and in May, 4,325. The percentage of missions flown against targets in Route Pack VI rose from 8 percent in March to 15 percent in April, to 16 percent in May. This resulted from the increase in approved targets. Twenty targets in Route Pack VI were struck over five weeks from late April through May, in contrast to only 22 targets in Route Pack VI struck in all of 1966.

In a meeting with President Johnson on April 27, General Wheeler stated that *Rolling Thunder* was "reaching the point where we will have struck all worthwhile fixed targets except the ports. At this time we will have to address the requirement to deny to the Democratic Republic of Vietnam the use of the ports." Attacking Haiphong again raised the possibility of provoking the Soviet Union and China by an accidental bombing of their ships. Additionally, Pentagon analysts raised questions over the cost-effectiveness of strikes in Route Pack VI, since the loss rate in pilots and aircraft was five times that of attacks in southern North Vietnam.

Despite having approved almost all of the *Rolling Thunder* 55 and 56 targets submitted by the JCS, McNamara now renewed his campaign to de-escalate the bombing. Meeting with the president on May 9, he and Deputy Secretary of Defense Cyrus Vance cited General Wheeler's statement about all major targets except the ports having been hit as reason to de-escalate, stating that the United States should "finish off major targets and then cut back to the 20th parallel." The two also stated their belief that missions against movement on roads, railways, and waterways in Route Pack VI were not worth additional losses and there was no evidence that bombing targets in and around Hanoi and Haiphong was weakening the enemy's will. McNamara recommended that after a strike on the Hanoi thermal power plant, further bombing should be concentrated on the transportation system in southern North Vietnam supporting the flow of men and supplies to South Vietnam.

Seeking to cast this position as continued resolution to fight on, McNamara said the administration should reserve "the option and intention to strike as necessary to keep the enemy's investment in defense and repair crews high throughout the country." They concluded by emphasizing that the Soviets should be informed of the new policy in hopes that they would urge the North to seize this opportunity to de-escalate the war "by talks or otherwise."

The proposal was supported by an informal group of second-tier White House, Defense, and State Department officials who had been meeting with the president's blessing since November 1966, to consider the major problems in Vietnam. Nicknamed the "No Committee" and the "Non-Group," National Security Adviser Walt Rostow, Under Secretary of Defense Vance, Assistant Secretary of Defense for International Security Affairs John T. McNaughton, and Assistant Secretary of State for Far Eastern Affairs William Bundy met weekly in the office of Under Secretary of State Nicholas DeB. Katzenbach. Secretaries McNamara and Rusk and CIA Director Richard Helms occasionally attended. Significantly, no military leaders were invited.

On May 19, General Wheeler presented the JCS response to McNamara's proposal. He declared that ceasing attacks in Route Pack VI would be an "aerial Dien Bien Phu," stating further that they were convinced that there was a net military gain by bombing the Hanoi–Haiphong area. He recommended continuing strikes on fixed targets, including bridges, roads, rail lines, depots, supply dumps, and POL facilities, and advocated reducing the restricted zone around Hanoi from 30 miles to ten, and that at Haiphong from ten to four miles, allowing additional strikes of previously bombed targets without specific authorization and a major campaign against all airfields, including Phuc Yen and Gia Lam. He concluded by advocating mining Haiphong Harbor, stating that this would cut the North off from continued resupply.

In the end, the president settled on a compromise designed to "hold our family together in ways that look after the nation's interests and make military sense." On May 22, the day after the strikes were completed on the Hanoi power plant, he reduced the Hanoi restricted zone to a ten-mile circle around Hanoi, as requested by the Joint Chiefs, and ordered a shift in attacks to the southern part of the country, as requested by the Secretary of Defense. The Soviets were informed of the change, but there were no productive diplomatic results.

The foremost dissenter against these changes was Pacific Theater commander Admiral Sharp, who cabled General Wheeler on May 29, a week after the president's May 22 decision, stating his conviction that the intensified bombing since March was beginning to hurt the enemy. "If we want to get this war over with, we ought to keep the pressure on Hanoi and move in on Haiphong as JCS have recommended." He reported that missions in April and May had destroyed most of the major electric power resources for Hanoi, bringing several key war-supporting industries to a virtual standstill, and that increased attacks against transportation had disrupted assistance arriving by rail from China. He concluded, "It would be unfortunate to back off just when repeated attempts to secure authority for a systematic air campaign were showing results, the pressure was increasing because of this campaign, and the weather was optimum over North Vietnam." Wheeler replied that he agreed about the bombing effectiveness and said that foreign observers in Hanoi, who sent their reports to European superiors, confirmed this opinion.

The worst month for the VPAF during all of *Rolling Thunder* was May 1967. Following the return of the VPAF to full activity in April, US tactics were changed. Four F-105 flights were escorted by two F-4 flights, with the first Phantom flight between the second and third Thunderchief flights, while the second flight covered the rear. The Phantoms also carried bombs, which would be dropped on the target if enemy fighters were not encountered. This gave maximum flexibility in dealing with VPAF interceptors. Additionally, flights of Phantoms were stationed between the target and the nearest enemy airfield as a Barrier Combat Air Patrol (BARCAP) to block enemy fighters before they attacked the strike force.

The 366th Tactical Fighter Wing's F-4s began carrying the General Electric SUU-16/A gun pod. Crews had complained about the lack of an internal gun since the first F-4 missions; McDonnell was developing the F-4E which would carry an internally mounted M61, but it would not appear before October 1967, and was always in short supply for the rest of the war.

Power for the SUU-16/A was provided by a pop-out ram-air turbine which officially limited use to speeds below 350 knots. Carrying 1,200 rounds, the pod weighed 1,700 pounds, and was carried on the centerline pylon, though the F-4 could carry two more on the underwing pylons for strafing. The F-4D was wired to carry the SUU-23A, which was powered by gun gas.

The weapon was inaccurate mounted on the short centerline pylon due to pod vibration spreading the shell stream wider than would an internal gun. When firing at another airplane, the pilot also had to allow for the fact that it was mounted at a slight downward angle.

Korean War ace and author of the definitive book of aerial combat *No Guts, No Glory* Colonel Frederick C. "Boots" Blesse was 366th Wing operations boss. When the pods arrived, Blesse was enthusiastic for them. When the 366th began flying over the North in May, Blesse advocated arming the F-4s with the pod for escort missions. Unlike Blesse, Robin Olds' reaction to the gun was to tell General Momyer he wouldn't touch it with a ten-foot pole. Even 35 years later, he said:

The gun pod wasn't so much a speed penalty as an object of increased drag, and therefore increased fuel consumption. But that wasn't my objection. I refused to carry it for three basic reasons: one – it took the place of five or six 750-pound bombs. Two – only my older and more experienced fighter pilots had ever been trained in aerial gunnery, to say nothing of air-to-air fighting. There were perhaps a dozen of them in the 8th Tactical Fighter Wing. And, three – I had no intention of giving any of my young pilots the temptation to go charging off to engage MiG-17s with a gun. They would have been eaten alive. Instead, they fought the MiGs the way I taught them, and I might say they did so with notable success. They learned that there were times to fight and there were times to go home and come back the next day.

Olds' reservations were echoed by then-Captain, later Major General, Don Logeman, victor over a MiG in October 1967, who pointed out that drag caused by the 600-gallon centerline tank was less than that created by the gun pod: "The SUU-23/A was somewhat sleeker than the centerline 'tub,' but with the open-ended gun barrels and blast deflector on its front end, the pod was indeed cruel to the Phantom II's slipstream and its fuel consumption."

May saw increased enemy opposition because the rules of engagement were modified in April to allow attacks against the MiG airfields. The Navy strike against Kep on April 23 saw the destruction of nine MiGs. In May, US pilots claimed 26 MiGs in 35 engagements against a loss of two F-4Cs to MiG-17s. F-105 pilots claimed six victories.

On May 1 the 366th flew their first BARCAP to cover a RESCAP. Major Bob Dilger, with First Lieutenant Mack Thies, led the flight and spotted a flight of four MiGs approaching his twelve o'clock position. This flight was led by VPAF ace Captain Nguyen Van Bay (the elder), with wingman Lieutenant Le Sy Diep, and element leader Senior Lieutenant Vo Van Mau with wingman Lieutenant Nguyen Ba Dich.

The MiGs approached head-on, suddenly entering a vertical climb and turning away to the right, likely not having seen the F-4s. Dilger and his wingman set off after Vo Van Mau and Nguyen Ba Dich and soon had a boresight lock on Dich's MiG. He was alerted to Dilger's presence by the missile plume from the AIM-7 that Thies fired, evading it and an AIM-9B that Dilger fired by diving and turning hard. Dilger reported, "I yo-yoed and fired two more missiles from his six o'clock. On each attack he would violently break into the missile. On the fourth pass he broke hard right and struck the ground while trying to avoid the missile, which was tracking toward his six o'clock. He spread in flames across a large area."

The fight demonstrated that the MiG-17's maneuverability was limited flying at high speed and low altitude. It could roll uncontrollably above 400 knots, with the flying controls ineffective above 575 knots, and severe vibration and buffeting in turns exceeding 3.5Gs.

On May 12, four MiG-17s flown by Cao Thanh Tinh, Le Hai, Ngo Duc Mai, and Hoang Van Ky, all of whom had scored against the Americans, attacked F-105 flights escorted by a flight of F-4s led by "Boots" Blesse that were carrying SUU-16 gun pods for the first time. In a confusing fight in and out of the heavy clouds, Ngo Duc Mai set Colonel Norman Gaddis's F-4 on fire. Gaddis ejected and was captured, while backseater First Lieutenant James M. Jefferson ejected but was killed when his parachute failed to deploy. Four other MiG-17s and two MiG-21s attacked the force and claimed four more shot down for no VPAF losses. The losses were admitted, but US records claimed that, other than Gaddis, they were the result of AAA and SAMs.

The one US success came when Crossbow Flight of the 333rd Tactical Fighter Squadron encountered a flight of MiG-17s and the flight leader shot down one with a Sidewinder. This was again likely a flight of the secret North Korean fighter group, since the VPAF admitted no losses. On May 13, two F-4Cs and five F-105Ds claimed seven MiG-17s shot down. Two flights of 355th Tactical Fighter Wing F-105s flew air strikes against the Yen Vien railroad yard, with a flight of F4Cs from the 433rd Tactical Fighter Squadron for MiGCAP, while a third flight of F-105s from the 388th Tactical Fighter Wing struck the Vinh Yen army barracks. After bombing the railyard, the 355th's Chevrolet Flight leader Lieutenant Colonel Philip C. Gast spotted MiG-17s ten miles away at an altitude of 1,000 feet, climbing to the right. Chevrolet Flight turned left as the North Vietnamese commenced a head-on pass. Gast concentrated on the lead MiG while element leader Captain Charles W. Couch attacked the third MiG. Gast fired a Sidewinder that lost thrust and passed about 200 feet away from the target.

Gast later reported, "As they approached head-on, I began firing my Vulcan gun at 3,000 feet and fired down to minimum range. The MiG-17 did not return fire. I think we really caught them off guard." Wingman Major Alonzo L. Ferguson supported Gast's claim: "As I looked to the rear after the MiGs passed below, I noted a gray cloud of smoke, tinged with pink, receding in the distance."

Couch recalled:

> I lined up on their number three man and fired a long burst from my 20mm cannon. The MiG and I were closing head-on at this time, and at very close range he broke hard left and disappeared from my view. Another flight in trail with us observed a MiG pilot eject and another MiG in a spin. Major Ferguson saw pinkish smoke trailing from one MiG, presumably the one fired on by Colonel Gast. The MiG-17 I was firing at took violent evasive action to avoid a head-on collision with me, and very likely could have entered a spin.

The 355th's Random Flight, led by Major Robert G. Rilling, encountered MiGs in a high and low Lufbery circle after they struck the Yen Vien railroad. Rilling reported:

I called for afterburners and we closed on two of the MiGs, and when I was in range, I fired my AIM-9. The missile detonated just to the right and under the tail of the MiG, which caught fire immediately and pieces were observed falling off. I followed the MiG through a 180-degree left turn in an attempt to use the Vulcan cannon. After completing the turn, the MiG rolled hard right and down and impacted.

Element lead Major Carl D. Osborne lit his afterburner and rolled in behind the second enemy fighter. The MiG turned left, and he fired his AIM-9B from a range of 4,000 feet:

I rolled into a slight right bank and the tone on the AIM-9 peaked up normally. Only a ten-degree left bank was required to hold the gunsight reticle on the MiG. I fired and the missile began tracking and detonated at the MiG's three o'clock position. He immediately turned left and began trailing smoke. I made a hard left turn and observed the MiG I had fired at still trailing smoke and descending.

My turn caused a great loss of airspeed and allowed a third MiG-17 to turn inside me by the time I had completed 180 degrees. He was now at my nine o'clock position and opened fire. I didn't believe he was either in range or had any lead on me. However, my wingman was in a more vulnerable position, so I dropped the nose and unloaded the Gs and began accelerating to 550–600 knots. As I began to dive, I saw the MiG stop firing and the pilot broke right and away from my element. He would have been in a good position to make a pass on myself and Random 04, but I saw Captain Seymour, who had lagged in the left climbing turn and stayed low, in a good firing position on this MiG. He was firing, but I was unable to assess any damage except that my attacker broke off and stopped firing.

Seymour, who had become separated from Osborne, joined up with Rilling after opening fire on the MiG firing at Osborne. He was able to confirm both victories, the first Sidewinder kills by F-105s.

The "Wolfpack"'s Harpoon Flight, led by Major William L. Kirk and First Lieutenant Stephen A. Wayne, was leaving the target when he spotted two MiG-17s attacking an F-105. Kirk later reported, "I observed two MiG-17s firing at an F-105 which was in a hard left turn. The F-105 reversed underneath and dove for the deck. The MiGs started to reverse, then pulled up and started a left turn again." Kirk and wingman Charlie Woods immediately went after the MiGs while Harpoon 03 and 04 stayed high to provide cover. Kirk switched to "heat" and got a good tone. "I fired two Sidewinders. The first tracked well and exploded approximately 30 feet behind the MiG, which started a very tight left diving spiral turn. He was on fire from the trailing edge of his left wing to the tail section. I lost sight of the MiG in this spiral, as he went underneath my aircraft."

Backseater Steve Wayne reported:

The F-105 quickly accelerated away. An F-4 could easily out-run a MiG-17 at low altitude, but not as easily as an F-105 could. Our minimum airspeed rule when fighting a MiG-17 was 400 knots. This meant that a MiG-17 could not close on us to get a guns position. We were already in position to launch an AIM-9, and in fact had already radioed to the F-105 to get out of the way so that we could shoot.

Wayne recalled what happened after Kirk got the first MiG:

The MiGs were flying in close fighting wing formation. When his wingman burst into flames, it was probably the MiG leader's first clue that he had two F-4s on his tail. As the remaining MiG then dived for the undercast, I was able to get a full-systems lock-on and we launched two AIM-7Es at him well within parameters. The radar lock was maintained for the missile's time of flight, at which time the radar return disappeared and lock-on was broken. It is my opinion that the break-lock and disappearance of the radar blip were due to the AIM-7(s) impacting the MiG. However, it had gone into low cloud, and we did not attempt to follow in order to try and confirm the kill. Thus, we were credited with one confirmed and one probable kill.

As this was happening, Lieutenant Colonel Fred A. Haeffner and First Lieutenant Michael R. Bever in Harpoon 03 dove after two other MiGs chasing F-105s. When Haeffner attempted to fire two AIM-7s from an overhead position, he fired three. The first missed by 100 feet. Haeffner and Bever saw the second hit the MiG just behind the canopy and it disintegrated in the explosion. Major Ronald E. Catton, Harpoon 04, reported, "The MiG seemed to blow up on the spot. The second missile powdered the MiG and it broke up into many disorganized pieces."

The seventh MiG-17 of the day was destroyed by Major Maurice E. Seaver, Jr., leading the 388th Tactical Fighter Wing's Tamale Flight, last to hit the target. Pulling out from his bomb run, Seaver observed a camouflaged MiG-17 below at his ten o'clock position. It was the first enemy aircraft he had ever seen. Most MiG-17s were silver, so he waited until he saw the North Vietnamese insignia on the wing to make an attack. Realizing that the enemy pilot hadn't spotted him because he was focused on other F-105s, Seaver pulled in behind and opened fire with his 20mm cannon, but saw no hits; his gunsight was still set for bombing. The MiG reversed as Seaver tried to re-set the sight, and he had to turn hard to stay with it. He fired ahead of the MiG, guessing at the lead. It passed through his shells. The pilot was probably hit, because it made a sharp right turn just before there was an explosion. Seaver recorded the MiG's destruction with his gun camera. The entire event had lasted less than 90 seconds.

The official VPAF history claims that all pilots returned safely. There is no official record from the North Korean unit, which had become the 927th Fighter Regiment of the VPAF, though the Koreans still fought separately.

The next day, the 366th scored two of their three MiG kills with the SUU-16 pods. The wing provided two flights as MiGCAP for an F-105 strike force attacking the Ha Dong army barracks and supply depot, with Speedo Flight sandwiched between the four F-105 flights between the second and third, while Elgin Flight trailed the Thunderchiefs. Speedo Flight ran into 16 MiG-17s, destroying two with their guns while Elgin fought ten MiGs and scored one with a missile.

Following the SUU-16 successes, Blesse embarked on a publicity campaign, pointing out that the MiG killed by Bakke and Lambert, using an AIM-7E and an AIM-9B, cost the taxpayers $46,000, while the two gun kills used only 336 rounds of 20mm, a cost of only $1,680. With the 8th Tactical Fighter Wing garnering a lot of publicity with their name, "the Wolfpack," Blesse held a competition to find a new name for the 366th, later recalling:

> After a three-minute discussion, I told them that no one was going to leave the room until we had a new insignia and a new name. Finally, one of the guys blurted out, "I've got it! How about the Gunfighters of Da Nang?" Maj Ed Lipsey of the weapons section suggested using the McDonnell "spook" cartoon, originally featured in the F-4 maintenance manual.

Captain Terry Talley recalled, "Before our kills on May 14, the Gunfighters idea didn't exist. My squadron mate Captain Chuck Colton, who was pretty good at drawing things, sketched the figure of a 'Phantom' holding an underarm gun pod, and things took off from there." McDonnell donated 60 large decals of the new insignia for application to the wing's aircraft.

The enemy avoided combat until May 20. This time, Phantoms were responsible for all victories. In addition to Robin Olds' two MiG-17s, the "Wolfpack" scored two more while covering a strike on the Bac Le railyards. The "Gunfighters" scored two MiG-21s while covering a strike attacking the Kinh No repair yards.

The "Wolfpack" sent Tampa Flight led by Robin Olds and Ballot Flight led by Major Phil Combies. MiG-17s were sighted by both flights as they approached Kep. The eight F-4s were up against as many as 14 MiG-17s.

Robin Olds described how the fight began:

> F-105s were bombing along the northeast railroad. We were in our escort position, coming in from the Gulf of Tonkin. We just cleared the last of the low hills lying north of Haiphong, in an east–west direction, when about ten or twelve MiG-17s came in low from the left and, I believe, from the right. They tried to attack the F-105s before they got to the target. We engaged MiGs approximately 15 miles short of the target. The ensuing battle was an exact replica of the dogfights in World War II. Our flights of F-4s piled into the MiGs like a sledge hammer, and for about a minute and a half or two minutes that was the most confused, vicious dogfight I have ever been in. There were eight F-4Cs, 12 MiG-17s, and one odd flight of F-105s on their way out from the target, who flashed through the battle area.

Shortly after they crossed the coastline, the "Wolfpack" flights dropped their centerline tanks. Twenty miles east of Kep, two SAMs were launched; the Iron Hand flight attacked the radar trailer with Shrike missiles. The attack was successful, since the SAMs immediately stopped guiding. The F-105 force split in two to strike different targets at the railyards. Olds' Tampa Flight stayed with the first group while Combies' Ballot Flight went in with the other. Olds' flight made the first MiG sighting 15 miles short of the target. Minutes later, Combies' flight sighted more MiGs several miles away. While the Phantoms engaged them, the F-105s hit their assigned targets.

The first MiG fell to a Sidewinder from Major John R. Pardo and First Lieutenant Stephen A. Wayne, element lead in Olds' Tampa Flight. Pardo reported:

As our flight approached the area of the sighting, I observed four MiG-17s turning in behind the F-105s. Colonel Olds fired one missile and told me to "go get him."

I launched one Sparrow, which did not guide. I then launched one Sidewinder which struck the fourth MiG. I broke left to evade other MiGs at my eight o'clock. I continued a 360 turn while positioning on another MiG and observed an aircraft burning on the ground near where my Sidewinder hit the first MiG. The remainder of the missiles I fired did not guide or were not observed due to evasive action necessitated by the tactical situation. Simultaneously with this hit, my back-seater called, "Two MiGs shooting at us from eight o'clock high!" I called for our element to break left. We went into afterburner and started a climbing turn at 6–7Gs. We evaded the MiG attack, and started descending back into the "wheel." We dropped down to an altitude of just 100 feet to get below a MiG we had selected as he started a left climbing turn. There was so much ground clutter on the radarscope that we went full boresight, put the pipper on him and got a burn through on the radar for a full systems lock-on. As we were tracking him in his turn, we saw van Loan's F-4 going straight up with fire streaming out of its fuselage and exhausts, the flames extending some 50 to 100 feet. We pressed to within 200 feet of his jet.

Major Jack Lee van Loan and First Lieutenant Joseph "Hoss" Milligan were protecting Olds' tail when they were hit in the wing by a missile fired by 921st Regiment commander Nguyen Nhat Chieu, who led two MiG-21s that got into the air battle unobserved by the US pilots. Both van Loan and Milligan ejected and were soon captured. Pardo fired at the second MiG, then turned into the attack from the two MiG-21s Wayne had spotted: "After negating the first attack, I came out of afterburner and didn't use it again. I knew if this was the way the fight was going to progress, I could fly in military power and leave reheat for my wingman to handle the heavy maneuvering that was bound to follow each attack." In the meantime, the AIM-7 appeared to guide. "Because we were evading two attackers I did not see whether the missile hit the MiG or not. We descended into the wheel to push one of the MiGs up and out of the circle so we could get a shot."

This time a MiG-17 pulled up before Pardo could get below him:

He wasn't pulling many Gs, and we had no trouble getting behind him. We got a lock-on and were about to fire when he saw us and made a maximum-G turn to the left. As we started to go with him, I saw van Loan and Milligan floating down beneath their parachutes. The MiG's turn was too tight to follow without hitting our guys, so we broke off to the right and went past them at a distance of no more than 200 feet. After we were clear, we resumed our left turn and went back down to get another MiG.

After their first three passes, Pardo and Wayne made seven more attempting to get their second kill. On the fourth pass they fired an AIM-7 that went ballistic; the last Sparrow didn't launch. Pass number six was frustrated when Tampa 04 got in the way. Pardo remembered:

I fired a Sidewinder which went ballistic because my wingman flew across my nose, between me and the MiG I was tracking – he was so close it caused me to flinch. The missile had broken lock because his airplane blanked out the heat source. Luckily for him, he was so close the AIM-9 didn't have time to switch to him because he was also inside minimum range.

Pardo made two more unsuccessful Sidewinder passes. Steve Wayne reported, "Our other missiles were fired with too much overtake or were inside minimum range. Our confirmed kill came when the MiG was so low he had to pull up to clear a hill, which gave a perfect clear sky background for a successful AIM-9 launch."

After he had fired all his missiles, Pardo made two final dry passes:

The dry passes were just like the hot ones except we had our speed up to about 650 knots. As we got in close, we would move just to the right as we went by a MiG, passing as close as ten feet and rolling into a 90-degree bank as we went by. Steve would give the pilot the finger, and as soon as we had clearance I would pull across his nose with about 7Gs trying to create enough turbulence to throw him out of control. To our knowledge it didn't work. During our second dry pass Colonel Olds called bingo fuel, and as we started outbound my wingman joined up on us.

Robin Olds and 1st Lieutenant Stephen B. Croker scored the next two victories, which made the colonel the leading MiG-killer with four. Olds described the fight: "Quite frankly, there was not only danger from the guns of the MiGs, but the ever-present danger of a collision to contend with. We went round and round that day with the battles lasting 12 to 14 minutes, which is a long time." Olds got a nasty surprise from the new MiG-17 "wheel" tactic:

This particular day we found that they went into a defensive battle down low, about 500 to 1,000 feet. In the middle of this circle, there were two or three MiGs circling sort of in figure-eight patterns. They were in small groups of two, three, and sometimes four in a very wide circle. Each time we went in to engage one of these groups, a group on the opposite side of the circle would go full power, pull across the circle, and be in firing position on our tails almost before we could get into firing position with our missiles. This is very distressing, to say the least.

The first MiG I lined up was in a gentle left turn, range about 7,000 feet. Croker achieved a boresight lock-on, went full system, narrow gate, interlocks in. One of the two Sparrows fired in ripple guided true and exploded near the MiG.

Croker confirmed that the MiG erupted in flame and fell off to the left:

We attacked again and again, trying to break up that defensive wheel. Finally, once again, fuel considerations necessitated departure. As I left the area by myself, I saw that lone MiG still circling and so I ran out about ten miles and said that even if I ran out of fuel, he is going to know he was in a fight.

Olds dropped down to 50 feet as he turned back toward the MiG:

I got down on the deck and headed right for him. I don't think he saw me for quite a while. But when he did, he went mad, twisting, turning, dodging and trying to get away. I kept my speed down so I wouldn't overrun him and I stayed behind him. He headed up a narrow little valley to a low ridge of hills. I knew he was either going to hit that ridge up ahead or pop over the ridge to save himself. The minute he popped over I was going to get him with a Sidewinder.

Olds fired one AIM-9 which failed to track and the enemy pulled up over a ridge and turned left:

With that, he gave me a dead astern shot. I obtained a good growl. I fired from about 25 to 50 feet off the grass and he was clear of the ridge by only another 50 to 100 feet when the Sidewinder caught him on the right side of the aft fuselage. He spewed pieces and broke hard left and down from about 200 feet. I overshot and lost sight of him.

I was almost out of fuel and all out of missiles and pretty deep in enemy territory all by myself, so it was high time to leave. We learned quite a bit from this fight. We learned you don't pile into these fellows with eight airplanes all at once. You are only a detriment to yourself.

Pardo recalled, "When I got to the tanker I had 1,000 pounds of fuel left, as did my wingman. Colonel Olds had about 600 pounds – about six minutes' flying time – when he got there." Pardo remembered May 20, 1967 as the most exciting day of his life. "The thing that surprised me most was the absence of fear. I was finally doing what I had wanted to do, and had trained to do, for so many years, and I was doing it with Robin Olds. What more could a young fighter pilot ask for?"

Major Combies and First Lieutenant Daniel L. Lafferty scored the final "Wolfpack" MiG kill of the day, which gave Combies a score of two. Having engaged several MiGs without results, Combies saw one in hot pursuit of Olds, who was about a mile and a half away. When Olds broke hard left, the MiG overshot and headed toward Kep, eight miles distant. Combies got behind it and fired an AIM-9 with good tone: "The MiG was flying at approximately 1,500 feet. The missile impacted in the tailpipe and it caught on fire then went belly up into an uncontrollable dive and impacted into the ground."

According to the VPAF, Tampa and Ballot flights had engaged MiG-17s flown by the North Korean-manned 927th Regiment. All VPAF MiG-17s were grounded that day while the pilots underwent further training.

After he shot down van Loan and Milligan, 921st commander Chieu was directed to return to Noi Bai. As he did, he was joined by Vu Ngoc Dinh and Nghiem Dinh Hieu. Vu Ngoc Dinh spotted four F-4s closing on them.

The F-4s were from the 480th Squadron, which was on TDY from the 35th Tactical Fighter Wing. Squadron commander Lieutenant Colonel Robert F. Titus had scheduled himself to lead the flight, but was pulled by Blesse. Titus recalled:

"Boots" told me I could not lead the mission, which I had scheduled myself. I had just returned the night before from the Fighter Symposium at Nellis AFB. He informed me the wing had changed tactics during my one week absence, and therefore I could not lead. I woke up Bob Janca and told him to get ready to fly lead. He objected, claiming a hangover, whereupon I told him to report for duty or he wouldn't fly again. I wanted him on the mission as he was one of my best.

Thus, Titus was flying element lead as Elgin 03 with First Lieutenant Milan Zimer, while Major Robert D. Janca and First Lieutenant William E. Roberts, Jr., flew lead as Elgin 01.

As the strike force headed in to the target, Titus spotted the two MiG-21s flown by Vu Ngoc Dinh and Nghiem Dinh Hieu that were attacking the departing strike. They soon joined up with Nguyen Nhat Chieu while Elgin Flight immediately accelerated to attack them. Major Janca later reported:

I spotted a MiG-21 at my nine or ten o'clock high position. The MiG started turning left into us. I lowered the nose and began a left turn into the MiG, at which time he reversed to the right and started to climb. I continued in the left descending turn to close and then commenced a climbing turn. As the MiG continued to climb, I put the pipper on him, received a good tone, and fired an AIM-9 with the MiG about 4,000 feet ahead, zero angle-off, and framed against the blue sky. The missile guided straight with very little flutter and detonated about ten to fifteen feet to the right of the MiG's tail. It appeared that a large piece of the tail came off along with other small pieces. The MiG pitched up and began a roll off to the right from about 8,000 feet, and then appeared to enter a spin. I continued my turn, watching as he disappeared from my line of sight at approximately 1,000 feet AGL.

Vu Ngoc Dinh had seen the F-4s fire their missiles and shouted to Hieu to take immediate evasive action. As he turned left, Janca's first missile exploded off his right side. Making quick evasive maneuvers, Dinh pulled up into a climb, at which point he felt another explosion. When he attempted to level out, he found his aircraft was difficult to control as it dropped its left wing and began spiraling down. It had no engine thrust and no control since the hydraulic fluid was gone. He was pushed forward against his seatbelt and there was a lot of smoke in the cockpit. When he ejected, he lost consciousness for a few moments. Coming too, he discovered his parachute lines were tangled. Untangling them in a desperate move to deploy the parachute in time to save his life, he successfully landed in the village of Thanh Van.

While Janca was shooting down Vu Ngoc Dinh, Titus, who had initiated the attack, with wingman Captain Stuart Bowen in Elgin 04, pursued the remaining MiGs. Titus remembered, "I had to let the first one go when my wingman Stu Bowen called a break." The MiGs turned away, so Titus and Bowen turned back to rejoin the strike force. Titus spotted the MiG flown by Nghiem Dinh Hieu. Lieutenant Zimer reported:

> While en route to target and at the north end of Thud Ridge, the strike flight was attacked by several enemy aircraft. Colonel Titus and I engaged three MiGs, of which we shot down a MiG-21C with a Sparrow missile. We were moving in for the kill on the first MiG we engaged with a full system lock-on, when Elgin 04 called MiGs at six o'clock. Colonel Titus immediately broke off the attack. We then rejoined the strike flight. We observed another MiG-21C and engaged him.

Titus fired a Sparrow, but before he could observe the result, he had to break off because his wingman Bowen was so short of fuel that, had the tanker not broken its track and moved closer, Bowen and his backseater would have been forced to eject over Laos.

Janca confirmed Colonel Titus' victory, observing how "the AIM-7 missile impacted on the right side of the MiG-21. The MiG exploded in flame and a short time later I observed the pilot, who had ejected, floating down in his chute." Although his parachute had automatically deployed, Lieutenant Hieu died of his wounds before he could touch ground.

The 366th Wing confirmed themselves as "the Gunfighters of Da Nang" two days later on May 22 when Lieutenant Colonel Titus and First Lieutenant Zimer became the first Phantom crew to shoot down one MiG with a missile and another with their gun on the same mission. Titus' Wander Flight was MiGCAP for a strike force directed against the Ha Dong army barracks and supply depot. He later related:

I was carrying a SUU-16 gun pod when I got two more MiGs, the second with the gun. We were escorting the Thuds inbound to the target, headed for the heart of Hanoi, and I had a feeling that we would get some kind of reaction. The MiGs had been flying a lot that month and, of course, with the strike force headed for Hanoi it did seem to be a fruitful mission to get on, although I had just happened to chum up on the mission that day.

I was leading the first flight that time, and we were south of formation, line abreast of the first two flights at about 16,000 feet, headed west to east, when suddenly I spotted a couple of MiGs 11 miles out in front because of the sun reflecting off them. I called my backseater and told him to go boresight, and immediately called that I was Padlocked and accelerating. I went into afterburner. Because of numerous MiG calls in the area, I had already cleaned off my external tanks, so we were in a good fighting configuration.

These two MiG-21s were flown by Lieutenants Tran Ngoc Siu and Dang Ngoc Ngu. Titus had locked onto Siu's MiG:

The MiG that we locked onto started a left turn; I lost sight of him and followed on the radar. He made a hard climbing turn. I was unable to get lead on him. I could merely keep him on the right hand of the scope. He stopped his climb and we leveled off. He descended then climbed again. Finally I told my back-seater that I thought there was something wrong with the radar. He agreed and we joined the Thud formation.

We came alongside the formation and came out of burner. I looked over my left shoulder and a MiG was making a pass on the formation. He fired a missile. I called him and turned into him just about the time he fired the missile. Having fired the missile, he started to climb, possibly after he saw me coming at him. In that particular area there was a scattered overcast condition, a cirrus deck. It must have been around 20,000 feet. As I closed, he went through the cirrus at a very high climb angle. I was in close pursuit, had a very strong Sidewinder tone, and I fired the missile.

This was the MiG-21 flown by Lieutenant Tran Ngoc Siu:

The missile was tracking as he disappeared into the cloud. The missile went through the same hole. I deviated slightly to the right, came out on top of the cloud deck, and noted some debris in the air and smoke off to the left. I don't know what it was, but there was some foreign matter in the air, very discernible. I mentioned it to my backseater.

Above the clouds, the missile exploded near Siu's MiG and damaged it, but he was able to land back at Gia Lam.

Titus then saw Dang Ngoc Ngu's MiG-21:

I saw another MiG-21 about a mile away at my one o'clock. I turned toward him and put the pipper on him and got another Sidewinder tone and fired another missile. Almost immediately the MiG started a hard descending left turn and we went from, I would guess, 25,000 feet down to about 2,000 feet while he was doing all sorts of twisting, turning reversals, rolling, all sorts of hard maneuvers. It was very impressive to see the rapid roll response and directional change ability of that airplane. I proceeded into the dive with him. We could not obtain a radar lock-on, presumably because of the ground return. We were right in the vicinity of the Hoa Lac airfield. There was quite a bit of flak and SAMs were going off. The MiG made a very high 4-G pull-out and leveled at approximately 1,500 to 2,000 feet. He was wings-level so I got the pipper on him and fired a long burst of the SUU-16. I did not observe any impacts and thought I had missed him. However, he did slow down quite rapidly. I overshot, pulled up to the left, did a reversal, came back around and called for my number two to take him. About this time number two had overshot and came up to my right. I turned off watching the MiG and called for number three, and as I did so I observed the MiG was in a shallow, wing-rocking maneuver and continued on down in the shallow dive and impacted the ground. Where he was hit I don't know, but apparently he was out of it after the first hits were taken.

With these two kills, Titus was right behind Olds in the race to see who might be the first ace of the war.

Following nearly a month of intense air combat activity, the end of May saw the enemy keep their distance from US formations. On June 2, Colonel Olds scored a probable that might have become the victory that made him an ace in this war, had he not been flying a new F-4D armed with the nearly useless AIM-4 Falcon in place of the Sidewinder.

The first examples of the new F-4D arrived at Ubon in late May and were assigned to the 555th Tactical Fighter Squadron. The F-4D emphasized bombing capability, carrying the General Electrics AN/ASG-22 lead-computing optical sight set (LCOSS) which replaced the primitive sight in the F-4C. The F-4Ds were also wired for the new SUU-23/A gun pod. While it was designed to be a better tactical bomber, it ultimately became the most successful MiG-killer of the war, credited with 44 kills by 1972. However, at first it was deficient in air combat, due to the fact the AIM-9 Sidewinder was replaced with the Hughes AIM-4D Falcon, with the Sidewinder wiring removed to prevent its use. The Falcons were the primary air-to-air missile in ADC and were mounted in pairs on LAU-42 launchers equipped with piping for gaseous nitrogen cryogenics to cool the infrared seeker heads. On paper, the AIM-4D provided better detection capability than the AIM-9B. Air Force selection of the Falcon as its close-in, dogfighting missile was seen by many as the result of inter-service rivalry; the AIM-9 had been developed by the Navy, which had been using the improved AIM-9D since the summer of 1966.

The AIM-4D Falcon missile presented difficult technical problems from the outset. The major problem was the minimum 4.2 seconds needed to cool the infrared seeker head, which prevented the missile's capacity for as quick a lock-on and launch during a dogfight as the Sidewinder could achieve. This was exacerbated by the missile becoming inoperative when the coolant was used up, which happened where the pilot might have more than one opportunity to fire it. The Red Baron report stated that firing the AIM-4D was the most complex for any missile in the inventory.

Additionally, unlike the AIM-9, the Falcon lacked a proximity fuse. The small 7.5-pound warhead required a direct hit for success. The AIM-4 record with the 8th Tactical Fighter Wing was so disappointing that development of an improved version was dropped and the F-4Ds were rewired for the AIM-9B.

Robin Olds later recalled, "The word was the Air Force wanted an air-to-air missile they could call their own. The powers in Systems Command tired of kowtowing to the Navy in testing and improving the AIM-9. They wanted a missile of their own, and picked the existing AIM-4 as a solution. What a farce!"

Dick Pascoe, who had experience with the AIM-4 when he flew the F-102A, explained the difficulty of using it in combat over North Vietnam:

In the F-4D application, the pilot had to decide to fire the weapon 90 seconds prior to it actually leaving the aircraft, as he had to push a button to discharge the nitrogen and then fire the missile within a lapsed time of between two to three minutes after the nitrogen had been discharged! Not an easy task to complete in a 6-G turning fight.

June 2 saw the first use of AIM-4D-armed F-4Ds by the "Wolfpack." A MiGCAP flight of two F-4Cs with AIM-9Bs and two F-4Ds carrying AIM-4Ds led by Robin Olds engaged MiG-17s in a defensive "wheel" formation of eight fighters. The Phantoms fired two Falcons, four Sparrows, and three Sidewinders, with no hits. Olds, whose F-4D carried Falcons, was understandably upset that what might have been the victory that made him the first Vietnam ace was a "probable" due to the Falcon's deficiencies; he was upset that the rest of his pilots were forced to use this defective missile.

F-105s of the 388th's Hambone Flight became involved with two flights of MiG-17s during a June 3 attack on the Bac Giang Bridge.

Ngo Duc Mai led the first, with Phan Tan Duan and element leader Truong Van Cung and Ha Dinh Bon. Phan Van Tuc led the second with Le Van Phong, and element leader Hoang Van Ky and Bui Van Suu.

After evading F-4 escorts, the first flight spotted two F-105 flights and attacked from ahead as the Thunderchiefs accelerated for their getaway. Phan Tan Duan fired at the fourth F-105 of the second flight, but the lead flight, led by Hambone 01, Major John Rowan, made a 180-degree turn. Hambone 03, Captain Larry D. Wiggins, was unaware that Hambone 04 had barely avoided a collision with the second F-105 flight and had stayed with them. Wiggins got behind Phan Tan Duan just as Duan ignited his afterburner, firing a Sidewinder at a range of 2,500 feet. The AIM-9B was 400 feet behind when he spotted it; Duan turned left, increasing his bank, when the missile exploded beside his tailpipe. Dense white vapor streamed as Duan tried to dive away with Wiggins pursuing him. "I had my gunsight aimed up and I worked it right down through him." Although he saw no hits and soon overshot, Kuster and Rowan saw the MiG explode in a fireball and crash, killing Duan.

Leader Ngo Duc Mai descended to low altitude, followed by Truong Van Cung and Ha Dinh Bon, where they could outmaneuver the Thunderchiefs. Rowan, Wiggins, and Major Ralph D. Kuster, Jr., followed them but Rowan and Wiggins overshot. Their canopies fogged up from the warm most air. Kuster cleared his canopy by turning off his cockpit ventilation.

The three MiGs loosened their turns after the first orbit and took up a "V" formation as Kuster aimed at Ha Dinh Bon's MiG. Before he could fire, Mai closed on Rowan from eleven o'clock while Truong Van Cung crossed his 1:30 a half mile distant. Kuster reported them and to Rowan responded, "If you can get one, go get him!" Kuster went after Mai while Rowan attacked Truong Van Cung.

Kuster quickly fired a short burst at Mai's MiG, but did not have enough lead. He started a high-speed yo-yo to reduce his overshoot, as Mai reversed into a hard right turn that solved Kuster's tracking problem. The two jets were in a left turn, with Kuster slightly behind. Mai turned across again and Kuster fired a few bursts but got no hits.

When Mai banked into a steep dive, Kuster closed rapidly, but Mai reduced power to force him into an overshoot. Pulling maximum Gs just short of blackout, Kuster rolled and put the sight well in front of the MiG. When he opened fire, Mai flew through the cannon shells. The underside of Mai's wing exploded between the fuselage and the external fuel tank. The fire and debris engulfed the F-105, which passed 25 feet below Mai while melted aluminum from his MiG partially coated the windscreen and the MiG debris punched an inch-wide hole inside the F-105's left air intake duct. The MiG rolled inverted and crashed, killing Mai. Meanwhile, Kuster's J75 surged violently after ingesting flames and the F-105 rapidly decelerated. Wingman Wiggins stayed with him as he turned away to head for a tanker and the engine recovered full power 30 miles from the tanker.

On June 5, three MiGs were shot down in what turned out to be the final battle of this part of *Rolling Thunder*. The first was claimed by Major Durwood K. Priester and Captain John E. Pankhurst, leading a flight of four 480th Squadron F-4Cs. Priester observed MiG-17s below, led by Ho Van Quy with Le Van Phong, and element leader Hoang Van Ky with Ha Dinh Bon. Priester led the flight in a dive to the enemy's altitude:

The number three MiG pulled up vertically as I started my dive. I pulled up in trail with him as he executed a hard right turn. I fired a short burst but saw no evidence of anything hitting the MiG. I did not have a gun sight and relaxed stick pressure, assuming I had overled him. He started to reverse his turn and I fired another burst. Two large balls of flame exited the tailpipe, but the MiG failed to burn. I rolled over and observed the damaged MiG as it impacted the ground and exploded.

Pilot Hoang Van Ky died in the crash.

Robin Olds, leading Chicago Flight, was covering the F-105s' departure when he heard the radio chatter of Priester's engagement and reversed course to join the fight. Proceeding south along Thud Ridge, wingman Dick Pascoe saw Priester's flight engaging two two-plane elements of MiG-17s at nine o'clock and three o'clock. These were flown by Tran Huyen with Nguyen Dinh Phuc, and element leader Truong Van Cung with newcomer Nguyen Quang Sinh. Olds and Pascoe went after the MiGs at nine o'clock while the second element attacked the second pair at three o'clock. Chasing the first MiGs, Olds fired an AIM-4 that failed to guide, while the second didn't leave the launch-rail, despite both being fired in perfect parameters. He then fired all four Sparrows and none guided. Frustrated, he passed lead to Pascoe, who later recalled: "It had been decided to fly F-4Ds with AIM-4s in positions 1 and 3 with F-4Cs with AIM-9s in positions 2 and 4 in each flight to back up the Falcons with Sidewinders if the Falcons didn't perform."

Pascoe closed on Tran Huyen:

We picked up a single MiG-17 at approximately five nautical miles in front of us, and I fired two AIM-9's as he started a slight climb and observed the first impact at the extreme tail end and the second about three feet up the fuselage. The MiG continued in his left descending turn and struck the ground as the canopy was seen to leave the aircraft. The aircraft was totally destroyed.

Olds and First Lieutenant James L. Thibodeaux saw the pilot eject just before it crashed "with a large fireball," but Tran Huyen had been killed. Once again Olds was denied his fifth kill.

That afternoon, Drill Flight of the 555th Tactical Fighter Squadron was MiGCAP for an F-105 Iron Hand flight in the vicinity of Thud Ridge. MiG-17s jumped Drill 03 and 04 and the two F-4Ds became separated and departed the combat area. Major Everett T. Raspberry, Jr., flying Drill 01 with Captain Francis M. Gullick, attacked eight other MiGs in a Wagon Wheel maneuver with Drill 02. Raspberry later recalled: "Upon sighting the MiG-17s, I immediately engaged them to prevent them attacking an Iron Hand flight. After making several turns with them, I disengaged and flew southeast some 3–4 miles, then turned back into them." Closing a second time, he spotted a MiG at twelve o'clock high and fired an AIM-4, which failed to guide. Pulling away to gain separation, he came back in at low altitude. Closing on a MiG ahead, he fired a second AIM-4, which also missed. Continuing to chase the MiG, he fired another AIM-4, but it failed to leave the rails.

Determined to get a MiG, Raspberry came back in a third time, engaging the three surviving MiG-17s that Olds had engaged. "I was between 500 and 1,000 feet on a northwesterly heading. I could see three MiG-17s – slightly high at my twelve o'clock, and two more slightly low at my 11 o'clock." Gullick obtained a radar lock-on. "I fired an AIM-7 that headed straight for the oncoming MiG. I was unable to watch the impact because Colonel Olds called me to break right as a MiG was in my 4 o'clock and firing." Wingman Captain Douglas B. Cairns witnessed the AIM-7 hit the MiG and observed it strike the ground, killing Nguyen Quang Sinh. This was the first of 44 F-4D aerial victories and further proof of the Falcon's unsuitability for close-in air combat.

The Falcon's failure in this mission, in which six had been fired and all failed, compounded by an additional 15 fired in July and August of which only ten left their rails and no hits were achieved, eventually prompted changes. Captain Don Logeman recalled, "Colonel Olds had very little use for, or anything good to say, about the AIM-4, and his disdain was well known. Most of us lined up four-square behind him on that issue." In August 1967, shortly before the end of his tour, Olds ordered rewiring of the F-4Ds' inner pylons to allow them to use Sidewinders. Following his departure, Seventh Air Force ordered the wing to cease field modifications of F-4Ds. However, by December the AIM-4's ineffectiveness was so well proven that F-4Ds were rewired for the Sidewinder and the factory made a similar change on all new-production F-4s.

11

THE HOT SUMMER OF 1967

By mid-1967, US commanders believed that *Rolling Thunder*, which began as an attempt to convince the North Vietnamese to cease operations in South Vietnam and enter negotiations for a political resolution, was beginning to show results. The battles of spring and early summer resulted in the VPAF sustaining heavy losses that seriously undermined effectiveness. Following the engagements on June 5, the VPAF stood down while the spring engagements were examined and new tactics developed to counter the Americans. During late June and July, a few MiGs intercepted US formations outside Route Pack VI. While there were no losses to MiGs, the increased SAM and AAA sites took a heavy toll.

Following the increase of approved targets in early 1967 through the summer, F-105s took heavy losses. Six were lost in January; two in February; ten in March, including three on March 11 attacking the Thai Nguyen steel factory. April was the worst with 12 lost, including three in the April 30 Hanoi power station strike. May saw ten gone, including three in ten minutes over Hanoi on May 5. Five went down in June, and ten in July, three to AAA within four minutes on July 5 while bombing rail targets near Kep. Three of the nine losses in August happened on August 3, when AAA took one and the others collided while refueling from a KC-135A.

A major crisis erupted in June when the 355th Wing's Major Ted Tolman attacked AAA positions near the port of Cam Pha that opened fire on his flight. In the midst of his strafing run, Tolman hit the Soviet freighter *Turkestan*, resulting in high-level protests, including presentation of a 20mm shell that allegedly hit the ship by Soviet Premier Alexei Kosygin to President Johnson during the Glassboro Summit in July.

When he landed at Ubon, Tolman stated that he hadn't fired his cannon. Back at Takhli, he told Jack Broughton the truth. Broughton helped him destroy the gun camera film used by Seventh Air Force to monitor compliance with the rules of engagement. Following the president's humiliation at Glassboro, PACAF commander General John D. Ryan ordered courts-martial for Broughton for destroying the gun camera film and for Tolman and wingman Major Lonnie Ferguson for violating the rules of engagement. Tolman and Ferguson were acquitted while Broughton was convicted of destroying evidence. He was relieved of command and returned to Washington. When the conviction was overturned and expunged by the Air Force Board for the Correction of Military Records, citing "undue command influence" and censuring Ryan for a gross miscarriage of justice, the war's most successful F-105 combat leader had already resigned. As Broughton put it, "I had been shot down by our own people."

Karl Richter was lost on July 28, 1967. He had requested a second 100-mission tour and specialized in defense suppression, being awarded the Air Force Cross for an April 20 mission in which his flight destroyed AAA and SAM sites despite intense fire. Flying with a new pilot over Laos, he spotted a bridge. Instructing the new pilot to stay high and watch, he attacked the bridge; AAA erupted from the jungle-covered hills, setting him on fire. He got some distance away before ejecting, but his parachute disappeared into the cloud cover. A nearby Jolly Green Giant homed on his beeper signal. The parajumper (PJ) went down the line, finding him badly injured from swinging into the side of the nearby sandstone cliff. He was recovered but died en route to Ubon. His record of 198 officially credited missions was the highest of any during the war.

From the campaign's beginning, pilots had complained about their inability to obtain early warning of possible MiG attacks. Such warnings were limited to the "Bullseye" broadcast on the guard frequency by the RC-121s orbiting over the Gulf of Tonkin. These reports only warned that MiGs were airborne, without guidance regarding location and possible intent. The nonspecific warnings were frequent and loud, swamping transmissions between flights. The inability of the

RC-121s' radar to detect or follow MiGs at low altitude became more important that spring with the enemy's adoption of low-altitude tactics. The College Eye EC-121Ds were updated with the QRC-248 that allowed operators to interrogate the Soviet-supplied SRO-1 Barly-M IFF (identify friend or foe) transponders in the MiGs, providing information on a formation's location, heading, and speed, allowing them to give more specific warnings.

Beginning in July, the EC-121Ds were joined by an EC-121K Rivet Top carrying a modified QRC-248 that monitored radio conversations between pilots and ground controllers, giving highly detailed information about intentions. Unfortunately, US pilots received little information due to the need to preserve secrecy. Operators could not actively interrogate the transponders to prevent the QRC-248 capability being accidentally revealed; thus, they waited for the GCI controllers to do this, then intercept the response passively.

On August 23, the EC-121K operators knew the MiG operations but could not provide a timely warning. This resulted in what the "Wolfpack" called "Black Wednesday," in which they suffered their heaviest single-day losses of the war. Thus, the North Vietnamese had the decisive advantage of knowing the enemy's location and when to make a surprise attack. The MiGs' elusiveness and the difficulty of bringing them into a successful engagement was the primary problem the US forces confronted over the rest of the year.

Following the spring air battles, Seventh Air Force took the drop in enemy activity after June 5 as proof that they had finally established air supremacy over North Vietnam. The belief was so strong that Seventh Air Force commander General Momyer stated, "We have driven the MiGs out of the sky for all practical purposes," when he testified to the Senate Armed Services Committee's Preparedness Investigating Subcommittee on August 16. Like every other optimistic military report during the war, the inaccuracy was soon evident on the battlefield.

The US strikes on the power plants at Uong Bi and Hanoi, and the Thai Nguyen industrial complex, and continuing strikes against POL targets, were temporarily productive, but the enemy's repair capability, reinforced by Chinese and North Korean experts, meant the results were not lasting. Powerplants thought to be battered ruins quickly came back on line, as had happened in the 1952–53 campaign against the North Korean hydroelectric complex.

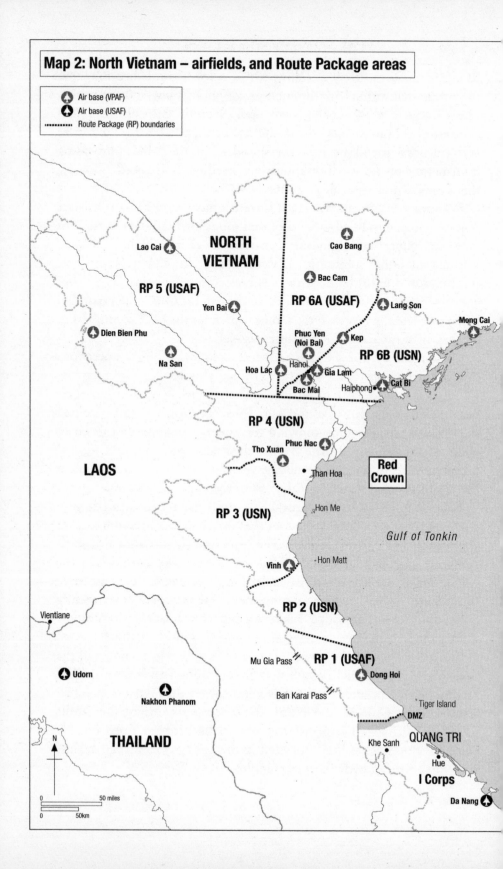

Map 2: North Vietnam – airfields, and Route Package areas

- ✈ Air base (VPAF)
- ✈ Air base (USAF)
- ·········· Route Package (RP) boundaries

NORTH VIETNAM

LAOS

THAILAND

Lao Cai

Cao Bang

Bac Cam

RP 5 (USAF)

RP 6A (USAF)

Yen Bai

Lang Son

Mong Cai

Dien Bien Phu

Phuc Yen (Noi Bai)

Kep

Na San

RP 6B (USN)

Hoa Lac

Hanoi

Gia Lam

Bac Mai

Haiphong

Cat Bi

RP 4 (USN)

Phuc Nac

Tho Xuan

Than Hoa

Red Crown

RP 3 (USN)

Hon Me

Gulf of Tonkin

Vinh

Hon Matt

Vientiane

RP 2 (USN)

Udorn

Mu Gia Pass

RP 1 (USAF)

Dong Hoi

Nakhon Phanom

Ban Karai Pass

Tiger Island

DMZ

N

QUANG TRI

Khe Sanh

Hue

I Corps

0   50 miles

0   50km

Da Nang

In the POL campaign, the North Vietnamese countered the bombing by changing from centralized storage to using many dispersed small storage facilities. Coupled with the US political decision to block strikes on Haiphong where the oil was offloaded from Soviet ships, the campaign had no effect on the North's ability to wage war and seemed to continue for lack of an alternative.

A 1968 report by the Central Intelligence Agency's Office of Economic Research, stated:

> During the early months of the *Rolling Thunder* program, the North Vietnamese were unable to repair bridges as fast as they were damaged. It took them several months to organize their labor force and pre-position materials near anticipated areas of attack.
>
> After two years of bombing, however, they had so organized their construction effort that they built and repaired bridges and other bypasses faster than the crossings could be interdicted... They stockpiled stone, bamboo, and timber near expected targets and assigned construction personnel to nearby semi-permanent work camps. As the campaign neared its end the North Vietnamese countermeasures had been perfected to a point that serious damage could be repaired in hours rather than days. The main reason for its ultimate success, however, was the strategy of building multiple bypasses for all important crossing points.
>
> The use of bypasses also made subsequent attacks more difficult. Thus, while an initial single raid might interdict an entire crossing, later raids to attack the repairs would require two or three raids to block the same crossing and increased the probability that at least one crossing at a site would always remain serviceable. The cost of bombing a water crossing increased much faster than the cost of repairing it. At the same time, attacking aircraft were subjected to the same risks when attacking bypasses as when attacking the original bridge.

CIA economists calculated that a dollar in damage cost US taxpayers $8.70 ($69.00 in 2021). This did not include aircraft losses. There was no way to compute economic loss/gain when comparing a North Vietnamese truck with a value of $5,000 against the $1.8 million cost of an F-105D, or the cost of training a pilot who was either killed or made prisoner, which was more than $750,000 in the early 1960s.

For the pilots, the only change they saw in the summer of 1967 was that the sortie rate intensified while the defenses were more formidable. Targets like Yen Bai became notorious hot spots. Jack Broughton recalled:

No place was worse than the 15-mile stretch of the northeast railway that ran between the Chinese buffer zone and the Hanoi forbidden circle. Each of the two F-105 wings was forced to send a morning flight into the area on a daily basis to reconnoiter this desolate stretch of track. The flights went every day, at the same time, same altitude, same airspeed and same heading. The enemy moved every available gun into position along that track. There was nothing there except a massive number of guns. By 1967 it averaged one gun every 18 feet.

The new VPAF strategy of "aerial guerilla warfare" was highly successful. A small formation made one pass in a usually successful attempt to provoke the bombers into jettisoning their loads before reaching their targets, breaking away before the escorts could respond. By September, nearly half of all US missions failed because the bombers jettisoned their ordnance due to the enemy activity. The small VPAF had an effect out of proportion to its numbers in protecting targets by preventing the bombing.

In July, the VPAF received 50 MiG-21F-13 fighters from the Soviet Union. This was the earliest model of the MiG-21; while it did not have an effective radar like the MiG-21PF that the VPAF was already using, it had an internally mounted 30mm cannon in addition to the two underwing Atoll missiles. It was also lighter than later models, and could dogfight if necessary. The gun was also useful for the new tactics, since a pilot could fire at more than one target as they passed through the enemy bombers. The lack of onboard radar was not a problem since the GCI system was able to place the fighters at an advantageous position to initiate attacks.

On July 1, President Johnson sent Secretary McNamara, General Wheeler, and Under Secretary of State Nicholas DeB. Katzenbach to Saigon to confer with the on-scene commanders. Most of the visit involved Westmoreland's request for additional troops, but briefings by Pacific commander Admiral Sharp, the Air Force's General Momyer, and Seventh Fleet commander Vice Admiral John Hyland regarding

Rolling Thunder were much more contentious. They advocated that the campaign be escalated, citing real military pain that had been inflicted on North Vietnam. McNamara was especially angered by Admiral Sharp's presentation. He wanted military support for his cutback proposals and so disliked Sharp that he went out of his way to pointedly ignore the admiral while congratulating Westmoreland on MACV's presentation.

The delegation met with the president on July 12. Also present were Secretary of State Rusk, Director of Central Intelligence Richard Helms, and General Taylor. Acknowledging that all favored expansion of *Rolling Thunder*, McNamara maintained that, even if expanded, it would have little effect on the war in South Vietnam. General Wheeler expressly disagreed with him and made a strong statement in favor of expanded bombing. The next day, the president approved the negotiated troop increase and said nothing about *Rolling Thunder*.

On July 20, Johnson approved *Rolling Thunder 57*, Air Force Secretary Brown's March position of "continuation of the present level of operations with certain targets added in the Hanoi–Haiphong area." Sixteen new targets were added in Route Pack VI and attacks were approved on selected rail lines, highways, and waterways inside the 30-mile Hanoi restricted zone but not within the ten-mile prohibited zone, the four-mile Haiphong prohibited zone, or the China buffer zone. Proposed attacks on the Paul Doumer Bridge and the Phuc Yen MiG base were specifically disapproved. While still overall another attempt by the president to "steer a middle course," the decision signaled the end of administration support for McNamara's position.

These disagreements between the administration and military leaders finally led in August to hearings by Senator John Stennis, Chairman of the Preparedness Investigating Subcommittee of the Senate Armed Services Committee. Admirals Sharp and Hyland and General Momyer were called as witnesses and all of the Joint Chiefs participated. Known as "the Stennis Committee Hearings," they were perhaps the most incendiary military hearings since the "Revolt of the Admirals" in 1949, when the Navy had challenged the effectiveness of the B-36 and the Air Force attempt to become the primary service through possession of the most effective delivery system, at the expense of naval aviation. McNamara, who privately believed he was waging a critical battle against "hawks" in both parties, was closely questioned. He presented the merits of bombing south of the 20th parallel as the primary focus, but his command of statistics did not have the success of earlier performances. Three years of inconclusive war had ruined his credibility, discredited his policies and destroyed his aura of infallibility. The hearings strengthened the position of the Joint Chiefs; afterwards, Chairman Wheeler attended the White House's Tuesday targeting luncheons as a regular. Johnson privately decided he needed a new Secretary of Defense and began looking to replace McNamara without looking as if he was changing policy. He rightly took the hearings as an attack on his Vietnam policy and reversed his July 20 decision against bombing the Hanoi thermal power plant and Paul Doumer Bridge, which had been cited by Admiral Sharp as crucial targets. The bridge was the only railway crossing over the Red River and was thus the main route for supplies brought into Hanoi from both the port of Haiphong and China.

The bridge had been built by the French colonial administration between 1899 and 1902, by the architects Daydé & Pillé of Paris, and was opened in 1903. With a length of 8,437 feet – over one and a half miles – and a width of 38 feet, the bridge was one of the largest in Asia. Hundreds of trucks and 26 trains crossed every day, carrying more than 6,000 tons of supplies; it was surrounded by AAA, from light 23mm and 37mm automatic weapons to 100mm heavy artillery, with several SAM sites and MiG bases nearby.

The 355th Tactical Fighter Wing received the attack order at 1000 hours on August 11 – to be executed that afternoon! Wing commander Colonel John C. "Big Kahuna" Giraudo was appointed deputy operations commander, Colonel Robert M. White as mission commander. As primary pilot for the X-15, White had set a new world air speed record of 2,275 miles per hour, following that up with flights at Mach 4 and later Mach 5 before setting the all-time winged aircraft speed record of 4,095 miles per hour – Mach 6 – on November 9, 1961. He was the first pilot of a winged aircraft designated an astronaut, for flying to an altitude of 314,750 feet (59 miles) on July 17, 1962.

The most experienced squadron commander, 333rd Tactical Fighter Squadron CO Lieutenant Colonel Bill Norris, was assigned as mission planner. Recalling the mission after the war, White said: "The intensity in the 355th rose to a higher level than I had seen since joining the wing." The risks were obvious, yet it seemed everyone wanted to go. Three squadron commanders not on the flight schedule volunteered as flight leaders. There were only a few hours to ready aircraft and plan the mission.

Previously mounted ordnance loads of M117 750-pound bombs and 450-gallon underwing tanks had to be removed so 3,000-pound M118 bombs could be carried in their place, while 600-gallon centerline tanks were attached and fueled. This normally took an hour per aircraft, but White recalled, "It was completed in about twenty minutes for each plane by waiving regulations against arming and refueling simultaneously. You'd have had to be there to understand how the support people and planners did what seemed impossible when the mission order came in."

The plan called for a strike force of five flights with the wing's most experienced pilots: a Wild Weasel flight for SAM suppression; two AAA-suppression flights; two additional flights of bomb-carrying F-105s from the 388th Tactical Fighter Wing, and two flights of bomb-carrying F-4s from the 8th Tactical Fighter Wing led by wing commander Robin Olds, as well as three MiGCAP flights.

Start-engines was 1350 hours; the strike force took off at 1418 hours and arrived at the target at 1558 hours. The skies over the route were clear. After tanking over Laos, the Wild Weasels, led by Lieutenant Colonel James McInerney and EWO Captain Fred Shannon, and the flak-suppression flights led the way as the formation headed toward Hanoi. As they approached the bridge, two flights of MiG-17s made ineffective head-on attacks.

AAA was intense. The Weasels took out two SAM sites immediately and hit four others during the attack. Moments later, Colonel White rolled into his bomb run. AAA filled the sky with the white streaks of several SAM launches as his four F-105s released their bombs at 8,000 feet. Eight more were dropped by the second flight, scoring the decisive hit when the central railroad span dropped into the river. More direct hits were scored by the F-4s and the two 388th Wing flights. 469th Tactical Fighter Squadron commander Lieutenant Colonel Harry Schurr reported, "You could see the 3000-pounders popping like big orange balls as they struck the bridge." The 94 tons of bombs destroyed two road spans as well as the one rail span.

Colonel White broke hard to the left, flying down the Red River as he led the force west, the F-105s flying low and fast across the plain to the hills 20 miles away and there were no losses on the way out. All aircraft returned safely from a mission that was a textbook demonstration of professionalism. A follow-up strike the next day planned and led by Lieutenant Colonel Norris was also successful. The Paul Doumer Bridge was closed for the next two months.

The bridge was repaired by early October, but bad weather prevented a third attack until October 25, when 21 355th Wing F-105s dropped two newly repaired spans with 63 tons of M118s for the loss of the 354th Tactical Fighter Squadron's Major Richard Smith, who ejected into captivity. A follow-up attack on December 14, with a final strike on December 18, left the bridge inoperable until November 1968. Several pontoon bridges were built to allow truck traffic. With the halt of all bombing of the North above the 20th parallel declared in April 1968, when President Johnson took his final step in attempting to end the war, a final strike would not be flown against the bridge until May 10, 1972.

Colonel White, Colonel Olds, 469th Squadron commander Lieutenant Colonel Harry Schurr, and Wild Weasel leader Colonel James McInerney, and his EWO, Captain Fred Shannon, were all awarded the Air Force Cross for the August 11 attack. The next morning, White trooped the line at Takhli with a large photo of the downed bridge "to show the people who worked so hard to ready the aircraft how their efforts paid off."

The new VPAF MiG tactics paid off with an interception of the "Wolfpack" on August 23, 1967 that saw the worst F-4 losses to date when the 555th Tactical Fighter Squadron lost four F-4Ds, while a fifth was lucky to escape with some minor damage.

The target was the Yen Vien railyards near Hanoi. The strike force was composed of five F-105 flights from the 388th Wing – three bomber flights, one combined flak-suppression and strike flight, and one Wild Weasel flight – and three F-4 strike flights from the "Wolfpack," which also provided one MiGCAP flight, led by Robin Olds. After tanking over Laos, the force headed down Thud Ridge to the target with the Weasels – two F-105Fs and two F-105Ds – in the lead. Approaching the target, the F-105s and F-4s split into separate formations. The single F-4 MiGCAP flight was positioned behind the F-105s.

Two MiG-21s flown by Captain Nguyen Nhat Chieu and Lieutenant Nguyen Van Coc took off to attack the formation between Thanh Son and Noi Bai airfield, while four MiG-17s from the secret North Korean unit took off to engage in the area from Yen Vien to Da Phuc. Shortly after the North Koreans took off, four VPAF MiG-17s flown by Cao Thanh Tinh, Le Van Phong, Nguyen Van Tho, and Le Hong Diep took off to reinforce the North Koreans. SAM batteries and AAA were ordered not to fire in order to give the fighters free rein.

The two MiG-21s flew west at 6,000 feet until they found the approaching formation above them. They zoom-climbed to 28,000 feet and executed a single pass against the F-4s. The MiGCAP failed to spot them. The two MiGs appeared out of the overcast at 25,000 feet and attacked Ford Flight from six o'clock. Nguyen Nhat Chieu fired first.

The crew of Ford 02 saw the white missile trail pass over their left wing before it impacted Ford 01, flown by Major Charles Tyler and Captain Ron Sittner, which "burst into a ball of flames" as Ford 03 later reported, victim of Chieu's Atoll. An instant later, Ford 04, flown by Captain Larry E. Carrigan and First Lieutenant Charles Lane, exploded when hit by Nguyen Van Coc's Atoll. He was so close that his MiG ingested pieces of the exploding Phantom, damaging the engine. Both crews ejected as the two MiG-21s chandelled back into the high overcast before the MiGCAP could respond. Tyler, Sittner, and Carrigan were captured while Lieutenant Lane was killed when his airplane exploded.

Hearing Nguyen Van Coc report that his airplane was damaged, flight leader Chieu turned back to cover him, but he was already diving back to Noi Bai. The Phantoms of Falcon Flight flew past Chieu without spotting him. He turned in and fired his other Atoll at Falcon 04, flown by Major Robert R. Sawhill and First Lieutenant Gerald L. Gerndt. It exploded and both ejected successfully to be captured. The other three jettisoned their bombs and turned back after Chieu, but he climbed through the overcast and lost them.

The North Koreans found the F-105s just as they commenced their attack and in a confused dogfight one F-4 aircrew fired two Sparrows at what they thought was a MiG but was quickly identified as another F-4. The pilot recalled, "I told the guy in the backseat to break lock. It was no problem." One of the Sparrows was tracking well and went ballistic when the lock-on was broken.

AAA caught another F-4 over the target and it turned away streaming fuel from a damaged tank. Unable to reach a tanker before running out of fuel, the two crewmen ejected over Laos. Their wingman was hit by AAA over the target and blew up with no survivors.

Coming off the target, First Lieutenant David B. Waldrop III, spotted two MiG-17s below:

As I rolled to the right, I looked down and saw two MIG-17s. One was on the tail of an F-105 at the time. I picked up one and broke in on him. I plugged in my afterburner, picked up a little airspeed, closed in, and started hosing off my cannon at him. Shortly afterwards, some fire shot out from his wingtips and about midway across the wing and he started a slow roll over to the right. I backed off and fired again. He continued rolling right on in and blew up when he hit the ground.

This MiG-17 was flown by Le Van Phong, who with his element leader Cao Thanh Tinh had shot down one F-105 and one F-4 before being shot down and killed by Waldrop.

Robin Olds witnessed Waldrop's victory. "It was beautiful. The MiG-17 was diving toward the ground with flames coming out of his tailpipe. It wasn't the afterburner; he was on fire. There was that great, great, huge Thud right behind him with fire coming out of his nose. It looked like a shark chasing a minnow."

Waldrop's flight leader, Major Billy R. Givens, engaged a MiG which was chasing another F-105 and damaged it. This was Phong's element leader, Cao Thanh Tinh, who managed to return to Noi Bai with his damaged fighter.

Waldrop and his wingman pursued two more MiG-17s, which were likely flown by North Koreans since the VPAF has no record of the engagement. Waldrop opened fire on the rear MiG at a range of 3,000 feet, getting hits before ceasing fire. The MiG disappeared into the clouds pursued by Waldrop. Reacquiring visual contact, he found his gun sight had failed. Opening fire from a range of 2,000 feet, he hosed 250 rounds that struck from the canopy to the tail. The MiG exploded and hit the ground. Waldrop was certain he had two victories. The 388th Wing's Enemy Aircraft Claims Board validated both, but the Seventh Air Force Enemy Aircraft Claims Evaluation Board confirmed the second and denied the first; the VPAF records validate both.

The new MiG tactics and victories were an unpleasant surprise for the "Wolfpack"; August 23, 1967 entered wing records as "Black Wednesday." The discovery that this had been anticipated after the

THE HOT SUMMER OF 1967

Seventh Air Force intelligence staff in Saigon had learned of the VPAF training from electronic eavesdropping of their radio transmissions made things worse. Robin Olds was still livid when interviewed about the mission several years later:

> The Intelligence people were constrained by their erudite peers in the nether regions of the Pentagon. It was feared that giving immediate intelligence to the fighting troops would jeopardize the fact that our people had some kind of clue as to what was happening. Of course both the North Vietnamese and the Russians knew we had information relating to the VPAF's impending change in tactics, but our crews in the frontline were not to be trusted with such intelligence. As a consequence, we were struck by a supersonic attack from our deep six just as we turned down Thud Ridge. We lost two F-4s there, and another over the target. Needless to say, I was furious when I found out that the spooks in Saigon knew that the North Vietnamese had practiced for over a week to get in position to do what they did – and they couldn't warn me.

In the aftermath of "Black Wednesday," Robin Olds and the rest of the "Wolfpack" leadership argued with Seventh Air Force over this policy of using the QRC-248 only passively. Finally, on October 6 a decision was made allowing the Rivet Top and College Eye EC-121 crews to actively interrogate the North Vietnamese system, and give strike force crews better information using secure communications that the North Vietnamese could not listen in on. The decision came just in time to save the air war by giving the pilots better real-time intelligence of the enemy's actions.

After August 23, the VPAF MiG-21 force refrained from engagements while they trained for an offensive against reconnaissance and electronic warfare aircraft. On August 31, two MiG-21s led by Nguyen Hong Nhi took off to intercept two RF-4C Phantoms flying a bomb damage assessment mission. After being routed to several locations by ground control, Nhi spotted the two reconnaissance jets. Each pilot pursued one jet after the Phantoms spotted them and split up. Just before the lead RF-4C made it into clouds over the mountains, Nhi fired an Atoll that hit in its engine area; it caught fire and crashed without survivors. Nhi followed this up on September 10, intercepting an RF-101C Voodoo which he shot down.

On September 16, the MiGs went after a pair of RF-101Cs. Senior Lieutenant Nguyen Ngoc Do and wingman Pham Thanh Ngan found them after they completed their photo runs. In order to maximize the chance of shooting down both, Nguyen Ngoc Do fired at the second while his wingman fired at the leader. Do's missile set the Voodoo on fire and Captain R.E. Patterson of the 432nd Tactical Reconnaissance Wing's 20th Tactical Reconnaissance Squadron successfully ejected. He was rescued by a combat search and rescue (CSAR) flight, marking his second successful rescue after being shot down on June 21. Pham Thanh Ngan shot down the lead RF-101, flown by Major Bobby Ray Bagley, who ejected 60 miles southwest of Yen Bai, and was captured. This was the first time the VPAF had shot down an entire US reconnaissance flight. By September 21, seven RF-101C and RF-4Cs had been shot down. After this, US reconnaissance aircraft only flew with fighter escort; the days of "alone, unarmed and unafraid" were over. All these successful interceptions were made by the older MiG-21F-13s that the VPAF had taken into their inventory over the summer.

12

ROLLING THUNDER'S ZENITH

The increase in MiG-21 hit-and-run attacks during the fall led to requests for permission to strike the MiG-21 base at Phuc Yen to go after the fighters there since they were so elusive in the air. Approval was suddenly given for an attack on October 23, along with approval for strikes on the Hanoi thermal power plant.

This was the result of increasing domestic antiwar political pressure; the antiwar movement had staged a massive national campaign against the draft, which found support from those whose son was subject to being called unwillingly to fight a war that had lost its purpose, to whom the president felt he must appear resolute. It was also rumored to result from a very frank conversation with Robin Olds, who had visited the White House on October 2 before becoming Commandant of Cadets at the Air Force Academy. Originally this was a "grab and grin" photo opportunity; however, Johnson invited Olds to lunch, where he was asked his real views on the war. Olds spoke in detail about the price paid by aircrews for the restrictions that kept the MiG bases off-limits. Johnson thanked him for his candor. Meeting his advisors on October 18, Johnson told them he was approving strikes against Phuc Yen.

By this time, the increased enemy defense capability was reflected in F-105 losses, which rose from five in September to a staggering 22 in October. More would come with 14 in November and three in December. By the end of 1967, total F-105 losses since April 1965 were 307, nearly 40 percent of the production total, with 80 percent of the losses over North Vietnam.

As with the Paul Doumer Bridge, approval to hit Phuc Yen gave little time for planning.

Phuc Yen was bombed by Air Force and Navy strikes on October 24 and 25. All bombs were reported on target; post-strike bomb damage assessment flights confirmed that the airfield was unserviceable, with four MiG-21s, four MiG-17s, and a MiG-15 destroyed or badly damaged. Major Bill Kirk, 8th Tactical Fighter Wing chief of tactics, and First Lieutenant Ted Bongartz shot down a MiG-17 that had just taken off, using an SUU-23 gun pod for the first time in an air engagement.

In its official history, *Historic Confrontations*, the VPAF says of the bombing of Phuc Yen and its result:

> Because of the ferocious American bombing attacks on Noi Bai, Phuc Yen, and other airfields, our MiG-21s were in trouble because they could not take off from their primary airbase. For this reason during the period from 23 to 30 October the Vietnamese Air Force's air combat missions were flown primarily by MiG-17s. However, none of the battles fought by our MiG-17s in late October 1967 were successful. Five MiGs were lost and no American aircraft were shot down.

The AIM-4 Falcon finally saw success on October 26. Captain John D. Logeman, Jr., and First Lieutenant Frederick E. McCoy II in Ford 01 led Ford Flight as escort for two RF-4Cs, Random 01 and 02, on a mission into the Red River Valley. Logeman spotted six MiG-17s, two camouflaged with the other four still unpainted, climbing through the clouds. The four silver MiGs were flown by Lieutenants Duong Trung Tan, Nguyen Hong Thai, Bui Van Suu, and Le Sy Diep. Ford 01 and 02 had Sidewinders, while Ford 03 and 04 carried Falcons.

Logeman told the RF-4Cs to leave the areas as the MiGs approached. Captain Bill Gordon and First Lieutenant James H. Monsees in Ford 03 and Captains Larry D. Cobb and Alan A. Lavoy in Ford 04 flew through the MiGs, then turned to re-engage. Logeman and wingman Major John A. Hall and First Lieutenant Albert Hamilton in Ford 02 closed on the enemy; Logeman ripple-fired two Sparrows, though only the second guided. Two MiGs forced Logeman to evade. Hall and Hamilton spotted one MiG beneath them spiraling down trailing sparks. Gordon and Monsees in Ford 03 spotted a white parachute drifting down. Logeman had hit Duong Trung Tan's MiG.

Observing another MiG about two miles distant, McCoy locked on it and fired a third Sparrow. It appeared to be tracking but Logeman had to break radar lock when they were fired on by another MiG-17. With "Bingo" fuel, he was forced to find a tanker.

Gordon and Monsees in Ford 03 closed head-on with a pair of MiGs. At a range of two and a half miles, Gordon attempted to ripple-fire two Sparrows, but only one launched. He then had to evade a gun attack from the oncoming MiGs.

Turning back into the fight, Gordon spotted a second parachute. This was Le Sy Diep, who had banked too tightly and put his MiG into a spin, forcing him to eject. Gordon made two more runs at the MiGs; on the second, he obtained position behind one MiG and selected a Falcon. Cooling it, he heard the tone and fired. By that time, the MiG had turned for a head-on gun pass; the Falcon had a lock-on at a range of 6,000 feet. Warned by Cobb of another MiG closing, he was forced to break off and the MiG had space to evade.

The MiGs were ordered to return to base, but Nguyen Hong Thai turned back to find Le Sy Diep. Cobb and Lavoy got behind him and Cobb prepared an AIM-4D for a self-track launch, pulled lead, fired optically, and watched the Falcon guide to Thai's tail, where it exploded. The MiG pitched 90 degrees right and Thai immediately ejected. Five months after the first had been fired in combat, the AIM-4 had scored a kill.

While Cobb demonstrated that, with luck, the AIM-4 could perform as advertised, his experience was singular. Don Logeman recalled:

I had the opportunity to engage MiGs on four other occasions. I experienced unsuccessful launches of the AIM-7E on three occasions and an AIM-4 on another. During the latter, I quite suddenly, and unexpectedly, found myself about a mile and a half behind a MiG-17. He came out of nowhere, turning in front of me and obviously didn't notice me at first. But by the time I had dealt with the various AIM-4 aiming, cooling, tracking and firing switchology and button pushing, the MiG saw me, performed the tightest 180-degree turn I ever saw, before or since, and passed the AIM-4 and me head-to-head!

The heavy VPAF losses resulted in the surviving fighters flying to southern China to avoid further US attacks. Only four MiG-21s and four MiG-17s remained in North Vietnam and were shuttled between Gia Lam and Kep to avoid being caught on the ground by other US strikes flown against every jet-capable airfield north of the 20th parallel except Gia Lam as US losses mounted. More targets were released from the restricted list in November. In the final two months of 1967, the battle between the two air forces reached the highest intensity of the war, despite increasingly poor weather after November 10. The period from the first Phuc Yen strike through November 8 marked the campaign's most productive period since it began.

On the afternoon of November 6, the 8th Tactical Fighter Wing provided MiGCAP for a strike on Kep. Captain Darrell D. "Dee" Simmonds and First Lieutenant George H. McKinney, Jr., led Sapphire Flight in an F-4D armed with an SUU-23. As the Iron Hand flight pulled up from its Shrike release, the first warning of "Blue Bandits" – MiG-21s – came from Rivet Top.

Simmonds called for the flight to drop tanks and turned to screen the strike. Red Crown reported that the MiGs had beaten a hasty retreat back to Phuc Yen. McKinney recalled, "The Thuds started checking in as they came off the target. Mixed in with their 'off target' calls were several calls of MiG sightings, and of MiGs shooting at Thuds." McKinney then spotted a MiG-17 shooting at a flight of F-105s below and warned Simmonds:

"Tally ho!" screamed Dee and the fight was on! He slammed the throttles to full burner and did a 135-degree slice down to a position a mile and a half behind the MiG at an altitude of about 1,000 feet. He was so smooth on the controls that we lost very little airspeed during the maneuver, and found ourselves overtaking said MiG at the proverbial "speed of heat."

Dee fired a very short burst from our gun just to ensure the MiG driver lost interest in the F-105. Boy, did he ever lose interest! I had heard all the briefings about how a MiG-17 could turn, but there is nothing like seeing it first hand. From my perch in the rear seat, it appeared that the MiG immediately went into a 90-degree left bank, stopped its nose on a single molecule of air and simply swapped ends!

Simmonds slammed the throttles to idle and soared into a near-vertical climb. As the airspeed decreased, he pulled around into a dive and re-engaged in full afterburner. McKinney remembered:

Quicker than one could say "You Gotta Be Shittin' Me," we were in a 60-degree dive with airspeed rapidly accelerating through 450 knots. I had kept the MiG in sight throughout. When we were about half-a-mile in trail the MiG began a hard, level left turn. Dee pulled lead and fired a three-second burst. At the instant of firing I lost sight of the MiG below the nose, but while we were gaining altitude I saw it in a 90-degree bank, just above the treetops and trailing heavy, gray smoke. At that instant the canopy flew off and I saw the ejection seat come out just as it collided with the trees. I screamed an egress heading and we were on our way out of North Vietnam with over 10,500 pounds of gas in our jet and an honest-to-God MiG kill under our belt.

The battle wasn't over:

Less than five minutes later we were half way to feet wet [over the Tonkin Gulf] when I turned to check six over my left shoulder. A silver flash, well below us, fought its way through to become a conscious realization that I had just seen *another* MiG! I informed Dee with the words, "Hey, there's another one!" When he quite naturally enquired "Where?" my response was, "Right down there!" After a two-second pause to regain a modicum of professionalism I added, "Nine o'clock, very low, going eight-thirty."

Simmonds pulled around and punched in afterburner:

We rolled out less than a mile behind at an altitude of just under 200 feet and an overtake speed in excess of 100 knots. In scant seconds, I could see a silver wingtip with a red star past either side of our front ejection seat, and even with my three whole minutes of air combat experience, I thought – aloud, as it turned out – that it was about time we took a shot, or did something!

The MiG went into a shallow left bank to avoid an upcoming hill. Simmonds pulled lead and fired, hitting the MiG's fuel tank and turning it into a massive fireball in the sky. The Phantom was so close, it flew through the explosion:

Fire on both sides of the canopy, two heavy thumps and we were out of the fireball and executing a climbing left turn. However, unexcelled exhilaration swiftly turned to serious concern, for both of us were convinced that our jet had just eaten about half of a MiG-17. The gauges remained steady, the jet flew fine and we were soon on our way to the coast, and safety. We headed to the tanker, then on to Ubon and a major celebration.

The double gun kill was so unusual that Simmonds and McKinney were flown to Saigon for a round of "meet the press." Simmonds was later awarded the Silver Star while McKinney received a Distinguished Flying Cross as a result of his third MiG gun kill on December 19.

During these fall missions, the 388th Wing saw their worst losses, with 29 F-105s shot down, including seven between November 18 and 20. Among the losses was wing commander Colonel Edward Burdett, shot down on November 18 in a ground-controlled radar-bombing mission during the second major strike on Phuc Yen.

Burdett led 16 F-105Ds from the 34th and 469th squadrons, controlled by Lima Site 85, a radar station atop an 8,500-foot tall mountain on the Laotian–Vietnamese border 100 miles from Hanoi with a clear radar view of the Red River Valley. The bombers were preceded by a four-plane Wild Weasel flight for SAM suppression. Unfortunately, the monsoonal weather kept the Weasels from spotting the SAM sites, while the clouds prevented the strike force pilots from seeing a launch in time to successfully evade. They were also vulnerable to attacks by MiGs.

Captain Pham Thanh Ngan and Lieutenant Nguyen Van Coc were vectored for a fast attack single pass against the F-105s. Ngan attacked the number four Weasel, flown by Major Oscar M. Dardeau and EWO Captain Edward W. Lehnhoff, firing a missile from 1,800 feet behind the F-105F, which caught fire, fell into a spin, and exploded on impact, killing both crewmen.

At the same time, Nguyen Van Coc pursued the F-105D flown by wing deputy commander Lieutenant Colonel William N. Reed. Closing to around 2,500 feet he fired an Atoll and the F-105 caught fire when hit. Reed attempted to fly his damaged aircraft to the Laotian border but was forced to eject 12 miles from the border and was rescued. US sources believed he was a victim of the intense AAA.

Colonel Burdett was lost when he was hit by a SAM that damaged his F-105. He tried to fly to the border, but the Thunderchief exploded 12 miles west of Hanoi, killing Burdett. The loss of the wing commander, deputy wing commander, and an experienced Weasel crew was a heavy blow.

The North Vietnamese had recognized the EB-66 and RC-121 electronic warfare aircraft that supported *Rolling Thunder* as primary threats from the beginning. The VPAF attempted to target them unsuccessfully. The RC-121s orbited over the Tonkin Gulf, with fighter escort, and could withdraw out of range before fighters could threaten them. The EB-66s only ventured across the Laos–Vietnam borders with strong fighter escort. The one time VPAF fighters had come close to intercepting one, the escorts had exacted heavy losses and the EB-66 had escaped to the relative safety of Laos.

On November 19, the VPAF finally scored. When an EB-66 formation was pinpointed on radar southwest of Hanoi, two MiG-21s, flown by Vu Ngoc Dinh and Nguyen Dang Kinh, flew at very low altitude to evade the RC-121D off the coast spotting them. They were vectored by GCI to the EB-66s, which were over western Thanh Hoa Province. As they closed, they were directed to climb to 30,000 feet. Spotted by the RC-121, the warning gave the EB-66s no chance to escape over Laos.

The MiGs dove on the DB-66s and their F-4 escorts head-on. Element leader Vu Ngoc Dinh realized he was approaching too fast; he was soon within minimum range and unable to open fire. Nguyen Dang Kinh approached from the rear and set up a shot as his speed carried him past the F-4s before they realized he was there. At a range of 7,000 feet, he fired his Atoll, which exploded on the EB-66's right side. Kinh fired his second Atoll from 3,500 feet. It hit the upper side of the wing and the EB-66 spun toward the jungle below. Both MiGs escaped and returned to Kep. After this, EB-66s no longer penetrated as deep into North Vietnam, resulting in less effective jamming of the North Vietnamese radars that controlled interceptors, SAMs, and AAA, and GCI radio communications to airborne fighters.

On November 20, Pham Thanh Ngan and Nguyen Van Coc flew three missions against US formations. On the first, they were guided toward what was thought to be another EB-66 with escorts, but turned out to be a pair of F-4s, both of which spotted the approaching MiG-21s and evaded them. Their second scramble never found the enemy in the poor weather, but the third time was the charm.

On the third scramble, Ngan and Coc intercepted four flights of F-105 bombers, escorted by two F-4 flights. Neither MiG was spotted, and they shot past the escorts and closed on the bombers. Ngan closed on an F-105, flown by Captain William Wallace Butler from the 388th Wing's 469th Squadron, which caught fire when hit; Butler ejected and was captured soon after he touched down. Turning away, Ngan suddenly found Butler's wingman in front of him and fired his second Atoll. As the F-4s closed in, he broke away and returned to Noi Bai safely.

Nguyen Van Coc fired an Atoll and saw it hit an F-105, but was also forced by the escorts to turn away and was unable to verify a victory. With two F-105s shot down, the rest jettisoned their bombs and turned back.

Bad weather through the rest of November and the first part of December reduced the number of US strike missions. On November 28, Pham Than Ngan and wingman Nguyen Van Coc intercepted a large formation of F-105s escorted by F-4s, but this time they were spotted before they could attack and were lucky to return to Noi Bai.

Nguyen Van Coc flew his first mission as element lead on December 12, with wingman Nguyen Van Ly. They intercepted 12 F-105s escorted by four F-4s. Coc closed on the fourth F-105 of the trailing flight and fired an Atoll; the F-105 exploded when hit. Accelerating in afterburner, he evaded the F-4s and disappeared in the cloudy skies.

At 1513 hours on December 17, US jamming signals were picked up from the Thud Ridge approach route. Vu Ngoc Dinh and Nguyen Dang Kinh took off while Nguyen Hong Nhi experienced a mechanical problem. Just past Doan Hung–Phu Tho, they spotted five flights of F-105s and an F-4 flight from the "Wolfpack" as MiGCAP. Dinh turned in to attack the first F-105 flight and fired an Atoll at number four from a range of 5,500 feet; hit, the F-105 fell away toward the jungle below. Dinh broke away and targeted a second flight that he misidentified as F-105s. He closed on number three, which caught fire when hit.

Dinh claimed it as a second F-105, but it was actually the F-4D flown by Major Kenneth Fleenor and First Lieutenant Terry L. Boyer, who became the 8th Wing's final loss of the year. The two MiGs disappeared above a cloud layer before the other escorts could catch them.

Nguyen Hong Nhi took off a few minutes after Dinh and Kinh, but couldn't catch up to them. Searching for them, he spotted two flights of F-105s below. He closed on the trailing bomber and fired an Atoll. The F-105 caught fire and the others immediately jettisoned their ordnance. As he pulled up, he spotted another formation and went into afterburner to catch them. Approaching from the rear, he fired his second Atoll but it failed to launch; spotting F-4s, he dived away. All three MiG-21s returned to Noi Bai airfield.

A third US formation included Marine Corps Captain Doyle Baker and First Lieutenant John D. Ryan, Jr., son of PACAF commander General John Ryan. Baker was on exchange duty with the 13th Tactical Fighter Squadron of the 432nd Tactical Reconnaissance Wing. He was flying an F-4D as element lead in Gambit Flight, which was trying out a new strategy in which the flight member who first spotted the enemy would take lead for the attack.

Four MiG-17s of the 923rd Regiment, flown by veterans Luu Huy Chao, Nguyen Hong Thai, Bui Van Suu, and Le Hai, took off from Kep. They soon spotted the F-105s escorted by Gambit Flight. Baker was first to spot the MiGs and he accelerated toward them, followed by his wingman, Gambit 04. Armed with an SUU-23 gun pod, when he came into gun range he opened fire on the MiG flown by ace Le Hai, making three gun passes before he ran out of ammunition, but failed to knock it down. Le Hai managed to dive away with only minor damage, accompanied by wingman Nguyen Hong Thai with Baker in pursuit. Le Hai accelerated away and Baker closed on Nguyen Hong Thai. He later recalled, "I ignited the afterburners and rolled, increasing speed to keep the MiG in sight. The forces of acceleration were so great that I could hardly see anything. Finally, at 500 feet and 600 knots I fired. The Falcon worked perfectly, going directly up the MiG-17's tailpipe and exploding." Baker had just scored the Falcon's second victory.

Despite Baker's victory, the December 17 strikes had all been defeated. Twenty MiG-17s and three MiG-21s had forced the bombers to jettison their bomb loads to avoid the attackers.

A strike mission on December 19 saw an F-105F from the 355th Wing's 357th Squadron, flown by Captain Philip M. Drew and EWO Major William H. Wheeler, and an F-105F from the 333rd Squadron flown by Major William Dalton and EWO Major James L. Graham, claim a MiG-17 between them, though the VPAF recorded no loss.

The final mission of 1967, flown on December 30, saw the MiGs unsuccessfully hunt for the attackers in the poor weather. Six MiG-21s and eight MiG-17s made multiple passes against two American formations. The F-105s in the first were forced to jettison ordnance when attacked by the MiGs, while the second managed to reach and bomb their target successfully.

The first formation was covered by Nash Flight. Lieutenant George H. McKinney was flying with Major Joseph D. Moore as Nash 01 in the same F-4 in which he and Simmonds had scored two MiG-21s in November. Moore spotted four MiG-17s and went after them. McKinney recalled:

This time the strike force was entering from northeast Laos. Our CAP flight and another F-4 formation were just joining up with the F-105s near the elbow in the Black River when the Thuds were jumped by a large number of MiG-17s. A giant "furball" ensued. All types of aircraft were going every which way, there were missiles in the air and bombs and tanks were being hastily jettisoned. In the midst of this "fog of war" Major Moore spotted a MiG-17 approximately three miles ahead at our twelve o'clock, and I obtained a radar lock-on. As we were closing to maximum Sparrow range, an F-105 with a MiG-17 in hot pursuit flew directly across our flightpath, about a mile in front of us. Immediately forsaking what appeared to be a sure kill, Joe Moore turned hard right to help the Thud with his MiG problem. They were in a descending right turn, passing through 6,000 feet. Major Moore arced the circle, performed a beautiful left barrel roll and obtained a moderate deflection gun shot at the MiG from about 1500 yards. I saw at least two "sparkles" from the MiG's aft fuselage, whereupon he seemed to relax all Gs and began to trail wispy, white smoke.

As Joe went into the vertical to avoid an overshoot, that little voice in my head said "Check six!" I did so and spotted a MiG-17 about two miles behind us. I mentioned our new playmate to Major Moore, whereupon he broke hard into the MiG, totally defeating its attack. Joe then unloaded the F-4 to zero-G and put a lot of distance between us and the threat by continuing downhill into the Black River Valley. By the time we separated and pitched back into the fight it was all over. Not a MiG to be seen anywhere! Lots of plumes of smoke from jettisoned ordnance, and no way to identify the grave of the MiG we had fired on.

We returned to Ubon, debriefed, wrote our narrative for the Claims Evaluation Board and went to the bar, not knowing how happy we ought to be. About 2130 hours that evening we received a call from Seventh Air Force saying that there were conflicting claims, and we and an F-105F driver would be awarded half a MiG each. That's how I became the only "half ace" of the Vietnam War.

The battle had indeed been confused. While Moore and McKinney were involved in their engagement, the second strike entered the area. The Iron Hand flight, composed of four F-105Fs from the 388th Wing, was led by Major Robert R. Huntley with EWO Captain Ralph W. Stearman. Spotting the MiGs that Moore and McKinney had first seen, Huntley turned into one that was attempting to gain position on another US aircraft and opened fire with his M61. Pieces flew off the enemy fighter and then he had to turn away when another MiG got in position on him. Huntley and Stearman put in a claim on return to Korat but it was downgraded to "damaged."

In the meantime, as Moore and McKinney zoomed away from the MiG they had attacked and then got involved in evading the second one, Huntley's wingman, Majors William M. Dalton and EWO James L. Graham, spotted the MiG Moore had hit and closed on it. Major Dalton later reported:

I saw a MiG pull up in a steep climb approximately five or six miles away at 12 o'clock and called it out. As we continued on course, several aircraft came into view – F-4s, F-105's, and four to six MiGs. At this time I saw a MiG-17 low and right, apparently going after Huntley. I called him and started turning to get behind him. I closed and fired but was not tracking him, so I let up on the trigger, repositioned the pipper ahead of the MiG, let him fly up to it, and tracked him. Again I opened fire. As verified by my gun camera film, I observed impacts on the left wing and left side of the fuselage under the cockpit, at which time the MiG broke up and left. I turned to follow him but he rolled and started down inverted off to my left. At this time my EWO, Major Graham, called another MiG at our seven o'clock coming down. I broke left into him and noted that two F-4's were in pursuit. The MiG rolled inverted and headed for the deck; the F-4s followed and fired a missile. I did not see the missile impact the MIG. At this time we contacted lead again but were unable to rejoin, and started to leave the area to rejoin aircraft three and four. During egress, I observed two impact points, which I assumed were downed MiGs.

While Graham was involved with his engagement, Iron Hand element leader Captain Philip M. Drew and EWO Major William H. Wheeler downed a MiG-17 for themselves. Drew later reported:

Major Wheeler warned me that there were two MiGs closing at our seven o'clock position. I turned hard into them, dived down into a valley, picked up my airspeed, and did a hard 180 degree turn back to the south. I picked up a MiG at my one o'clock high position going about the same direction that I was going. He appeared to be alone. I was low on him and I don't believe he ever saw me. As he started a gentle right turn, about 40 degrees of bank, I started my attack. I had no problem tracking him, so I continued my attack, firing 756 rounds of 20-mm, until I could see the end of the MiG's wing tips on each side of the canopy bow which put him about 100 feet away. Prior to breaking off my attack, I saw numerous 20-mm rounds impacting in his fuselage and his right wing root area. As I crossed over the top of him, I clearly saw the aircraft markings on the top of his left wing. Major Wheeler, my EWO, called that we had another MiG attacking us from our left and that he was shooting. I looked to my left and picked up the new attacker about 1,000 feet out at nine o'clock with his guns ablaze. I looked back at my target one last time and saw him rolling further right into a 120 degree bank turn and a 30 degree dive from about 7,000 feet altitude. Due to my position, I could not see beyond the tail of the MiG that I had fired on to observe the intensity of the smoke and fire. I was still close to him, though, since I could now clearly see the red star on his fuselage and the same insignia on the under side of his left wing as was on the top. I then pushed over, obtained two negative Gs, and continued rolling to the left until I reached 50 feet above the ground and lost my attacker.

I made a slow 360 degree turn back to the area, looking for more MiGs and to pick up my wingman, who joined up as I completed my turn. I looked back at my four o'clock position and saw black and gray smoke mushrooming up from where an aircraft had impacted the ground. This is a point that coincided exactly with the direction and altitude of flight from my MiG. By this time we were all well below Bingo fuel and there were no other aircraft, friendly or enemy, in the area.

1967 had seen the most air combat of the campaign. Unfortunately, the enemy made no move to enter into a negotiated settlement. Dissatisfied with what had been achieved, Secretary McNamara requested a further Air Staff study of available options. The report was submitted in November. In it, the staff argued strongly that increased US action was unlikely to provoke a Soviet or Chinese military response. McNamara presented plans for a four-month campaign in 1968 that lifted restrictions against mining Haiphong Harbor and bombing warehouses in the port area, as well as lifting restrictions for targets in Hanoi. This was turned down in late December. One planner said, "It was clear they desired no major change in military policy in Southeast Asia."

The belief on the part of the Washington leadership in a winnable war was based on the increasingly optimistic reports made by General Westmoreland, who announced during a visit to Washington in late November that there was "light at the end of the tunnel," and that he had "never been more encouraged in my four years in Vietnam." The CIA figures showed that US forces in South Vietnam had been able to increase "pacification" of most of the rural areas. New Ambassador to South Vietnam Ellsworth P. Bunker cited higher enemy casualties and their failure to win any major battles during 1967 and called for greater cooperation between US military units and what he called a "rejuvenated ARVN." There was confidence that 1968 would see the US prevail. In testimony to Congress shortly after New Year's, Secretary McNamara stated his belief that all "militarily significant targets" in North Vietnam had been struck and that what was left of the "agrarian economy" could not be collapsed by bombing.

13

THE END OF *ROLLING THUNDER*

With the upbeat and highly optimistic reports made by senior US commanders and diplomats regarding the war's future, the events of the first three months of 1968 would literally upend everything that had been said and drastically change US policy and the way the war was fought. General Westmoreland's promise that January 1968 would "mark a new phase in the conflict" was about to come true, just not in the way he had foreseen.

Rolling Thunder continued in early January 1968 as it had in the past three years, though the northeast monsoon severely restricted missions. According to Air Force historical records, "American airmen had to deal with the worst bombing weather over North Vietnam that they had encountered thus far in the war." The VPAF fighters that had fled to China in November returned to their North Vietnamese bases, and became more aggressive. The MiG-17s and MiG-21s operated in concert with each other, with the MiG-21s seeking to drive aircraft they attacked to lower altitudes where the MiG-17s could take them on under competitive terms with their American opponents.

The first encounter of the new year occurred on the morning of January 3 and saw a third claim of success using the AIM-4 and a second kill with a gun for the "Wolfpack." Bad weather prevented missions for several days, and the strike saw two separate forces launched in an effort to "catch up." Alpha Force was composed of four F-105 strike flights, two F-105 Iron Hand flights, and two F-4D "Wolfpack" MiGCAP flights, with their target the Dong Dau railroad bridge near Hanoi. Bravo Force was all-"Wolfpack," with three F-4D strike flights, one

F-4D flak-suppression flight, and two F-4D MiGCAP flights, tasked with bombing the Trung Quang railroad yard.

Alpha Force was spotted by two MiG-21s flown by Nguyen Dang Kinh and Bui Duc Nhu. Approaching the MiGCAP, they spotted the F-105s; element leader Nguyen Dang Kinh decided to engage them. Closing on the second F-105 in the third flight, he fired an Atoll that hit the F-105. As the formation came in range of SAMs and AAA, Kinh turned away and did not see the hit set the F-105 on fire. Other F-105s jettisoned their ordnance. Wingman Bui Duc Nhu closed on the second flight, firing an Atoll at close range that set the F-105 on fire. At that point, the formation broke into individual flights and turned back while the two MiGs landed back at Kep.

MiG-17s flown by Luu Huy Chao, Le Sy Diep, Bui Van Suu, and Le Hai spotted Bravo Force and attacked the Phantoms on withdrawal. Lieutenant Colonel Clayton K. Squier and First Lieutenant Michael D. Muldoon of the 435th Tactical Fighter Squadron led the strike in Olds 01. Pulling off their run, they encountered the MiGs. Squier later reported:

I engaged four MiG-17 aircraft in a head-on pass during egress from the strike target approximately six miles south of Bac Giang. The MiGs passed within 200–300 feet of my aircraft, going the opposite direction. I chandelled in afterburner to the left, cooling an AIM-4 missile for the re-engagement. After making a 360-degree turn, I visually acquired two MiG-17s three miles ahead in trail and in a gentle left turn. I selected the trailing aircraft, closed to positively identify the type of aircraft, and launched the AIM-4. The missile tracked directly to the aft section of the MiG-17, impacting in a ball of fire and smoke. The MiG immediately started a solid trail of gray-white smoke and continued in a gentle left turn with no maneuvering observed as I passed to the right rear and slid to the outside of the turn.

Another MiG-17 opened fire on Squier from 1,000 feet behind. Olds 02 was also fired on by a pair of MiGs but evaded the attack. The small Falcon warhead only damaged the MiG-17 flown by flight leader Luu Huy Chao, who returned to Gia Lam.

Meanwhile, the 433rd Tactical Fighter Squadron's Major Bernard J. Bogoslofski and Captain Richard L. Huskey, leading the MiGCAP in Tampa 01, spotted a MiG-17 firing on Olds 02 and went after it. Bogoslofski later reported, "The MiG-17 was tracking one F-4 in a tight left turn and gunfire was observed coming from the MiG. I was high and at five o'clock to the MiG and rolled in on him from 11,000 feet at an estimated 80 degree dive angle." Bogoslofski closed on the MiG, flown by Le Sy Diep, and opened fire with his SUU-23. "The MiG tightened his left turn and I performed a vertical pirouette left in order to continue tracking him, using high-G and high angle off. I fired another burst that hit the MiG's left wing and it disintegrated under my fire. I broke off and initiated a recovery." Major Albert S. Borchik, Jr., Tampa 04, and Major Ronald L. Markey, Tampa 03, saw Le Sy Diep eject and the MiG hit the ground.

The 921st Regiment had one operational MiG-21, after the other ran off the end of the runway, damaging the nose gear. Despite having only one airplane, Lieutenant Ha Van Chuc took off when an incoming strike was spotted on radar. Routed by GCI to an advantageous position, he spotted three F-105 flights escorted by an F-4 flight. He turned in behind and closed in on the number one F-105 of the first flight. He fired an Atoll from 3,000 feet which exploded in the tailpipe and set the bomber afire. Colonel James E. Bean, the 388th's deputy wing commander for combat operations, ejected as the others salvoed their bombs and was captured soon after he touched ground. Lieutenant Chuc zoomed to 30,000 feet before the escorts could catch him and returned safely. Two other F-105s were shot down by SAMs.

The next two days saw inconclusive engagements, then a week of bad weather, before January 14, when two MiG-21s flown by Ha Van Chuc and Nguyen Van Thuan intercepted an F-105 strike. Chuc led Thuan in a dive past the escorts. Closing on the F-105s, his Atoll didn't leave the rail. He found success a second time and the Atoll hit Major Stanley H. Horne of 469th Squadron. The F-105D caught fire, going down near Yan Bay. Horne was killed in the crash. Horne's wingman fired at Chuc as he flashed past. Though not shot down, Chuc died of wounds after returning to Noi Bai. The other F-105s salvoed ordnance and turned back.

That afternoon, MiG-21 pilots Nguyen Dang Kinh and Dong Van Song attacked two unescorted EB-66s. Kinh fired an Atoll that did launch. Closing to 2,000 feet, he tried again and the missile exploded near the EB-66, damaging it. Song fired on the second EB-66 and hit the right engine. He saw the EB-66 erupt in a ball of flames.

All seven crewmen of the EB-66 ejected successfully. A rescue mission the next day saw one Jolly Green Giant helicopter shot down with two damaged. Two days later, Jolly Green 71 rescued the shot-down helicopter crew and EB-66 pilot Major Merce, First Lieutenant Thompson, and First Lieutenant Pedroli; the other four had been captured. Merce died of his wounds after transfer to Clark AFB. Following this loss, EB-66s were ordered not to enter enemy airspace, which lessened their jamming and electronic warfare support to strike missions.

On January 18, the weather cleared. Three large strike forces were launched against targets in North Vietnam. The results demonstrated the determination of the VPAF defenders.

Alpha Force – one F-105 Iron Hand flight, one F-4D flak-suppression flight, one F-4D strike flight, and two F-4Ds flying MiGCAP – was sent against the Bac Giang thermal power plant. They met opposition from SAMs, AAA, and MiG-17s. The strike leader and wingman were lost, but not before the leader destroyed a MiG-17.

Bravo Force – four F-105 strike flights, one F-105 Iron Hand flight, and one F-4D MiGCAP flight – went for the Ha Gia railroad siding, but coordinated attacks by two MiG-17s and two MiG-21s forced the F-105s to jettison ordnance and turn back.

Only the Charlie Force, composed of four F-105 strike flights, one F-105 Iron Hand flight, and two F-4D MiGCAP flights, was able to successfully hit the Dap Cau railroad bypass.

On February 3, Pham Thanh Ngan and Nguyen Van Coc were vectored to what was believed were two EB-66s near the Laotian border, but they found two F-102A Delta Daggers that were used as tanker escorts. Ngan closed on the second F-102; his Atoll flew up the exhaust and exploded, killing First Lieutenant Wallace L. Wiggins of the 509th Squadron. The lead F-102A managed to evade the missile fired by Nguyen Van Coc and escaped in the cloudy sky.

The last Falcon victory was scored on February 5. A small force of one F-105D flight, one Iron Hand flight, and two F-4D MiGCAP flights from the 13th Tactical Fighter Squadron were intercepted near the Thai Nguyen works. A MiG-21 shot down one F-105, while his wingman was destroyed by Captain Robert G. Hill and First Lieutenant Bruce V. Huneke in Gambit 03.

The strike was warned by the College Eye EC-121 that two "Blue Bandits" were airborne. Flown by Lieutenants Nguyen Ngoc Do and Hoang Bieu, the MiGs were spotted by Hill. The flight leader ordered him to take lead and he went after Nguyen Ngoc Do. Hill momentarily lost sight of Do, who shot down Captain Carl W. Lasiter; he successfully ejected and was captured. Hill then spotted Hoang Bieu as he climbed toward the force. He reported:

> I sighted a MiG-21 at my ten o'clock position, low, as he was breaking off from an attack on an F-105. I immediately attacked and positioned myself in his six o'clock. The initial engagement was with the SUU-23 and 100 rounds were expended with no visible effects. I then cooled an AIM-4D. It never got a high tone. But I fired it, thinking it might track, but the missile did not appear to guide. I fired a second AIM-4D that worked exactly as advertised, and was observed to detonate on the MiG's aft section.

The small Falcon warhead damaged but didn't kill the MiG:

> I then selected radar. The first AIM-7E was fired in boresight and did not guide. The second was fired with full lock-on and appeared to guide. The third did not fire. The MiG exploded in a large red fireball, blowing off the tail section. It fell straight down and impacted. No parachute was observed.

The Falcon's poor record of five kills out of 48 attempts did not justify its being continued by the F-4. It was withdrawn and F-4Ds were re-wired for AIM-9s.

The next day, four MiGCAP F-4Ds of Buick Flight escorting an F-105 strike were leaving the target when two MiG-21s made a pass from the high rear quarter. The flight broke up; Buick 01, 02, and 03 fired Sparrows at the trailing MiG and all missed. Buick 04, Captain Robert H. Boles and First Lieutenant Robert B. Battista, acquired one MiG. Element lead Captain Joel S. Aronoff in Buick 03 cleared Boles to fire. Boles recalled:

> When Captain Aronoff cleared me to fire, I was line abreast, 1,500–2,000 feet out from his plane. I attempted to fire two AIM-7's. The first missile did not come off the rail. The second fired as advertised

and guided toward the MiG. I watched the missile guide and just prior to impact the MiG either initiated a left turn or rocked his wings to the left in order to look back at our flight. The missile detonated at the left aft wing root section, and he exploded. I then exclaimed over the radio that I got the MiG and asked Captain Aronoff to confirm it. He acknowledged the MiG's destruction. At that time the flight leader called for the egress.

Action continued on February 12. Buick Flight of the 435th squadron – one of two "Wolfpack" MiGCAP flights that escorted an F-105 strike against Kep airfield – was diverted from the attack on Kep to their alternate target, the Cao Nung railroad yard. After escorting the F-105s out of the area, the two MiGCAP flights returned to sweep the target and Buick Flight picked up two MiGs on radar. Buick 01, flight leader Lieutenant Colonel Alfred E. Lang and First Lieutenant Randy P. Moss, got a bogey on radar. Guided by Moss, Lang closed to six miles and identified a MiG-21. He reported:

I identified the bogey as a MiG-21 and fired two AIM-7E's at four miles with a full system lock-on. The first missile exploded in the MiG's seven o'clock position and the second in its ten o'clock position. He rolled inverted, then entered a tumbling spin. The pilot did not eject and the aircraft continued in an uncontrollable spin. I then sighted the other MiG, which had been approximately three miles in front of the destroyed MiG. We acquired lock-on from dead astern and closed to ten miles, but had to break off the attack because Buick 04 was at bingo fuel. We recovered at our home base.

Colonel Robert V. Spencer and First Lieutenant Richard Cahill in Buick 03 accelerated past Buick 01 and fired two Sparrows at the lead MiG. Spencer later reported that both seemed to explode close enough to cause the enemy fighter to spin out of control. Captain Alexander D. Kelly and First Lieutenant Allan R. Sweeny in Buick 02 confirmed the shoot-down. Seventh Air Force later confirmed Lang's and Moss' kill but denied Spencer and Cahill's.

The last *Rolling Thunder* mission that engaged enemy fighters occurred on February 14. Two "Wolfpack" flights, a "Fast CAP" led by deputy operations commander David O. Williams, and a "slow CAP" led by 555th Squadron commander Lieutenant Colonel

Wesley D. "Red" Kimball, with flight and element leaders in both packing SUU-23s, covered two flights of Iron Hand F-105s and one F-4D strike flight striking Phuc Yen airfield.

On approach, the strike force received accurate Rivet Top warnings of two MiG-21s approaching. Colonel Williams later reported:

> They were well above us, and since they were pulling contrails, we acquired them quickly and I turned my flight to intercept them. They must have been under tight ground radar control because when we began closing on them, they made a hasty 180-degree turn to the north in the direction of the sacrosanct buffer zone abutting the Chinese border with North Vietnam. Perhaps they were attempting to sucker us away from a trap they were hoping to spring against our strike flight because at about that time we received warning calls from radar surveillance aircraft that "Red Bandits" [i.e., MiG-17s] were airborne in the vicinity of Thud Ridge. This put them athwart the strike force's route. Hearing that, I turned my flight back to join the strike force, and shortly thereafter heard a "Tally ho" from "Red" Kimball's Nash Flight.

After avoiding Williams' flight, the MiG-21s attacked the trailing Iron Hand flight. Following a brief engagement, one element of the second Iron Hand flight returned to Korat while the other headed on to the target area.

Kimball's Nash Flight sighted four MiG-17s, flown by veterans Luu Huy Chao, Nguyen Chiem, Bui Van Suu, and Le Hai. They entered a left-hand Wagon Wheel at 8,000 feet over the flats northeast of Phuc Yen. Kimball and Nash 02, Major Ray M. Burgess, flew through the wheel as Kimball attempted to get a MiG with an AIM-4. Since it didn't get a high tone, he didn't fire. Nash 03, Major Rex D. Howerton and First Lieutenant Ted L. Voigt II, spotted the MiG flown by Nguyen Chiem trying to fall in behind Kimball and Burgess. Howerton recalled:

> Observing this, I began my attack and rolled in approximately 2,500 feet behind the MiG and fired an AIM-4D. It appeared to guide, but thinking that I might be inside minimum parameters I selected guns and began firing the SUU-23 cannon. Hits were seen

on the MiG and shortly thereafter it exploded and began to break up. The missile was not seen to impact or destruct. The MiG went down in flames with one wing and the tail section separated.

Luu Huy Chao, pursued by Kimball and Burgess, looked back just in time to see Chiem's MiG explode.

Kimball and Burgess made another pass at Chao's MiG, firing 350 rounds from his SUU-23 from a range of 2,000 feet, but saw no hits. Very low on fuel at this point, his flight left the area.

Williams spotted Kimball's flight engaged with the MiGs:

Almost at the same time, my GIB, First Lieutenant Jim Feighny, called that we had four Red Bandits at two o'clock low. I quickly spotted them and noted that they were in the Wagon Wheel defensive maneuver. I plugged in both afterburners to go max power, pulled up into a steep climbing right turn, rolled inverted so as to keep my eyes on the MiGs and then did a split-s and dived down, rolling out to a position astern and slightly below a silver-gray MiG-17 in a lazy, right-hand orbit. I don't think he ever saw me.

Approaching the MiG at about 1.2 Mach, I asked Feighny if his radar was locked on to the target. He replied that he was locked onto a target, but wasn't sure if it was the target I was looking at, so he asked me to put the pipper on my target, selected gyro-out mode and re-locked. I fired one AIM-7E in full-systems lock-on, interlocks in and in-range light on from about three to four nautical miles, almost minimum range for the missile to arm properly. The Sparrow tracked perfectly and appeared to approach the port side of the MiG's fuselage when the proximity fuse detonated the missile's warhead with a huge orange fireball, severing the MiG's empennage. The forward fuselage and wing section began snapping violently end-over-end, falling forward and downward.

Passing to the port side of the fireball and debris, I commenced a steep, high-speed yo-yo to clear my tail, and when I looked to the rear I observed a parachute with orange and white panels billowing above the MiG pilot. I was amazed that he had escaped the violent break-up of his aircraft and the fireball.

When I topped out of my climb, I rolled out in a right turn to attempt to acquire the other MiGs. As I did, Feighny called out another bandit at about one o'clock, slightly high, about two nautical miles distant. He quickly locked onto the MiG-17, which was in a slight turn to starboard, and I fired one AIM-7E well within range of the target. The missile was tracking the MiG well, as I kept the steering circle on the target, when Feighny called out rather emphatically that we had a Bandit approaching us fast from four o'clock low.

I diverted my attention to look back at this new threat, and sure enough one of the MiG-17s had tried to zoom up to our perch. He was well in gun range of us, but apparently couldn't pull enough lead to hit us. He was stalling out, and had to perform a wing-over to keep from departing controlled flight. Unfortunately, while my attention was diverted from attacking the second target MiG, I had let the steering circle drift slightly aft of the target while the Sparrow was tracking. Consequently, the missile detonated just aft of the MiG's tailpipe without damaging him perceptibly. I was so upset that I wanted to keep on pursuing the MiGs – both the one I had missed and the one that had tried to attack us from below. But at that moment my wingman called and said he was at "no shit bingo" fuel state, which was understandable since we had been running in afterburner for about five minutes or so. As a leader, it was my responsibility to give paramount importance to the safety of my wingman, so we reformed the flight and began our egress from the area of hostilities.

The VPAF listed Nguyen Chiem as shot down. Flight leader Chao had seen him eject when his MiG was hit and exploded. Given that Kimball's and Williams' flights were both engaged with the same flight of MiG-17s, it is possible that, in the confusion of battle, Williams actually hit Chiem's MiG with the Sparrow an instant before or after Howerton claimed to shoot him down with his gun. The accounts of Chao, Howerton, and Williams all sound as if they are speaking of the same event, glimpsed by each mere instants apart.

Although Navy pilots scored victories on May 23 and July 19, this was the last *Rolling Thunder* engagement involving Air Force fighters. During January and February 1968, the VPAF emerged a much stronger and better-organized force, accounting for 17 percent of Air Force aircraft lost during that period. Between August 1967 and the end of February 1968, the USAF lost 22 aircraft to MiG-21s and MiG-17s, claiming 20 MiGs, a 1.1-to-1 ratio in favor of the Vietnamese. Six F-4s were lost against four MiG-21s. The "Wolfpack" shot down three of the MiG-21s for loss of two F-4Ds, a victory ratio of only 1.5-to-1.

The MiG-21PF and MiG-21PFM dominated F-105s by 16-to-1. The MiG-21PF was equipped with an internal 30mm cannon that was used with great effect since the gunfire on a supersonic pass through an F-105 formation was sure to result in the bombers salvoing their ordnance. Only one of 16 F-105s was shot down by gunfire.

The MiG-17 was not as successful, scoring no victories between May and December 1967, while losing 20.

While 18 percent of F-4s hit by AAA and 59 percent hit by SAMs were total losses, 88 percent hit by MiGs were lost. The MiG pilots' success was totally dependent on GCI controllers positioning them for a single, supersonic attack from the rear quarter, accelerating away at 1.8 Mach. The MiGs made full use of their small size, speed, and smokeless engines to strike and escape unseen. However, a MiG that stayed to fight the Phantoms invariably came off worst.

While MiG-21 pilots shot down 19 aircraft between August 1967 and February 23, 1968 for the loss of only five, between November 1966 when MiG-21s first entered combat and February 1968, they shot down 24 while losing 25. The figures demonstrate, however, that the MiG pilots learned fast against experienced opponents with qualitatively superior aircraft.

Tet, the Vietnamese New Year's celebration, traditionally began with the first new moon after January 20 and lasted for three days. In 1968, it began on January 31. Shortly after midnight, the National Liberation Front carried out attacks throughout South Vietnam, including the Long Binh army base, Bien Hoa air base, Tan Son Nhut air base, and the new US Embassy in Saigon. An estimated 67,000 enemy troops, approximately 45,000 NLF and the remaining 22,000-plus North Vietnamese PAVN regulars shelled or tried to seize US and South Vietnamese military facilities, towns, and government facilities from Khe Sanh in the Central Highlands to Ca Mau in the southernmost tip of South Vietnam. Five major cities, including Saigon, the capitals of 27 of the nation's 44 provinces, 58 lesser towns, and some 50 hamlets saw fighting.

Out of the ten major air bases used by the United States in South Vietnam, only four emerged unscathed: Cam Ranh Bay, Phu Cat, Phan Rang, and Tuy Hoa. At Tan Son Nhut and Bien Hoa, the two largest and most important bases, enemy troops got onto the fields but were all killed or captured by the end of the day. Air bases at Pleiku, Nha Trang, Da Nang, and Binh Thuy were attacked with rockets and mortars. By the afternoon, aircraft were able to use all the airfields to mount air support for the American and South Vietnamese counterattacks.

Surprise was initially complete, but American and South Vietnamese forces were able to prevail over the next several days. However, the attack's goal was primarily political. In the United States, it destroyed all previous claims for optimism. Newsman Walter Cronkite, called "the most trusted man in America," visited South Vietnam after the Tet Offensive. When he returned, his historic broadcast, stating that the United States had lost whatever reason it had for fighting the war, so dismayed President Johnson that he told his aides, "If I've lost Walter Cronkite, I've lost the whole thing."

The primary reason US forces were not ready for the possibility of enemy action throughout South Vietnam, despite intelligence warnings first sounded in mid-December 1967 by a team of analysts working for National Security Advisor Walt W. Rostow, who managed to penetrate the "noise" in intelligence reports and enemy interrogations to spot the possibility of a major urban offensive, and the few analysts in Saigon who tried to warn of "something big," was that the campaign against Khe Sanh had captivated nearly all military leaders and intelligence analysts, who saw that as a possible North Vietnamese replay of the battle at Dien Bien Phu in 1954 that led to the end of the First Indochina War.

Because the northeast monsoon created bad weather over North Vietnam, only a few missions had been flown over the North in January before the monsoon hit. In the aftermath of Tet and with the continuing requirement to provide air support at Khe Sanh, there were no US air attacks on North Vietnam until April.

In the end, the kind of determined ground assault that resulted in the surrender at Dien Bien Phu never happened, perhaps as a result of the failure of the Tet Offensive. However, while the enemy failed to stimulate an urban uprising, the fact that American death totals exceeded 400 a week during the Battle of Hue had a major effect on public opinion across the United States and more importantly among decision-makers in Washington. McNamara, who had become increasingly and publicly disillusioned with the war, left office on February 29 to become President of the World Bank. Clark Clifford, who replaced McNamara as Secretary of Defense, also chaired the "A to Z" project, involving an examination of every aspect of the war effort – military, budgetary, economic, diplomatic, and political. On March 4, the committee recommended activation of 262,000 reserve and national guard troops.

News of the report was leaked to the press. Soon, the question of whether anything done since 1965 had been of any value split the administration and Congress. When Senator Eugene McCarthy's antiwar campaign made an unexpected showing in the New Hampshire primary election in early February, despite the president still winning the vote, Johnson's vulnerability on the war was demonstrated. By the end of the month, Senator Robert F. Kennedy, the man Johnson feared most, entered the campaign.

The president invited a panel known as "the Wise Men" to review the war's conduct. It included Dean Acheson, Secretary of State to President Harry S. Truman; C. Douglas Dillon, President John F. Kennedy's Secretary of the Treasury; and two former Chairmen of the Joint Chiefs of Staff, Generals Maxwell Taylor and Omar N. Bradley. Representatives of State and Defense, the JCS, and the CIA presented reports. There was no reasonable increase in the war presented that did not risk intervention by China or the Soviet Union, or that would compel North Vietnam to abandon the war.

Westmoreland was told there would be no more troops past the 10,500 sent during Tet, though Air National Guard units activated in the January *Pueblo* Crisis would be sent to South Vietnam to increase air support.

The entire war changed on the evening of March 31, when President Johnson unexpectedly announced during a televised address to the nation that "I will not seek, nor will I accept, the nomination for another term as your president."

With that, bombing of North Vietnam north of the 20th parallel ended, with effect on April 1, in an attempt to stimulate peace negotiations. The position McNamara had advocated since 1966 was official US policy.

Following the enemy withdrawal from Khe Sanh, operations were planned to drive the enemy out of the Ashau Valley. Twenty-two miles long and less than six miles from Laos, Ashau was one of two strongholds for the PAVN in South Vietnam, the other being the

U Minh Forest north of Saigon. It had belonged to the North since March 1966 when the Special Forces camp there was overrun. Known to the North Vietnamese as Base Area 611, it was a major route on the Ho Chi Minh Trail for infiltration into Thua Thien Province and northern I Corps, the launch point for the offensive against the Marines at Khe Sanh.

In late February, what was perhaps the strangest aerial engagement of the Vietnam War took place above the clouds over the Ashau Valley's triple-canopy jungle.

On the morning of February 24, two US Army OV-1A Mohawks "threaded the needle" through the pass at the western end of the Ashau that led to the Laotian plain beyond. The Mohawk was a strange-looking airplane, reminiscent in shape of a dragonfly, and the only fixed-wing US Army airplane that carried underwing ordnance, in the form of a .50-caliber gun pod and two Zuni pods under each wing. Captain Ken Lee, who had first flown Mohawks with the 73rd Aviation Company from December 1964 to November 1965, when they "wrote the book" about Mohawk operations in Vietnam, flew lead. The two flew high, since under the riot of green below were more than 6,000 PAVN troops. The enemy disliked the bug-headed OV-1, having learned the hard way what happened when they were discovered by the Mohawk's side-looking radar and infrared detection gear. If they were forced down, Lee and his wingman could expect leech-infested streams, cliffs, and hills with 60-degree slopes, jungle so dense one could not see more than a few feet in any direction, populated by 140 varieties of poisonous snakes and the most unusual insects in the world – and that was if the NVA didn't find them.

Many years later, Lee recounted:

All of a sudden, I felt the airplane taking hits, but it felt different from before, not like the usual ground fire. I didn't know why, so I commenced a clearing turn to the right, but then my wingman – who was maybe half a mile behind me in trail – shouted "You got a MiG behind you!" I immediately leveled my wings, just as a silver, swept-wing airplane dove past on my left about sixty feet away at around 275 knots. My first thought was it was an Australian Sabre, since they were based in Thailand, but then I saw the red star and knew I was in trouble.

The MiG-17 pulled out 200 feet below Lee and turned back. "I was a sitting duck. With our full load of ordnance and extra fuel, I was so heavy I'd stall at about 165 knots in a 30 degree bank, so I sure couldn't dogfight him." Lee ordered his wingman to break left and over the mountain range into a cloud bank, since there was no reason for two Mohawks to be shot down that day.

The MiG pilot then made a major error as he slowed to make his attack. The OV-1A might have looked like a dragonfly, but it was a thoroughly competent warplane. More than half the wing span was within the wake of the big, reversible pitch propellers, and the wing incorporated a pair of hydraulically operated auxiliary ailerons that worked only when the flaps were down, for better low-speed control. It was fully aerobatic, rated at +5G and -1.5G.

Lee decided the best defense was a good offense and turned toward the approaching MiG:

I fired 38 rockets in two shots, and got what looked like four hits. I put about 100 rounds into him – I could see the tracers going into the fuselage. Hitting his engine killed his power. His right wing dropped when he got hit, and he went into a cloud bank. I pulled out of the clouds to the right, and saw him come out about three to five seconds later. His right wing was low and his nose was pitched over, with flickers of red flame, followed by white smoke, then black smoke, and then orange flames.

The MiG turned into what Lee knew was a blind valley. "He was so low, he could not have gotten out of that valley without impacting the hillside. The clouds were dense and I didn't follow him in there."

Back at base at Phu Bai Lee recalled:

I didn't get scared from the fight till I climbed out and saw the bullet holes in the tail and the aft fuselage, but the unit leaders were also worried that maybe it had been an Aussie Sabre, plus nobody could explain how a MiG could be down over South Vietnam when they never came that far south before. The doubt continued for days.

The two pilots, neither of whom was trained for air combat, were accused of trying to cover themselves from the repercussions of being involved in a second friendly fire incident. "Three weeks earlier, my wingman was accused of hitting my airplane when we made a strafing run up in Ashau," Lee explained. The doubts ended when incontrovertible evidence of an air battle was produced:

> My crew chief measured those 39 holes in my rear section, and found they'd all struck at about a 45-degree angle, which would mean my wingman would have had to have been diving on me to do that. And then there was the fact that the holes were bigger than a .50 cal. They were about 20 millimeter. After my chief reported that, they started taking the story seriously.

For the Army, Lee's "victory" could turn into a major defeat if it became widely known that an Army airplane had shot down a MiG, which the Air Force considered its prerogative. As Lee explained, "The Army was terrified the Air Force would force them to either disarm the Mohawks or even turn them over to the Air Force." The event was officially forgotten until 2004, when Lee's story was published in an aviation history magazine and the Army confirmed it had happened. "I always knew I'd got him, because a month later I flew into Ubon, and the guys at the Wolfpack found out who I was and told me 'We know it happened, don't ask how.' They even let me take a victory flight around the bar in the officer's club." Ken Lee is the only Army aviator to have shot down an enemy airplane in combat since the US Air Force was founded as a separate service; the flight suit he wore that day is now on display at the Fort Rucker Army Aviation museum.

Air action over North Vietnam was now limited to striking the enemy in the panhandle below the 20th parallel. The 60 B-52 sorties a day that had been flown in the area during Operation *Niagara*, the air campaign to support Khe Sanh, were maintained, with the hope that the bombers could also overwhelm the operation of the Ho Chi Minh Trail. This was maintained during the rest of what remained of *Rolling Thunder* through to November 1 when all bombing ceased. Over the course of the seven-month campaign, the enemy maintained their infiltration and supplies.

The VPAF air bases north of the 20th parallel effectively became sanctuaries once again as they had been prior to the first airfield attacks in April 1967. Those bases the VPAF had south of the parallel were unused. Beginning on April 3, 72 hours after the restrictions went into effect, the MiGs began making forays south of the bomb line. They would operate under radio and radar silence, flying at low level to avoid being picked up by the College Eye RC-121s that still flew off the coast. Their goal was to harass American strike missions in the panhandle, maneuvering to make a single pass in an attempt to get the bombers to salvo their ordnance as before, with the MiGs quickly flying back across the bomb line in afterburner before the escorts could engage them. After September 28, VPAF activity south of the bomb line completely ceased.

Between the first missions of March 1965, and the final missions that ceased on November 1, 1968, *Rolling Thunder* cost a total of 881 aircraft lost "up North," almost 24 per month; the Vietnamese Air Defense Forces and VPAF claimed 1,331, "572 of which crashed on the spot." Losses of 163 in 1965 jumped to 280 in 1966, 329 in 1967, and finally 109 in 1968. Of these, 475 were Air Force while the Navy lost 382, with the remaining 24 being Marine Corps aircraft. The SA-2s shot down 112 aircraft, while MiGs shot down 50. The massive numbers of heavy, medium, and light AAA, as well as small arms fire, were responsible for the loss of the remaining 719, which confirmed the traditional lethality of conventional antiaircraft fire demonstrated in World War I, World War II, and Korea. The worst loss rate was recorded in 1965, with an aircraft loss rate of 6.42 aircraft lost per 1,000 sorties. At the climax of *Rolling Thunder* in 1967, total losses were 329 aircraft: 188 Air Force, 129 Navy, and 12 Marine Corps. That year SA-2s shot down 62 while MiGs were responsible for 25. The overwhelming numbers of heavy, medium and light AAA, and small arms fire, claimed 205. Operational losses due to breakdown and pilot error were 32, while five simply disappeared in the terrible weather that could happen in an instant. At an average cost of $1.43 million each in then-year dollars, the 881 aircraft lost over North Vietnam totaled $1.26 billion (equivalent to $9.5 billion in 2021). At the same time, the CIA estimated that overall damage to North Vietnam in the three and a half years of bombing came to a total of $300 billion in then-year dollars.

Over the course of *Rolling Thunder*, aircrew deaths were 413 Air Force, 92 Marine Corps, and 83 Navy, 1.61 percent of the 36,540 American deaths in Southeast Asia from 1965 through 1968. This does not include those killed in accidents, such as 178 naval personnel killed in the fires aboard USS *Oriskany* and *Forrestal*. The air warfare ratio of killed to wounded has always been higher than land warfare, where the wounded traditionally greatly exceed those killed. In Vietnam, the killed-to-wounded ratio for all services was two dead for each one wounded. In comparison, the Army ratio was one dead for three wounded, while the Marine Corps ratio was one dead for eight wounded. In air combat over North Vietnam, 40 percent of aircrews shot down were killed. Of those who survived, 53 percent were rescued, a testament to the dedication of the CSAR forces who completed 276 combat rescues, over 68 under fire, in return for 45 aircraft lost, over 50 rescue aircraft crewmen killed in action, and the capture of ten. The other 47 percent who bailed out over the North were either captured and made prisoners of war, or missing in action. The MIAs were most likely dead, given the threats facing a man in triple-canopy jungle so thick it was impossible to know there might be a trail five feet away through the thick cover. There are more than 300 species of poisonous snakes in Southeast Asia, not to mention several varieties of large predators, as well as poisonous plants.

For some, *Rolling Thunder* represents wasted effort. To others, it is a textbook study of the limitations to air power. For many who fought in the campaign, the results demonstrate not the limits of air power, but rather the result of limitations imposed upon air power. The campaign was poorly planned from the beginning and provided vague and ill-defined goals. It was defined by politically induced limitations and outright meddling from the senior levels of government, sporadic in execution, and undertaken in the last years of "dumb bombs."

14

INTERREGNUM – 1968–72

The temporary ban on all air and naval bombardment of North Vietnam that had been imposed in April by President Johnson overshadowed all US operations in the southern panhandle of North Vietnam, following the commencement of peace talks between the United States and North Vietnam, which began in Paris in May 1968. President Johnson's advisers recommended offering a permanent bombing halt in exchange for three concessions by the North Vietnamese: respect the demilitarized zone (DMZ); refrain from attacking South Vietnamese cities; and accept the government of South Vietnam as a party to truce negotiations. The Paris talks quickly became mired in procedural questions, most importantly participation by the South Vietnamese government. A bombing halt appeared to offer a means of resolving this issue and obtaining the other assurances of North Vietnamese cooperation, assuming, of course, that the North Vietnamese would agree.

However, the North Vietnamese insisted that the United States stop bombing, unconditionally refusing even to consider offering concessions in return. As negotiations continued, signs appeared that North Vietnam would agree to negotiate with the South, if the bombing ended and the reality of Hanoi's concession was somehow camouflaged. President Johnson consulted General Abrams, the new MACV commander, and Ambassador Bunker; both agreed that a bombing halt was militarily and politically acceptable. President Thieu agreed, which he later tried to disavow, provided that the United States would renew air attacks if Hanoi intensified the war.

As resolution for participation by the Thieu government, the North Vietnamese accepted an "our side, your side" formula: representatives of both the NLF's Provisional Government of South Vietnam and the Thieu government, though neither was recognized as a separate party to the negotiations, would accompany the respective North Vietnamese and American delegations. Sparing South Vietnamese cities and respecting the DMZ were tacitly agreed; the fact that enemy rockets rarely exploded in the cities seemed to reinforce the notion that an unwritten agreement stopped the attacks.

The bombing halt began on November 1, just before the US presidential election pitting Republican Richard M. Nixon against Vice President Hubert H. Humphrey, and immediately closed the gap between the two candidates. The Thieu government delayed the expanded negotiations until the end of November. The United States invoked another "tacit understanding" to continue aerial reconnaissance missions over parts of North Vietnam.

In 2017, notes by Nixon's Chief of Staff, H.R. Haldeman, were publicly released, clearly demonstrating that candidate Nixon tried to delay the negotiations to prevent an end to the war being announced just before the election, which he believed would give victory to Vice President Humphrey. According to the Haldeman notes, Nixon called Anna Chennault, widow of "Flying Tigers" founder Claire Chennault and a Republican operative with close contacts to the South Vietnamese, on October 22, 1968, and instructed her to keep "working on" Thieu to prevent a deal before the election. While the campaign's intervention was known by President Johnson at the time, the Haldeman notes prove Nixon's direct involvement, despite his denial when Johnson confronted him.

The JCS also discussed appropriate responses to violations of the DMZ, ranging from air strikes to artillery shelling to ground combat, depending on the severity of the provocations.

Nixon's shenanigans resulted in victory; his administration was publicly committed to "peace with honor." This resulted in what was called "Vietnamization" of the war, decreasing direct US involvement in ground combat in the South and air combat throughout Southeast Asia. While there were only a few US "protective reaction strikes" in North Vietnam, the bombing campaign in Laos continued despite being illegal under international law and treaty and thus remained "secret."

On January 21, 1969, the day after his inauguration, President Nixon requested that the JCS present a program to halt the infiltration of supplies and personnel through Cambodia to South Vietnam. The result was a diplomatic attempt to persuade Cambodia's leader, Prince Sihanouk, to allow air and ground attacks against bases and supply routes in sparsely inhabited parts of Cambodia. General Abrams suggested "unacknowledged" B-52 strikes against the Central Office for South Vietnam, the communist headquarters that US intelligence believed was located in the "Fishhook" region of Cambodia. In response to enemy shelling of Saigon seen as a "second Tet," the president considered ordering this bombing in March, then delayed it from concern that it could ignite protests during his tour of Western Europe.

With bombing in North Vietnam ruled out due to its likely impact on domestic opposition to the war, and invasion of Laos to cut the Ho Chi Minh Trail being a violation of both treaty and international law, Nixon considered a Cambodian campaign for three weeks. Secretary of State Rogers reportedly opposed this because of an adverse impact on the Paris talks. Secretary of Defense Laird favored the idea but did not think it would remain secret. National Security Advisor Henry Kissinger believed the strikes would be worthwhile despite objections by Cambodia or the antiwar movement, or an increase in the war's tempo in the South, or Soviet reaction. News of rockets exploding in Saigon on March 14, 1969 resulted in the launch of Operation *Menu*, bombing Cambodian bases. The first mission, Operation *Breakfast*, was flown the night of March 18/19; 59 B-52s bombed the Fishhook, resulting in many secondary explosions. Strict secrecy was maintained.

Each raid was made by SAC, concealed with the mission identifier and time assigned to a nearby South Vietnamese target. The bombers were routed near the cover target, which was the alternate if there was bad weather or equipment failure. The missions were flown at night, with Combat Skyspot radar controlling bomb release. Crews were briefed as if the attack would occur in South Vietnam; only the pilot and navigator knew they were over Cambodia, and their silence was expected. The Skyspot operators knew that the targets were in Cambodia. A SAC representative arrived at the Skyspot site and gave the operator the necessary information. At the same time, an officer from Seventh Air Force went to the GCI radar site tracking the mission and warned technicians not to alert the bombers when they neared the border, which was standard operating procedure (SOP) to prevent violation of Cambodian airspace. Radar teams did not record border violations, and the Combat Skyspot controllers submitted summaries of flight patterns that the B-52s would have followed to hit the cover target. The actual report, including an initial assessment of damage, was sent over secure channels.

The bombing did not deter a May offensive, but General Abrams reported that the strikes had relieved pressure on Special Forces camps in the Central Highlands, and forced the enemy to put time and manpower into dispersing supplies and constructing blast-resistant storage bunkers.

Two reports by the Associated Press and *New York Times* revealed that Abrams had requested authority to bomb enemy sanctuaries in Cambodia, but there was no official response; the Cambodia campaign remained secret until former Air Force Major Hal Knight testified to the Senate Armed Services Committee in 1973 that he had destroyed records of strikes in Cambodia and substituted reports on cover targets in South Vietnam. This testimony later formed one of the articles of impeachment drawn up against Nixon in 1974.

North Vietnam used the years of the bombing halt as a breathing spell to improve and strengthen its air defenses with the material assistance of the Soviet Union and China. New AAA and SAM sites appeared, particularly in Quang Binh Province in the southern panhandle. New airfields were constructed, while GCI coverage extended south. MiG activity below the 20th parallel increased from five flights per day in late 1971 to ten per day early in 1972. When *Rolling Thunder* began in 1965, the VPAF had 36 pilots. By the end in 1968, there were 72 pilots and 80 aircraft. By May 1970, there were 140 MiG-17s, 95 MiG-21s, and 30 MiG-19/J-6s. In January 1972, the 921st Fighter Regiment converted to the improved MiG-21MF, with longer range and better radar, carrying four Atolls.

By early 1972 North Vietnam had what was recognized as the best air defense system in the world. It incorporated excellent radar integrated with the SA-2 SAM and the MiG-21, along with a massive number of light, medium, and heavy AAA throughout the country. By 1971 SAM sites were in the Laotian panhandle to cover the Ho Chi Minh Trail between the Mu Gia Pass and northern South Vietnam. The system wielded impressive firepower from ground level to 60,000 feet. Their radar operators were so experienced that they could determine the structure of American strike forces soon after the aircraft took off.

US forces also changed. The original assignment of two rated pilots as F-4 crew was altered. This was due to a pilot shortage and recognition that there was no need for a rated pilot to operate the radar and missiles. The Air Force had an excess of navigators, who already knew most of what the rear seater needed to know; additional training was easy. From this came the weapon systems officer (WSO), similar to the radar intercept officer (RIO), the rear-seater in Navy F-4s. This change also eliminated the situation where the lower-ranking pilot in the rear seat had more F-4 experience than the senior pilot in front, having likely gone directly to F-4 advanced training, while the senior pilot frequently did not have a fighter background. Once a "team" was created with the WSO, crews trained together.

The badly depleted F-105 force rapidly re-deployed to the United States following *Rolling Thunder*'s conclusion. The 388th Tactical Fighter Wing remained in-theater, with F-4s replacing F-105s. The Wild Weasel F-105F was updated to F-105G standard with detection gear that did not require overflying a SAM site to locate it. Close air support squadrons using F-100s and A-1s converted to the A-7D Corsair II, an Air Force-specific version of the Navy A-7. Sandy squadrons continued using the Skyraider since its loiter capability allowed it to perform RESCAP coverage better than any other available aircraft.

While the war saw many stirring stories of rescues of downed fliers in difficult circumstances, the largest, most difficult, and most hard-fought rescue operation of the entire period occurred between December 5 and 7, 1969.

At 0900 hours on December 5, two F-4Cs from the 558th Tactical Fighter Squadron, call signs "Boxer 21/22," took off from Cam Ranh Bay, South Vietnam. Boxer 22 was crewed by pilot Captain Benjamin Danielson, and WSO First Lieutenant Woodrow "Woodie" Bergeron, Jr., flying together for the first time. The mission involved dropping Mark 36 antipersonnel mines along a section of the Ho Chi Minh Trail in Laos that had seen increased traffic since the beginning of the dry season the month before. The two fighters met a KC-135 over the Tonkin Gulf, then headed toward central Laos.

They found the target weathered in and were unable to contact a FAC to direct the drop. The two were diverted to a target near the village of Ban Phanop, ten miles below Mu Gia Pass, where they were briefed to sow the Nam Ngo River ford with their mines. "Boxer 21" took lead with "Boxer 22" half a mile behind. Just after "Boxer 22" dropped their ordnance, previously unspotted AAA sites opened up. The Phantom suddenly pitched up, then down. "Boxer 21" radioed: "Boxer 22, you're hit! Eject! Eject! Eject!" The two crewmen punched out as the fire spread.

Bergeron recalled the ejection:

The windblast knocked my helmet off and got my nose. The 'chutes were fairly close. As I was coming down, there was a guy shooting at me with a 12.7 machine gun. When I got on the ground the shots were ricocheting over my head. I happened to land right at the edge of the river in a little cleared area about ten by ten. I hit the ground running. My 'chute was stuck in a ten-foot high bush. Ben's 'chute over across the river was in a tall tree.

Danielson and Bergeron, now Boxer 22 Alpha and Bravo, came down on opposite sides of the river. The valley was a mile wide and 1,000 feet deep, walled by limestone karst cliffs, ten miles from the North Vietnam border, but only 65 miles east of Nakhon Phanom RTAFB (NKP), the primary Air Force special operations SAR base. Most of the experienced rescue crews had rotated home; this was the first big rescue mission since *Rolling Thunder* had ended.

Boxer-22's Mayday and their beepers were picked up by the HC-130 rescue coordination aircraft, call sign "King," orbiting 60 miles west of the bailout area. King provided communications, controlled aircraft, and coordinated refueling. The Nail FAC ("Nail" being the call sign for USAF air controllers over the Ho Chi Minh Trail) overhead confirmed that two good parachutes and a SAR operation existed, that the survivors were on relatively flat ground at an altitude of 600 feet, in good condition, and that weather was clear. King contacted NKP and Udorn to scramble a Sandy flight, two HH-3 helicopters, and a second HC-130 for refueling.

King headed for the recovery area, expecting a normal rescue operation. SOP was to extract downed airmen before enemy forces could concentrate. This time, however, the enemy was already concentrated around Ban Phanop.

King and First Lieutenant James G. George in Sandy 01, leading four A-1Es, arrived overhead at 1100 hours. George assumed RESCAP lead from the FAC. Contacting the survivors, he learned that Danielson was near a work area between the west side of the river and Route 23. Bergeron was on the east side at the river's edge. There was a 20-foot high embankment that shielded him from being spotted by anyone above. A 1,200-foot karst ridge rose 300 feet behind him, extending north. The river was 50 feet wide and the two were about 70 feet apart. Danielson reported small arms fire on his side while Bergeron reported silence at his location.

Suddenly, Danielson called, "Sandy 1, this is Boxer 22 Alpha – I need help now! I've got bad guys only 15 yards away, and they are going to get me soon."

George replied, "22 Alpha, this is Sandy 1. Keep your head down. We're in hot with 20 mike-mike."

The four Skyraiders strafed the work site. The entire valley erupted in response. Bergeron saw 23, 37 and 57mm AAA open up from positions in the karst on both sides of the river. Pulling out of the valley after evading the fountain of fire, George called King 01, now 24,000 feet above. "King One – Sandy One. We are going to need everything you can get."

Seventh Air Force HQ at Tan Son Nhut and MACV HQ had received word of the Boxer 22 shoot-down. The carrier *Hancock* at Dixie Station launched A-6 Intruders, while F-100s from Bien Hoa, F-105 Wild Weasels from Takhli, and Phantoms from Korat and Udorn converged on Ban Thanop. The first A-1 reinforcements arrived at 1120 hours, followed by two flights each of F-100s and F-105s. For the next 80 minutes, the A-1s strafed and bombed the valley floor, while the jets attacked the larger guns on the karst to the north. It was soon apparent the ground threat was much greater than originally thought, as aircraft flying down the valley were caught in a crossfire. A 37mm gun located in a cave at the foot of the karst 300 yards directly behind Bergeron was particularly troublesome, and additional air support was requested. Six A-1s loaded with CBU 19/30 tear gas were launched from Da Nang, while four F-4s at Ubon were loaded with Paveway laser-guided bombs (LGBs) for use against the 37mm gun and launched at 1500 hours.

By 1240 hours, George determined that ground fire had died down sufficiently to try a pickup. Because the west side was flatter and the scene of the greatest ground activity, he decided to attempt rescuing

Danielson first and radioed, "We're going to lay CBU all around you, and then we are going to bring the choppers in to scarf you up and we'll all go home for a beer." Then he radioed the two HH-3 Jolly Greens hovering five miles west to move fast: "Let's get this done. I don't think we can waste any time."

At 1240 hours, Captain Charles Hoilman headed Jolly Green 37 into the valley. The crew reported increasing flak as they approached the pickup point. Hoilman became disoriented coming around the karst and had to slow while he regained Danielson's position. Moving into a hover over Danielson, Jolly Green 37 was a big, stationary target. Every enemy gun was brought to bear. With the fuselage riddled and the engines overheating, Hoilman radioed, "I've got to go home. I've burned the shit out of these engines." He pulled out, leaving a smoky trail.

Skyraiders spent the next 45 minutes dropping napalm and tear gas. But when Jolly Green 09 went in, small arms fire and two 23mm cannons firing from caves in the karst hit its rotor. Jolly Green 09 was driven off with a transmission leak, hot engine temperatures, and malfunctioning controls. The rescue was now a pitched battle. The enemy's battle plan was obvious: take cover in the karst caves, then emerge and let the rescue choppers have it with everything.

Four new HH-53E Super Jolly Greens that were bigger, more powerful, better armed and armored were called in. The first in was Captain Holly G. Bell's Jolly Green 76. He remembered, "It sounded like we were caught in a popcorn machine." As they hovered over Danielson, tail gunner Airman First Class David Davison hosed the valley with 4,000 rounds per minute from his M134 7.62mm Gatling gun, but was outgunned. Jolly Green 76 took multiple hits in the fuselage and rotor and began vibrating hard. Bell reported, "I knew if we took more hits, my Jolly would be shot down. During egress from the valley, I received notification that Davison had been badly hit." The tailgunner had been hit in the head, dying of blood loss during the return to NKP. He was posthumously awarded the Silver Star. In February 1970, Bell and his entire crew were shot down and killed in another rescue operation.

An hour later, Jolly Green 69, flown by Captain Jerald Brown, was the next to try after more "prep." A burst of 23mm fire cut a hydraulic line and the spraying fluid caught a spark. The big chopper climbed away with flames gushing from a window as the crew manned CO_2 sprayers.

More A-1s arrived to reinforce the reinforcements. The valley thundered with the sound of airplane engines, cannons, and bombs. Major Jerry Crupper's Jolly Green 79 headed in. A 37mm shell blew a two-by-four-foot hole in the helicopter's belly before it could get close to the pickup point.

After the A-1s dropped more napalm and tear gas, Major Hubert Berthold managed to bring Jolly Green 68 in to hover over Danielson and try for a pickup. Berthold remembered that before they could, "The entire area was lit up with tracers from both sides, from both the karst and the ground." Retreating, the Super Jolly was still taking ground fire five miles west of the rescue site.

With 45 minutes to sunset, Colonel Daryle Tripp, deputy operations commander of the 56th Special Operations Wing, assumed RESCAP lead in Sandy 07 as the sun lowered over the Laotian hills. He called for one last attempt, then led the Skyraiders on another napalm run into the valley, before calling in the last HH-53E.

Captain Donald Carty's Jolly Green 72 closed to within 30 feet of Danielson before they were driven off. He remembered, "We were so low and it was so dark on the egress that we almost hit the karst. I advised against making another attempt because it was too dark and our mini-guns were either jammed or out of ammo." Five of seven helicopters had been seriously damaged. It was unclear if the other two would ever fly again.

After the failed pickup attempt, Sandy 07 informed Danielson and Bergeron they would be back at first light. An instruction from Udorn, that the two inflate their Mae Wests after dark, cover themselves with branches and leaves, and float south down the river, was never received. Bergeron explained later:

> I couldn't have done it anyway because at night they had a ford south of us and they'd light flares to get a winch going to get the trucks across and with the flares lighting the river it was like a mirror. And also just right south down the river it turned sandy where the ford was. I'd have had to walk again. They were going to have to pound this particular area to get us and they were already pounding it and if we got any farther south they were going to have to do the same thing all over again.

The two stayed in radio contact overnight, but with the enemy searching through the bushes on the west bank, Danielson seldom came up on guard. Bergeron remained in the clump of bamboo he had hidden in when he landed, with a front-row view of the supply convoys crossing the river. "I learned how they got the trucks across the ford. They'd hold up flashlights one way to start the winch, another way to pull the truck across, and another way to stop it."

Skyraiders remained overhead all night. One pilot remembered, "The AAA was firing across the entire valley, with the tracers ricocheting off the side of the karst on the opposite side. It was like being in the bottom of a tunnel of fire."

The morning found both survivors still free and alive. Bergeron explained, "I could hear the enemy looking for Ben. They would go to a clump of trees or other spots where he might be hiding and fire off a few AK-47 rounds. No one came looking for me."

Seventh Air Force Commander General George S. Brown informed PACAF that all aircraft in theater, except those supporting troops in direct enemy contact, were assigned to the rescue effort. On December 6, nearly the entire air war in Southeast Asia was fought over Boxer 22.

Colonel Tripp arrived at 0600 hours with a flight of A-1Es. Several minutes later, Bergeron informed Tripp that the North Vietnamese had just killed Danielson. He later recalled, "They were talking in a fairly normal tone, and then all of a sudden they started yelling, like they found him. They shot a very long burst of AK-47 fire. I heard Ben scream. It was definitely him. I knew that he had been killed."

Enemy troops began wading the river toward Bergeron. "I decided they weren't taking prisoners. If they came over to where I was hiding, I was going to try to fight it out with my pistol." He called in Tripp's Skyraiders to strafe the river, killing the enemy troops.

The bombers arrived soon after; for the next five hours the valley was cluster-bombed, napalmed, rocketed, and strafed. Over 154 sorties were flown throughout the day. A controller aboard the HC-130 later remembered, "It was a wonder we didn't have mid-air collisions." Bergeron recalled, "The closest they came to me with 20mm cannon fire was about one foot." A tear gas cluster bomblet actually bounced off his chest. "One whiff was enough to make me urinate and retch all at the same time."

Finally, shortly before 1200 hours, the rescue was attempted. Skyraiders laid down a smoke corridor of gas and white phosphorus so massive it was recorded by a Nimbus III weather satellite. One pilot recalled he could see smoke on takeoff from NKP, 65 miles away. "At 5,000 feet, it looked like a Texas sandstorm." The airstrikes were so heavy that Seventh Air Force ran low on smoke bombs.

Visibility was close to zero. Before darkness fell, six rescue attempts were made, but whenever a Jolly Green Giant could hover over Bergeron, rotor wash swept the air clear and the enemy gunners had clear aim. At 1415 hours, one Jolly Green hovered four feet above the ridge behind Bergeron, but the crew were unable to see him over the hill. He climbed the seven-foot high sheer wall but just as he got to six feet from the helo's door, it had to leave because of incoming fire. The final attempt failed at 1800 hours when the pilot became disoriented in the smoke and ended up on the wrong side of the river.

As night fell, the planes flew off and the enemy closed in. Bergeron recalled, "I knew they were aware I was hiding somewhere on the east side of the river, and it was just a matter of time until they found me." Fifteen minutes after sunset, three soldiers emerged from cover, tossed a tear gas bomblet into the bamboo thicket where Bergeron had been hiding, and sprayed it with their AK-47s. All they found was his survival gear; just before they made their move he had moved 40 feet to the north, losing his revolver in the scramble, and was hiding under exposed tree roots. "If those guys had a flashlight, they could have found me."

The pilot of the last Skyraider had advised Bergeron that if the river was deep enough, he should get in and go downstream. After the soldiers departed, he waded into the river, but was too exhausted to swim. Dragging himself to an overhanging bush, he hid beneath it. In the dark, exhausted and hungry, he heard trucks roll past on both sides of the river, and drifted in and out of consciousness: "During the night I began to hallucinate. I envisioned two members of my squadron were with me, discussing my plans of action."

NKP's flight line was lit all night in an all-hands effort as aircraft were repaired, refueled, and reloaded to go again at dawn.

Dawn found Bergeron on his last legs. "I was drinking water out of the river and had only a little food." The lead Skyraider appeared overhead at 0515 hours and asked for authentication. "What's your best friend's name?" Bergeron replied "Weisdorfer." The pilot laughed, "I don't even have time to check it, but it's gotta be you."

Airstrikes began at 0600 hours. F-100s fired Zuni rockets against the karst walls to keep the gunners down, while Skyraiders laid a fresh smoke corridor and others strafed the valley floor. At 0830 hours, Lieutenant Colonel Clifton Shipman took Jolly Green 77 into the smoke for the pickup run. Sun angle and smoke density created IFR conditions. "When we got down over the river, we could see absolutely nothing." Taking fire from a camouflaged truck, Shipman spotted what he guessed was 500–1,000 troops to the northwest, massing for an attack. Jolly Green 77 was forced to abort.

After three more hours of strikes, RESCAP lead Major Tom Dayton ordered the 22 Skyraiders to fly two "daisy chain" formations to either side of Bergeron's position, ten to the west and 12 to the east, hitting the enemy with smoke, gas, and gunfire. They quickly silenced the gun truck, saturating the valley with smoke. As they did, Shipman refueled Jolly Green 77 from the HC-130 while his gunners reloaded. Dayton gave the go-ahead at 1140 hours.

With all the smoke, Shipman couldn't spot Bergeron. Overhead, Major Dayton talked them in. Bergeron remembered, "They flew over me, I called they'd overshot, so they did a 360, then lowered the penetrator." After days of popping smoke and flares, the only thing Bergeron had left to signal with was his vinyl escape chart. He bolted from his hiding place, waving the chart's white side. "The penetrator landed about four feet away from me in the water. I put the strap on first and then flung the penetrator beneath me."

Shipman's tail gunner hosed his mini-gun at 30 enemy soldiers 50 feet distant while the left-side gunner sprayed troops across the river. The PJ dragged Bergeron aboard and Shipman powered upward. "We've got him, and we're coming out!"

The radio circuit immediately jammed with cheers. Dayton ordered everyone home. When the helicopters arrived at NKP, they trailed red smoke from their tails in victory. Every member of the ground crew, air crew, and the entire command staff crowded around Shipman's helicopter. Bergeron climbed out to roaring applause.

Bergeron's rescue took 60 hours; 336 sorties were flown, expending 1,463 smart bombs, high-explosive bombs, cluster bombs, smoke bombs, napalm bombs, and rocket pods. The Skyraiders flew 242 sorties in which five were damaged. Ten helicopters were shot up; five never flew again. One crewman died. In 2003, a Laotian fisherman found human remains, a partial survival vest, a survival knife and Captain Danielson's dog tags beside the Nam Ngo River; he was buried in his hometown in 2007. Bergeron was awarded the Silver Star and remained in the Air Force. He flew A-10s before retiring as a lieutenant colonel in 1987.

B-52 strikes continued in Laos and Cambodia. Reconnaissance missions continued, to confirm that the North Vietnamese were also standing down. However, the rules of engagement established after the bombing halt prohibited US aircraft from firing at North Vietnamese targets unless they were fired at by AAA or SAMs, or unless enemy radar was activated and following them. Forbidden targets included any fighter base designated as a sanctuary, a fighter aircraft that did not have its landing gear retracted, any fighter not showing hostile intent, and any SAM site not in operation. A SAM had to be fired before the escorts could engage in what were called "protective reaction strikes." General John D. Lavelle said the reason that the F-4 had a two-man crew was so that one could fly the airplane while the other studied the briefcase full of rules regarding what could and could not be done.

By the summer of 1971, the North Vietnamese air defense system netted the Fan Song SAM fire control radars with their Bar Lock, Whiff, and Spoon Rest GCI radars, which then fed tracking data to Fan Song, with the result that it did not have to be turned on until just before missile launch. The radar homing and warning (RHAW) gear that American aircraft carried, which warned when Fan Song was tracking, could not detect the GCI radars. Thus pilots so targeted had virtually no warning before the missile was fired. Since the GCI radars were always on, General Lavelle later stated that this redefined the "activated against" criterion for protective reaction strikes. "As far as I'm concerned, from November on, no airplane ever went into North Vietnam when the system wasn't activated against them."

The North Vietnamese, in the midst of planning what became the Easter Offensive of 1972, were increasingly active. Between November 1971 and February 1972, they fired over 200 SAMs at US aircraft, compared with 20 for the year before, while MiG incursions into northern South Vietnam and Laos increased by a factor of 15. US commanders requested a change to the rules of engagement to allow pre-emptive attacks on SAM sites and MiG airfields instead of allowing a SAM site to fire a missile or a MiG attack. In September 1971, General Abrams requested JCS authorization for immediate strikes on Bai Thuong, Quan Lang, and Vinh airfields to destroy the MiG threat. The request was denied, but the Joint Chiefs urged that commanders on the scene make maximum use of the authority allowed under existing rules of engagement.

Joint Chiefs Chairman Admiral Thomas H. Moorer arrived in Vietnam on November 8, 1971, and personally approved General Lavelle's request to attack Dong Hoi airfield, which was carried out immediately. Moorer approved the bomb damage assessment photos before he departed. The results were also sent to the Pentagon. The strike had more than "stretched" the authority allowed under the rules of engagement. On November 12, Admiral John S. McCain, Jr., CinCPac, informed Moorer of the threat that new North Vietnamese tactics posed to the B-52s bombing the Ho Chi Minh Trail in Laos, stating "The enemy is more determined than ever to shoot down a B-52." On November 21, McCain asked Moorer for authority to bomb North Vietnamese targets, citing the preplanned strike Moorer had authorized on November 8. Moorer responded on November 28; he expressed understanding of the situation, but declined the request.

General Lavelle met Secretary of Defense Laird in Saigon on December 8. In later testimony to Congress, Lavelle stated, "He told me I should make a liberal interpretation of the rules of engagement in the field and not come to Washington and ask him, under the political climate, to come out with an interpretation; I should make them in the field and he would back me up... General Abrams agreed with Secretary Laird." Lavelle issued orders that crews were to assume that the air defense system was activated against them, providing authorization to fire under the rules of engagement. He also authorized planned protective reaction strikes in which the targets involved elements of the air defense system such as missile transporters and any SAM sites spotted while under construction. These orders were in direct contradiction to the rules of engagement.

In December, reconnaissance flights gave strong evidence that North Vietnam was preparing a massive conventional attack against the South. SAM firings increased. On December 18, three F-4s from the 432nd Tactical Reconnaissance Wing were lost to enemy action, two to AAA, and an F-4D flown by Major K.R. Johnson and WSO First Lieutenant S.R. Vaughan of the 555th Tactical Fighter Squadron was shot down by MiG-21 pilot Le Thanh Do. Both crewmen ejected and were captured.

In January 1972, Seventh Air Force vice commander and Korean War ace Major General Winton W. "Bones" Marshall attended a CinCPac conference at which Lieutenant General John W. Vogt, Jr., Director of the Joint Staff, told him, "field commanders were, in the opinion of the Chairman of the Joint Chiefs of Staff, not nearly as aggressive as they should have been." Lavelle later testified that Marshall reported Vogt said "field commanders had not been flexible enough in the use of existing authorities" and that "JCS would not question our aiming points on protective reaction strikes."

Early 1972 saw mounting US aircraft losses. On January 15, Pathet Lao and North Vietnamese "volunteers" launched an assault on General Vang Pao's Hmong army at Long Tien, Laos, supported by strikes flown by MiGs. Two AC-130 gunships operating over the Ho Chi Minh Trail were shot down by SAMs on January 17. Three days later, the 432nd Reconnaissance Wing lost an RF-4C flown by Major R.K. Mick and WSO First Lieutenant J.L. Stiles, shot down by MiG-21 pilot Nguyen Hong My. Both ejected and were picked up by an Air America helicopter.

Air Force intelligence learned on January 23 that the VPAF planned to attack "a large aircraft" that night. Concern immediately rose because B-52s would be bombing targets on the Ho Chi Minh Trail in Laos that night. A flight of MiG-21s was deployed to Dong Hoi airfield just north of the DMZ. General Lavelle decided to destroy the MiGs or at least interrupt the plan under the guise of a protective reaction strike.

A US strike by the 432nd Wing was sent to hit Dong Hoi. When reports came that weather was closing in, Lavelle ordered the pilots to cut the runway to prevent the MiGs' landing. The strike leader reported no enemy reaction when they hit the target. Major General Alton T. Slay, deputy operations commander, later reported that Lavelle said to him, "We cannot report 'no reaction.' Our authority was protective reaction, so we have to report there was some enemy action." Later, Lavelle used operation of the enemy GCI radar as the enemy action that the strike responded to, but did not explain this to Slay.

Slay informed 432nd Wing commander Colonel Charles A. Gabriel and vice commander Colonel Jerome F. O'Malley that, "You must assume by General Lavelle's direction that you have reaction." At subsequent preflight briefings on other missions, crews were ordered to record enemy "reaction," regardless of whether or not it occurred. Most missions did get reaction by SAMs, AAA, or MiGs, but some did not. Regardless, crews reported "hostile enemy fire." The wing intelligence office began falsifying after-action intelligence reports to record enemy action; a total of four false reports were filed. Lavelle did not learn this until March. The questionable missions were all attacks on SAM sites, SAMs on transporters, MiG airfields, 122mm and 130mm heavy AAA, and radars. Seventh Air Force was only flying reconnaissance missions over North Vietnam, but Lavelle's liberal interpretation of the rules of engagement allowed striking enemy assets which threatened the missions.

Speaking with US Ambassador to South Vietnam Ellsworth F. Bunker on February 3, 1972, President Nixon explained that he did not want Lavelle's liberal interpretation of the rules of engagement made public, saying:

> You've worked out the authority. He can hit SAM sites, period. OK? But he is not to do it with a public declaration. All right? And, if it does get out, to the extent it does, he says it's a protective reaction strike. He is to describe it as protective reaction. And he doesn't have to spell it out. They struck, that's all he needs, a SAM site. A protective reaction strike against a SAM site.

This presidential directive did not become public until it was released by the Nixon Library in 2007.

On February 5, General Abrams decided that the predicted enemy offensive in the South had in fact begun, based on intelligence of the continued buildup and positioning of major troop units. He ordered that everything available be brought to bear. Tactical air sorties, gunship missions, and B-52 strikes were flown practically nonstop in a 48-hour maximum effort, concentrating all available airpower against the B-3 Front in the Central Highlands. Following a 24-hour cease-fire for the Tet holiday, a similar maximum effort was made in Military Region 1 in northern South Vietnam.

On February 16, the Pentagon announced orders suspending the rules of engagement regarding any pre-strike need for enemy reaction. General Lavelle sent an RF-4C and 14 escorting F-4D fighter-bombers into North Vietnam. A first wave of US aircraft struck the defending SAM sites and another struck heavy gun emplacements north of the DMZ. More missions were flown against the "offensive" through March 8, 1972, when General Abrams was forced to admit to Peter

Osnos, a reporter for the *Washington Post*, that there was no North Vietnamese offensive. It was subsequently reported in the *Post* that the rules of engagement had been changed without a change in enemy actions.

What came to be known as "the Lavelle Affair" began when Air Force Sergeant Lonnie D. Franks, an intelligence specialist in the 432nd Wing wrote his senator, Harold Hughes of Iowa, a Democrat who was a member of the Senate Armed Services Committee, telling Hughes, "We have been reporting that our planes have received hostile reactions such as AAA and SAM firings, whether they have or not. We have also been falsifying targets struck and bomb damage assessments." Franks continued in detail, explaining how, two days after the January 25 strike on the MiG runway, he had debriefed a pilot and navigator who said they had not received any ground fire or hostile reaction, but had been instructed nevertheless to report hostile reaction. Franks explained how he then checked with his supervisor, Technical Sergeant John Voichita, who told him to fabricate the necessary details to "make it look real," and "just make up some sort of hostile reaction," then contacted Captain Douglas Murray, the intelligence officer in charge of his unit, who confirmed the instructions and said the orders came from the wing director of intelligence. Franks stated that he then created an intelligence report that said 10–15 rounds of 23mm antiaircraft artillery had been fired at the crew, and that he had done this on other occasions.

Senator Hughes had a copy of Franks' letter hand-carried to Air Force Chief of Staff General John D. Ryan on March 8. General Ryan sent the Air Force Inspector General, Lieutenant General Louis L. Wilson, Jr., to Saigon to investigate Franks' charge. There, General Lavelle told Wilson he had interpreted the rules of engagement liberally, as he had been told to do by Secretary Laird. He explained why he regarded the air defense system as always being activated against any aircraft flying into North Vietnam, thus providing grounds for protective reaction strikes and told people in the command they could not report "no reaction" to a mission over North Vietnam. He was reportedly astounded when Wilson showed him the false intelligence reports, stating he had never seen the reports before and had not known the detail that was required to complete one. Wilson's conclusion was that Lavelle had exceeded his command authority, specifically citing 147 sorties that violated the rules of engagement when they were reported as protective reaction strikes though there had been no enemy action.

Admiral Moorer sent a top secret message to Seventh Air Force on March 21, warning that "the increased number of protective reaction strikes since Jan 1, 1972 has attracted a considerable amount of high-level interest here and is receiving increasing attention from the press." Moorer ordered that all crews be "thoroughly briefed that current authority permits protective reaction to be taken only – repeat only – when enemy air defenses either fire at or activated against friendly forces."

On March 23, Wilson submitted his findings to General Ryan. Lavelle was immediately recalled to Washington, arriving on March 26 to find he was accused of filing four false reports and conducting 28 unauthorized bombing raids against enemy air defense positions. In his defense, Lavelle stated that he had been encouraged by Secretary Laird and other superiors to interpret the rules of engagement liberally and that the reports were falsified by subordinates who misconstrued his instructions. The general was presented with two alternatives: to take another assignment as a major general (i.e. loss of two stars), or to retire with a reduction to lieutenant general. He asked to meet personally with either Secretary Laird or Air Force Secretary Seamans, then waited in vain for a week for an audience at the Pentagon. Realizing his superiors were denying his statements, he agreed to retirement and the Pentagon announced it "for personal and health reasons" on April 7.

On May 4, Representative Otis Pike of New York called for a congressional investigation. Pressed by Congress and the news media, a revised statement was made on May 15 in which General Ryan stated that Lavelle "had been relieved of command of the Seventh Air Force by me because of irregularities in the conduct of his command responsibilities."

The next week, the House Armed Services Committee appointed a special subcommittee to investigate Lavelle's retirement. The "Lavelle Hearings" were held on June 12, 1972. While the morning session was open to the public, the afternoon session was closed to allow discussion of classified information. General Lavelle acknowledged he had made "a very liberal interpretation" of the rules of engagement. A committee member asked if he would do it again. "Absolutely. The strikes were specifically directed at air-defense targets, where the buildup had increased in preparation for the invasion." General Ryan disagreed with

Lavelle over the number of protective reaction strikes flown under the liberalized rules. He estimated that the strikes totaled about 147 sorties out of approximately 25,000 sorties flown during that period, and that all were directed against missile sites, missiles on transporters, airfields, heavy antiaircraft guns, and radars and that Lavelle's instructions were the "impetus" behind the falsified reports.

General Lavelle stated that there were no civilian-populated areas involved, and that no American planes or lives were lost. Asked if General Abrams was aware of the missions, Lavelle replied, "I believe General Abrams knew what I was doing." He assumed full responsibility for reporting the strikes as protective reaction, but testified that he was not aware of the four falsified after-action intelligence reports until they were brought to his attention by the Inspector General, stating:

> I accepted responsibility for it even though I did not do it and did not have any knowledge of the detail. It was my command and I should have known... my instructions were not clear and were subject to misinterpretation and, in retrospect, were apparently interpreted by my subordinates as an exhortation to report enemy fire when there was none. "Hostile action, enemy radar," would, in my judgment, have been an accurate report.

In February 2007, Lieutenant General (ret.) Aloysius Casey and his son Patrick published an article in *Air Force Magazine* about the Lavelle Affair which quoted then-recently released Nixon tapes confirming that President Nixon had authorized the liberal interpretation of the rules of engagement as implemented by Lavelle. In a letter responding to the Casey article, former Secretary of Defense Laird confirmed he had authorized Lavelle to implement a liberal interpretation of the rules, stating:

> Prior to my order, there was no authorization (under McNamara or Clifford) to destroy dangerous targets except when fired upon without special permission. General Bus Wheeler, Admiral Tom Moorer, and General Abrams all agreed with the liberal interpretation on my order on protective reaction. The new orders permitted hitting anti-aircraft installations and other dangerous targets if spotted on their missions, whether they were activated or not.

In an oral history interview recorded by the Air Force History Office in April 1978, Lavelle said he should not have acted on the basis of private assurances that he would be supported if the missions became known. He added, "Somewhere along there we just should have said, 'Hey, either fight it or quit, but let's not waste all the money and the lives the way we are.'"

The first US Air Force aerial victory in four years and, more significantly, the first at night took place on February 21, 1972 over northeast Laos, some 90 miles southwest of Hanoi. The VPAF had trained several MiG-21 pilots over the previous year to qualify them to fly the fighter at night, and there had been several attempts made towards the end of 1971 to intercept and shoot down AC-130 "Spectre" gunships over the Ho Chi Minh Trail. The hope at this time was that they might intercept a B-52 mission, since these were being flown at night over southern Laos to attack the Ho Chi Minh Trail. As a result of the fear on the part of the Air Force that the North Vietnamese might be able to score a public relations victory by shooting down a "Buff," F-4s at Da Nang and Udorn stood "hot pad" alerts to launch into the night sky if any enemy fighters were picked up on radar.

On the night of February 21, Major Robert A. Lodge and WSO First Lieutenant Roger C. Locher were airborne 5,000 feet over Laos as Falcon 62 in a two-plane MiGCAP. Lodge later reported:

> Red Crown called out bandits and proceeded to vector us on an intercept. My wingman Falcon 63 became separated at around this time. I descended to minimum en route altitude, and my WSO detected and locked on a target using the Combat Tree equipment at the position Red Crown was calling Bandit. I fired three AIM-7Es, the first at approximately 11 nautical miles, the second at eight nautical miles and the third at six nautical miles. The first missile appeared to guide and track level, and detonated in a small explosion. The second missile guided in a similar manner and detonated with another small explosion, followed immediately by a large explosion in the same area. No detonation was observed for the third missile.

This engagement saw the beginning of the final phase of aerial warfare over Southeast Asia that continued to the end of 1973. A week later, on March 1, the "Triple Nickel" squadron added another MiG-21 to its expanding list of aerial victories, which led the squadron to declare itself

"Largest distributor of MiG parts in Southeast Asia." Falcon Flight was led by Lieutenant Colonel Joseph W. Kittinger, Jr. His WSO, First Lieutenant Leigh A. Hodgdon, recalled:

> I didn't have any other MiG contacts prior to that one. Although I did a lot of night flying, there wasn't much MiG hunting involved. We were on "Papa Alert" that night, and were scrambled as one of two Combat Tree F-4Ds. With that gear and the help of the "Disco" EC-121s, we had a good chance of an intercept.

"Disco" was an upgraded version of College Eye, which had provided early warning of MiG activity during the final stages of *Rolling Thunder* in 1967–68. EC-121s orbiting over northern Thailand and Laos were able to increase radar coverage beyond what College Eye had provided, and continued the signals intelligence (SIGINT) role provided by the Rivet Top equipment. While better than nothing, the system suffered from a limited range of coverage, limited crew and equipment capacity, and the need for the EC-121Ts to remain in slow, controlled orbits.

Kittinger's wingman in Falcon 63 was crewed by Major Robert Carroll and WSO Captain David L. Hams. Prior to takeoff, they were briefed that there might be enemy diversionary flights attempting to lure unsuspecting F-4s into North Vietnam. American pilots were well aware that the North Vietnamese monitored all radio conversations between US ground control and airborne fighters and used such information to their advantage. Falcon Flight took up a MiGCAP position in northeastern Laos at 2000 hours. Disco soon called a MiG warning and vectored the two Phantoms to make contact. Kittinger later remembered:

> The number two aircraft was heading for the tanker, which I had just departed from. I made a radio call that I was having trouble with transferring my fuel and would have to return to the tanker. This was a coded message to confuse the enemy, as we knew that they monitored all of our radio transmissions. The controller on Disco recognized the bogus call and made the appropriate return call. I immediately dropped down to low level, skimming over the mountains as I flew towards the MiG. It was a very dark night, and I depended on my instruments and intimate knowledge of the terrain to avoid hitting the ground. Lieutenant Hodgdon remained cool,

performing his role professionally, even though we were flying at very high speed at night over mountains.

Using Combat Tree, Hodgdon was able to identify the MiGs, which turned to follow the two F-4s. They duly turned back into their pursuers, and Colonel Kittinger locked onto a MiG at a range of about 18 miles and shed the outboard fuel tanks. Hodgdon recalled:

> The one we shot down was head-on, which we could tell via the Vc circle on the radar display showing closing velocity. The in-range light illuminated at six miles, and we fired our first AIM-7E missile. We only had three Sparrows since we were carrying an ECM pod and the first one fell off the aircraft with motor ignition failure. The second one lit off and flew down at a 45-degree angle. Colonel Kittinger held the trigger down for another three seconds and the third Sparrow blasted off. I calculated that the closing distance to the MiG was such that we were a fraction of a second away from the missile not arming in time to hit the MiG.

Kittinger later reported:

> At approximately 18 miles the system broke lock but it was quickly reacquired. A slow left turn ensued to keep the dot centered. Altitudes were slowly increased from 8,200 feet to 11,500 feet. The Vc on the scope was extremely difficult to interpret; however, it appeared that we were not really overtaking the target, so the outboard tanks were dropped. Heading of the aircraft changed to approximately 360 degrees at time of firing. At approximately six miles the in-range light illuminated, followed by an increase in the ASE circle. I squeezed the trigger and felt a thump as the missile was ejected, but the missile motor did not ignite. I squeezed the trigger again and held it for approximately three seconds, but the missile did not fire. I squeezed again and missile number three fired. It made a small correction to the left then back to the right and guided straight away. I kept the dot centered. Approximately five–six seconds after launch, a detonation was observed. Almost simultaneously, two enemy missiles were observed coming from the vicinity of the detonation. Evasive action prevented more thorough observations of the detonation. The flight turned to a heading of 210 degrees, maintained 9,000 feet, airspeed 500 knots, and egressed the area.

Hodgdon recalled, "The missiles missed! What we didn't know, or didn't hear, was that there were three other MiGs after us from the side and one nearly behind us. Our wingman yelled at us repeatedly about multiple MiGs, but we were too focused to hear him." Kittinger and Hodgdon both received Silver Stars for the mission. The VPAF admitted the loss of a MiG-21 flown by Lieutenant Dang Van Dinh, who was able to eject and parachute safely despite his fighter catching fire when hit.

On March 30, 1973, the North Vietnamese invaded South Vietnam, quickly moving through the DMZ into Quang Tri Province. That evening, Captains Frederick S. Olmsted, Jr., and WSO Gerald R. Volloy of the 432nd's 13th Tactical Fighter Squadron led the two-plane Papa Flight in a scramble from Udorn to take up an orbit near the Laotian border, flying one of the wing's Combat Tree-equipped F-4Ds. Captain Stuart "Stu" Maas, who was on the mission as WSO in Papa 02, recalled:

There were three VPAF aircraft airborne, types unknown, at the time, and the weather over RP [Route Packs] I and II was bad. As we climbed out in the waning light on a north-easterly vector, GCI casually asked if we were "interested in running on a target." Fredo Olmsted's reply was "Yes," and we were off to the races. Flying through the "soup" in tight wingtip formation over the northern Steel Tiger area, we headed towards the Mu Gia Pass at about 18,000 feet, where we ran into our target.

Olmsted remembered, "There was no Visual ID since it was pitch black! We had flown through rain and cloud cover, directed by Red Crown. In fact, the Navy directed the entire low-altitude night fight."

Papa 01 didn't have the contact at first, but Papa 02 did. Maas explained:

The lead WSO (Volloy) at first had no contact, but we did. I had a full-system lock-on, and was giving intercept instructions to Volloy, as well as preparing to fire. At a range of about seven miles the flight lead abruptly banked left and was gone. We went on as lost wingmen, and without the certainty of a target, or of the location of our flight lead, we held our fire. Shortly afterwards we heard Fredo and Volloy say they had fired a missile, and there was a distant explosion.

My target was a single MiG-21, but at least three MiGs were up that night. Bobby Lodge also engaged a MiG at about the same time as we did, but without results. The entire fight took place below 1000 ft. Our radar altimeters were set at 1000 ft, and the red altitude alert light was constantly flashing on and off during the engagement. I remember Gerry saying, "Don't hit the ground, Fredo!" over and over. We did get a missile launch, but due to the parameters we probably didn't give the missile too much of a chance. The motor ignited but we didn't see any impact or explosion.

WSO Volloy reported:

Twenty minutes after reaching our orbit point, Red Crown called a bandit and vectored the flight to intercept. Red Crown provided vectors until approximately 20 nautical miles, and at 15 nautical miles I established radar contact with the bandit. A full system lock-on was acquired at 12 nautical miles, and all missile-firing parameters were satisfactory. We fired one AIM-7 at approximately eight nautical miles with no visible results. Another AIM-7 was fired at approximately six nautical miles; the missile appeared to fire properly and guided well, straight off the aircraft. When no visible results were seen, a third AIM-7 was fired at approximately four nautical miles. This missile appeared to guide well, appeared to track straight off the aircraft and then disappeared from view. A few seconds later both of us observed a large reddish-yellow fireball at one o'clock, almost level, approximately two nautical miles ahead, that sustained itself for a few seconds. The fireball first appeared, and then trailed what seemed to be sparks behind it. The fiery sparks paralleled our flight path, toward us, and the entire fire pattern was estimated to be 150–200 feet in length. Visual contact was lost with the fireball due to our breakaway. A subsequent query to Red Crown confirmed that the bandit had disappeared from their scopes as well. It was at this time that we left the area.

The larger war that everyone had expected since the end of *Rolling Thunder* was now on.

15

THE EASTER OFFENSIVE

On March 30, 1972, the long-expected North Vietnamese military offensive in South Vietnam began with PAVN forces overrunning the DMZ, followed by thrusts into Quang Tri Province from Laos. Known to the North Vietnamese as "the Nguyen Hue Offensive," to the United States as "the Easter Offensive," and to the South Vietnamese as "the Red Fiery Summer," the military event officially known in North Vietnam as "the 1972 Spring–Summer Offensive" was the largest military action in Asia since the Chinese People's Volunteer Army had crossed the Yalu River into North Korea and attacked United Nations forces there during the Korean War. The event came almost exactly a year after the disastrous South Vietnamese incursion into Laos known as Operation *Lam Son 719*, in which North Vietnamese forces had inflicted heavy losses on the ARVN invasion force.

Three years of progressive "Vietnamization" of the war saw withdrawal of nearly all US ground units. The 101st Airborne Division, the last major American unit in South Vietnam, completed withdrawal on March 10; by this time, most Air Force units had been withdrawn, leaving the smallest US force in the region since the spring of 1964. In 1971 President Nixon had announced an official visit to Beijing to commence normalizing a situation frozen in place since the communist victory in 1949, as well as a major summit with Leonid Brezhnev in Moscow in June, with expressed hopes of ratifying the second Strategic Arms Limitation Treaty (SALT II). Although this created hopes for reducing Cold War tensions, both communist powers had increased aid to North Vietnam to demonstrate their zealous support for the cause of anti-imperialism. While the US position had not been weaker since the war's beginning, that of North Vietnam had never been stronger.

There was increasing evidence of the North Vietnamese build-up throughout 1971. Between December 26 and 30, the US Air Force and Navy conducted Operation *Proud Deep*, the first major strikes against targets in the North since 1968, but the domestic political environment did not support a sustained campaign. The Lavelle Affair – which increased distrust of the military – had broken mere weeks before the Easter Offensive began.

The response to the intelligence reports of a coming invasion did not improve the situation. Secretary Laird had testified to Congress in late January that North Vietnamese military action "was not a serious possibility." MACV's launch of US air strikes around Tet in the mistaken belief that reported North Vietnamese actions presaged the invasion left General Abrams a subject of press ridicule as "the boy who cried wolf."

The success of the China trip in February and the positive Soviet attitude regarding the coming summit contributed to high-level belief that the major communist powers were keeping North Vietnam on a short leash. Days before the offensive began, the United States walked out of the Paris peace negotiations, citing North Vietnamese "intransigence." Despite continuing reports of enemy preparation, there was no concern that Ambassador Bunker and General Abrams would both be absent from Saigon at the end of March.

The opening phases of the invasion demonstrated how hollow "Vietnamization" was. The offensive took advantage of the seasonal monsoon, with 500-foot ceilings negating air support, while the invaders used the new ZSU-57-2 self-propelled vehicle armed with two deadly 57mm guns, as well as the SA-7 Grail shoulder-fired antiaircraft missile, which were both deadly against low-level air attacks.

Of 27,000 US troops in South Vietnam, only 10,000 were combat troops. Only three F-4 squadrons and an A-37 squadron were based in South Vietnam, with 114 F-4 fighter-bombers in Thailand. The entire heavy force was 83 B-52s at U-Tapao and Guam; the Thailand-based bombers were due to depart in April.

A week after the invasion began, a new front opened in III Corps, threatening the central Vietnamese coast and Saigon itself. Fortunately, the southern advance inexplicably halted for three crucial weeks, while the northern crisis waned as the reorganized ARVN held southern Quang Tri Province.

When first informed of the invasion, President Nixon's response was to order a three-day all-out bombing of Hanoi by B-52s. Secretary of State Henry Kissinger, aghast at the thought of destroying SALT II, managed to change this to B-52 use in North Vietnam south of the 18th parallel. Despite Kissinger's fears, Nixon determined that a total collapse in South Vietnam would cause a loss of prestige just before the coming summit that would be even more threatening to a successful outcome. US forces began to move toward Southeast Asia on April 6 and were largely in place by the end of the month.

Nixon made good on his threat to send B-52s north, when, on April 16, 17 B-52s bombed the Duc Giang fuel storage depot, located northeast of Hanoi, the first return to Route Pack VI since the 1968 bombing halt. Two hundred SAMs were fired at the Stratofortresses.

The mission also saw the first air combat over the North since 1968. Basco Flight, led by Captain Frederick S. "Fredo" Olmsted, Jr., victor over a MiG-21 two weeks earlier, with WSO Captain Stuart W. Maas, who had flown Olmsted's wing in the previous engagement, as Basco 01, Captain Steve Cuthbert as Basco 02, Major Dan Cherry and WSO Captain Jeff Feinstein in Basco 03, and Captain Greg Crane in Basco 04, took off from Udorn to escort F-4 fighter-bombers to hit oil storage tanks outside Hanoi.

At the same time, the MiG-21-equipped 921st Regiment put Nguyen Hong My and Le Khuong on alert while the MiG-19-equipped 927th Regiment did the same for Nguyen Ngoc Hung and Duong Dinh Nghi. The two flights took off, but did not encounter the bombers. Instead, they ran into Basco Flight.

Olmsted later recalled:

Red Crown initially pointed us in the right direction, calling out "White" and "Blue" bandits. Stu then picked them up using the newly installed Combat Tree gear. Since I didn't understand how it worked, or trusted it, I wasn't sure the bogeys weren't our guys merely heading our way. Plus, after nearly 300 missions where we had to absolutely visually identify our targets, I couldn't convince myself to shoot BVR. But the two bogeys marched right down the scope, with Stu screaming in my headset to "kill'em!" He was right. They were two MiG-21s head-on to us. As it turned out, there was also a "trailer" MiG-21 coming up from the weeds to act as shooter from behind.

WSO Maas explained:

The MiG two-ship we met up with was called out as being "Bullseye 270/40" [40 miles west of Hanoi on a bearing of 270 degrees – all GCI references to MiG bearings were relative to Hanoi, codenamed "Bullseye"]. We were southwest of Bullseye, and had just turned from our easterly heading to a northerly one. A quick mental calculation indicated to me that there were MiGs north of us, but they were not yet a threat. Keeping track of these "players" was a team effort, and with up to ten flights on the same combat frequency, it initially made inter-flight and sometimes intra-cockpit communication difficult.

These were MiG-21s, of the 927th Regiment, flown by Captain Nguyen Ngoc Hung and Lieutenant Duong Dinh Nghi:

I kept track of threats to us, as well as friendlies in our area, as I heard them, mentally cataloguing them and quickly explaining to my pilot what we ought to do next. In this specific case we jettisoned the external tanks using a special maneuver that got them off without them colliding with the airframe. We then began a shallow descent through the cloud deck into clear air and picked up Mach.

Basco Flight continued toward Hanoi. Dan Cherry recalled:

As we approached Hoa Binh two things happened almost simultaneously. Stu Maas picked up a bogie [this was Nguyen Hong My and Le Khuong] on his radar at 20 miles. About the same time our airborne controller called and directed us to proceed to a new orbit point down by the DMZ. Since we had contact, and an engagement seemed imminent, we disregarded their instructions and turned to put the bogies on our nose.

Stu Maas' work demonstrated the truth of what one pilot said, "Without the guy in back, the Phantom is just another cross-country airplane." Maas reported:

"Basco has bandits on the nose, 21 [nautical miles]." I did have Combat Tree "grass" at the bottom of the scope, indicating azimuth and presence, but just "grass" was not good enough. I soon had a full Tree indication, "grass" just above and just below a radar return at range and azimuth, and at 11 nautical miles I called out "Basco on the nose, 11 miles." We were fast, with full systems in range lock, good tracking and closure. I told Fredo to "shoot, shoot, shoot!" at seven miles. With rules of engagement allowing a full-lock on and Tree ID, we were authorized to shoot BVR, but Fredo did not.

In seconds the fight was on. Four clean, roaring Phantoms versus two MiG-21s. When Fredo visually ID'd them, they were slightly high at eleven o'clock, going in the opposite direction. The MiGs' reaction was to begin a slight climbing left turn and split. The wingman probably got spat out by the lead MiG's abrupt left turn. Fredo, with Captain Steve Cuthbert in a fighting wing position, worked on one side, while Dan Cherry and Captain Greg Crane worked the other. I recall checking Steve's position once during the first seconds of the engagement, and he was right in there at my eight o'clock, about 800–1,000 feet out.

Fredo never lost sight of that lonesome MiG. I think it was the wingman, because his turn eased off and he began a slight descent, indicating to me that he had lost sight of us and his partner. With a full radar lock and in a slight left turn, ten degrees nose low, we shot our first AIM-7. I watched as it guided towards the MiG's right wing-tip. AIM-7 number two's contrail sailed off to heaven at two o'clock high. Number three – our last AIM-7 –flew perfectly, colliding just behind the MiG's canopy as we maintained our descending left turn.

Generally, we could shoot all the AIM-7s we had aboard at a target aircraft without hesitation, but with a "shoot/brief look/ shoot" pattern, if the missile looked like it was guiding, we'd hold off with the next one. If the first indications were that there might be a tracking problem, the next missile was launched.

Their kill was the MiG-21 flown by flight leader Captain Nguyen Hong My, who successfully ejected.

Dan Cherry recalled his part of the engagement:

After using Basco 01's Combat Tree for the initial contact and identification, Stu maintained his radar contact and called them out as we closed to five miles and then picked them up visually. We saw two silver MiGs about 5,000 feet higher than we were. We cranked it around, trying to keep the MiGs in sight. I was on the outside of the turn, so I fell behind. Half way through the turn my wingman called a third, camouflaged, MiG-21 at twelve o'clock low to me, and climbing into position behind Olmsted's element. The VPAF had apparently been setting a trap, using the silver MiGs as bait. The camouflaged MiG had been at low altitude, and as we started our turn to chase the silver MiGs, he had climbed, hoping to roll in behind us. I rolled out of my turn and headed directly for him. He turned hard left away from me and into a cloud.

Cherry's opponent was Lieutenant Le Khuong.

Thinking they might have lost their target, Cherry followed the MiG into the cloud for some time, pulling up and out of it only at the possibility of unseen SAMs rising from below. As they turned back towards Olmsted's lead element, wingman Captain Greg Crane saw the camouflaged MiG above them in a climbing turn. Cherry went to afterburner and pulled around to go after him:

As I pulled the nose up, I had a beautiful set-up for a Sidewinder shot. The sun was more or less behind us, and there was nothing out in front except the MiG. I pulled the nose out in front of him as I selected "heat" and pulled the trigger. Nothing happened. The perfect shot and my airplane was broken! When I returned to base, the AIM-9s were gone, but there was no indication from my wingman or in the cockpit that they functioned properly. We did have serious reliability problems then, probably because of the missiles' age, and all the uploading and downloading that had gone on for several years.

As Cherry's MiG entered a diving spiral, wingman Crane called that he was taking lead. Cherry rolled into fighting wing formation as Crane lined up the MiG and fired his missiles. "His first weapon malfunctioned and fell away, and the next round went into a corkscrewing spiral and missed." Crane's final AIM-7 guided well, but just prior to impact, the MiG broke hard and the Sparrow flew past without exploding. The turn meant that the MiG quickly bled off energy; both F-4s were determined to nail him even though only Cherry had missiles.

Crane chased the bandit in full afterburner. His radio had failed so he didn't hear Cherry call that he was taking back lead. With Crane ahead of them, Cherry and Feinstein could not risk an AIM-7 shot. They were a little faster and pulled level with him. Cherry recalled the climax:

> I called Jeff and told him, "I've got the sight right on the MiG. Lock him up." He did, and I clamped down on the trigger again, never expecting the missile to come off, but suddenly, Whoosh! That big AIM-7 smoked out in front of us as we accelerated through 500 knots in a descending turn to the right. It did a big barrel roll, and at first I thought it would miss him as it appeared to be going too far out in front of him.

The missile blew the MiG's wing off and it went into a hard spiral, trailing fire and smoke as Le Khuong ejected. "The pilot ejected and his 'chute opened right in front of me. I turned hard left to make sure I didn't fly through it. We were close to supersonic with the afterburners cooking, and I know we weren't more than 30 feet away from him when we passed." Cherry noticed the pilot's black flying suit and white parachute with one red stripe. "By this time we were low on fuel, and I had but one thought at that point: let's get out of here before more MiGs show up."

Basco Flight headed back to Udorn at treetop level, hoping to find a tanker so they would have fuel "to show off a bit when we got back," as Maas remembered. They arrived with less than 1,000 pounds of fuel, with each peeling off quickly from their overhead entry and shutting down as soon as they pulled off the runway.

A third kill was scored by an F-4 flown by Captain James C. Null and WSO Captain Michael D. Vahue, flying element lead as Papa 03 in a standby MiGCAP flight, and vectored into northern Laos to investigate a possible hostile track. The target was declared hostile shortly after they reached their designated orbit over Laos. Vahue remembered:

> I had a cockpit problem. Back-seaters carry so much junk, maps, checklists etc., that something got in the way of my radar cursor control stick so that I couldn't get the cursor on the MiGs for a radar lock-on, so we lost them. We came round again and Jim cleared our wingman, Gary Lorenz, to shoot. I don't know why, maybe he had a switching problem, but all his missiles fell off. Then we got a vector,

which I think was from "Teaball" [the aircraft monitoring VPAF communications] that gave us the info we needed. We came up behind the MiGs in their six o'clock. We were "down in the weeds" at less than 1,000 feet, headed for Hanoi. We had all the parameters we needed, and Jim loosed off all three AIM-7Es at the second MiG.

Null reported:

Aircraft four acquired a radar lock-on when the target was 19 miles out. He was given the lead and attempted to fire, but all AIM-7s malfunctioned. A flight of two MiG-21s passed overhead, and we started a hard right turn. A vector of 275 degrees for 12 miles was received and visual and radar contact was made at that point. We closed on the target, confirmed it was a flight of two MiG-21s, and maneuvered to their twelve o'clock position. Radar lock-on was acquired and when in range three AIM-7's were fired, the second of which exploded on the left side of the wingman's tail section, tearing it from the fuselage. We then passed overhead and observed the MiG to be on fire in the aft section of the fuselage and out of control at approximately 2,000 feet altitude. No chutes were observed. We then egressed and heard from a controlling agency that a single hostile aircraft was orbiting in the vicinity of the engagement.

Their kill was a MiG-21 from the 927th Regiment flown by Lieutenant Duong Dinh Nghi.

In the final years of *Rolling Thunder*, a revolution had played out in the development of what came to be called "smart bombs." More accurately, they were "precision-guided munitions" (PGM). The first "smart bomb" was the Navy's Walleye, a free-fall bomb steered by a television tracking system that required a sharp visual contrast in order to lock on to the target, and was thus often foiled by Southeast Asian weather and the nature of targets in Vietnam. The Air Force developed an electro-optical glide bomb, called HOBO (HOming BOmb System), which was more accurate and carried a bigger warhead than Walleye.

The real breakthrough in PGM technology was the laser-guided bomb. The key players in the creation of the LGB were Colonel Joseph Davis, Jr., vice commander of the Air Proving Ground at Eglin AFB, and Texas Instruments engineer Weldon Word. Davis had come to Eglin in search of a weapon accurate enough to routinely hit within 30 feet of a target that was powerful enough to destroy it. The colonel saw promise in a concept suggested by Word that used earlier research for laser guidance of missiles. His idea was a laser kit of seeker and guidance components that could be bolted on to standard "dumb" bombs. The system would require two airplanes. One focused a tight laser beam to designate the target, painting it continuously and reflecting a cone of laser energy called "the basket" back outward. The second aircraft would drop a bomb fitted with a seeker head into the basket, which would lock on to the laser illumination and home on the target.

The guidance system and control fins for the bomb were adapted from the Shrike missile. The bomb would fly a zigzag course to the target as the fins made a corrective switch every few seconds to bring the laser reflection back to the center of the seeker head's field of view.

The sighting and steering device was created by two Air Force officers at Eglin. Mounted on the left canopy rail of the rear cockpit of an F-4, it was called the "Zot box." The designator orbited the target in a pylon turn and fixed its laser beam on the target. At bombing altitude, the cone of laser energy radiating outward was almost a mile in diameter. Any number of shooter aircraft could drop their bombs into the basket while the designator held its illumination of the target until the bombs hit the target about 30 seconds after release. The advantage of the LGB over the E/O system was that the aircraft dropping the weapon was not required to stick around to guide it.

An LGB known as "Paveway" was combat-tested from May to August 1968 by the 8th Tactical Fighter Wing. Two variants were used. One bolted the laser kit onto a Mark 117 750-pound bomb, with the control fins in the rear due to the bomb's bulbous shape. The other used a Mark 84 2,000-pound bomb, which had a more dynamic shape that allowed the control fins to be bolted on the nose. The Mark 117 Paveway was a disappointment, with an accuracy of 75 feet, but the Mark 84 Paveway had a spectacular average accuracy of 20 feet, with one in every four scoring a direct hit. At $3,000 each, Paveway was cheap compared to the $35,000 Walleye.

The bombing halt in November 1968 had prevented the use of Paveway in North Vietnam, but the intervening years had seen enough Paveways used that there was a cadre of experienced crews when bombing began anew in May 1972. The initial results clearly demonstrated the weapon's effectiveness. Importantly, by 1972 the Pave Knife laser designator pod had been created. Hanging from an F-4's wing rather than mounted in the cockpit, it was on a gimbal that swiveled to keep the beam on the target, thus freeing the designator airplane to maneuver at will without being forced to fly a fixed orbit. This allowed the designator to also act as the shooter, dropping the LGB as well as illuminating the target. By May, 1972, the 8th Tactical Fighter Wing had seven Pave Knife F-4s and 12 equipped with Zot boxes.

The "Dragon's Jaw" was the first "smart bomb" target. By the time strikes against the bridge were canceled in 1966, the Air Force and Navy had flown 871 sorties against it, losing 11 aircraft and failing to even seriously damage it. On April 27, 1972, the 8th Tactical Fighter Wing attacked the bridge, but heavy cloud cover prevented use of the Paveway illuminators and the strike force had to employ HOBO bombs instead of LGBs; these damaged the highway sections but failed to drop any bridge spans.

The North Vietnamese offensive continued in the face of the US return. On May 8, President Nixon announced in a televised address to the nation that he had authorized the resumption of bombing in North Vietnam, as well as the mining of Haiphong Harbor. The Easter Offensive had been significantly slowed, if not stopped, through the use of air power to stop North Vietnamese military action in South Vietnam. Now, the objective was to destroy the military supplies stored in the North, and the infrastructure that might be used in a future invasion, in order to bring about a resumption of peace negotiations. The president's orders put airfields, SAM sites, and other targets that were previously off-limits on the strike list. While Operation *Linebacker* would not commence until the morning of May 10, action was being taken to prepare.

16

OPERATION *LINEBACKER*

Both the Soviet Union and China publicly denounced the US response to the Easter Offensive, but neither was willing to jeopardize the opportunity of reducing the continuing Cold War confrontation. North Vietnamese requests for additional support met cool responses. The leaders in Hanoi saw that they would face the final act of American military action alone.

By early May, the situation in the South was such that it was decided the United States would bomb North Vietnam again to slow the rapid advance. This time, the Johnson Administration rules of engagement were removed for Operation *Linebacker*. Nixon privately announced, "These bastards have never been bombed like they're going to be bombed this time."

Linebacker began on May 10, 1972, with day-long alternating strikes by Air Force units from Thailand and strikes by naval air wings from the four aircraft carriers operating from Yankee Station. The main Air Force strike was against the Paul Doumer Bridge which had been hit repeatedly in 1967, but had been repaired in the years after the November 1968 bombing halt. On May 10, the bridge was targeted by 16 F-4 Phantoms from the 8th Wing, using first-generation "smart" bombs. The lead flight each carried two 2,000-pound electro-optical guided bombs (EOGBs) while the second and third flights each carried two Mark 84 2,000-pound laser-guided bombs. All eight EOGBs missed the target, some by wide margins. The LGBs did much better, scoring several direct hits that displaced one span without dropping it but rendered the bridge impassable to wheeled traffic. On May 11, four Phantoms paid a return visit and concentrated their LGBs on the damaged section, dropping it into the river.

Linebacker's first day saw Captain Steve Ritchie score the first of his five victories to become the only Air Force pilot ace of the Vietnam War. Graduating first in his class at the Air Force Academy, Ritchie was described by Robin Olds as "brilliant" but thinking himself "God's gift" – cocky and egotistical. Other squadron members recalled Ritchie as often lacking in self-discipline, with a personal trademark of using too much Old Spice cologne, for which his retort was that the pilots' locker room smelled too bad.

The opening day saw 120 Air Force aircraft launched, including 32 F-4 bombers, eight F-4s dropping "chaff" – thin aluminum strips designed to degrade the enemy radar system – and 28 air-to-air configured F-4s for a strike on Hanoi. Oyster Flight from the 555th and Balter Flight from the 13th Tactical Fighter Squadron formed the pre-strike MiGCAPs, entering North Vietnamese airspace ahead of the strike formation. As they crossed in from Laos, two Balter F-4Ds were forced to abort due to Combat Tree failures, while First Lieutenant Tommy Feezel and WSO Captain Larry "Doc" Pettit in Oyster 04 lost their radar, but stayed with the flight.

Major Robert Lodge and WSO Roger Locher in Oyster 01 led the four F-4Ds at low altitude to form a BARCAP to catch any MiGs heading for Balter Flight, 22,000 feet above. Lodge's F-4D and the F-4D flown by element leader Captains Steve Ritchie and WSO Charles B. "Chuck" DeBellvue, carried Combat Tree and a full air-to-air armament of four AIM-9 Sidewinders and four AIM-7 Sparrows. They received reports of MiGs taking off from Kep from the Disco EC-121T. As they neared Hanoi, the Navy's Red Crown, manned by chief radarman Larry Nowell on USS *Chicago* (CG-11), who was considered the best US controller by both Air Force and Navy aircrews, reported four separate two-MiG formations airborne. The enemy fighters repeatedly flew towards the oncoming strike formation, then drew back, trying to draw off the escorts. At 0942 hours, the MiGs closed on Oyster and Balter flights as they flew their figure-eight orbits 50 miles south of Yen Bai. WSO Locher's Combat Tree gear got two separate hostile contacts on the nose at 40 miles.

What neither Oyster lead Lodge nor chief Nowell realized was that the two "hostile contacts" were the two MiG-21s flown by Nguyen

Cong Huy and Cao Son Khao, and a flight of four MiG-19s from the 925th Regiment led by Hoang Cao Bong and Pham Cao Ha, and element leader Nguyen Van Cuong and Le Van Tuong. The two MiG-21s, which had been launched to provide cover for the J-6s, separated as they engaged the Phantoms.

Lodge turned Oyster Flight toward the MiG-21s, and climbed to meet them. Lodge set up for the impending engagement as Locher watched the MiGs on the scope while Lodge accelerated to Mach 1.4. When they were 20 nautical miles from contact, Locher armed the Sparrows. At 13 nautical miles the "in-range" light came on. Lodge fired one AIM-7 at a range of eight nautical miles at the MiGs. The missile began climbing and tracking, but when the motor burned out, it detonated prematurely. Lodge immediately fired a second AIM-7 at six nautical miles that left a contrail for eight seconds, then detonated, in a huge reddish-orange fireball. Lodge continued his climb and five seconds later Locher saw a MiG-21 with the left wing missing, trailing fire with pieces falling off and out of control pass 1,000 feet away. The pilot had ejected. The kill was Lodge's third victory.

First Lieutenant John D. Markle and WSO Captain Stephen D. Eaves in Oyster 02 caught the second MiG-21, flown by Cao Son Khao. Eaves remembered:

> We engaged a MiG-21 with a full system radar lock-on. I fired both our AIM-7s and observed the second missile to climb slightly and turn right approximately 15 degrees. Soon after launch, I visually identified a MiG-21 passing from my left to right. The AIM-7 continued on a collision course. Upon impact, the missile detonated and a large yellow fireball resulted. The right wing of the MiG departed the aircraft and the airframe immediately began to descend out of control. The kill was witnessed by Oyster 04, First Lieutenant Tommy L. Feezel and WSO Captain Lawrence H. Pettit.

Cao Son Khao ejected but he died when his parachute failed to fully deploy.

Major Lodge set off after what he thought was another MiG-21, but was in fact the MiG-19 flown by Nguyen Van Cuong, while Ritchie and DeBellvue, with Oyster 04, pursued what they thought was the fourth MiG-21 but was actually Pham Cao Ha, the wingman of Hoang Cao Bong.

Ritchie later reported:

Upon reaching our patrol area west of Phu Tho and south of Yen Bai, Red Crown advised us of bandits approaching from the northeast. Shortly thereafter, both Lodge and I obtained a radar contact. The bandits were declared hostile and our flight engaged the flight of four MiG-21s. Lodge fired two missiles at the attacking MiGs from a front-quarter aspect, utilizing a full system radar lock-on. A detonation and fireball were seen as one of the missiles impacted the number two MiG. Meanwhile, Markle achieved a radar lock-on on the number three MiG-21 and fired two AIM-7 missiles. Another yellow fireball was observed and the number three MiG began to disintegrate. At this time, we switched the attack to the number four MiG, which was now a threat to Lodge and Markle, while Lodge pursued the number one MiG. As we converted to the rear, I achieved a radar lock-on and fired two AIM-7s at a range of approximately 6,000 feet. The first missile guided to the target and appeared to pass just under it. The second guided perfectly and impacted the target, causing another yellow fireball. As we flew past the falling debris, my weapon systems officer observed a dirty yellow parachute and what is believed to be the MiG-21 pilot.

Lodge was on the tail of element leader Nguyen Van Cuong's MiG-19, which he misidentified as a MiG-21, and was seconds away from his fourth kill when Le Van Tuong maneuvered onto Lodge's tail, unseen by either Lodge or Locher. Tuong, due to his inexperience, overshot the Phantom on their left side, making himself what would have been an easy shot if Oyster 01 had been an F-4E with a gun. Markle yelled a warning to reverse right, but Lodge stayed on the enemy fighter's tail and fired his third AIM-7. In the meantime, Tuong dropped back, took position behind Lodge and opened fire with his three 30mm NR-30 cannon.

Locher saw their target accelerating away unscathed as his own aircraft seemed to slow after what felt like a mid-air collision. Tuong fired again. The F-4's hydraulics were disabled and its right engine seemed to explode. Locher remembered, "We immediately went out of control, flopping from side to side. Then fire started coming in the back of the cockpit. It seared my canopy with bubbles and I couldn't see out any more. The airplane slowed down and we went into a flat spin." Turning on full oxygen as the Phantom descended through 8,000 feet, he advised Lodge to eject, but he refused and ordered Locher to punch out. In desperation, Locher ejected himself, with the Phantom inverted in its death dive with Lodge still aboard. Three weeks earlier, Lodge had told squadron members that he would not allow himself to be captured because of his extensive knowledge of the top secret Combat Tree system and his fear that he might break and reveal the secret under torture.

The three remaining Phantoms of Oyster Flight departed when they spotted a second MiG-19 flight. In a bizarre twist, Le Van Tuong, elated after shooting down Lodge's F-4 in the first victory for the 925th Regiment, returned to Yen Bai and ran out of fuel on final approach. He landed too fast and over-ran the end of the runway, at which point his J-6 flipped over and he died in the resulting fire.

As he hung in his parachute, Locher was afraid to use his URC-64 rescue radio since it was difficult to remove from the zippered pocket of his survival vest and he was unsure whether he could get it back in. He managed to steer towards a nearby mountainside about 2,000 yards away from the burning Phantom. On landing, he was unable to hide his parachute which was stuck in the trees. Knowing he needed to put distance between himself and the parachute, he had a pistol, two pints of water, a first aid kit, insect repellent, mosquito netting, and a knife in his survival vest and knew he could not expect rescue this deep in North Vietnam, north of the Red River. When he tried his radio, the signal was received by a friendly aircraft, but because there was no voice transmission, it was believed it was a North Vietnamese using a captured radio. Locher camouflaged his trail while he listened to hear if a search party was looking for him. Climbing the mountain's eastern side to its peak, he got his bearings, then found a hiding place in the bushes on the western side. Over the next three days, a search party of local farmers beat the bushes up and down the east side of the mountain looking for him. At one point, a boy came within 30 feet of his hiding place. The next day, the search party finally gave up.

Locher decided his best chance of rescue was to cross the Red River Valley, swim the river, then work his way to the sparsely inhabited mountains on the southern side of the valley. He estimated it would take him 45 days, traveling at first light and at dusk, avoiding local farmers, and living off the land.

Evading capture, Locher was able to cover 12 miles over ten days. The morning of the tenth day, he was nearly discovered when he suddenly heard local farmers around the bend. Hiding in a nearby field, he lay there all day as children from the village played nearby. At one point, he was nearly stepped on by a water buffalo, and had to hold his breath as a boy came to fetch the animal. That evening he climbed a hill and saw the open fields of the Red River basin. To his west was Yen Bai airfield, five miles distant.

Locher managed to remain hidden on the hill for the next 13 days. while he dodged people and watched for American aircraft. On June 1, he saw a flight of F-4s and called "Any US aircraft, if you read Oyster One Bravo, come up on Guard." Incredibly, the flight was led by Steve Ritchie, who recognized the call sign. The fact that Ritchie recognized Locher's voice would be the deciding element in the decision to go for a rescue, since others back at Udorn doubted he could have remained free that deep in North Vietnam for 23 days and argued that the North Vietnamese might have manipulated a prisoner of war into impersonating him to set a trap.

Once identification was confirmed, a small rescue force was on its way from NKP in a few hours. This was the deepest penetration into North Vietnam ever made by rescue forces. Fortunately, a bombing raid earlier that week had forced the 925th Regiment to redeploy to Hanoi's Gia Lam Airport. The A-1 Sandys arrived over Locher's position, established radio contact and were satisfied from personal questions that they were indeed talking to him. The HH-53C Super Jolly Green helicopter flown by Captain Dale Stovall of the 40th Aerospace Rescue and Recovery Squadron started in for the pickup.

At that moment, a flight of two MiG-21s flown by Pham Phu Thai and Nguyen Cong Huy spotted the four F-4s of the rescue MiGCAP and turned to attack. The F-4s spotted the incoming MiGs. The first element climbed to meet them while the second dived away. Thai went after them. Diving from 40,000 feet to 6,000 feet, he closed on the lead F-4. Closing to 3,000 feet, he fired an Atoll that exploded just behind the F-4's tail. He banked away, pulling an amazing 9.5Gs accidentally, and was about to fire a second missile when the MiG shook hard twice. Thai looked out and realized his pitot had broken under the G-force.

As he turned away, Captains G.W. Hawks and WSO David B. Dingee ejected. Fortunately, with Captain Stovall's HH-53C at hand, they were quickly rescued. In the face of this opposition, the attempt to rescue Locher was called off for the day.

In the light of the failed attempt on June 1, there were questions whether such a deep-penetration rescue could be carried out. Seventh Air Force commander General John W. Vogt informed MACV that he was canceling the strikes set for Hanoi the next day to dedicate all available resources to rescuing Locher. He later explained:

> I had to decide whether we should risk the loss of maybe a dozen airplanes and crews just to get one man out. Finally I said to myself, goddamn it, the one thing that keeps our boys motivated is the certain belief that if they go down, we will do absolutely everything we can to get them out. If that is ever in doubt, morale would tumble. That was my major consideration. So I took it on myself. I didn't ask anybody for permission. I just said, go do it!

The rescue involved 119 aircraft, including two HH-53C rescue helicopters, four flights of F-4 fighter-bombers, six A-1E and A-1H Sandys, two flights of F-105G Wild Weasels to deal with SAMS, EB-66 jammers, eight flights of F-4 escorts, and KC-135 tankers. The pickup point was 60 miles northwest of Hanoi. It was the largest rescue force ever assembled, to make the deepest-penetration rescue ever attempted.

The fighter-bombers struck Yen Bai and wrecked the runway. Captains Ronald E. Smith and "Buck" Buchanan took their A-1Es in to locate Locher. Light and medium AAA opened up and flak-suppression F-4s went after the guns. Locher guided Smith and Buchanan with his rescue radio. Smith told Locher to flash his signal mirror, which was spotted by Buchanan. Smith guided Captain Stovall's HH-53C to the location and Buchanan told Locher to "pop smoke." His flare went unseen and Stovall overflew him. Locher guided Stovall back as enemy fire increased. Stovall hovered and lowered the penetrator. When it touched ground, Locher broke cover and ran to it. Cheers erupted over the radios when he popped out of the jungle canopy aboard the penetrator. Once he was clear, Stovall turned to escape. Locher later remembered that he was struck by how young the PJs who pulled him aboard were. The three crewmen manned their Vulcan miniguns, hosing the enemy as Stovall flew out of the valley. Despite the heavy AAA, there had been no losses.

With Locher aboard Stovall's helicopter, the rest of the force turned away. On arrival at Udorn, Locher was greeted by General Vogt, who had flown over from Saigon in a T-39. For their efforts, both Sandy leader Smith and Jolly Green pilot Stovall, who had twice flown his helicopter further into North Vietnam than had ever been done before, were awarded the Air Force Cross.

During the rescue, Major Phillip W. Handley and WSO First Lieutenant John J. Smallwood, flying F-4E Brenda 01, and wingman Captains Stan Green and WSO Douglas Eden in Brenda 02, got separated from the other flight element, which was forced to head for the tankers when they reached "Bingo" fuel. After circling the area once, Handley also headed for the tankers. As he turned west, he received a MiG warning from Red Crown and moments later spotted the MiG-19s flown by Phan Trong Van and Phung Van Quang when they appeared out of the undercast. Brenda 01 and 02 accelerated to Mach 1.2 and immediately turned in to the enemy fighters.

Phan Trong Van and Phung Van Quang spotted the oncoming Phantoms and dived back into the clouds to evade. Handley followed and opened fire with his M61 cannon in what he later called a "snap shot" when he was unable to get a missile tone. Phung Van Quang's MiG caught fire as its wing came off. Brenda 02 spotted two MiG-19s flown by Nguyen Hong Son (Son A) and wingman Pham Hung Son (Son C) as they turned toward the Phantoms. The two Phantoms pulled up and turned west for the tankers while Phung Van Quang's MiG-19 hit the ground and exploded. Handley's kill was the second gun kill for the F-4E and the only supersonic gun kill ever recorded.

For the 432nd, the loss of Robert Lodge was hard. He had initiated many new ideas as wing weapons and tactics officer. John Markle recalled:

Bob and Roger were innovative in their attempts to both provide proper mission coverage and give the MiGs some incentive to fly. We tried erroneous radio transmissions, claiming weapons systems or aircraft problems, in the hope of duping them into thinking we were crippled. At times we tried flying close formation to create a radar image of a single aircraft on CAP. He was dedicated to getting the job done as effectively as possible.

During Locher's 23 days on the run in North Vietnam, the Air Force engaged in an air war with the VPAF that resulted in the destruction of no fewer than 11 enemy fighters during the month of May.

On May 11, Captain Stephen E. Nichols and First Lieutenant James Bell were flying Gopher 02, to wing deputy commander Lieutenant Colonel Joe Kittinger and WSO First Lieutenant Bill Reich in Gopher 01, when Kittinger spotted two bogeys and accelerated to close and get a visual ID, identifying them as MiG-21s. They were flown by Lieutenants Ngo Van Phu and Ngo Duy Thu, neither of whom was aware of the presence of Gopher flight. Ngo Duy Thu broke away to attack F-105G Wild Weasels just before Kittinger closed on them. His speed was such that he overtook and passed the enemy fighters. As he did, he handed off lead to Nichols and Bell, telling them to shoot. Ngo Van Phu was about to go after the Wild Weasels when Kittinger's Phantom passed, putting him suddenly on the Phantom's tail. Closing on Phu's MiG-21, Nichols pulled the trigger to fire a Sparrow. An instant later, Nichols and Bell were horrified to see Kittinger's Phantom catch fire, hit by an Atoll fired by Phu at the same time they fired. Kittinger and Reich immediately ejected and were captured. Before the Sparrow hit its target, Bell called an approaching MiG and Nichols pulled up to evade and was unable to confirm that the Sparrow he had fired hit Phu, who ejected immediately. Their kill was unconfirmed for two years, until Seventh Air Force awarded Nichols and Bell the credit in 1974.

The next day, 555th Squadron commander Lieutenant Colonel Wayne T. "Fossil" Frye and WSO Lieutenant Colonel James P. "Granny" Cooney, wing operations and tactics officer, shot down the "Triple Nickel"'s first MiG-19 while flying as Harlow 02 to flight leader Harlow 01 Major Sidney Hudson and WSO Captain Larry H. "Doc" Pettit after Harlow 01 lost their radar. Frye, 41, and Cooney, 44, were the oldest MiG killers, as well as the highest-ranking team to score in the war.

With better weather on May 13, the invulnerability of the Dragon's Jaw finally came to an end. The F-105 Wild Weasels went after the AAA as the F-4 strikers hit the bridge with 26 laser-guided bombs. They accomplished what all previous attacks had failed to do. The Bomb Damage Assessment read, "The western span of the bridge had been knocked completely off its 40-foot thick concrete abutment and the bridge superstructure was so critically disfigured and twisted that rail traffic came to a standstill for at least several months." The Dragon's Jaw was still knocked out when *Linebacker* ended in December 1972.

The next kills came on May 23, when two crews of Balter Flight from the F-4E-equipped 35th Tactical Fighter Squadron, operating with the 366th Tactical Fighter Wing on TDY, engaged eight MiG-19s. Balter 01, Lieutenant Colonel Lyle C. Beckers and WSO Captain John Huwe, shot down a MiG-19 flown by Vu Chinh Nghi with a Sparrow. Nghi ejected and managed to land safely despite the fact that his parachute lines had tangled, successfully untangling them when he was 500 feet from the ground. Balter 02, Captain James Beatty and WSO First Lieutenant James M. Sumner, spotted a MiG-21 attempting to get position on Balter 01. Closing on the MiG's tail, Beatty was too close for missiles and instead shot down the enemy fighter with his nose-mounted M61 cannon. The kills marked the first two credited victories for the F-4E, though the VPAF states in its history that there were no MiG-21s in the air at the time of this engagement and that the only MiG-21s that did engage US aircraft on May 23 attacked Navy A-7s.

On May 31, the 555th's Gopher Flight, with element leader Gopher 03, Captains Bruce Leonard and WSO Jeff Feinstein, was able to shoot down a MiG-21 while flying MiGCAP for a strike mission to Kep. Gopher Flight became involved with several flights of J-6s and elements of MiG-21s, and Gopher 01, Major John Lessenberg and WSO Captain John Bullock, managed to fire all four of their AIM-7s without scoring a hit. When another MiG-21 approached, Lessenberg gave Leonard lead and Gopher 03 shot the enemy fighter with a new AIM-9J for that missile's first kill. The MiG was Feinstein's second credited MiG after his victory on May 8.

In the meantime, the Triple Nickel's Icebag Flight, led by Steve Ritchie with WSO "Doc" Pettit, got involved in an engagement with a pair of MiG-21s from the 927th Regiment, led by Captain Nguyen Van Lung, leader of the 9th Company. Luring the MiGs by posing as a "chaff" flight, "Icebag" was warned of approaching MiGs by Red Crown and Ritchie turned into them. Captain John Madden, flying as Icebag 03 in his first MiG engagement, recalled:

We went up over the Gulf of Tonkin and came in over Cam Pha, north of Phantom Ridge. We had slowed down to drop our centerline tanks. We were headed west, and they ran MiGs around in a left turn to get behind some bombers below us. One pilot saw he had overshot the target and climbed to 40,000 feet, getting out of the fight. The other MiG was a mile and a half from us at our eleven o'clock, high in a 2-G turn. I called to Steve Ritchie and he was able to pick him up and turn into him. Steve got him – his second kill.

By the end of *Linebacker*, Madden would be credited with three kills. Ritchie described the fight:

Shortly after crossing the coast northeast of Haiphong, heading generally northwest, Red Crown advised us of blue bandits 40 nautical miles west-southwest of our position. Red Crown continued to give excellent information on the position of the bandits. With the bandits at 7 o'clock, 14 miles range, I began a descending left turn. Shortly thereafter I spotted a flight of two MiG-21s at 10 o'clock high. I continued the left turn and maneuvered to a seven o'clock position on the number two MiG. The lead MiG broke up and away. At this time my weapon systems officer, Captain Larry Pettit, achieved a full-system lock-on and I fired four AIM-7 missiles. The first missile corkscrewed to the right. The next two missiles detonated early. The fourth missile guided perfectly and impacted the MiG in the forward fuselage area. The fuselage from the wings forward broke off and the remainder of the MiG entered a flat left spin until impacting the ground.

The Sparrow that struck behind the MiG's cockpit killed Nguyen Van Lung.

The month of May had been a disaster for the VPAF, which lost 11 fighters to Air Force Phantom crews and 16 to Navy Phantom crews.

On June 13, Spark Flight, a MiGCAP flight from the 308th Tactical Fighter Squadron, engaged a formation of MiG-19s near Yen Bai. As the MiGs evaded their pursuers, two MiG-21s flown by Pham Phu Thai and Nguyen Cong Huy spotted the Phantoms and made a rear attack. Pham Phu Thai shot down Spark 04, flown by First Lieutenants Gregg O. Hanson and WSO Richard J. Fulto, who both ejected successfully and were captured. Their loss cast further doubt over the "fluid four" fighting wing strategy that too often resulted in number four being placed in a vulnerable position.

Bombing Hanoi was suspended between June 14 and 18 when Soviet Premier Alexei Kosygin made a state visit to North Vietnam. For the next 20 days, the ratio of kills was reversed in favor of the MiGs.

Phantom crews were only able to claim two kills while enemy fighters and SAMs were responsible for the loss of seven Air Force F-4s.

On June 21, a flight of MiG-21PFMs from the 927th Regiment led by Le Thanh Dao with wingman Mai Van Tue engaged Iceman Flight from the 469th Tactical Fighter Squadron. After several minutes of maneuvering to get in position, Le Thanh Do realized the two MiGs were in an unfavorable position and broke off. Wingman Mai Van Tue found himself behind Iceman 01 and 02. Tue fired one Atoll that exploded just to the right of Iceman 02. Iceman 01, flown by squadron commander Colonel Mele Vojvodich, Jr., and WSO Major Robert M. Maltbie, had got a warning call from Iceman 03, and the two F-4s had broken left at the last moment. As Tue maneuvered to fire his second missile at Iceman 01, his aircraft shook hard and nosed over. He had been shot down by Iceman 03, Lieutenant Colonel Von R. Christiansen and WSO Major Kaye M. Harden. After shouting to Iceman 01 to break hard just in time to avoid Tue's first Atoll, Christiansen had pulled in behind Tue and fired three AIM-9s that didn't come off the rails. Christiansen reported, "We locked-on in boresight and fired two AIM-7s. The first AIM-7 guided to a direct hit and the second guided into the wreckage. The MiG's right wing was blown off and the fuselage tumbled end over end. No chute was observed." In fact, Tue had fired his ejection seat and landed safely in the Son Dong area.

On July 8, three MiG-21s were lost. The 366th Tactical Fighter Wing Brenda Flight, flying MiGCAP for "chaffers" escorted the chaff-droppers out of the area on one of the first missions flown by the wing since their transfer from Da Nang to Takhli. After the chaff-droppers were safe, Brenda Flight returned for a MiG sweep. Not spotting any enemy aircraft and getting close to "Bingo" fuel, the four F-4s turned to head out of the area when two MiG-21s led by six-victory ace Captain Dang Ngoc Ngu and wingman Lieutenant Tran Viet attempted to catch them from the rear, a tactic based on the assumption that the F-4s would be short of fuel. At the time, the formation was flying in trail, with Brenda 03 and 04 following Brenda 01 and 02 at a slightly higher altitude.

When Ngu and Viet spotted Brenda Flight, they dropped their fuel tanks and Ngu took aim at the lead pair. Diving from the rear, he fired an Atoll at the lead F-4, but turned away before seeing that it had failed to guide. Because his turnaway was at high speed, he ended up sliding in front of Brenda 03, flown by Captains Richard "Tuna" Hardy and

WSO Paul Lewinski. Hardy launched an AIM-9E that failed to guide, then tried to ripple-fire the other three Sidewinders, all of which failed to launch. Lewinski set up a boresight launch and Hardy fired a pair of AIM-7E-2s. The first blew off Ngu's right wing, while the second hit the wreck, compounding its destruction.

The VPAF confirmed that Captain Ngu died in the engagement. This was the first MiG kill for the 4th Tactical Fighter Squadron.

Wingman Tran Viet suddenly found Brenda 01 and 02 in front of him. He fired an Atoll that hit Brenda 01's left engine. Lieutenant Colonel R.E. Rosse managed to fly the damaged F-4E into Thailand before he and WSO Captain Stanley M. Imaye were forced to eject. They were soon rescued by a Jolly Green Giant from NKP.

Lieutenant Tran Viet survived the war and remained in the VPAF, retiring after a 30-year career as a major general. In 2008, he recalled Captain Ngu, "For a young pilot like me to be selected to fly number two to an experienced, courageous, and skilled pilot like Ngu was a very fortunate thing. Ngu always provided very concrete guidance based on combat experience and always tried to make our young pilots feel self-confident and to give them a chance to score victories."

The other two MiG-21s were victories scored by the team of Steve Ritchie and Chuck DeBellvue. Paula Flight was covering the departure of a strike force when they were advised by both Disco and Red Crown that MiGs had been vectored towards them. The two MiG-21s were flown by the 927th Regiment's Nguyen Ngoc Hung and Vu Van Hop. While they were actually unaware of the presence of the Disco EC-121 radar picket as it circled at low altitude, they were on an interception course for the early warning Constellation and both Disco and Red Crown warned Ritchie in Paula 01 of the potential threat. Ritchie recalled, "Disco and Red Crown advised our flight of bandits southeast of our position, approximately 35–40 nautical miles. The flight headed toward the threat in patrol formation and crossed the Black River on a southerly course. Red Crown advised that the bandits and our flight had merged." Ritchie saw a MiG pass overhead. Paula Flight remained on their northerly heading until he saw a trailing MiG as the two turned to trap the F-4s.

At this point, Ritchie pulled hard left and gained position low in the wingman's six o'clock. DeBellvue set up a boresight and Ritchie fired a pair of Sparrows. The MiG pilot finally spotted his adversary, but he was seconds too late. As he attempted to turn away, the first Sparrow hit him. "The first missile impacted the number two MiG, causing a large yellow fireball as it broke into parts. It continued to disintegrate until it hit the ground."

Ritchie then spotted the lead MiG as it turned to threaten Paula 04. Unloading to gain energy, he led the flight into a hard right turn to engage the enemy fighter. As he held a 5-G turn below the MiG-21 in its five o'clock position, he fired another AIM-7 at the very edges of the missile's envelope. Not expecting the missile to guide under such a high G-force, he and DeBellvue immediately prepared for a follow-up gun attack. However, the Sparrow made the sharp right turn and guided perfectly to its target. "The missile impacted the MiG, resulting in a large yellow fireball. This MiG also broke into parts and began to disintegrate. The front of the aircraft was observed impacting the ground in a large fireball." The victory was DeBellvue's third and Ritchie's fourth. As had happened in Korea in 1951 with James Jabara, the Air Force began to apply pressure to enable Ritchie to become the first USAF MiG ace of the Vietnam War.

As the force engaged in Operation *Linebacker* became "all F-4" over the summer of 1972, the units involved began to specialize. Of the four squadrons operated by the 8th Tactical Fighter Wing at Ubon, the 25th and 433rd Tactical Fighter Squadrons were dedicated day-bomber units, with the 433rd also pioneering the use of LGB delivery, while the 435th and 497th squadrons concentrated on night operations. The 388th Tactical Fighter Wing at Korat, which had transitioned from F-105s to F-4s in 1969, retained a primary mission as bombers. Additional units from the 13th and 3rd Air Forces were assigned on TDY throughout the period of increased operations. The 366th Wing, which transferred from Da Nang to Takhli in June, was primarily a day strike outfit. The 432nd Tactical Reconnaissance Wing at Udorn operated the 555th Tactical Fighter Squadron which had transferred from the 8th Tactical Fighter Wing in June 1968 and retained its primary air-to-air mission with its F-4Ds modified with Combat Tree. Along with their fellow 432nd Wing 13th Tactical Fighter Squadron, the "Black Panthers," the two squadrons provided dedicated air combat capability for defense of the bombers.

Unfortunately, there was an ever-diminishing number of crews with any substantial air-to-air experience or training. TAC continued to resist the facts revealed by Project Feather Duster back in 1965, claiming that the primary mission of TAC crews in Southeast Asia was bombing, and that ACM training was thus a "diversion." Major General Alton D. Slay, Seventh Air Force deputy chief of staff for operations, stated the policy clearly: "MiG killing was not our objective. The objective was to protect the strike force. Any MiG kills obtained were considered a bonus. A shoot-down of a strike aircraft was considered a mission failure, regardless of the number of MiGs killed."

By 1972, there were very few *Rolling Thunder* veterans still in the Air Force, with many having left on completion of their minimum required service out of a desire to avoid continuing to fight a war that anyone on the front line knew was not being fought to win. The rapidly trained replacement aircrews, many of whom had never sat in a fighter aircraft, let alone flown one, until they received orders to Southeast Asia and were put through a fast conversion training course, often received their only air-to-air training in the unit they served with after they arrived in-theater, a program that was always limited by operational responsibilities of the individual unit.

In August 1972, Lieutenant Commander John B. Nichols, a Navy F-8 Crusader MiG-killer, was sent with three other Crusader pilots from VF-211 and VF-24 squadrons from USS *Hancock* to teach air combat maneuvering to the Air Force F-4 crews of the 555th and 13th squadrons at Udorn, after the poor performance during June and July. Nichols later recalled that the Air Force crews were "terrible," stating that the students in the two F-8 training squadrons could have flown circles around the best crews he found at Udorn. Experienced in the Navy's "loose deuce" fighting formation, Nichols was amazed to find the Air Force pilots still using the World War II "finger four," which he considered nothing but a waste of two wingmen, a fact borne out by the losses of numbers two and four crews over North Vietnam. Nichols and the other three Navy pilots soon realized they could only help the Air Force crews to improve by putting them through ACM training. When he departed at the end of his time at Udorn in early September, Nichols believed that he had persuaded only about a third of the pilots there of the value of ACM. When one considers that during *Linebacker*, Navy crews who had undergone ACM training through the Top Gun program scored a 6-to-1 kill ratio during May and June, after which the VPAF largely avoided Navy fighters, while the Air Force recorded a 1-to-1 ratio during the same period, the facts demonstrate the validity of Nichols' criticism.

Thus, during *Linebacker*, the number of crews qualified to fly MiGCAPs was quite small. This caused problems for squadron schedulers, who needed to avoid overworking the highly qualified crews and the experts who killed MiGs, while insuring that no MiGCAP went out without an adequate level of expertise in the flight. As MiG-killer Bruce Leonard observed after the campaign, "relying on a succession of crews who visited the war for relatively short TDYs was a funny way to run a war."

On July 18, the 13th Tactical Fighter Squadron "Black Panthers" scored when WSO Captain Jeff Feinstein got his third MiG-21, flying with squadron commander Lieutenant Colonel Carl Baily, who recalled:

> As we were heading toward Hanoi, aircraft number four called out bandits and broke hard right. This caused our elements to be separated, but I elected to continue inbound as the other flight was requesting our assistance. They were low on fuel and were being pursued by MiGs. Captain Feinstein got a radar contact and vectored me and our wingman toward it. At a range of three miles I got a visual contact with a single silver MiG.

Feinstein locked on the enemy fighter and Baily fired four AIM-7s as it dived in an attempt to evade them. Feinstein later recalled, "The missiles missed their mark, but he quickly followed with an AIM-9, which did not miss. It blew off the MiG's right wing and caused the enemy aircraft to snap-roll to the right. During the second snap it hit the ground and disintegrated." The MiG-21 was flown by Lieutenant Nguyen The Duc of the 927th Regiment, who was unable to eject and died in the crash.

On July 29, Baily and Feinstein were flying lead in Cadillac Flight, a MiGCAP that was sent into North Vietnam during the early morning hours to protect forces attacking targets on the Northeast Railway near Kep when they repeated their performance with another MiG-21. The 927th Regiment had launched two MiG-21s flown by ace Captain Nguyen Tien Sam, and Lieutenant Nguyen Thanh Xuan. Sam had been credited with shooting down the F-4E flown by Captain S.A. Hodnett and WSO First Lieutenant D. Fallert of the 366th Wing's 421st Squadron while they were engaged in a strike near Kep on July 24. Both crewmen had ejected successfully and were rescued by an HH-3C Jolly Green Giant. Just before Sam and Xuan encountered Cadillac

Flight, Sam had shot down the F-4E flown by Captain James D. Kul and Captain Melvin K. Matsui of the 366th Wing's 4th Squadron, who had both ejected and been captured, for his sixth victory.

Captain Feinstein recalled his fourth victory:

> While proceeding to our assigned orbit point near Kep, Red Crown gave the code words for MiG activity. A minute-and-a-half later, I picked up radar contacts in the vicinity of Phuc Yen. Red Crown began vectoring our flight toward the southwest onto two bandits and I had radar contacts at that position. I obtained a radar lock-on, and the flight began a hard left turn, attempting to close within firing range. Lieutenant Colonel Baily was able to close to five miles but could not get in range due to the bandit's high speed. We lost the radar lock-on at six miles. After completing the turn, we reacquired another contact which was probably the same bandit.

They were closing on wingman Nguyen Thanh Xuan, who was having trouble keeping up with his leader, Nguyen Tien Sam:

> We called the position of the contact – on the nose for eight miles – to Red Crown, and Red Crown confirmed it was a bandit. We closed in on an attack as Red Crown continued to call the bandit's position. At about four miles, Lieutenant Kirchner and Captain Rogers had visual contact with a silver MiG and called his position in front of the flight as the MiG went into a descending turn. Colonel Baily began firing AIM-7s. The first did not ignite. The second and third were ripple-fired at two-and-three-quarters miles range. They guided down and to the left, bursting into a large fireball. This was observed by other members of the flight.

Lieutenant Kirchner stated that after visually acquiring the MiG, he observed the two missiles guide to it and explode. He observed it emerge from the fireball in flames:

> We continued our turn, and seven members of our flight observed an F-4 in a spin at our nine o'clock position at approximately the same altitude. After a hard reversal turn to check an unidentified single aircraft which I saw at our six o'clock, we observed the F-4 crash into a hillside and explode. Red Crown was still calling a MiG in our immediate vicinity and the flight egressed after a futile attempt to engage this bandit.

This was the F-4 shot down moments earlier by Nguyen Tien Sam, who evaded the Phantoms, while wingman Nguyen Thanh Xuan was able to eject successfully.

Baily later described the aerial victory to newsmen, giving proper credit to WSO Feinstein:

> The MiGs were coming at us at a very high rate of speed. They managed to get by us before we engaged them. We turned as hard as we could, started toward them, and got them right in front of us, coming head-on. Jeff locked on the MiG and I fired two missiles. They both guided right in and splashed him good. The credit all goes to Jeff. When you get them head-on, the guy with the radar does all the work. I just sat up front and squeezed the trigger.

Moments after Feinstein's kill, WSO Captain Stan Imaye, who had been forced to eject with Lieutenant Colonel R.E. Rosse on July 8 when their F-4E was damaged in air combat, was flying as lead WSO in Pistol 01 of the 4th Tactical Fighter Squadron's "chaffer" escort flight with pilot Lieutenant Colonel Gene Taft. With numerous SAMs fired and several MiG warnings from Red Crown, the chaff flights pulled out. Pistol Flight was attacked by a pair of MiG-21s, and Taft managed to get behind one. Imaye initially had difficulty in acquiring a lock-on, but was able to lock in boresight mode when the MiG leveled out. Taft squeezed the trigger and the AIM-7 flew straight, striking the MiG's wing and starting a fire. The enemy fighter went into an uncontrollable roll, but Taft and the flight had to turn away when they got another MiG warning before they saw it impact the ground.

The air battles of June and July saw the Air Force shoot down eight enemy fighters for the loss of 13 Phantoms, a horrific 0.6-to-1 kill ratio in favor of the enemy. During *Rolling Thunder*, the National Security Agency (NSA) had monitored North Vietnamese radio traffic between ground controllers and pilots. This information was not shared with aircrews, out of fear that the North Vietnamese would realize their communications had been compromised if air crews acted on such guidance too often. When the crews learned in late 1967 that such information was available and was not passed on, combat leaders such as Robin Olds vociferously opposed the situation. However, Major General George Keegan, Director of Air Force Intelligence, refused to change the system at the time.

The heavy losses of June and July resulted in a demand from Seventh Air Force commander General John Vogt for the NSA information to be provided in some manner to his crews. The request was backed up by Air Force Chief of Staff General John Ryan, and met a favorable response from the new head of the NSA, Admiral Noel Gaylor, a World War II Navy fighter ace. NSA analyst Delmar Lang, who had created an operational SIGINT system that provided guidance to F-86 pilots in MiG Alley in Korea in 1953, and who had offered to create such a system for the Air Force as far back as 1965, was assigned to work with Lieutenant Colonel William Kirk to establish a new system as quickly as possible.

The result was Project Teaball, a GCI system in which analysts at NKP were able to track enemy ground–air communications in real-time and provide that information to crews over North Vietnam. The network included Olympic Torch, a SIGINT U-2 orbiting over North Vietnam at an altitude "in excess of" 70,000 feet; Burning Pipe and Combat Apple, RC-135 SIGINT aircraft operating over Laos; information from the Navy's Red Crown and Deep Sea EKA-3B SIGINT aircraft operating off the North Vietnamese coast; and Big Look EC-121M aircraft orbiting over the Gulf of Tonkin. The information was fed to NKP where it was combined with classified NSA intercepts from spy satellites and fed into "Iron Horse," a computer that synthesized all the information and put it into a composite display that showed a near real-time picture of the location of all friendly and enemy aircraft over North Vietnam.

The information was sent directly to aircrews via UHF radio relayed through a KC-135 aircraft operating off the coast just north of the DMZ code named "Luzon." Because the Iron Horse computer took on average two minutes to process all the SIGINT and radar inputs, the system was only used to provide early warning, after which Disco or Red Crown directed the engagement. Teaball went operational in the last week of July, 1972, literally operating out of the back of a van behind a hangar at NKP.

The first result of the new system was a victory on August 12 by a Navy/Marine exchange crew flying with the 58th Tactical Fighter Squadron as leaders of Dodge Flight, a weather reconnaissance RF-4C escorted by three F-4Es. Flight leader Dodge 01 Marine Captain Larry Richard and WSO Navy Lieutenant Commander Mike Ettel received a

Teaball warning of two MiG-21s 30 miles distant that had just taken off from Gia Lam with orders to intercept the flight. The two enemy fighters were flown by Luong The Phuc and Nguyen Cong Huy. Dodge 01 and the RF-4C dropped their tanks while Red Crown provided guidance on the oncoming enemy fighters. Dodge 03, Lieutenant Colonel Lee Williams and WSO Major Tom Leach, gave cover with Dodge 04 when Dodge 01 headed for the MiGs. Richard reported:

> As I crossed the Red River, I was informed by Red Crown that bandits were airborne out of Bullseye heading 180. At this time I was 35 nautical miles northwest of them heading 020, proceeding on my fragged route. The bandits then turned to a heading of 360 and commenced an attack. At this time, with the bandits at my six o'clock at 30 nautical miles, I turned the flight to a heading of 180 and accelerated. Red Crown continued giving bandit information and I visually acquired two aircraft at about four nautical miles, starting a turn to my six o'clock.

Richard turned in behind the two MiGs as they banked away and Ettel obtained a lock-on with the leader's silver MiG. Richard then fired an AIM-7 from a range of 1,300 feet. Just before impact, wingman Nguyen Cong Huy spotted the missile and warned leader Luong The Phuc, who broke hard toward the Phantoms, passing Richard and Ettel canopy to canopy. The leader then broke down and away as Richard unloaded and locked on Nguyen Cong Huy's green-camouflaged fighter, firing a second AIM-7 at a range of one mile that blew the tail off Huy's fighter. With the MiG tumbling out of control, Huy managed to eject successfully. The kill was confirmed by Dodge 03. With Teaball warnings of other MiGs, Dodge Flight departed the area.

Three days later on August 15, both Teaball and Red Crown were down due to equipment failure and an eight-plane "chaff" mission composed of Date Flight, led by squadron commander Lieutenant Colonel D.C. Vest, and Palm Flight, led by Captain Rudy V. Zuberbuhler from the 4th Tactical Fighter Wing's 336th "Rocketeers" Squadron, demonstrated the system's value when they were surprised by two MiG-21s, flown by ace Captain Nguyen Tien Sam and Nguyen Hung Thong, with the only warning of their presence being a radioed shout from the MiGCAP Pistol Flight to "Take it to the right, Date!"

Captain Fred Sheffler, in Date 04 with WSO Captain Mark A. Massen, suddenly spotted Nguyen Tien Sam's MiG as it flashed past 200 feet away. He recalled:

Had Pistol flight not spotted the MiGs and engaged them before they could attack, I might have ended up in the Hanoi Hilton, or worse. I immediately banked right and he sped by at Mach 1.1, not turning, while we were at 0.95 Mach. Pistol told us that there were now two MiGs in the attack. We continued our turn, trying to visually pick up the MiGs. A camouflaged MiG-21 overshot at this time. Captain Massen, my WSO, called for me to auto-acquire. I placed my pipper on the MiG and toggled the proper switch on my throttles. We achieved an immediate radar lock-on. I continued our turn to the right, striving to pick up the second MiG.

Unable to gain position on either enemy fighter, element leader Captain Harv Smith in Date 03 yelled to Sheffler to take lead:

Captain Massen cleared me to fire. I made a quick check to see if the MiG was still at my twelve o'clock and then squeezed off an AIM-7 at a range of 4–5,000 feet. For the next ten seconds, until impact, I divided my attention between monitoring the AIM-7 and checking our six for his partner. The missile made two minor corrections in flight; one just prior to impact.

The Sparrow hit Nguyen Hung Thong's MiG just forward of the tail section. "He did not appear to take any evasive action up until the last second, when he hardened up his turn to the left. After impact and explosion, the MIG-21 entered a 45-degree dive, trailing smoke and flames." Thong was able to successfully eject.

Seeing what had happened to his wingman, Nguyen Tien Sam turned back to engage the F-4s:

At this time, the second MiG-21 came by on our right in a hard left turn and went between our two flights head on. We continued our turn and egressed the area at low altitude. Because of the ensuing engagement with the second MiG, I was unable to observe a 'chute or the impact of the MiG-21 with the ground. However, the back-seater of an aircraft of the follow-on strike flight observed a large fire on the side of a hill near the area of the engagement during ingress, and it was still burning during his egress some 15 minutes later.

Date and Palm flights had been fortunate. During the time that Teaball was operational, between August and the end of October, the Air Force lost six F-4s in combat with the MiGs. Five of those six happened when Teaball was non-operational due to technical failure, which demonstrated how valuable the system was.

On August 19, Teaball was working and another MiG was destroyed. Captain Sammy C. White, flying his 204th and final mission over two Southeast Asian combat tours, with WSO First Lieutenant Frank J. Bettine, were flying element lead in Pistol 03, a flight of four chaff-dispensing aircraft. Teaball was able to provide a warning when Le Thanh Dao and Nguyen Thang Duoc took off in their MiG-21PFMs from Gia Lam to intercept the flight. Captain White later reported, "Not long after entering North Vietnam, the WSO in Pistol 02, Captain Forrest Penney, saw a MiG-21 in Pistol 01's six o'clock position and called for a break." As the two flights broke away from each other, Le Thanh Dao realized he had lost the advantage and requested permission to break off. Receiving permission, he started to bank away, but his momentary indecision allowed White to come in on his wingman's rear, unseen. "We rolled into his six o'clock and, following some maneuvering, fired an AIM-7 which tracked on the MiG and detonated." Nguyen Thang Duoc ejected, but while he hung below his parachute, one of the Phantoms flew past so close that its wingtip ripped his parachute. He fell over 1,000 feet into a tree, where he sustained injuries so bad that, despite being rescued, he died in the hospital on August 20.

Throughout the month of August, attention fell on Captains Steve Ritchie and Jeff Feinstein as to which would score a fifth victory first to become the Air Force's first MiG ace of the war. Both already had claims that would have given them their fifth victory disallowed. A claim by Feinstein on June 9 was disallowed for insufficient evidence, as was Ritchie's claim of a kill on June 13. Many crews at Udorn believed the Air Force wanted a pilot as the first ace. Stories became common around the base that Ritchie's chances were being enhanced by the commanders placing him in the best-maintained F-4s with the latest equipment and weapons on board. Those whose memories went back 20 years recalled the effort made then to insure that Captain James Jabara would become the first MiG ace of the Korean War. On August 25, Lieutenant Colonel Carl Baily and Captain Jeff Feinstein were hit at 3,000 feet by 37mm AAA during a strike on Haiphong. They managed to hold their F-4D together long enough to get a mile out into the Tonkin Gulf before ejecting, and were picked up by an HH-53E Jolly Green Giant from the 37th Aerospace Rescue and Recovery Squadron after 20 minutes in the water.

The issue of who would be first was settled on August 28, 1972. Captains Ritchie and DeBellvue were flying as Buick 01 on a MiGCAP for a strike north of Hanoi, leading Buick, Vega, and Olds flights. They were flying F-4D 66-7463, the same Phantom they had flown on May 10 when they scored their first MiG kill. On their way up to North Vietnam from Udorn, Teaball had suffered another equipment failure, and the mission was flying under control from the Disco EC-121 over Laos. The strike formation was picked up on radar at 0922 hours by the North Vietnamese 291st Radar Regiment as they left Laotian airspace, headed for "Bullseye." When the strike force neared Hanoi, control was handed off to Red Crown, aboard the nuclear-powered guided missile cruiser USS *Long Beach* (CGN- 9).

At Gia Lam, the 921st Regiment ordered the MiG-21PFMs flown by Pham Phu Thai and Bui Thanh Liem that were on combat alert to take off at 0942 hours and intercept the enemy. Soon after takeoff, they were identified as "Blue Bandits" by Red Crown and a warning was flashed to Buick lead. North Vietnamese GCI positioned the two fighters behind the oncoming strike and they popped through the broken overcast at 25,000 feet, in position for a fast slashing dive through the Phantoms to force them to jettison their bombs. Moments later, Bui Thanh Liem visually identified the formation of F-4 fighter-bombers and their escorts.

Warned of the threat by Red Crown, which was unable to provide altitude information, DeBellvue picked up the MiGs using the Combat Tree gear and pinpointed them ten miles behind Olds Flight. Ritchie and DeBellvue led the three MiGCAP flights as they turned toward the two MiGs. No one in the 12 cockpits could spot the enemy. Recalling that the MiG-21s had been reported reverting to the high-altitude patrols they had flown during *Rolling Thunder*, Ritchie and DeBellvue searched the sky above them. Suddenly they spotted the two MiGs through a gap in the overcast. Ritchie went into afterburner and climbed toward the enemy. DeBellvue gave him constant updates as the Phantom strained in its climb to catch up to the MiGs.

Finally, with the enemy four miles away, Ritchie fired two AIM-7E-2s at extreme range, hoping they would force the enemy to turn and engage. Not only did both Sparrows miss, but their explosions failed to get a response from either MiG pilot. Moments later he rolled out at the same altitude as the two MiGs and accelerated into a stern chase. At that moment, Pham Phu Thai banked sharply to initiate an attack on the bombers. Bui Thanh Liem was a fatal moment late in following his leader. Ritchie fired his third and fourth Sparrows. The third missed, but the fourth went through the right wing of Bui Thanh Liem's MiG, exploding an instant later as Liem successfully ejected. Ritchie's kill was witnessed by Captain John Madden in Buick 03.

Unlike James Jabara, whose claims of five victories were not supported by loss reports from his Soviet opponents, one of whom actually claimed him as a shoot-down during his "ace making" mission, with the Soviets crediting him with a maximum of two possible victories in the air battles over MiG Alley in April and May 1951, the VPAF confirmed all five of Ritchie's victories.

On September 9, flying with pilot Captain John Madden as Olds 01, Captain Chuck DeBellvue added two MiG-19s to his score of four MiG-21s with Steve Ritchie, to become the top Air Force ace of the war. During the engagement, Olds 03, Captain Calvin B. Tibbett and WSO First Lieutenant William S. Hargrove, also shot down a MiG-19. Teaball warned the flight of MiGs some 50 miles distant. Madden later reported, "We knew they would be returning soon to land at Phuc Yen, so we just kind of sat back and waited for them." When DeBellvue picked the enemy fighters up with his Combat Tree gear, Olds Flight maneuvered to attack. Madden made the first move:

We got a visual on a MiG about five miles out on final approach with his gear and flaps down. Getting a lock, I fired my missiles but they missed. We were coming in on his right side from the rear and slipped up next to him at no more than 500 feet apart. He got a visual on us, snatched up his flaps, hit afterburner and accelerated out. It became obvious that I wasn't going to get another shot at him. That's when Captain Tibbett closed in.

Tibbett, who had been watching the engagement, recalled:

Madden then cleared us to fire, since we were in a good position for an AIM-9 attack. We fired two AIM-9s which appeared not to guide, closed to gun range, and fired the cannon. The MiG sustained numerous hits along the fuselage and left wing. The pilot ejected, and the aircraft started a gentle roll into a nosedown attitude toward the ground. The altitude was approximately 1,000 feet.

As Tibbett's MiG-19 exploded on the airfield, Madden started to lead Olds Flight away, but Teaball warned them of two airborne MiG-19s 20 miles distant, headed toward Phuc Yen to land, so they turned back to try and repeat the performance. DeBellvue picked the enemy fighters up at 15 miles and reported:

> We acquired the MiGs on radar and positioned as we picked them up visually. We used a slicing low-speed yo-yo to get behind them and started turning hard. We fired one AIM-9, which detonated 25 feet from one of the MiGs. We then switched the attack to the other MiG and one turn later we fired an AIM-9 at him. I observed the missile impact the tail. He continued on normally for the next few seconds, then began a slow roll and spiraled downward, impacting the ground with a large fireball.

Madden and DeBellvue returned to Udorn and claimed the second MiG-19. Captains Daleky and Murphy in Olds 04 were hit by AAA as the flight departed Phuc Yen, and were forced to eject over northern Laos, where they were rescued. When they returned to Udorn, they confirmed that Madden and DeBellvue had also destroyed the first MiG-19.

On October 13, in one of the final *Linebacker* missions, Captain Jeff Feinstein became the third and last Air Force ace when he scored his fifth kill with newly arrived 13th Tactical Fighter Squadron commander Lieutenant Colonel Curtis D. Westphal, shooting down a MiG-21 with a Sparrow in an engagement near Kep. Feinstein later recalled: "We received a call that bandits were in the area and heading our way. There were two of them and I got a visual on them when they were about two miles off."

Westphal described the engagement:

> We received initial word that two bandits were airborne from the vicinity of Hanoi, heading north. At 1324 hours our flight, under Red Crown control, turned to engage the MiGs. Shortly thereafter Captain Feinstein obtained radar contact at 17 nautical miles. Red

Crown confirmed the contact as being the bandits, and our flight closed on a front quarter attack. Due to the presence of friendlies in the area, we decided not to fire at that point. After closing to one mile, Captain Feinstein obtained a visual contact on one of the two MiG-21s. We turned left to engage. At 1328 hours we fired three AIM-7 missiles. All eight members of the flight observed the second AIM-7 hit the MiG-21 in the aft section, at which time it burst into flames. We saw the MiG pilot eject approximately five seconds after missile impact. The entire flight then observed the MiG-21 going down in flames until it disappeared through the undercast.

During the three months it was operational, Teaball was responsible for 16 of the 21 victories scored by Air Force fighter crews. The system was discarded after the war, but the concept of an air controller guiding fighters lives on with the use of the Airborne Warning and Command System (AWACS) aircraft, which have been responsible for all other air victories scored by Air Force pilots in engagements since Vietnam. The *Linebacker* engagements also demonstrated that the crews had been right all along to ask for an internal gun in the Phantom, since half the kills credited to F-4Es were accomplished with the onboard M61.

As the North Vietnamese offensive stalled in the South and Operation *Linebacker* inflicted unprecedented destruction in North Vietnam, the North Vietnamese returned to the Paris peace talks in early August, where they ended the deadlock over demands for the ouster of South Vietnamese President Nguyen Van Thieu and installation of a coalition government. For its part, the United States agreed to a cease-fire in place that allowed North Vietnamese troops to remain in South Vietnam after a peace agreement was signed and came into effect. With this basic agreement made between Henry Kissinger and North Vietnam's Le Duc Tho in mid-October, Nixon halted all bombing above the 20th parallel on October 23 and on October 26 Henry Kissinger publicly announced that "peace is at hand." There were many who thought the terms were "peace at any price" to insure Nixon's re-election. On November 7, the president won re-election with 60.7 percent of the popular vote and the largest Electoral College margin ever, 520–17, carrying 49 of the 50 states.

17

THE CHRISTMAS BOMBING

President Nixon's re-election victory was made certain by Henry Kissinger's announcement on October 26, 1972, that "peace is at hand." The country was well and truly tired of the war in Vietnam. Nixon knew he had to deliver an exit from the war by the time he was sworn in on January 20, 1973. With the breakdown in negotiations that delayed signing the peace treaty by October 31, the president knew his options were limited by public opinion in the United States.

Following the agreement on October 8, 1972 between US Secretary of State Henry Kissinger and North Vietnamese Foreign Minister Le Duc Tho to end the war in Vietnam, further negotiations to finalize the agreement commenced on October 17; at issue was the South Vietnamese release of political prisoners and continued American military assistance to the Saigon government. The North Vietnamese made significant concessions, and the treaty was to be signed on October 31. However, South Vietnamese president Thieu proposed 129 textual changes and demanded that South Vietnam be recognized as a sovereign state. The supreme irony, in the words of Stanley Karnow, had now arrived: "having fought a war to defend South Vietnam's independence, the United States was now denying its legitimacy." On October 26, Thieu publicly released the South Vietnamese demands. The North Vietnamese leadership, believing they had been hoodwinked by Kissinger, responded by broadcasting portions of the agreement that gave the impression that the agreement conformed to Washington and Saigon's objectives. Kissinger, hoping both to reassure the North Vietnamese of American sincerity and to convince Thieu of the administration's dedication to a compromise, held a televised press conference at the White House during which he announced "We believe that peace is at hand."

On November 20, Kissinger presented the South Vietnamese revisions, and 44 additional changes demanded by Nixon, to the North Vietnamese delegation. They included: acceptance of the DMZ as a true international boundary; a token withdrawal of North Vietnamese troops; that the North Vietnamese guarantee an Indochina-wide cease-fire; and that a strong international peace-keeping force (the International Commission of Control and Supervision) be created for supervising and enforcing the cease-fire. Once the North Vietnamese saw these demands, they began to retract their own concessions and wanted to bargain anew. Kissinger proclaimed that they were "stalling." The talks resumed on December 3 and ended on December 13, with both parties agreeing to resume negotiations. Teams of experts met to discuss technicalities and protocols on December 14, at which time the North Vietnamese submitted a Vietnamese-language text of the protocol on prisoners containing several important changes that Hanoi had failed to gain in the main sessions. At a subsequent meeting of experts on 16 December, the North Vietnamese side "stone-walled from beginning to end." The talks broke down that day, and the Hanoi negotiators refused to set a date for the resumption of negotiations.

Kissinger's "peace is at hand" statement had raised expectations of a settlement in the US. Nixon feared the new 93rd Congress, which would go into session on January 3, would preempt his pledge of "peace with honor" by legislating an end to the war. He was also under pressure from the cost of the mobilization for the Operation *Linebacker* "augmentation force," which totaled more than $4 billion by mid-autumn. Secretary Laird insisted that the president request a supplementary defense appropriation from Congress to pay for it. Nixon and Kissinger were convinced that the legislative branch would seize the opportunity to write the United States out of the war.

On December 14, after consultations with Nixon, Kissinger sent an ultimatum to Hanoi, threatening "grave consequences" if negotiations did not resume within 72 hours. That day, Nixon ordered the reseeding of North Vietnamese ports with air-dropped naval mines and that the Joint Chiefs of Staff direct the Air Force to begin planning for a three-day "maximum effort" bombing campaign to begin by December 16.

On December 18, the United States began bombing Hanoi.

The force of 207 B-52 bombers available for use in Southeast Asia represented nearly half of the Air Force's manned bomber fleet, and SAC commanders were initially reluctant to risk the aircraft and their highly trained crews in such an operation. The production line for B-52s had been long shut down; losses could not be replaced. However, many in SAC welcomed the opportunity to fly into the heavily defended North Vietnamese airspace, to finally prove the viability of manned bombers in a sophisticated Soviet-style air defense network.

An additional reason for using B-52s was the September–May monsoon weather that made visual bombing by tactical fighter-bombers difficult. The B-52s were equipped with their own radar bomb-navigation systems and supporting fighter-bombers would be able to strike targets either with the newly deployed laser-guided bombs (in clear weather) or by utilizing LORAN and radar-guided bombing systems.

Linebacker II was marked by top-down planning from SAC headquarters. The plan called for all bombers to approach Hanoi at night in three distinct waves, each using identical approach paths and flying at the same altitude. The aircraft themselves were to fly in three-plane formations known as "cells" for more effective electronic warfare jamming coverage. Once they had dropped their bombs, they were to execute "post-target turns" (PTTs) to the west. The turns had two unfortunate consequences: the B-52s would turn into a strong headwind, slowing their ground speed by 100 knots and prolonging their stay in the target area, and the turn would point the antennas of their electronic warfare systems away from the radars they were attempting to jam; this would also show the largest radar cross-section to the SAM guidance radars. Lieutenant Colonel Earl W. Tucker, a veteran bomber pilot of both World War II and Korea who was a senior planning staffer for Eighth Air Force headquarters on Guam, later recalled that when he was told how the mission would be flown, "I nearly resigned on the spot, because this was a perfect way to lose men and airplanes."

The first three missions were flown as planned on three consecutive nights, December 18–20, 1972. Seventh Air Force, Task Force 77, and the Marines provided F-4 fighter escorts; F-105 Wild Weasel SAM-suppression; Air Force EB-66 and Navy EA-6 radar-jamming aircraft; KC-135 tankers; and SAR aircraft.

On December 18, 129 B-52s were launched, 87 from Andersen AFB on Guam and 42 from U-Tapao, Thailand. Targets for the first wave were the North Vietnamese airfields at Kep, Phuc Yen, and Hoa Loc and a warehouse complex at Yen Vien; the second and third waves struck targets around Hanoi. The North Vietnamese fired 68 SAMs and shot down two B-52Gs from Guam and a B-52D from U-Tapao, while two Andersen B-52Ds were heavily damaged and managed to limp into U-Tapao. Only one of the three downed crews was rescued. An F-111A was shot down on a mission to bomb Radio Hanoi.

On December 19, 93 sorties were flown. Targets included the Kinh No railroad complex, the Thai Nguyen thermal power plant, and the Yen Vien complex. Twenty SAMs were launched. Several bombers were damaged but none were lost.

On December 20, 99 bombers struck the Yen Vien railyards, the Ai Mo warehouse complex, the Thai Nguyen power plant, a transshipment point at Boc Giang, the Kinh No railroad complex, and the Hanoi petroleum storage area – all in or near Hanoi. A combination of repetitive tactics, degraded electronic warfare systems, and limited jamming capability created dire consequences when "all hell broke loose." The repetitious nature of the previous strike profiles allowed North Vietnamese air defense to anticipate strike patterns; 34 SAMs were salvoed into the formation without radar usage, preventing attacks by the Wild Weasels. Four B-52Gs and three B-52Ds were lost in the first and third waves. A fourth B-52D, returning to Thailand, crashed in Laos. Only two of the eight crews were recovered.

Colonel Tucker remembered, "The repercussions were fast and furious. SAC was under pressure from the administration to stop the carnage, which was being reported as a blood bath – which it was." SAC leaders held the position that if the missions continued they "would lose too many bombers and that airpower doctrine would be proven fallacious... or, if the bombing were stopped, the same thing would occur."

Tucker explained:

The main problem was that SAC based its tactics on a MiG threat that did not materialize. The flight paths, altitudes, formations, and timing had not varied. The official explanation was that the similarity would be helpful to the crews, who were inexperienced in flying in a high-threat environment. The truth was that SAC had spent years dropping bombs on undefended jungle and planning for nuclear war, which created a mind-set that didn't understand the mission. Those of us with previous combat experience from World War II predicted this would happen, and our prescience was not well-received when we were proven right.

Lieutenant Colonel Earl McGill, who had flown his first bombing mission as pilot on the disastrous "Black Tuesday" mission of October 23, 1951, that had seen Soviet-flown MiG-15s permanently drive the B-29s from the daylight skies of North Korea, flew all three missions. He described the mission of December 20 as "The worst losses suffered by the Air Force since my first mission back in Korea."

Despite the losses, President Nixon ordered that the effort be extended past its original three-day deadline. Since the radar jamming equipment of the B-52Gs was designed for use in the air defense environment of the Soviet Union, not against the more antiquated SA-2 and Fan Song radar systems utilized by the North Vietnamese, only the aircraft at U-Tapao, which were equipped with more powerful and sophisticated ECM gear, could be used over the North. Thus, the attack waves were smaller, though the tactics did not change.

On December 21, 30 U-Tapao B-52Ds struck the Van Dinh storage depot, and Quang Te airfield. The SAMs knocked down two more B-52s.

The next night, 30 B-52s struck the petroleum storage facilities in Haiphong; there were no losses, but an errant string of bombs from a B-52 damaged by a SAM hit the Bach Mai Hospital in the southern suburbs of Hanoi. The hospital was just over half a mile from Bach Mai airfield and a major fuel storage facility was only 200 yards distant. The patients had been evacuated, but 28 doctors and nurses were killed.

On December 23, SAM sites and airfields were added to the target list. F-111s were sent in before the bombers to strike the airfields and reduce the fighter threat. The F-111s finally lived up to the original hopes of the design and proved so successful that they were shifted to SAM site suppression for the rest of the campaign, since there were no losses among the B-52s that night. On Christmas Eve, 30 B-52s supported by 69 tactical aircraft struck the railyards at Thai Nguyen and Kep without losses.

The campaign then took a 36-hour Christmas stand-down. Tucker recalled, "We at Guam were finally allowed to create revised plans while SAC HQ stepped back. When we went back on December 26, we launched an all-out attack on the air defenses." The Eighth Air Force planning staff, which had several World War II veterans in its number, dropped the use of multiple attacking waves. Instead, the B-52s would approach in seven streams, four of which were from the east over the Gulf of Tonkin, with all at different altitudes, thus preventing the North Vietnamese salvoing SAMs. The bombers would enter and exit the target area in 20 minutes, with each formation exiting in different directions. B-52Gs with additional jammers installed would return to the operation.

On December 26, 78 B-52s took off from Andersen AFB at one time, the largest combat launch in SAC history; 42 others flew from U-Tapao. The force was supported by 113 tactical aircraft creating chaff corridors, Wild Weasel SAM suppression, and ECM support. The B-52s struck Thai Nguyen, the Kinh No petroleum complex, the Duc Noi, Hanoi, and Haiphong railroads, and a vehicle storage area at Van Dinh. The North Vietnamese air defense system was overwhelmed by the number of aircraft and the dense blanket of chaff laid down by the fighter-bombers. The defenses had fired so many SAMs between December 18 and 24 that their inventory was so low that only 68 were fired. One B-52 was shot down near Hanoi while a damaged B-52 crashed just short of the runway at U-Tapao with only two crewmen surviving.

On December 27, the bombers struck Lang Dang, Duc Noi, the Trung Quang railroad, and Van Dinh. One B-52 was so heavily damaged that the crew ejected over Laos, where they were rescued. A second B-52 took a direct hit and went down over the Trung Quang railroad yards. Two F-4s and an HH-53 Jolly Green SAR helicopter were also shot down.

On December 28, 15 B-52Gs and 15 B-52Ds from Andersen and 30 B-52Ds from U-Tapao attacked five targets. Four waves struck targets in Hanoi while the fifth hit the Lang Dang railroad yards southwest of Lang Son. No aircraft were lost.

By December 29, there were few strategic targets left unhit. The targets were two SAM storage areas at Phuc Yen and the Lang Dang railroad yards. U-Tapao again sent 30 B-52Ds, while Andersen sent 12

B-52Gs and 18 B-52Ds against Hanoi, while 30 B-52Gs from Andersen flew Arc Light missions, bombing the jungle in the southern panhandle of North Vietnam and in South Vietnam. This final day of attacks also saw no losses.

According to Air Force records, during Operation *Linebacker II*, 741 B-52 sorties were dispatched; 729 completed their missions. B-52s dropped a total 15,237 tons of bombs on 18 industrial and 14 military targets, including eight SAM sites; fighter-bombers added another 5,000 tons of bombs. Ten B-52s were shot down and five others were damaged and crashed in Laos or Thailand. Thirty-three B-52 crewmen were killed or missing in action, another 33 became prisoners of war, and 26 were rescued. In *The 11 Days of Christmas: America's Last Vietnam Battle*, author Marshall Michel used mission records to confirm that "15 B-52s were shot down... 10 crashed 'on the spot' in North Vietnam and 5 were able to fly out of the Hanoi area and into Laos or Thailand before they crashed." According to Dana Drenkowski and Lester W. Grau, the number of B-52s lost is unconfirmed since the USAF figures are suspect. If a plane was badly damaged, but managed to land, it was not counted as a combat loss, even if it was too damaged to fly again. During the operation, Air Force spokesmen told the press that 17 B-52s were lost, but later told Congress that only 13 B-52s were lost. Nine B-52s that returned to U-Tapao were too badly damaged to fly again. The number of B-52s that managed to return to Guam but were combat losses remains unknown. The overall B-52 loss is probably between 22 and 27, making *Linebacker II* one of the most expensive bombing campaigns in Air Force history.

The VPAF flew 27 sorties by MiG-21s and four by MiG-17s. They entered eight aerial engagements, and claimed two B-52s, four F-4s, and one RA-5C shot down, for a loss of three MiG-21s. The two B-52s claimed by MiG-21 pilots were attributed to SAMs by the Air Force.

On December 22, the Nixon Administration asked Hanoi to return to the talks with the terms offered in October. On December 23, Hanoi notified Washington that they were willing to re-start negotiations with a bombing halt as a precondition; this was done to "impress upon Nixon that the bombing was not the reason for this decision." Nixon responded that he wanted the technical discussions to resume on January 2, 1973 and would halt the bombing if Hanoi agreed. When they did, Nixon suspended aerial operations north of the 20th parallel on December 30.

He then ordered Kissinger to agree to the terms previously offered in October, if that was what it took to get the agreement signed before the new Congress convened. On January 9, Kissinger and Le Duc Tho returned to Paris. The agreement struck was basically the same one that had been reached in October. The additional demands made by the United States in December were generally discarded. As Kissinger's deputy John Negroponte put it, "We bombed the North Vietnamese into accepting our concessions."

Nixon tried to placate President Thieu by writing on January 5, 1973 that "you have my assurance of continued assistance in the post-settlement period and that we will respond with full force should the settlement be violated by North Vietnam." By this time, however, he was in no position to make such a promise, since the possibility of obtaining the requisite congressional appropriations was non-existent. Thieu still refused to agree. On January 14, Nixon made his most serious threat: "I have therefore irrevocably decided to proceed to initial the agreement on 23 January 1973... I will do so, if necessary, alone." On January 22, Thieu bowed to the inevitable and consented to the agreement.

The American part of the war in Vietnam was over.

18

THE FINAL WARS IN SOUTHEAST ASIA

Following the signing of the Paris Peace Accords, most Americans believed that US armed forces were no longer involved in the continuing wars in Southeast Asia. Such belief was mistaken. Although US ground forces had been withdrawn from Vietnam in accordance with the Paris Accords amid domestic political and economic pressures, the Nixon Administration still tried to increase South Vietnam's chances of survival against the North. The heart of these efforts involved keeping US airpower in Thailand, whence missions could be flown if necessary to support the South Vietnamese. Thus, US air involvement continued in the ongoing wars in Laos and Cambodia until a final withdrawal came in late October, 1973. The B-52 units remained in Thailand to threaten North Vietnam with another *Linebacker II* bombing campaign if they failed to live up to their responsibilities in the Paris Peace Accords.

In addition, the United States attempted to end the continuing wars in Cambodia and Laos under terms by which the North Vietnamese would withdraw from these countries, in order to cut off the Ho Chi Minh Trail and continued supply of PAVN and NLF units in South Vietnam. The goal was to establish South Vietnam as another South Korea or Taiwan, with pro-United States governments in power in both Cambodia and Laos. In fact, following the January 27, 1973 effective date of the Paris Peace Accords, the fighting increased in both Laos and Cambodia, while both sides engaged in "land-grabbing" activities in South Vietnam. In light of this, the B-52s continued to fly Arc Light-style missions to bomb suspected enemy positions in the jungle in both Cambodia and Laos while other Air Force units provided direct air support to the pro-US forces, all unknown to Congress or the American people. President Nixon was anxious to capitalize on having achieved "peace with honor," especially as questions continued to swirl over what would come to be known as "Watergate," which led to both the president and Secretary Kissinger maintaining secrecy regarding continued US involvement in Southeast Asia.

The new US military command, replacing Military Assistance Command Vietnam (MACV), was US Support Activities Group/ Seventh Air Force Command, located at RTAFB Nakhon Phanom in Thailand, which was activated on February 10, 1973. The command was responsible for planning any resumption in bombing and for maintaining contact with the South Vietnamese forces. Forces available to USSAG/7AF were 18 tactical fighter squadrons operating F-4s, F-111s, A-7Ds, and Marine A-6As; one reconnaissance squadron equipped with RF-4Cs; and one AC-130 gunship squadron. These units operated from Ubon, Udorn, Korat, Nam Phong, Takhli, and Nakhon Phanom. The B-52 force, which numbered 203 bombers at U-Tapao in Thailand, Andersen AFB on Guam, and Kadena AFB on Okinawa, was under the direct command of SAC. During the first two weeks of January, B-52 attacks continued against targets in North Vietnam south of the 20th parallel, during which one B-52 and one A-6A were shot down by SAMs. USSAG/7AF also was responsible for the United States Defense Attaché's Office (DAO) in Saigon, which coordinated US activities with the South Vietnamese armed forces with emphasis on military assistance, logistics, and intelligence reporting. The DAO was unlike any other defense attaché's office in any other diplomatic mission, with a staff of 1,200 Department of Defense civilians, 5,500 contractors, and 50 military personnel.

The situations in Laos and Cambodia following the signing of the Paris Peace Accords were not quickly resolved. In Laos, the 1962 Geneva Agreement prohibited any in-country US military command, which resulted in military matters being directed by the US ambassador in Vientiane. PACOM in Hawaii controlled airpower used in *Barrel Roll* bombing operations, though all such strike missions required approval by the ambassador. The CIA-operated Air America airline had its headquarters at Udorn in Thailand, though its paramilitary officers were with Vang Pao's Hmong paramilitary force at Long Tieng and other locations in Laos.

B-52s had bombed Laos since 1970. Over the two years between 1968 and 1970, half of all US bombing missions flown in all Southeast Asia were flown in Laos, which by the time of the Paris Peace Accords was the most-bombed country on earth.

Following the capture of the Plaine des Jarres by Vang Pao's Hmong force in July 1971, the Western position in Laos had steadily deteriorated, with the North Vietnamese-backed Pathet Lao forces steadily gaining territory. The Paris Peace Accords contained an agreement by North Vietnam to withdraw their troops and respect the 1962 Geneva Accords. A cease-fire was to take effect on February 22, 1973. On that date, the United States stopped all offensive air operations over Laos, but the North Vietnamese forces remained in the country. A total of 499 B-52 sorties had been flown in northern Laos to bomb suspected North Vietnamese and Pathet Lao positions, with another 948 sorties in southern Laos by the time the cease-fire went into effect. Between April 15 and 17, an additional 41 B-52 strikes hit enemy positions south of the Plaine des Jarres, which were the last US bombing missions in the country.

In Cambodia, the government of President Lon Nol, which had come into existence through the machinations of the CIA in 1970, attempted to negotiate a cease-fire with their Khmer Rouge opponents, but this failed. The United States resumed bombing, with 168 B-52 sorties against 59 targets between January 20 and 23. When the negotiations failed on January 29, the United States responded to Cambodian requests for air support of their forces with limited missions during the first half of February. However, on February 24–25, in response to increased activity by the Khmer Rouge, 200 tactical fighter and 60 B-52 sorties were flown to help break the Khmer Rouge siege of Kampong Thom. With evidence of increased North Vietnamese infiltration into Cambodia in support of the Khmer Rouge, the US embassy – which was the controlling US authority for air operations in Cambodia – approved additional air strikes. There were 4,700 sorties in March and 5,700 in April, growing to 6,200 in May and 6,400 in June.

Among the 37,499 US Air Force personnel authorized to be in Southeast Asia with the end of the war in Vietnam was First Lieutenant Thomas E. Rodgers, who with the other pilots and WSOs of the 474th Tactical Fighter Wing's 428th Tactical Fighter Squadron stepped out of the C-141 that brought them from Nellis AFB, Nevada, into the humid tropic heat at Clark AFB in the Philippines on Thursday, January 4, 1973. The crews expected to be in Thailand for 90 days of TDY while they took over the F-111As that had been flown to Southeast Asia by the crews of the 429th and 430th squadrons in September 1972. As Rodgers later recalled:

> The Air Force really wanted to get the F-111 back into combat after that poor start back in 1968, so they alerted the 474th, which had the most time in the airplane of any of the F-111 wings. The wing took all the experienced crews and put them into the 429th and 430th squadrons, and they flew out to Thailand, but they got there just when *Linebacker I* stopped. Then when *Linebacker II* came along, they supported the B-52s and really turned the airplane's reputation around. The group of us who I came out with were the guys just out of combat crew training when the first deployment happened. We didn't really expect to see much action since the war was obviously ending. Boy, were we wrong!

The men of the 428th went through three quick days of escape and evasion training, and flew to Takhli on January 9. The F-111s were flying air support missions into Laos, where war still raged. Rodgers remembered:

> By the time peace was declared at the end of February, I had flown 22 combat missions. My last mission prior to "peace" breaking out was on February 22, when the C-130 Airborne Command and Control Center (ABCCC) diverted me to some nebulous target on the edge of the Plaine des Jarres where I dropped 24 Mark 82s without any obvious result. February was still the dry season in Laos, and there was a lot of fighting on what we called "PDJ" between Vang Pao's Hmong troops and the Pathet Lao.

The 428th Tactical Fighter Squadron got a three-day stand down after what they later called "The first 'End of the War' party," then started flying training missions:

> These sorties had to stay within the boundaries of Thailand due to the constraints of the peace treaty. Some low-level training routes went past Bangkok south over the Gulf of Thailand and then headed inland over the southern Thai peninsula, simulating an over-water ingress.

Other routes went around the more mountainous northwestern areas of Thailand. For the most part, the attack profiles were "dry" radar camera attacks in which there was no actual weapons delivery. We did, however, get to drop 25-pound practice bombs occasionally on the Thai-owned Chandi Bombing Range situated between Takhli and Korat.

For the 428th and 430th squadrons, "peace in Southeast Asia" lasted two weeks:

I flew my first combat mission into Cambodia on March 14, 1973, during which I dropped 24 Mark 82s on a "military complex" – that was Seventh Air Force targeting jargon for where they thought the bad guys might be. I called this "bombing suspected jungle," which was the description for a lot of our targets: "military complex," "suspected truck park," "known enemy location." Occasionally, we might get a "Troops in Contact" situation, but this was not very common unless it was a night or the weather was bad and the F-4s and A-7s couldn't work those targets with an airborne FAC.

Given the F-111's capabilities, operating parameters were different from other aircraft, though the full capability of the F-111 was not put to the test since another objective of the campaign was to minimize losses to keep things out of the newspapers back in the United States. Rodgers explained:

Our missions were always single ship. Inbound, we would check-in with ABCCC with our mission status and weapons load. They would then clear us to strike our primary target or have us divert to another target. I got diverted about half the time. I don't really know if things were that fluid on the ground or if the powers-that-be were just making things up as they went. Our standard weapons load was twenty-four Mark 82 500-pound bombs, which is equal to about three B-17's worth. In some cases, we would carry four Mark 84 2,000-pound bombs when attacking bunkers or bridge abutments. All of our missions were level drops from medium altitude, 15,000–18,000 feet AGL in order to stay above the AAA. The biggest guns the Khmer Rouge had were 37mm and this also kept us above any possible SA-7 threat. There was no SA-2 threat. All the bombs were dropped in the "low drag" configuration and from early summer till the final cease fire on August 15, we carried what we called "Banded

Snake Eyes" – Mark 82s with high drag Snake Eye fins that were banded with metal straps so the fins would not deploy on release and they would fall in a low drag configuration. We used these because of a shortage of low drag fin units and the need to get rid of the high drag fins before we left town after the war. As a side note, once in a while one of the bands would snap and the high drag fins would deploy resulting in a bomb impacting "unbelievable at six" from the target area... oh well.

Almost all of our bombing was done using "radar offset" from a ground radar beacon for target aiming, i.e., we knew the location of the beacon – on the roof of the US embassy in Phnom Penh – and the bearing and distance from it to the target. Put the radar crosshairs on the beacon return and the computer did the rest. This allowed us to bomb day and night, in any type of weather. As far as accuracy was concerned, that is most likely buried somewhere in the Pentagon's archives. The weather in Cambodia could really be nasty at times and the other fighters would be unable to work with the FACs. In these cases, we would be "pathfinders" for them so they didn't have to return home with their bombs or jettison them somewhere. You could pretty much tell if you would be needed to pathfind when the weather was bad. You would get a call from ABCCC with the other flight's data and rejoin info. You would join up, usually with two F-4s or A-7s on each wing. They would give us their target coordinates and their ballistic data. We would plug that info into our computer, make the bomb run, and give them a count down when to pickle their bombs off. In many cases, I would lead more than one flight. On one eight-and-a-half hour mission, I dropped my twenty-four bombs and then led several other flights for a total of a hundred Mark 82s – twenty-five B-17s worth of bombs.

Several years later, Rodgers discovered that the bombing system that would be used in the event that war broke out in Western Europe was the beacon system that had been used in Cambodia. "It appeared we had been the 'beta test' there in Cambodia for the system they were going to use along the East German border."

Despite official American statements that there were no actions involving US forces with the North Vietnamese, and statements by Secretary Kissinger that there were no Vietnamese forces now involved in the fighting that continued in Cambodia, Rodgers recalled one mission that challenged those statements:

> We had one mission that involved supporting the weekly convoy that brought supplies up the Mekong from Saigon to Phnom Penh and further upstream to Kampong Cham. The bad guys (the Khmer Rouge) were dug in, in bunkers at various places along the river and would fire on the boats and barges with 105mm recoilless rifles and RPGs [rocket propelled grenades] as they came upstream. We would get assignments to attack these "known enemy locations" ahead of the arrival of the convoy at that position. During one of these, the fragged target description was a "known enemy location" on the Mekong, just south of Kampong Cham. On further target study and talks with intel, they determined it was a North Vietnamese R&R [rest and recreation] camp/resort – no matter what Kissinger was saying about the other side observing the terms of the Paris Peace Accords. My bomb load was the standard twenty-four Mark 82s and the Time Over Target (TOT) was just at sunrise when everyone should be still asleep. We made a first dry pass over the target just for curiosity's sake to see what was on the ground. It was a beautiful complex of about ten white buildings with red tile roofs, right on the river beach. The next pass was for real. The first bomb hit in the river. The second hit on the beach. And the rest hit the red tile roofs.

While Cambodia was considered a "benign" air environment – so long as aircraft stayed out of range of the light AAA and the shoulder-fired SA-7 SAMs – during the summer of 1973 several crews reported picking up Fan Song radar warning signals, indicating the presence of one or more SA-2 SAM sites, just east of Phnom Penh:

> This made the F-105 Wild Weasel guys at Korat happy because they were just flying local training missions and not getting combat pay. The Weasels were now fragged to fly CAP over our target areas, just in case a SAM came up and tried to engage us. It was a good feeling to have them around but led to a humorous occurrence one night.
>
> On the F-111, we carried our bombs on BRU-3 bomb racks, a supersonic-capable version of the standard MER [Multiple Ejector Rack]. On quite a few occasions, due to switch sensor problems,

the weapons panel would show that the racks were empty, but on visual inspection of the racks, we would find a hung bomb. A visual check was the only valid safety check. At night, this was a problem, since there was no outside light to enable us to check the racks. This is where the F-111's ability to "Torch" – dump fuel, light the afterburners, and light up the sky with a giant plume of burning JP-4 – came in handy. After we came off target, we would torch and check the racks to make sure they were clean.

One night, we dropped our bombs and had just torched when we got a high pitched "SAM Launch" radio call from the Weasel guys. We were between thin cloud layers and all the Weasel crew was able to see was the plume from our jet and they thought it was an SA-2 booster. They got quite a ribbing for that call. As things turned out, the SAM radar warnings were actually being triggered by the Precision Approach Radar (PAR) at Tan Son Nhut airport in Saigon.

During June and July, with a congressional cutoff in funding authorization for use of US military force in Cambodia looming on August 15, the F-111s, F-4s, A-7s, and B-52s controlled by Seventh Air Force supported attempts to drive the communist forces back from their advance on Phnom Penh, and to clear the Mekong from the border to Neak Leong to allow the Lon Nol Cambodians a chance to survive after US airpower was withdrawn. There was great pessimism that this would actually be possible among senior American commanders in Thailand, with many believing that the communists would take control of the entire country within 60 days of the withdrawal of US air support. An all-out air campaign conducted August 4–12 was mounted to support the Cambodian army as it cleared Route 1. Between August 4–6, 103 B-52 and 30 F-111 sorties were flown. On August 7–8 there were 28 F-111 and 58 B-52 strikes as the Cambodian army moved south on Route 1 from Phnom Penh. Over the final days of the operation, 60 tactical sorties with F-4s and A-7s, 28 F-111 sorties, and 43 B-52 sorties were flown as the Cambodian army gained control of the west bank of the Mekong without suffering a single casualty, while communist units experienced "heavy losses." Overall, the 45 days before August 15 saw the US Air Force fly 1,908 B-52 sorties and 10,360 tactical sorties. As a result, the Khmer Rouge forces fell back from their advance on the capital.

In early September 1973, there was a "war scare" when the 474th's commander called the crews to a briefing where he announced they would be "going back to Hanoi." As Rodgers recalled,

> There were a lot of us who thought our Wing King was like the "General Jack D. Ripper" character in "Dr. Strangelove" and that he might be making this up on his own. But there were more rumors over the next few days, then everything quieted down. That was right when Watergate started being a big problem back home, and we concluded maybe Nixon had been planning to do something, but now with the hearings going on, he couldn't.

On October 22, the ten crews Rodgers had deployed with boarded C-141s for the flight from Takhli back to Nellis AFB. The "90-day tour" had extended to 280 days. In the seven months between mid-January and mid-August, Tom Rodgers had flown 101 combat missions, a full Southeast Asia combat tour; 79 were flown in Cambodia, after the Paris Peace Treaty went into effect.

Following the end of the US air campaign with the congressional funding cut-off, US support for the pro-Western governments in Laos, Cambodia, and Vietnam over the next 21 months was limited to use of the psychological effect of US airpower that remained in Thailand and the possibility that it would be unleashed again if communist forces were to start any offensive operations in order to keep what passed for "peace" in the region.

Thai public opinion began to turn against the continued presence of US military forces in the country. Additionally, the Thai government was under pressure from both Hanoi and other Southeast Asian governments to end this arrangement. On October 14, 1973, the Thanom Kittikachorn government was overthrown, leading to increased popular opposition to the US presence. The US realignment of forces following the effective date of the peace accords had led to there being more US personnel in Thailand than was allowed by the mutual defense agreement. As a result, the Marine A-6 squadron, three other tactical fighter squadrons on TDY, and ten KC-135 aerial refueling tankers were withdrawn shortly before the Thai coup; this left 15 tactical fighter squadrons, one C-130 gunship squadron, and 43 KC-135s in Thailand. With the withdrawal of 83 B-52s from Thailand and Guam to meet the crisis of the October 1973 Yom Kippur War, there were 75 B-52s left in Southeast Asia, 50 at U-Tapao in Thailand and the remaining 25 on Guam. In December, the Joint Chiefs recommended maintaining Seventh Air Force in the region through the end of FY 1974, i.e., September 30, 1974.

US aerial reconnaissance capability remained active throughout this period, with RC-135 missions flown over the Gulf of Tonkin on a daily basis after April 1, 1973. Operation *Giant Scale* saw a once-a-week photo reconnaissance mission flown over North Vietnam beginning that May. Daily reconnaissance missions flown over South Vietnam detected the siting of seven SAM sites by the North Vietnamese in the mountains surrounding Khe Sanh in the Central Highlands in March 1973, a clear violation of the Paris Peace Accords. Further photo reconnaissance over the South was restricted following damage to an RF-4C on a *Steel Tiger* mission over South Vietnam/Laos by AAA in late March.

In the wake of the Paris Peace Accords, North Vietnamese losses in the 1972 battles were made good in 1973 by the Soviet Union and China, with an increase in support by 50 percent over 1972, to $330 million, followed by an increase in 1974 to $400 million. At the same time, aid to the Saigon government dropped from $2.2 billion in 1972 to $965 million in 1974.

A political debate over future military policy developed among the North Vietnamese leadership in December 1973 when the Central Committee of the Communist Party of Vietnam convened to review the progress of military actions in the South. PAVN Chief of Staff General Van Tien Dung reported:

> We then improved our anti-pacification operations. The enemy became passive and utterly weakened. The morale and combat strength of the troops were clearly declining. Their total manpower had decreased by 15,000 men since 1973, with a heavy loss in combat strength. Their mobile strategic forces had bogged down. The reduction of US aid made it impossible for the troops to carry out their combat plan and build up their forces. Nguyen Van Thieu was forced to fight a poor man's war. Enemy firepower had decreased by nearly 60 percent because of bomb and ammunition shortages. Its mobility was also reduced by half due to lack of aircraft, vehicles and fuel. Thus, the enemy had to shift from large-scale operations

and heliborne deep-thrust and tank mounted attacks to small scale blocking, nibbling and searching operations.

Defense Minister Vo Nguyen Giap and General Dung urged an increase in military operations while Premier Pham Van Dong believed that this would reduce reconstruction in the North. Resolution 21, which charted a middle course, calling for "strategic raids" to regain territory taken by the ARVN, resolved the dispute. The approved action was seen as a test of South Vietnamese and US government resolve. Between March and November 1974, when the monsoon limited aerial response, ARVN forces in Quang Duc Province and at Bien Hoa were attacked, resulting in the regaining of PAVN control of jump-off points for any new offensive. Most importantly, the B-52s did not return. The resignation of President Nixon in August ended any lingering American desire for further involvement in Southeast Asia.

In October 1974, the North Vietnamese Politburo agreed that the war had reached its "final stage" and passed the Resolution of 1975, outlining strategy for 1975 and 1976: the army would consolidate gains and continue the southern build-up in the South, followed by the final offensive to take South Vietnam occurring in 1976. Lieutenant General Tran Van Tra, PAVN commander in the South, proposed a "test" attack in Phuoc Long Province to test ARVN fighting ability and determine how the United States would respond. The plan had potential for great gain at low risk. First Party Secretary Le Duan warned General Tra: "Go ahead and attack... [But] you must be sure of victory."

Morale in the South was hit hard by inflation, which reached over 100 percent in 1974 from existing prices in January 1973, in part a result of the Arab Oil Embargo following the Yom Kippur War. This had a particular impact on the army, since their already-low pay could not be increased; this led to increased desertion as well as increased corruption as both officers and men attempted to supplement their salaries. Nguyen Ngoc Huy, who had represented the South Vietnamese government in the Paris negotiations, reported to the CIA:

Except for a few special cases, in which officers look out for their troops and help them surmount financial difficulties, the soldiers are unable to feed their families and no longer possess the will to fight. They are demoralized by the shameless exploitation of their superiors. Generally speaking, the army has become a vast enterprise for corruption; even artillery support must be paid for.

US Air Attaché in South Vietnam Colonel Garvin McCurdy reported:

No U.S. aid should be directed to upkeep of the Vietnamese armed forces; this is a function of the Vietnamese government. But the government deliberately cut corners here in order to make the budget balance; the pay for even senior officers was insufficient to feed, clothe, house and educate their families. The effect was to build in what we've called corruption, and it's not a wonder why the Vietnamese were as dishonest as they were. There were no pay cuts but there was constant inflation. There were young Vietnamese officers who were continually hungry. This includes pilots. And that was one of the very basic problems the VNAF had to face.

Among other things, the 157 percent increase in fuel costs over the six months from October 1973 to April 1974 saw a forced 22 percent reduction in fuel availability for the South Vietnamese armed forces, despite aid for fuel being increased from $42 million to $78 million during that period. The issue of corruption became so important that in October 1974 Thieu was forced to fire three of his four regional corps commanders, despite two being considered the best battlefield commanders in the army, as well as demoting 400 field-grade officers, all of which led to a further worsening of morale in the military leadership.

With the end of fiscal year 1974 approaching, US leaders questioned the reasoning behind maintaining US air power in Thailand, particularly since congressional restraints largely negated any possibility of its being used in response to what was going on in South Vietnam. William R. Kintner, the US ambassador to Thailand, argued in favor of maintaining the US presence, because it added an "uncertainty factor" to any North Vietnamese plans, since they could not be sure that Congress would forbid use of US airpower in the face of a renewed northern drive to control the South.

Over the course of 1974, most US air assets in Thailand had been withdrawn, including the EB-66 squadron, with those aircraft removed from the Air Force inventory afterwards. One A-7 squadron was rotated back to the United States in April, while the second A-7 squadron was withdrawn in May. US use of Nakhon Phanom and Takhli ended, with some squadrons transferred to Korat RTAB, and others withdrawn to the United States. By July, half the B-52s in Thailand had returned to the United States; there were a total 48 B-52s at U-Tapao and Guam, and this force was reduced in October–November to 29, all on Guam. The 429th and 430th squadrons moved their F-111s from Takhli to Udorn in June. The F-105G Wild Weasel squadron was withdrawn at the end of September. At the end of 1974, there were eight tactical fighter-bomber squadrons, one tactical reconnaissance squadron, two special duties squadrons, and one tactical air support squadron left in Thailand, and plans called for a reduction to only two tactical squadrons by the summer of 1975. Only Ubon remained as an operational airfield. The decline in the military fortunes of South Vietnam was matched by the decline in US military support capability.

In August 1974, General Murray completed his tour of duty as Defense Attaché in Saigon and returned to the United States. On his way, he stopped in Honolulu to meet with Pacific Forces Commander Admiral Noel Gayler, and informed the admiral that, in his opinion, "South Vietnam will not fall next week or next month, but certainly next year."

In his State of the Union address in January 1975, President Ford told the US Congress, "Last year, some believed that cutting back our military assistance to South Vietnam would induce negotiations for a political settlement. Instead, the opposite has happened. North Vietnam is refusing negotiations and has increased its military presence."

In addition to the US Air Force reductions in 1974, congressionally imposed reductions in military aid to South Vietnam resulted in the return of all F-5E fighters that had been sent to replace F-5As in the VNAF, and a reduction in aid to $700 million total, with only $159 million for the VNAF. Admiral Gayler testified before the Senate Foreign Relations Committee that this amount would not allow the VNAF to even maintain and operate the force it had. As a result, by December 1974, the VNAF had been reduced from 2,073 aircraft of all types to 1,484 aircraft of all types. All remaining A-1H, AC-119G, and AC-47 aircraft were to be removed from operational service by the end of March 1975. The cutback in funds eliminated all US contractor maintenance support, which meant that most advanced aircraft in the force would soon go out of service due to lack of maintenance, and total flying time allotted was cut 40 percent.

At the end of 1974, CIA Director William Colby informed Secretary Kissinger that it was the considered judgement of US intelligence that South Vietnam could survive with this reduced aid if the North did not increase its present commitment in the South, and that at least a symbolic level of US air support should be maintained in the region to be used if there was a change in circumstances. He concluded:

> I would add that Hanoi's perception of future changes in U.S. support and of trends in the strength and stability of GVN [Government of Vietnam] will be key factors determining North Vietnam's future policies. If Hanoi came to believe that a major decline either of US support or of GVN's own strength was occurring, these factors alone would stimulate more aggressive action by North Vietnam.

All parties – North, South, and US – were surprised when the 1975 Spring Offensive rapidly turned into a war-ending campaign following its initial success in Phuoc Long Province, which saw Phuoc Long became the first provincial capital permanently taken by the PAVN. The lack of US response led General Cao Van Vien, Chief of the ARVN General Staff, to say, "Almost gone was the hope that the United States would forcibly punish the North Vietnamese for their brazen violations of the cease-fire agreement... What more encouragement could the communists have asked for?" News of the victory reached the Politburo during their Twenty-third Plenum; Le Duan declared: "Never have we had military and political conditions so perfect or a strategic advantage so great as we have now."

By March 25, South Vietnamese defenses were in collapse in the I and II Corps regions that comprised the northern half of the country. Finally, even the CIA was forced to amend the rosy forecasts it had provided that one more infusion of aid would save the day. A report on March 25 stated:

> In the face of recent supply losses and continuing NVA pressure on all fronts, government forces are not likely to regain the initiative or recoup their strength in the near future, since the very factors that

sparked the current crisis are still operating unchecked in Saigon, Hanoi and Washington. The entire complexion of the Vietnam war has altered in a matter of weeks, and the government is in imminent danger of decisive military defeat.

As the retreat from the Central Highlands became a rout, South Vietnamese President Thieu was forced to realize that there was no hope of the United States approving the $300 million supplemental aid package he had requested. On March 10, he informed the ARVN military leaders that they should redeploy the army to "hold and defend only those populous and flourishing areas which were most important." These were the III and IV Corps zones, which he called "Our untouchable heartland, the irreducible national stronghold." By March 25, 1975, the Politburo decided it was no longer necessary to wait to begin the final offensive. On April 7, Le Duc Tho – who had shared the 1973 Nobel Peace Prize with Henry Kissinger for the Paris Peace Accords – arrived at PAVN headquarters near Loc Ninh to oversee the final offensive.

The US intelligence community entertained no doubt that the South Vietnamese government would fail to meet the challenge, regardless of any actions the United States might take, though no US intelligence agency realized how fast the collapse would happen. It was not until April 6 that Secretary Kissinger informed President Ford that evacuation plans must be set up to deal with the emergency. This was the week that TV sets in America were treated to footage of flight crews forcing ARVN soldiers off airliners at gunpoint. On April 21, President Thieu resigned in hopes that a new leader could reopen negotiations with the North. It was too late.

Throughout this period, there were Americans who had a more clear-eyed view of the ultimate fate of American involvement in Southeast Asia. During the military interregnum between the end of US bombing missions on August 15, 1973, and the outbreak of the 1975 general offensive in South Vietnam, planners at USSAG/7AF had worked on evacuation plans for Cambodia (code name "Eagle Pull") and Laos (code name "Talon Blade"). A plan titled "Talon Vise" was developed in May 1974 regarding Air Force participation in an emergency evacuation of US personnel from South Vietnam. The plan was completed in July and approved by CinCPac in December.

While these events were playing out in South Vietnam, the war in Cambodia that had begun in May 1970 with the US invasion of the then-neutral country came to an abrupt end. On February 17, the US-allied Khmer Republic armed forces were forced to retreat from the villages and strongpoints they held along the Mekong River that provided the only connection to outside support from South Vietnam. The capital of Phnom Penh was quickly surrounded by the Khmer Rouge, leaving the city completely dependent on aerial resupply through Pochentong Airport. The United States mobilized an airlift of food, fuel, and ammunition, but military support was limited by the Case–Church Amendment. Bird Air operated the airlift under contract to the United States, flying C-130 and DC-8 cargo planes into Pochentong from U-Tapao. On March 22, two aircraft were hit by Khmer Rouge rockets which forced a suspension of the airlift the next day, but it was resumed on March 24, in the desperate hope that the Khmer Rouge could be held off until the monsoon began in May. Khmer Republic president Lon Nol resigned on April 1 and left for exile in Thailand in hopes that his departure could lead to peace negotiations. That day the final Khmer Republic position at Neak Luong fell and its captured artillery soon made its presence felt as Phnom Penh came under bombardment.

On April 12, the United States executed Operation *Eagle Pull*, using Marine CH-53s aboard USS *Okinawa* (LPH-3) to land the 2nd Battalion 4th Marines Battalion Landing Team to hold the landing zone in Phnom Penh while 84 Americans and 205 Cambodians and third country nationals were evacuated to the fleet. By 1040 hours, the last were aboard the helicopters and headed out to sea and the last Marines departed at 1059 hours to the accompaniment of rocket fire from the Khmer Rouge as USAF OV-10s from Thailand maintained air cover overhead. The Cambodian government was surprised by the evacuation since Phnom Penh and the provincial capitals that government forces still held were filled with refugees. Khmer Rouge forces closed in by the end of the day.

Over the course of April 15, the Khmer Rouge refused attempts to negotiate peace through China. On April 16, the Khmer Republic Air Force flew its last mission, using T-28Ds to bomb Phnom Penh Airport to cover the departure of 97 other aircraft loaded with civilian dependents, which escaped to Thailand.

On April 17, the Khmer Rouge occupied Phnom Penh, then ordered its evacuation, emptying the city. With that, Cambodia descended into a dark age of mass genocide that would end only in 1979 after the deaths of some two million Cambodians when forces supported by Vietnam took control.

US Air Force C-141s from Military Airlift Command and C-130s from Thailand began evacuating US personnel from South Vietnam on April 20. These flights were supplemented by airliners from World Airways, which could take non-US personnel who could not be evacuated by the Air Force. Nearly 100 flights carried refugees out of Saigon, but plans to fully institute Operation *Talon Vise* in South Vietnam were disrupted by an air attack on Tan Son Nhut Airport on April 28 by former VNAF A-37s flown by VPAF pilots in a special operation. After that, operations at the field ceased with the approach of North Vietnamese forces that brought the airfield under artillery fire. Instead, Operation *Frequent Wind* saw US and third country personnel evacuated by helicopter to ships of the Seventh Fleet operating offshore on April 30, 1975. Eight Air Force CH-53 and two HH-3 Jolly Green Giant helicopters participated in this evacuation, operating from the deck of the aircraft carrier *Midway* (CVA-41).

During the April 30 evacuation of Saigon, an Air Force C-130 ABCCC aircraft orbited over the city, controlling all air operations. In addition to US Navy tactical aircraft, Air Force F-4s and A-7s from Thailand were overhead, while KC-135s offshore provided refueling. Several F-4C Wild Weasel aircraft were also involved, as there was fear that the North Vietnamese would emplace SAMs around the city to prevent the evacuation. The only Air Force air strike during the day involved one Wild Weasel F-4C and an accompanying F-4D from the 388th Tactical Fighter Wing which were north of Tan Son Nhut during the first stage of the helicopter evacuation when the Weasel detected a SAM radar, then came under fire from 57mm AAA. The Weasel F-4C marked the location with a Shrike and the F-4D bombed the guns, silencing them. This was the last Air Force combat strike in Vietnam.

The final USAF involvement in active combat in Southeast Asia involved the effort to rescue the crew of the container ship *Mayaguez*, which was detained by the Khmer Rouge on May 12, 1975. The next day, the ship was spotted by a US Navy P-3 patrol plane and plans were put into effect to rescue the crew and recover the ship. A decision was made in Washington to take military action to obtain release of the crew and ship.

The Air Force planned to retake the ship with an assault force of 75 troops from the 56th Security Police Squadron dropped onto the containers on deck on the morning of May 14. Five HH-53C Jolly Green Giants from the 40th Aerospace Rescue and Recovery Squadron and seven CH-53 Knives of the 21st Special Operations Squadron at Nakhon Phanom RTNB were ordered to proceed to U-Tapao for staging, but CH-53 Knife 13 crashed en route; the crew and 18 security policemen were lost. After it was discovered that the containers would collapse if the helicopters landed on them while the men would be exposed if they rappelled to the deck, the plan was canceled. The rescue was put on hold until the carrier USS *Coral Sea* (CVA-43) arrived off Koh Tang and a special Marine battalion landing team arrived in Thailand. The rescue attempt was set to occur on May 15.

The rescue force included five CH-53 Knives and three HH-53 Jolly Greens carrying Marines of Echo and Golf companies which would seize and hold Koh Tang Island. Two helicopters would make a diversionary assault on the West Beach to cover the six that put the main assault on the wider East Beach. Two more waves of helicopters would land all of the battalion landing team on Koh Tang. Due to fear of harming the crew, there would be no preparatory air strike.

After *Mayaguez* was seized by 57 Marines from Delta Company, volunteers from Military Sealift Command would be brought in by the destroyer *Holt* an hour after the assault on Koh Tang. With *Mayaguez* retaken, a strike force from *Coral Sea* would bomb the mainland. The Air Force plan for B-52s to bomb the port facilities at Kampong Som and Ream Naval Base was dropped.

In the event, the rescue mission turned into one of the bloodiest battles Air Force helicopter crews engaged in during the wars in Southeast Asia. Khmer Rouge forces on Koh Tang Island were more numerous, better armed, and more willing to fight than expected, and the assault was disastrous. At 0630 hours, the two CH-53s approaching East Beach came under intense fire. Two RPGs hit Knife-31 and it crashed in a fireball 150 feet offshore, killing the copilot, five Marines, and two Navy corpsmen while a sixth Marine drowned swimming from the wreck; three Marines were killed trying to reach the beach and a tenth died clinging to the burning wreckage. Ten surviving Marines and three helicopter crewmen were in the water for two hours before they were picked up. Among the survivors was the Marine FAC, who called in air strikes from the water with a survival radio until the battery failed.

Knife-23's tail was blown off by another RPG and it crash-landed on the beach; the 20 Marines and five crewmen got out and set up a defensive perimeter. Cut off for 12 hours, they were saved by the copilot, who called in air strikes with his survival radio.

The remaining four helicopters diverted to West Beach and their Marines managed to land between 0630 and 0700 hours. Jolly Green 41 took five tries and finally got in with support from an AC-130 gunship. Knife-32 and Jolly Green 41 and 42 landed 81 Marines on West Beach while half a mile away to the southwest Jolly Green 43 landed 29 Marines of the battalion command and mortar platoon, led by company executive officer Major Randall Austin. There were 109 Marines and five Air Force crewmen on Koh Tang in three isolated positions and under enemy fire.

With Knife 21, 23, and 31 destroyed and Knife 22 and 32 and Jolly Green 41 and 42 too badly damaged to continue, only Jolly Green 11, 12, and 43 along with Knife 51 and 52 were left to bring in the follow-up force.

Covered by suppressive fire from the AC-130, Jolly Green 13 landed on East Beach in a hail of enemy fire at 0815 hours, 300 feet from the surrounded Marines. When they were reluctant to break cover and run through the heavy fire to the helicopter, it managed to lift off with its fuel line ruptured and made an emergency landing in Rayong, Thailand.

Between 0900 and 1000 hours, three HH-53s and two CH-53s picked up 127 Marines of the second wave at U-Tapao. Knife 51 and 52 and Jolly Green 43 arrived over Koh Tang at 1130 hours and prepared to land on East Beach, but Knife-52's fuel tanks were punctured by enemy fire; the pilot aborted the landing and managed to return to U-Tapao. Knife 51 and Jolly Green 43 took up a holding pattern.

In the face of the attack, the Khmer Rouge announced that they were freeing the crew. At 0935 hours, the fishing boat they were on was spotted by a P-3; they were taken aboard the destroyer *Wilson* at 0953 hours. President Ford refused to call off the air strike by the *Coral Sea* and the strike force bombed barges and oil storage facilities at Kompong

Som, cargo planes and T-28s at Ream airfield, and other boats at Ream naval base starting at 0905 hours. Fortunately the defenses were poorly organized and all aircraft returned safely.

The Joint Chiefs issued an order at 1155 hours to withdraw. The orbiting EC-130 ABCCC sent a recall to the second assault wave which turned back. Major Austin managed to convince Air Force General Burns that he needed reinforcement to keep his separated units from being overrun; the helicopters headed back to Koh Tang. Knife 51, followed by Jolly Green 43, 11, and 12 landed 100 Marines on West Beach at 1210 hours. With 205 Marines on West Beach and 20 Marines and five airmen on East Beach, A-7s provided close air support that allowed Major Austin and his Marines to reach Golf Company on northern West Beach at 1245 hours.

Gunfire at West Beach slowed by 1400 hours. Jolly Green 11 and 43 approached East Beach at 1415 hours but heavy fire damaged Jolly Green 43, forcing it to make an emergency landing on *Coral Sea* at 1436 hours. Nail-68, an Air Force OV-10 FAC, took over control of air support at 1623 hours but the battle regained intensity at 1700 hours.

With the sun setting at 1800 hours, a third rescue attempt was made at East Beach. Jolly Green 11, supported by fire from Jolly Green 12, Knife-51, and *Wilson*'s whaleboat armed with four M60s, ran in to the beach after Nail-68 directed an AC-130 and *Coral Sea* F-4s and A-7s to hit the enemy. At 1815 hours, Jolly Green 11 was over East Beach. The wreckage of Knife-23 blocked the original landing zone, but pilot First Lieutenant Donald Backlund see-sawed up and down to present a difficult target for the enemy. The Marines timed their jumps aboard with the downward moves. Despite being hit repeatedly, Jolly Green 11 got all 20 Marines and the five Air Force crewmen and delivered them to *Coral Sea*.

Just after the pickup, the FAC ordered five C-130s that had arrived with BLU-82 "Daisy Cutters" to make their drop. The 15,000-pound BLU-82 was the largest conventional bomb in existence at the time. The first was dropped well south of the Marines on West Beach, but the enormous blast sent a shockwave so strong that Major Austin radioed that no more should be dropped and the other C-130s departed with their weapons.

Word came that one Marine might still be in the wreckage of Knife 31. Jolly Green 12 went in and lowered a crewman to check, but no one was there. The helicopter took several hits and was forced to fly to *Coral Sea*.

The moonless night provided cover to extract the remaining Marines. The withdrawal began at 1840 hours, protected by gunfire from the AC-130 and *Wilson*. Knife 51 lifted out 41 Marines, followed by Jolly Green picking up 54. As Jolly Green 44 loaded 44 Marines, the shrinking perimeter came under attack and the remaining Marines were in danger of being overrun. Pilot First Lieutenant Bob Blough took the Marines to the nearby destroyer *Holt*, hovering over the ship in total darkness with only the front wheels touching down as the Marines dropped onto the ship. Five minutes later, Blough returned to West Beach and picked up 34 more Marines. Due to engine trouble, he had to fly out to *Coral Sea*. There were still 32 Marines left.

At 2000 hours, Knife 51 landed under fire and began loading in the dark. Parajumper Tech Sergeant Wayne Fisk made a final search for stragglers. Finding none, Knife 51 left Koh Tang at 2010 hours, headed for the *Coral Sea*.

Total American losses included 18 dead and 50 wounded. Thirteen dead were left on the beach. Two hours later, Echo Company commander Captain Stahl found that Lance Corporal Joseph N. Hargrove, Private First Class Gary L. Hall, and Private Danny G. Marshall, all members of a machine gun team that had been protecting the constantly shrinking perimeter's right flank, were missing.

The next morning, *Wilson* cruised between the beaches broadcasting in English, French, and Khmer that they had no hostile intent and only wished to retrieve any Americans dead or alive and would send an unarmed boat ashore. No answer was received and no one spotted the missing Marines. After three hours, *Wilson* departed the area. Hargrove, Hall, and Marshall were declared missing in action; their status was changed to Killed in Action (Body Not Recovered) on July 21, 1976. In 1985, the Khmer Rouge commander in the fight revealed that the next morning he conducted a search, during which his men came under fire and one was wounded. They captured one Marine; on learning that his soldier had died, the commander ordered the American shot. A week later, his men noticed that their leftover food was being disturbed and found bootprints in the mud. Two Americans whose descriptions matched Gary Hall and Danny Marshall were caught. They were delivered to the mainland, where they were taken to the Ti Nean

Pagoda above Sihanoukville and shackled after being stripped to their underwear. On orders from Phnom Penh a week later, each was beaten to death with an RPG launcher. They were the last American casualties in Southeast Asia.

While the North Vietnamese Army moved into Saigon, the Pathet Lao, supported by more than 50,000 North Vietnamese troops still in Laos, seized power in Vientiane.

Neutralist Prime Minister Prince Souvanna Phouma "retired." The 600-year old Laotian monarchy ended with the abdication of King Savang Vatthana, and the Lao People's Democratic Republic was proclaimed on December 2, 1975. The majority of Vang Pao's Hmong force ended up in refugee camps in Thailand, from where they were eventually allowed to emigrate to the United States.

The new regime curtailed the practice of Buddhism in 1976, while King Savang Vatthana and his family were imprisoned in a cave in a remote area of northern Laos, where they died in 1978 from lack of food and medical care.

To this day, unexploded bombs are a hazard on the Plaine des Jarres, though parts of the area have been cleared of explosives and have become an attraction for tourists drawn by the several hundred ancient stone burial jars that survived 15 years of war.

BIBLIOGRAPHY

Baker, Peter, "Nixon Tried to Spoil Johnson's Vietnam Peace Talks in '68, Notes Show," *New York Times*, January 3, 2017, p. 11

Biggio, Charles P. Jr., "The USSR and the National Liberation Movement," unpublished Master's thesis, US Army War College, April 1966

Boyne, Walter J., "Air Power at Khe Sanh," *Air Force Magazine*, August 1998, pp. 49–51

Boyne, Walter J., "Breaking The Dragon's Jaw," *Air Force Magazine*, August 2001, pp. 58–60

Churchill, Jan, *Hit My Smoke! Forward Air Controllers in Southeast Asia* (Sunflower University Press, 1997)

Correll, John T., "Against the MiGs in Vietnam," *Air Force Magazine*, October 2019, pp. 14–18

Cosmas, Graham A., *The Joint Chiefs of Staff and the War in Vietnam, 1960–68, Part 3: 1967–68* (Washington DC, Office of the Chairman of the Joint Chiefs of Staff, 2009)

Davies, Peter E., *USAF F-4 Phantom II MiG Killers: 1965–68* (Osprey Publishing, 2004)

Davies, Peter E., *USAF F-4 Phantom II MiG Killers: 1972–73* (Osprey Publishing, 2005)

Davies, Peter E., *F-105 Thunderchief Units of the Vietnam War* (Osprey Publishing, 2010)

Davies, Peter E., *F-105 Thunderchief MiG Killers of the Vietnam War* (Osprey Publishing, 2014)

Futrell, R. Frank, William H. Greenhalgh, Carl Grubb, Gerard E. Hasselwander, Robert F. Jakob, Charles A. Ravenstein, *Aces and Aerial Victories: The United States Air Force in Vietnam – 1965–73* (Washington DC, Office of Air Force History, 1976)

Grant, Rebecca, "The Missing Aces," *Air Force Magazine*, September 2004, pp. 28–30

Hallion, Richard P., *Rolling Thunder: 1965–68 – Johnson's Air War Over Vietnam* (Osprey Publishing, 2018)

Hankins, Michael, "The Phantom Menace: The F-4 in Combat in Vietnam," unpublished Master's thesis, University of North Texas, August 2013

Hankins, Michael, "Making a MiG-Killer: Technology and Signals Intelligence for Air-to-Air Combat in Vietnam, *Balloons to Drones*, August 15, 2019, found at https://balloonstodrones.com/2019/08/15/airwarvietnam-making-a-mig-killer-technology-and-signals-intelligence-for-air-to-air-combat-in-vietnam/ [accessed 1 November 2021]

Hartook, E.H., *The Air Force in Southeast Asia: The End of U.S. Involvement – 1973–1975* (Washington DC, Office of Air Force History, 1980)

Hastings, Sir Max, *Vietnam: An Epic Tragedy 1945–75* (HarperCollins, 2018)

Herring, George, *American's Longest War: The United States and Vietnam, 1950–1975* (McGraw-Hill Education, 2014)

Hung, Nguyen Sy, *Historic Confrontations: Air Battles between VNP Air Force and U.S. Airpower* (The People's Army Publishing House, 2021)

Keating, Susan K., "Plausible Denial," *Air & Space Magazine*, Smithsonian Institution, May 1997

Marrett, George J., *Cheating Death: Combat Air Rescues in Vietnam and Laos* (Pen & Sword Books Ltd, 2003)

Mrozek, Donald J., *Air Power and the Ground War in Vietnam* (Air University Press, 1988)

Nalty, Bernard C., *The War Against Trucks: Aerial Interdiction in Southern Laos 1968–72* (Washington DC, Air Force History and Museums Program, declassified 2005)

Nalty, Bernard C., *Air War Over South Vietnam: 1968–73* (Washington DC, Air Force History and Museums Program, declassified 2018)

National Security Agency, "Spartans in Darkness: American SIGINT and the Indochina War – 1945–75," Washington DC, Top Secret, declassified 2007

Rasimus, Ed, *When Thunder Rolled: An F-105 Pilot Over North Vietnam* (Smithsonian Institution Press, 2003)

Toperczer, Istvan, *MiG 17/19 Aces of the Vietnam War* (Osprey Publishing, 2016)

Van Staaveren, Jacob, "USAF Plans and Policies in South Vietnam, 1961–1963," US Air Force Historical Division Liaison Office, June 1965, Top Secret, declassified 2018

Van Staaveren, Jacob, "USAF Plans and Policies in South Vietnam and Laos, 1964," US Air Force Historical Division Liaison Office (date not given), Top Secret, declassified 2018

Van Staaveren, Jacob, "USAF Plans and Operations in Southeast Asia, 1965," US Air Force Historical Division Liaison Office, October 1966, Top Secret, declassified 2018

Van Staaveren, Jacob, "The Air Force in Vietnam: The Search for Military Alternatives, 1967," Office of Air Force History, December 1969, Top Secret, declassified 2018

Van Staaveren, Jacob, "The Air Force in Southeast Asia: Toward a Bombing Halt, 1968," Office of Air Force History, September 1970, Top Secret, declassified 2018

Weaver, Michael E., "Missed Opportunities before Top Gun and Red Flag," *Air Power History*, Vol. 60, No. 4, Winter 2013, pp. 18–31

Wetterhahn, Ralph, "Nguyen Van Bay and the Aces From the North," *Air & Space Magazine*, November 2000

Whitcomb, Darrell, "Farm Gate," *Air Force Magazine*, December 1, 2005

INTERVIEWS WITH THE AUTHOR

Wetterhahn, First Lieutenant Ralph: 112ff, 121, 161, 170ff, 2020
Lee, Captain Ken: 278-280, 2004
Tucker, Lt. Colonel Earl W.: 357, 358, 2002
Rodgers, First Lieutenant Thomas D.: 363ff, 2021

GLOSSARY

AAA	antiaircraft artillery
ABCCC	Airborne Command and Control Center
ACG	Air Commando Group
ACM	air combat maneuvering
ACT	air combat training
ADC	Air Defense Command
ADD	Aviatsiya Dal'nego Deystviya (the Soviet strategic bombing force)
ADVON	Advanced Echelon
AFB	Air Force Base
AGL	above ground level
AMC	Air Materiel Command
ANG	Air National Guard
ARVN	Army of the Republic of Vietnam
BARCAP	Barrier Combat Air Patrol
BDA	bomb damage assessment
BVR	beyond visual range
CAS	close air support
CAT	Civil Air Transport
CIA	Central Intelligence Agency
CinCPac	Commander in Chief, Pacific
CNO	Chief of Naval Operations
CO	Commanding Officer
CSAR	combat search and rescue

GLOSSARY

DACT	dissimilar air combat training
DMZ	Demilitarized Zone (the border zone between North and South Vietnam between 1954 and 1976)
DRV	Democratic Republic of Vietnam (= North Vietnam)
ECM	electronic countermeasures
EOGB	electro-optical guided bomb
EWO	electronic warfare officer
FAC	forward air controller
FWS	Fighter Weapons School
GCI	ground controlled interception
GIB	"Guy in Back"
GP	general-purpose
helo	helicopter
HOBO	HOming BOmb System (an electro-optical glide bomb)
IAS	indicated air speed
IRAN	Inspect or Repair As Necessary
JCS	Joint Chiefs of Staff
LGB	laser-guided bomb
MAAG	Military Assistance Advisory Group
MACV	Military Assistance Command – Vietnam
MIA	missing in action
MiGCAP	MiG Combat Air Patrol
NIE	National Intelligence Estimate
NKP	Nakhon Phanom (Royal Thai airbase)
NLF	National Liberation Front (also known as the "Viet Cong")
NSA	National Security Agency (US)
NSAM	National Security Action Memorandum
NSC	National Security Council
NVA	North Vietnamese Army
OSS	Office of Strategic Services
PACAF	Pacific Air Forces
PACOM	Pacific Command

PAVN	People's Army of Vietnam
PCS	permanent change of station
PGM	precision-guided munitions
PJ	parajumper
POL	petroleum-oil-lubricant
POW	prisoner of war
RAAF	Royal Australian Air Force
RESCAP	Rescue Combat Air Patrol
RIO	radar intercept officer
ROE	rules of engagement
RPG	rocket propelled grenade
RTAFB	Royal Thai Air Force Base
RVN	Republic of Vietnam (= South Vietnam)
SAC	Strategic Air Command
SAM	surface-to-air missile
SAR	search and rescue
SEATO	South East Asia Treaty Organization
SIGINT	signals intelligence
SOP	standard operating procedure
TAC	Tactical Air Command

ACKNOWLEDGMENTS

This book could not exist without the assistance and support of the following people:

My "brother from another mother," the late Eric Hammell, spent his last years convincing me that I needed to write about Vietnam. Eric was the first of a new generation of aviation historians to search for the truth in the first-person memories of participants, tracking down and interviewing those the public had already forgotten, bringing their memories and accounts into history's record before they were lost forever. His example always guides me and I miss him every day since he lost his battle with Parkinson's.

My other "brother from another mother," Barrett Tillman, was – as always – a rock of support in this project, putting me in touch with people he knew whom I should interview, reading the work in progress and providing feedback that always improved what was there. His body of work in aviation history over the past nearly 50 years has always been an example of how one goes about doing this.

The presence of my now-friend and fellow aviation historian, Colonel Ralph Wetterhahn, with his "been there/done that" perspective from his time as wingman to Robin Olds in the Wolfpack, was crucial to understanding the way the air war was fought on the US side. His willingness to read and critique the work in progress was invaluable to ensuring everything stayed on track. I wouldn't have known to go looking for the reports on Project Featherduster had he not told me what it was and why it was important. Thanks to the internet, declassified reports like that are now at a historian's fingertips through the magic of Google.

I would never have been able to document the story of "the other side" without the help of Dr. Nguyen Sy Hung, historian of the Vietnam People's Air Force and the author of that air force's official history, *Historic Confrontations in the Skies of Vietnam*, who provided me with a copy of the first English translation of this important work.

Thank you to all. As the old saying goes, "I couldn't have done it without you."

INDEX

Reference to maps are in **bold**.

Dong, Pham Van   19, 29–30, 327
Dong Hoi airfield   262, 263
Drew, Capt Philip M.   228, 230–31
Duan, Le   327, 330
Duan, Phan Tan   201
Dulles, John Foster   28–29, 32, 33
Dung, Gen Van Tien   326–27

East Germany *see* German Democratic
Republic
Easter Offensive (1972)   261, 273–82
Eastern Europe   86
economics   209, 327–28
Eisenhower, Dwight D.   28, 29, 30, 32,
33, 39; and aircraft   45, 46; and Laos
34–35, 37
Ély, Gen Paul   31
Eskew, Capt William   174–75
Ettel, Lt Cmdr Mike   301–2
Everest, Lt Col Frank K. "Pete"   47, 50

Fall, Bernard: *Street Without Joy*   40
Farr, Maj Jack   128–29
Feather Duster project   106–10
Feinstein, Capt Jeff   275, 278–79, 292,
298–300, 304–5, 307–8
Felt, Adm Harry D.   72, 89–90
Ferguson, Maj Alonzo L. "Lonnie"   186, 206
Fighter Weapons School (FWS)   104
First Indochina War (1946–54)   17, 25–29,
40, 72
flares   75–76
Ford, Gerald   329, 331
Foreign Legion   22, 28
formations   107–8, 112, 114
Fosdick, Raymond   26
France   18–21, 22, 24–25, 30–31, 32, 70; *see
also* First Indochina War
Franks, Sgt Lonnie D.   265
French Indochina *see* Indochina

Gaddis, Col Norman   185–86
Garrison, Vermont   145, 149–50
Gast, Lt Col Philip C.   186
Gayler, Adm Noel   301, 329
Geneva Accords (1954/62)   29–32, 39–40,
71, 319
German Democratic Republic (GDR)   39,
86
Germany   21, 23, 24; *see also* Berlin
Gia Long, Emperor   18, 19
Giap, Vo Nguyen   19, 23–24, 27, 28, 89,
327
Gilpatric, Roswell   38
Gleason, Lt Col Robert L.   67, 76
Glenn L. Martin Company   43
Gordon, Capt Bill   220–21

Gorski, Capt Frank   75–76
Graham, Maj James L.   228, 229–30
Great Britain   24, 28, 29, 31, 32
Greene, Graham   17, 84
Greene, Gen Wallace   90
Gullick, Capt Francis M.   203–4

Ha, Pham Cao   285, 286
Haeffner, Lt Col Fred A.   188–89
Hai, Lt Le   173, 185, 227, 233
Haiphong   182, 183, 211, 212
Halberstam, David   35, 40, 74
Hall, Pvt 1C Gary L.   337–38
Hall, Maj John A.   220–21
Halsey, Adm William F., Jr.   23
Handley, Maj Phillip W.   290
Hanh, Lt Tran   101, 102–3, 132, 166
Hanoi   182–83, 211, 212, 310–16
Hardy, Capt Richard "Tuna"   294–95
Hargrove, Lance Cpl Joseph N.   337
Harriman, Averell   36, 87
Helms, Richard   182, 211
Hieu, Nghiem Dinh   195, 196, 197
Higgins, Maj Harry E.   177
Hill, Capt Robert G.   235–36
Hirsch, Maj Thomas M.   165–66
Ho Chi Minh   19–20, 23–24, 25, 32,
33, 86
Ho Chi Minh Trail   16, 83, 253–54
Hoa Lac airfield   164–65, 169–70
Hodgdon, 1Lt Leigh A.   269–71
Holcombe, Capt Kenneth   116, 117
Holloway, Gen Bruce K.   110
Hosmer, Maj James   129–30
Howerton, Maj Rex D.   238–39
Huan, Lt Le Minh   101, 102–3
Hue   18, 23, 242
Hughes, Harold   265
Huneke, 1Lt Bruce V.   235–36
Hung, Nguyen Ngoc   275, 276
Huskey, Capt Richard L.   233–34
Huy, Nguyen Cong   284–85, 288, 302
Hyland, Vice Adm John   210–11

Imaye, Capt Stanley M.   295, 300
India   24, 30
Indochina   19, 20, 21–22, 23–25; *see also*
First Indochina War
Indonesia   26, 80
intelligence   89–90, 242, 263–65, 274,
300–1, 331; *see also* CIA

James, Col Daniel "Chappie," Jr.   145, 148,
149–51, 154, 157–58, 161
Janca, Maj Robert D.   195–97
Japan   20–22, 23–24, 32, 42
Johnson, Gen Harold   90, 171–72, 179